passion to win

passion to win

How Winning Companies Develop And Sustain Competitive Edge

Abad Ahmad
O P Chopra

Based on
A Path Breaking Research Study by
All India Management Association

EXCEL BOOKS PRIVATE LIMITED

ISBN: PB-81-7446-389-5
HB-81-7446-390-9

First Edition: New Delhi, 2004
Reprint: 2010

Published by
EXCEL BOOKS PRIVATE LIMITED
A-45, Naraina, Phase-I
New Delhi-110028
in association with
ALL INDIA MANAGEMENT ASSOCIATION
14, Institutional Area, Lodi Road, New Delhi - 110 003

Published by Anurag Jain for Excel Books, A-45, Naraina, Phase-I, New Delhi -110 028 and printed by him at Excel Printers, C-205, Naraina, Phase-I, New Delhi -110 028

Contents

PREFACE VII

ACKNOWLEDGEMENTS XIII

FOREWORD XVII

CHAPTER ONE

The Key Questions and The Search for Answers 1

CHAPTER TWO

The Purposeful, Values-Driven Enterprise 11
Distinguishing Characteristics of Organizations that Demonstrated Sustained High Performance and Competitive Edge

CHAPTER THREE

Sustainable Competitive Edge 25
An Overview of the Key Factors

CHAPTER FOUR

Inspiring Leadership 37
The Energizing, Direction Providing and Driving Force

CHAPTER FIVE

Innovative Strategy 97
Conceptualizing Innovative Business Models, Distinctive Approaches and Initiatives for Competitiveness

CHAPTER SIX

Process-Driven Execution 169

CHAPTER SEVEN

'Win-Win' Relationships 191

CHAPTER EIGHT
Distinct Identity 215
Purpose, Values and Culture

CHAPTER NINE
The Firm as a Living System and the Emerging Modern Indian Corporation (EMIC) 253

CHAPTER TEN
Critical Analysis of Performance and Sustainability of the Companies Studied 263

CHAPTER ELEVEN
Learnings and Action Implications 277
Lessons For the Business Leaders, Entrepreneurs and Managers

RESEARCH APPENDIX I 299

RESEARCH APPENDIX II 315

INDEX 319

Preface

THIS BOOK IS ABOUT how business organizations become outstanding, achieve superior performance and competitive ability relative to others and sustain these over long spans of time. It focuses on the Indian context, and is aimed at developing Indian organizations as globally competitive organizations.

It is based on an empirical research covering some of the most admired, outstanding Indian companies and multinational companies operating in India, which have demonstrated that it is possible to achieve such performance against all odds. It is an attempt to identify the critical factors, characteristics and practices that make the difference, based on the insights and experience of some of the most successful organization builders, business leaders and professional managers. The findings have emerged from comprehensive analysis of data, field observations and case studies of these companies.

The genesis of this work goes back to the mid-seventies when we started jointly offering Business Policy and Strategic Management course at the Faculty of Management Studies at the University of Delhi. We strongly felt the need to have good quality Indian case studies, research-based books and articles that would familiarize the students with the Indian business environment. We had very little choice and had to depend largely on foreign textbooks, articles and cases. It was only in the late nineties that we found some good quality, comprehensive Indian cases and research-based books on strategic management.

It was all along our cherished dream that we shall write a research-based book on strategic management in the Indian context. Few years back, one of us who had taken up academic administration assignments for several years in the University, rejoined the Faculty and we again started jointly offering strategic management courses. Around this time, one of us was invited by AIMA (All India Management Association) to conduct a research study on 'Developing sustainable competitive edge in Indian business organizations', which we decided to take up, jointly. This offered us an excellent opportunity to take up this research, which not only provided financial support to meet the cost of field visits and technical support but also provided access to the leading Indian firms in addition to our own contacts.

When taking up this research, little did we realize how complex and difficult is the subject we have chosen. After carefully identifying the companies to be included in the sample for study in consultation with various opinion leaders, experts, professional managers and business leaders, first we thought of a research design consisting of comprehensive interviews combined with questionnaire-based study, with the traditional approach of testing hypotheses. After some preliminary work and a few interviews we realized that such research will be more of academic interest and is likely to end up in the library shelves, like other researches that are seldom used by practitioners. We found the depth interviews with the leading professional managers and business leaders so rich and insightful that we decided to utilize the Delphi and ethnographic type approach to develop a deep and holistic understanding of the various aspects of leadership, strategy and other aspects of management and organization that lead to outstanding performance, competitiveness and sustainability of organizations.

We travelled extensively across the country, visited most of the organizations and personally tape-recorded the depth interviews with the top management and a cross-section of members of the selected organizations. In addition, we collected and analyzed all relevant published case studies, annual reports; financial, marketing, operational and stock market performance data over a decade; and write-ups on the companies.

Having collected this voluminous data and sizeable scripts of the taped interviews, we found ourselves in an extremely difficult situation to analyze it and put it into a meaningful pattern. Traditional methods like content analysis did not help us. However, repeated and persistent attempts to identify patterns, careful analysis of data and thorough discussions among ourselves as well as with several professional colleagues, and our extensive experience in teaching, management development and consultancy work in organizations began to yield results. We began to notice that about twenty to twenty five distinctive factors, characteristics and practices seemed to come up in most of the outstanding companies. Since these were too many, we tried to put them in clusters. Interestingly, we found it difficult to put them in linear boxes, as these were overlapping and interactive. When we were struggling to do so, we began to discover the five clusters in a pattern of overlapping circles that led to the 5-I framework of the key elements that distinguish the outstanding organizations with sustainable competitiveness. These five key elements are:

1. Inspiring Leadership
2. Innovative Strategy

3. Implementation Skills and Process-driven Execution
4. Internal and External 'Win-Win' Relationships
5. Identity - Purpose, Values and Culture

These five clusters constitute the interactive, dynamic parts of the organization as an open system that is closely and continuously interacting with the changing, competitive and regulatory external business environment. The stable core that provides continuity consists of identity, purpose, values and culture; while the changing parts are leadership, strategy, implementation structures and processes, and relationships. Each cluster has several components with unique nuances in characteristics and practices that develop and sustain competitiveness and outstanding performance.

Among the various characteristics of Inspiring Leadership, a proactive, positive and optimistic mindset; clarity of purpose, vision and values; setting challenging and highly ambitious goals for the success and supremacy of the organization; willingness and ability to change; and the passion to win, were very conspicuous. Likewise, in other clusters, unique characteristics were noted, like in the cluster of Strategy; innovative business models for creating and delivering value to customers, internationalization of operations to develop competitiveness; redefining industry and creating new markets in situations which others saw as barriers and constraints. In Implementation and Execution, mastering technology; highly efficient and productive processes, systems and structures and great attention to details were some of the characteristics. In the cluster of Relationships a 'win-win' approach and an 'extended family' like ethos in relationships with stakeholders and an attempt to equitably share wealth with stakeholders were noted.

In the central core, we noted a strong sense of Identity of which members felt proud, based on clear, widely understood purpose and deeply shared values. These companies had developed distinct culture of high performance combined with genuine care for people and stakeholders in the organization. They had high level of openness, transparency and professionalism in governance as well as in management.

We discovered a distinctive paradigm being followed by the outstanding organizations that we have described as 'Purposeful, Values-driven Enterprises' (PVEs). Such organizations had long-term institution-building orientation and passion for supremacy that led to sustainability and competitiveness, as contrasted with the 'Commercial Money-making Outfit' (MCO) paradigm of the short-sighted business organizations, which could not survive tough competition in the long run.

At the theoretical level, we have conceptualized organizations as Open, Organic, Socio-Economic-Technical systems that are Co-evolving with the changing Business Environment. Each of their sub-systems, i.e., social, technical and economic, and their interfaces have to be understood and managed effectively. The organizations are, therefore, living and self-rejuvenating systems, and not mechanistic, inorganic systems - a tacit paradigm of most business leaders and managers. The mechanistic, impersonal and purely economic-aspects oriented paradigm has far-reaching implications in policies and practices of management and styles of leadership, that tends to make them prisoners of self-fulfilling prophecy, often leading to decline and demise of organization in the competitive environment.

We also noted unique characteristics in the outstanding emerging modern Indian organizations which were a class apart from the traditional Indian business organizations. In addition to being Purposeful, Values-driven Enterprises, they demonstrated a unique combination of Indian cultural ethos based on extended-family metaphor; Japanese practices for quality, productivity and efficiency; and Western techniques, systems and processes in management. We have described them as Emerging Modern Indian Corporations (EMICs). They operate on a global mindset, benchmarking with the best in the world, internationalizing their operations for competitiveness and aspiring to become Indian multinationals. They are creating brand equity of quality, reliability, and cost effectiveness for Indian products, services and organizations. These are critical minimum requirements for entry of Indian corporations in the global markets. The EMICs are role models for the future development of Indian corporations and will usher Indian business in the global markets.

An important point that clearly emerges from the research is that the barriers to growth and development are mostly within the mindset of the leaders and managers, and not so much in the external environment. On the contrary, the challenges and competition in the business environment bring out the best among leaders and managers who have the passion to win. Therefore, the will, vision and passion of leadership are more important than any other factor for developing outstanding competitive organizations. In fact, nothing great has ever been achieved without passion.

We have followed an unconventional style in writing this book. Instead of loading it with theoretical jargon, we have tried to place before the reader the insights of highly experienced business leaders and professional managers by quoting their views and observations directly as stated by them in the interviews. By developing conceptual frameworks based on such insights, we have attempted to bring to surface the tacit knowledge of highly experienced leaders and managers.

We have attempted to make this work relevant, easily understood, and applicable by the management practitioners, in addition to making it useful for the management teachers, trainers, and MBA-level students in general, and for courses and training programmes in Strategic Management, in particular. The book is also relevant for leaders and managers of other institutions and non-profit organizations.

We see Indian business organizations at a crucial juncture. The process of liberalization and globalization is exposing them to unprecedented competition. Many organizations that are showing profitability at present may disappear unless they gear up for global competition, and take steps to enhance and sustain their competitive edge. Although the awareness for change is increasing, the sense of urgency to initiate change is still not adequate. In this rapidly changing and turbulent scenario, only those organizations will survive that initiate steps for change well ahead of others. The best time to change, as pointed out by one distinguished business leader, is when change appears to be least needed. We hope this work will provide a framework for diagnosing organizations and initiating carefully thought actions for change to make Indian organizations competitive and sustainable.

We also hope that some of the propositions of this work will inspire more rigorous research to advance the field of empirical research and knowledge in management; and enrich management education and training to develop future business leaders, entrepreneurs and professional managers.

Abad Ahmad
O P Chopra

Acknowledgements

WE ARE EXTREMELY GRATEFUL to AIMA, especially to Major General D.N. Khurana, for sponsoring the research project that is the basis of this book. Major General Khurana initiated the research project, supported it throughout and demonstrated enormous patience to enable us to complete the work. He was very generous in helping us in getting appointments with the chairmen, CEOs, and other members of top management of the selected companies, often at a very short notice. It speaks volumes of the high esteem in which the industry leaders hold him, and the value he attaches to empirical research in management.

Prof. S.L. Rao has been a constant supporter of the research study. He provided very valuable suggestions at different stages of this work and appreciated the need to extend the time to complete the study. He also gave us valuable tips and feedback on the manuscript. We wish to express our deeply felt gratitude to him.

Mr. Subodh Bhargava, Former Chairman of Eicher Motors Ltd., was the first one we interviewed. The interview, in a way, set the tone of the research study. The manifestation of the same is our quoting him so frequently. Our special thanks to him.

We wish to make a special mention of our deeply felt appreciation and thanks to Mr. Brijmohan Lall Munjal, Chairman of Hero Honda Motors Ltd., Mr. R (Gopal) Gopalakrishnan, Executive Director of Tata Sons Ltd., Mr. Suresh Krishna, Chairman & Managing Director, Sundram Fasteners Ltd. (TVS), Dr. K. Dinesh, Co-founder and Member of the Board, Infosys, Mr. D.S. Brar, CEO and Managing Director of Ranbaxy Laboratories Ltd., Mr. G.V. Prasad, Executive Vice-Chairman & CEO, Dr. Reddy's Laboratories Ltd., Mr. Gunender Kapur, Executive Director-Foods of HLL, Mr. Bhaskar Bhatt, Managing Director of Titan Industries Ltd., Mr. L.H. Bhatia, Managing Director of B.S. Refrigerators Limited (BPL), Dr. U. Balaji, Vice-President, and Dr. P.S.S. Murthy of Satyam Learning Center, Mr. A. S. Murthy, Director & Sr. Vice-President of Satyam Computer Services Ltd., Mr. Pratik Kumar, Corporate Vice-President-HR, and Mr. J. Shankar, Corporate Treasurer, of Wipro Ltd., and some senior managers of Reliance for giving us a very incisive understanding of the working of their organizations, and for sharing with us their vast experience and their perception of what influences sustainability of competitive edge.

We owe, in no less measure, our thanks to Mr. Amineedu, Director, Bharat Electronics Ltd., Mr. P. Dwarkanath, Director-HR of GSK Consumer Healthcare Ltd., Mr. Aqil Busrai, Director-HR, India & SAARC Countries of Motorola India Ltd., Ms. Kalpana Morparia, Executive Director of ICICI Ltd., Mr. Gyan Prakash Gupta, ex-Chairman IDBI, Mr. A. M. Singhvi, President - World Class Manufacturing of Aditya Birla Group of Companies and Mr. L.N. Jhunjhunwala, Chairman Emeritus of LNJ Bhilwara Group for sharing with us their deep insights on management, general understanding of the economy and its linkages with the global system.

We were very fortunate to have intensive interviews and discussions with Mr. Yogi Sriram, Vice-President, Corporate HR & Personnel, Larsen & Toubro Ltd., Mr. Vijay K. Gupta, Vice President, Brand & Corporate Communication, Mr. C. R. Nagraj, Corporate Vice President, Mission Quality, Mr. L. Ramnath, Corporate Manager - Innovation & Mission Quality, of Wipro Ltd., and Mr. Tamal Dasgupta, Corporate Vice President & Chief Information Officer of Wipro Technologies, Mr. S. Sukumar, Manager - Corporate Planning of Infosys, and Mr. V.G. Jagannathan, President (Finance) of Sundram Fasteners.

In addition to the specific names given above, we are equally grateful to a number of other executives whom we interviewed, the distinguished thinkers, scholars, practitioners, teachers and alumni with whom we discussed the subject of this research, and got valuable ideas and suggestions from them.

Needless to state that any such research borrows a great deal from the writings, concepts, cases and theories developed by other thinkers and writers. We have tried to ensure that we acknowledge such contributions when we have utilized them at the appropriate place.

We also had the benefit of suggestions and comments on this report from some very senior professional managers and scholars who spared their valuable time to go through the manuscript and give their valuable observations. We wish to express our sincere thanks to them.

Mr. Kamal Singh and Ms. Sujita Khemka of AIMA were our immediate contacts for appointments with the interviewees. They have been extremely helpful in getting appointments and assisting us in logistics of the visits and other support required from the AIMA for our research work. We are highly thankful to them.

We are also grateful to various organizations and institutions that extended their kind hospitality during our field visits in different parts of the country. In this connection, we would like to specially thank the BEL at Bangalore, and IFMR/ ACME at Chennai.

Mr. S. Prabhakar has assisted us in statistical calculations, formatting and technical support of the text in a very efficient manner. But for his patience, help and dedicated work, it would not be possible for us to handle the enormous information and empirical data collected for this research. We wish to record our heart felt thanks to him.

We sincerely appreciate the meticulous care and enormous effort put in by Mr. Anurag Jain of Excel Books, and the editorial staff, especially Mr. Rajan Wadhwa and Ms. Preetika Anand, Ms. Sushmita also the designer Ms. Abha Bhatia and DTP Mr. Ashok Sharma for bringing out this book in its present form and releasing it in record time.

Finally, we are grateful to our families for bearing with us very patiently through the ups and downs of this study over an unanticipated extended period, and for giving us moral support when we faced difficult times in our work. If there is something worthwhile in the study, it is an index of their cooperation and appreciation.

Foreword

MANAGEMENT RESEARCH IS PICKING up in India. In order to give a boost to this activity, AIMA found it fit to support research on various management themes. The main objective is to bridge the gap between management theory and practice. 'Passion to Win' is a piece in this plan. The findings will also help us in strengthening the training programmes by enabling the executives to have an access to materials specific to the Indian context. I have great pleasure in introducing this research to our executives.

This study attempts to identify the factors, characteristics and practices that the most admired business organizations use for developing and maintaining sustainable competitive edge. It pinpoints the factors that lead to sustainability of excellence. The approach used for identifying the factors has been a Delphi type methodology combined with ethnographic type of research. The authors, Prof. Abad Ahmad and Prof. O P Chopra, studied 19 organisations and these were selected based on judgement. These were highly admired organizations operating in India. The deductions were substantiated by the performance of these companies during the period 1990 - 2003. The motivation to carry out such a study has been to provide the business leaders, professional leaders and management knowledge seekers with some propositions and insights that can stimulate their thinking.

The distinguishing characteristics of high performance organizations, as identified by the authors, are five fold namely:

- Inspiring Leadership: The Driving Force
- Innovative Strategy : Conceptualization of Business
- Distinct Identity : Purpose, Values and Culture
- Process-driven Execution : Processes, Logistics and Technology
- Win-Win Relationships : Satisfying all Stake holders

The core of value driven enterprise is the overarching element "identity" that binds other elements. The interconnectedness is the differentiating feature of high performance organizations.

Leadership comes out as the most pervasive element that makes performance the cornerstone of competitive advantage. Leadership also means collectivity of persons who utilize the process of influencing and inspiring people. Leadership sets the connection process and culture binds and gels the interconnecting elements. The study helps one to conceptualize the manner in which most admired organisations sustain their cohesiveness as well as purposiveness. This also shows the intercueing nature of soft aspects and their dominating influence on the long term performance.

Strategy is the manifestation of the leadership as action. Customer centric value creating propositions come from the strategy. Innovation, internationalization and change are brought about through this. This framework gives a basis for organizational action and indicates the role of individual in the organizational context. The linkages among context, task and role occur through strategy. This is sustained through process. Institutionalization, networking and coordination is the result of process driven execution of strategy. The studies like 'Built to Last' have shown that sustenance of superiority comes from process driven execution of strategy. The current study brings out the nature of relationship among the firm and stakeholders as the basis of sustainability of performance once processes are in place. The quality of relationship among stakeholders is yet another factor influencing long term performance. The pivotal element that glues everything is the organisational identity. The identity manifests as purpose, values and culture. This is the soul of the organization.

Using the framework proposed, the authors have been able to explain the basic organizational attributes that provide for sustainability of performance over long periods. The pervasiveness of leadership and the overarching influence of organizational culture have been brought out. This brings out clearly the need in Indian organizations for an overarching initiative for developing the leadership pipeline and creating a performance culture. These are essentially the soft aspects that make winning organizations very different. These are the sources of inimitable advantage of winning companies. This study, I am sure will motivate Indian management researchers to take up a series of studies on similar themes that could provide an insight into the context-specific elements of management.

R Gopalakrishnan

CHAPTER ONE

The Key Questions and The Search for Answers

'We do not need theories as much as the experience that is the source of theory'

R.D.LANG

THE KEY QUESTIONS

How are some companies able to survive and grow in spite of radical changes in the business environment? How are they able to face tough competition from the domestic and multinational firms? Why do a few distinguished companies continue to survive and grow, while most others become victims of declining performance, fall by the wayside, become sick, are taken over, or wither away? *How do some companies sustain outstanding performance over long spans of time?*

These are some of the questions that are probably of great interest to the business and industry leaders, professional managers, management knowledge seekers and many others who are deeply concerned with the development of a dynamic, competitive and responsible corporate sector in India.

When we undertook the research project to address some of these questions, a professional colleague, with a cynical twinkle in his eyes, said, 'Another search for excellence?' We said, 'No. Another search for the *sustainability* of excellence, and that too *in the Indian context!'*

Several well-known researches have been done and books have been written on the subject of corporate excellence. Many companies that were chosen and described as models of excellence in some of the studies, like in the well-known book *Search for Excellence*[1], faced crisis or disappeared. The major question, therefore, is of sustainability and not only of discovering the secret of excellence. Besides, our major concern has been to explore what factors are unique and relevant for developing and sustaining competitive edge in the *Indian context,* that have been relatively less researched.

Never before has the Indian industry faced the kind of challenge of global competition as presently. The increasingly tough competition from the large multinational companies on the one side and from the much cheaper Chinese products on the other side is threatening the survival of business organizations in India across the entire range of industries. A large number of companies are struggling hard to survive in this challenging environment. They are seriously apprehensive of more intense competition when the imperatives of the WTO will become fully operative and the international competitive challenge will become even more daunting. A large number of companies in several industries, especially the small and medium companies in the manufacturing sectors, are desperately searching to find ways to cope with such challenges. However, some companies have risen up to the challenge and are showing the way, not only how to survive, but to thrive and grow by developing their competitiveness.

If we examine the statistics of performance of the top hundred companies operating in India during the period 1991 – 2002, we will notice that a large number of companies had dwindling performance and slipped to lower ranks while, during the same period, a few companies not only sustained but also surpassed many others to achieve much higher rank within this list. (See Table A-1 in Appendix II). Table 1.1 shows that only 27 companies remained among the top hundred, while 73 companies which were among the top 100 companies in market capitalization in the year 1991, were no more in the list and were replaced by other companies in the year 2001. During this period, some companies that were at much lower ranks moved up significantly.

The issue of sustainability of organizations is becoming increasingly important in the highly dynamic, competitive and unpredictably changing business environment not only in India but also across the globe. According to Prof. Keyn Wyn Smith, 'the average age of new enterprises in the USA is 11 months - akin to a very high rate of infant mortality of organizations'.[2] Therefore, the need to search for factors and characteristics that lead to sustainability of organizations is universal.

There is no doubt that there have been significant national level policy changes, and changes in the domestic and global markets during the last decade. The technological and business environment, the domestic and global regulatory

Table 1.1: Companies that were Present in the Top 100 *Business Today* Rankings of 1991 and 2002 Based on Market Capitalization

Company Name	Rank 1991*	Rank 2002**
ABB	77	47
Asian Paints (India)	54	33
Bajaj Auto	12	19
Ballarpur Industries	30	94
Britannia Industries	46	41
Castrol India	31	31
Century Textiles & Inds.	4	82
Colgate-Palmolive (India)	10	37
Grasim Industries	7	27
Great Eastern Shipping Company	16	64
Gujarat Ambuja Cements	40	26
Hindalco Industries	11	18
Hindustan Lever	5	1
Indian Aluminium Co.	33	68
Indian Rayon & Inds.	32	92
Ingersoll-Rand India	34	80
ITC	2	5
Jaiprakash Industries	51	72
Larsen & Toubro	14	23
Nestle India	17	17
Ranbaxy Laboratories	65	6
Raymond	27	83
Reliance Industries	6	3
Siemens	37	56
Tata Motors+	3	21
Tata Power Co.	47	32
Tata Tea	23	54

Total Number of Companies that exited from the list of the top 100 by the year 2002:73

* Source: *Business Today,* March 7–21, 1992.

** Source: *Business Today,* November 9, 2003.

+ Company Name Changed from *Telco to Tata Motors*

Companies included in this research are shown in Bold letters.

framework and many other factors external to the companies have radically changed during this period. These external factors may have influenced changes in the performance and rating of most of the companies. But some key questions remain:

Why some companies continued to grow and excel, or started from the scratch, achieved and sustained extraordinary levels of performance in the same business environment? How did these few firms become highly admired companies?

What were the factors *within the control* of leadership and management of the companies, which, in the same business environment, achieved outstanding performance and growth?

What were the basic paradigms, values, strategic orientations, organizational characteristics, managerial processes and practices that made the difference?

More specifically, *how did some of the distinguished Indian and multinational companies operating in India develop a sustainable competitive edge in the context of the changing business environment?*

What can we learn from such companies to develop world-class organizations in India?

These are the questions that have inspired this research-based work.

As stated above, there is no dearth of writing and research on this subject. There are a number of well-known researches and studies that have attempted to answer questions pertaining to the excellence and sustainability of organizations. These questions are as eternal and complex as the search for survival, good health and longevity of human life. Each research throws up some new light and adds to the existing plethora of knowledge.

Sometimes the new researches question, challenge and change the existing paradigms. We took up this challenge to come up with a modest empirical work that would hopefully be in such a category of research.

The Search for Answers

We did not attempt a questionnaire-based research with a large sample, complex statistical analysis entailing quantitative testing of hypotheses. Instead, we opted for a qualitative research methodology that would provide holistic and meaningful insights to complex questions in the contemporary and changing Indian context.

We chose a simple Delphi-type methodology combined with ethnographic type of research and case study approach, utilizing in-depth interviews with key managers, field observations and analysis of various aspects of management and performance of selected companies from other available sources of data and information.

The interviews were open-ended and intensive, in some cases lasting for several hours. Each interview was tape-recorded and transcribed for comprehensive analysis. The data, information and views so obtained were supplemented by some field observations, study of published material, published case studies of these companies, and related research studies and literature. Further, the available data was rigorously analyzed on various parameters to examine the comparative level and sustainability of performance of the companies and validity of the sample.

The sample of companies chosen for the study was mainly based on judgment and opinions sought from some eminent Indian professional managers and management thinkers, keeping in view the companies' performance over a span of 10 – 15 years period, coverage across major sectors, ownership patterns, domestic and multinational companies, regions in the country and old and new industries, to the extent possible. The sample consisted, mostly, of highly admired organizations that were considered outstanding, as well as a few of those that were finding it difficult to cope with the challenges of change. The convenience and access in obtaining information within the limited time and resources were also some of the factors, which account for its limitations. A detailed analysis of the performance of these companies, during 1990 - 2003, to examine the validity of the sample has been given in Chapter 10 and Research Appendix I.

Companies Included in the Study

- INFOSYS
- WIPRO
- SATYAM
- RANBAXY
- DR. REDDY'S LAB
- HERO HONDA
- EICHER
- LARSEN & TOUBRO

- SUNDRAM FASTENERS (TVS)
- TITAN
- MOTOROLA
- BPL
- HINDUSTAN LEVER LIMITED
- GLAXO-SMITHKLINE BEECHAM
- TATA SONS
- RELIANCE
- HINDUSTAN ELECTRO-GRAPHITE
- ICICI
- BEL

Examining the track record of these companies in their relative compound rates of growth during the period 1990–2003 tested the relevance and significance of the sample. The parameters chosen for this purpose were compound rates of growth of net sales and profit (PBDIT), as compared to the selective industry averages; and change in their relative rank in market capitalization among the top hundred companies in India during this period, as shown in table numbers 1.1 to 1.4 [Companies included in the study are shown in bold letters in Table 1.1.]

It is interesting to note from these tables that most of the companies selected for this research registered a significant rise in their relative ranking in market capitalization, while 4 companies had a relative lower rank (Table 1.2). Further, from among the 10 companies (out of the 19 companies chosen for this research, whose data could be comparatively analyzed with *selected* industry averages), 8 companies significantly exceeded the selected industry average in compound rate of growth of sales, and 8 companies, by far, exceeded such industry average in compound rate of growth of profit (PBDIT). (Tables 1.2, 1.3 & 1.4.)

The purpose of this research-based work is to present to business leaders, professional managers and management knowledge seekers, some helpful propositions and insights based on an empirical study that may stimulate their thinking. We did not choose a 'methodology bound', narrow research approach purely for the academic purpose of testing a few propositions, though it has its own merits for the development of scientific knowledge. We were looking for a

Table 1.2: Companies included in the study for indepth Analysis Based on Market Capitalization in the year 1991 and 2002

Company Name	Rank 1991*	Rank 2002**	
Wipro	195	2	↗
Infosys technologies#	83	4	↗
Satyam Computer Services#	344	8	↗
Ranbaxy Laboratories	65	6	↗
Dr. Reddy's Laboratories	310	9	↗
Hero Honda Motors	115	12	↗
Eicher Motors	454	277	↗
Titan	70	151	↘
BPL+	233	235	↘
Reliance Industries	6	3	↗
Hindustan Lever	5	1	↗
Larsen & Toubro	14	23	↘
Sundram Fasteners	270	147	↗
HEG	280	294	↘
ICICI Bank##	62	10	↗
GSK Cons. Health Care#	47	39	↗

* Source: *Business Today,* March 7-21, 1992

** Source: *Business Today,* November 9, 2003

Source: Ranking for the year 1997 as Given in *Business Today,* Sept 7, 1997

Source: Ranking for the year 1998 as Given in *Business Today,* Sept 7, 1997

\+ Name Changed from BPL Sanyo (1991) to BPL.

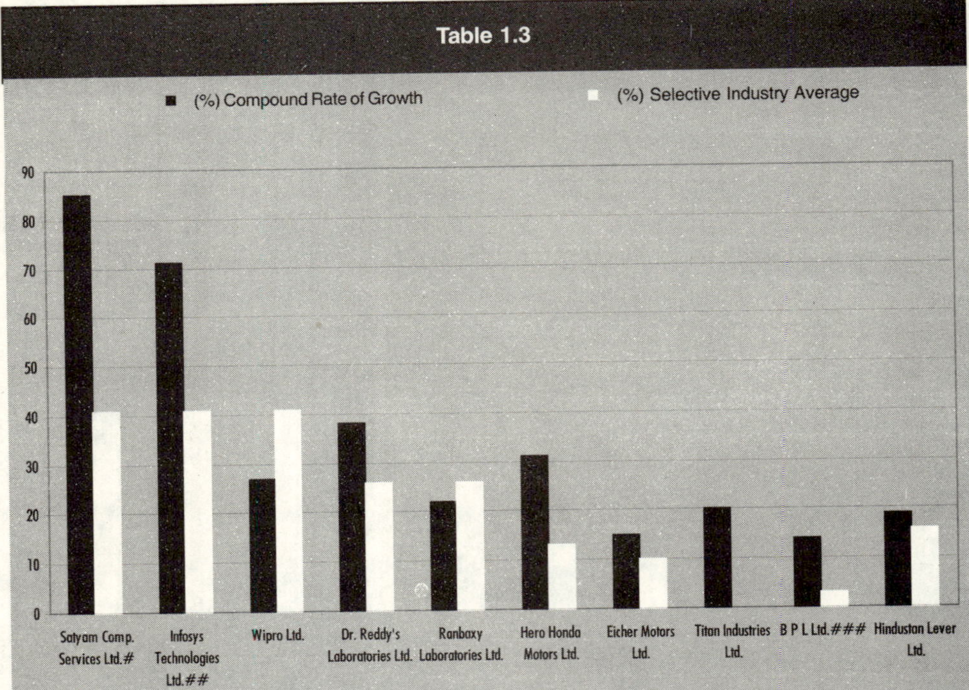

Compound Rate of Growth of Net Sales 1990 - 2003

Company name	Compound Rate of Growth (%)	Selective Industry Average* (%)
Satyam Comp. Services Ltd.#	85	41
Infosys Technologies Ltd.##	71	41
Wipro Ltd.	27	41
Dr. Reddy's Laboratories Ltd.	38	26
Ranbaxy Laboratories Ltd.	22	26
Hero Honda Motors Ltd.	31	13
Eicher Motors Ltd.	15	10
Titan Industries Ltd.	20	0
B P L Ltd.###	14	3
Hindustan Lever Ltd.	19	16

From Mar 94 - Mar 03
From Mar 92 - Mar 03
From Mar 90-Mar 02
*Based on data of top 20 companies whose data was available and excluding the companies under study

Table 1.4

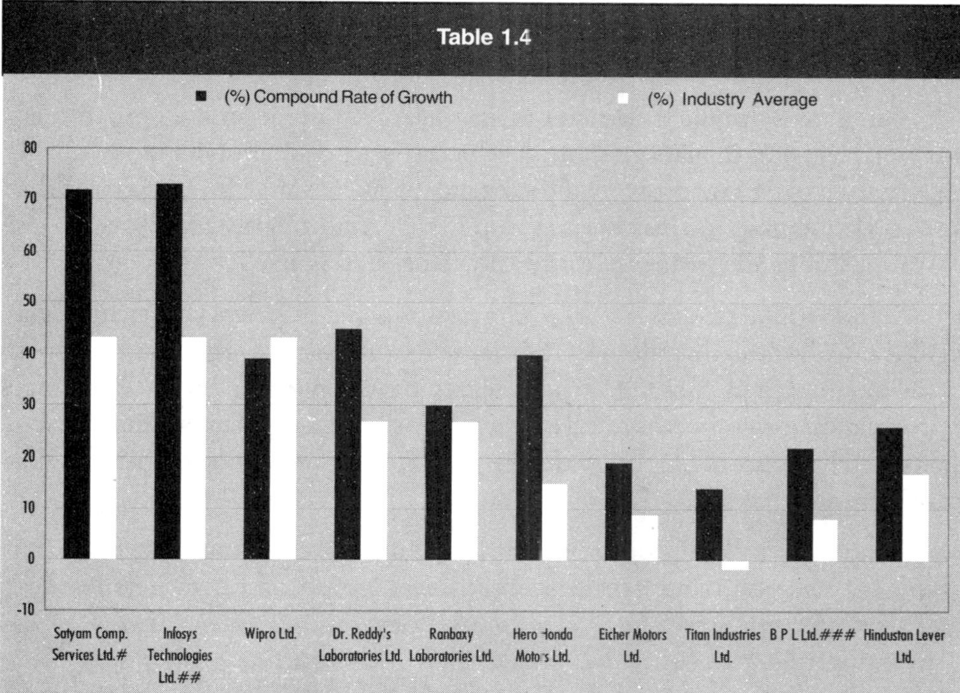

Compound Rate of Growth of Profits (PBDIT) 1990 - 2003

Company name	Compound Rate of Growth (%)	Selective Industry Average* (%)
Satyam Comp. Services Ltd.#	72	43
Infosys Technologies Ltd.##	73	43
Wipro Ltd.	39	43
Dr. Reddy's Laboratories Ltd.	45	27
Ranbaxy Laboratories Ltd.	30	27
Hero Honda Motors Ltd.	40	15
Eicher Motors Ltd.	19	9
Titan Industries Ltd.	14	-2
B P L Ltd.###	22	8
Hindustan Lever Ltd.	26	17

From Mar 94 - Mar 03
From Mar 92 - Mar 03
From Mar 90-Mar 02
*Based on data of top 20 companies whose data was available and excluding the companies under study

more holistic understanding of the phenomenon of organizational sustainability and competitiveness.

Our hope is that the understanding, insight and proposition developed through this work will help in managing and developing more competitive and sustainable organizations in the increasingly difficult and turbulent times. We also expect that some of the findings and insights may inspire more rigorous research works to test the propositions and further advance knowledge in this area.

We identified several factors, characteristics and practices that stand out as significant common threads in the fabric of the outstanding organizations. Most of the organizations chosen for this research have demonstrated sustained high performance and competitive edge over a reasonably long span of time of ten to fifteen years, in spite of significant changes and intense competition in their business environment.

We have based our propositions on the patterns observed and insights shared by highly successful and experienced business leaders and managers of these organizations. In a sense, *we have tried to make explicit and document the tacit knowledge of highly experienced and successful business leaders and professional managers in India.* Such knowledge was embedded in their insights and wisdom based on long years of experience of managing, leading and developing outstanding organizations, and sustaining high performance across different and changing business environments.

We found that the organizations that sustained high performance over long spans of time and consistently achieved high ratings had distinctive characteristics. We have chosen to describe them as 'Purposeful Values-driven Enterprises' (PVEs).

In the following chapters, we will present the findings, insights and propositions that evidently account for developing and sustaining competitive edge.

REFERENCES

1. Thomas J. Peters and Robert H. Waterman Jr., *Search for Excellence* (New York: Harper & Row Publishers, 1982).

2. Visiting Professor at the Wharton School of Finance, stated in a personal meeting in New Delhi on 3rd December, 2002.

CHAPTER TWO

The Purposeful, Values-Driven Enterprise

Distinguishing Characteristics of Organizations that Demonstrated Sustained High Performance and Competitive Edge

'We may affirm absolutely that nothing great in the world has ever been accomplished without passion'

FRIEDRICH WILHELM HEGEL

AT THE END OF our interview, we asked the chief executive officer of Dr. Reddy's Labs, one of the dynamic and leading Indian pharmaceutical companies, to give one message for young managers aspiring to be future business leaders. Without a moment's hesitation, he said:

> I have mentioned three platforms on which Dr. Reddy's Labs is becoming globally competitive, which are: Innovation and Entrepreneurship, Globalization and Focus on People. The fourth thing I will say is **Passion** – Passion for what you do. And I think only companies and leaders who are passionate about what they are doing will be able to create great organizations... *Without passion you cannot create great organizations.* You have to be excited about what you are doing. We believe we are very excited about what we are doing, because we are making a difference in people's lives.[1]

Passion stood out as a powerful driving factor for leading the organizations to success and sustainability in the companies included in this research. When we analyzed and reflected on our other interviews and observations, we recalled the involvement, commitment and passion of people across all the outstanding organizations for the purpose, values and identity of their company. It struck us as such an important factor that we chose to give the title **'Passion to Win'**.

As we repeatedly listened to the tape recordings of interviews with some of the most experienced and insightful business leaders and professional managers and did a close analysis of their interviews' manuscripts and other available information, we began to notice some deep and powerful common undercurrents in all highly admired companies. These undercurrents were: clarity of purpose with challenging goals, some distinctive principles and professional values, a high performance and learning culture and an identity of organization that generated a sense of pride. *A passion for these key elements set them apart from the other ordinary business organizations.*

The winning companies were guided by an over-arching and compelling purpose and vision. They were driven by a distinctive set of *values*, which they did not compromise even at the risk of losing short-term gains. The dominant motivation of their leadership was the passion to win in the most challenging and competitive environment. In addition to inspiring, transformational leadership, imaginative and innovative strategy, superior execution and 'win-win' relationship with all the stakeholders, *they were driven by the ambition, passion and vision to build a great enterprise.* They did not exist merely to make money in the protected markets, or by shortchanging their customers and stakeholders.

This was common to the relatively new first generation enterprises like Infosys, Wipro, Satyam, Ranbaxy, Dr. Reddy's Labs., Hero Honda, Eicher and BEL; as well as the older business houses and companies like Tata Sons, Larsen & Toubro, Hindustan Lever, Glaxo-Smithkline Beecham, TVS Group and several other well known business houses. Irrespective of the age, sector, region, type of ownership and country of origin, there seemed to be a driving purpose larger than only benefiting the owners. They almost religiously adhered to a set of guiding principles, values and purpose that endowed them with a distinctive identity, character and destiny. We have, therefore, chosen to describe such companies as **'Purposeful Values-driven Enterprises' (PVEs),** as contrasted with **'Money-making Commercial Outfits' (MCOs).**

It is not to deny or undermine the importance of profitability. As also pointed out by Peter Drucker, profitability is essential to cover the costs of being in business, costs of staying in business and to insure the supply of future capital for innovation and expansion, either directly or indirectly.[2] But he cautioned that "to emphasize only profit,... misdirects managers to the point where they may endanger the survival of the business. To obtain profit today they tend to undermine the future".[3]

"Profitability", as very lucidly explained by Collins and Porras, "is a necessary condition for existence and a means to more important ends, but it is not the end in itself for many of the visionary companies. Profit is like oxygen, food, water and blood for the body; they are not the *point* of life, but without them, there is no life."[4] They have quoted David Packard, co-founder of the famous Hewlett-Packard Company, who had said: "Profit is *not the proper end and aim of management - it is what makes all of the proper ends and aims possible*" [*emphasis* added]. Interestingly, in the same spirit, Mr. B.M.L. Munjal, chairman of Hero Honda, said: "Right from day one, the idea was to give full value for money to the customer, without having before us a very ambitious profitability factor. Profitability has been always behind us and it has seriously followed us because we have left it behind."

In short, profit is one of the key measures of success of an enterprise and a critical requirement for its survival, growth and sustainability, but it cannot be the 'be-all' or 'end-all' of business. If profit for making money is pursued as the only purpose, it can endanger sustainability of the organization in the long run. Factors like providing value to the customers, constant improvement in products and services, ensuring high commitment and motivation of employees are more vital for the survival of the firm than short-term profitability. So also is investment in developing competencies, R&D and innovation and maintaining goodwill of all stakeholders by adhering to the core values and business ethics critical for the long-term competitiveness and sustainability of an enterprise.

In the pre-liberalization phase of the Indian economy, most companies were busy cornering licenses to make monopoly profits, or giving shoddy products and service to the customers because of highly protected markets. Operating in the same business environment, most of the highly admired companies *opted* for providing better products and services and building enterprises with a vision to be among the best in their industry on various qualitative, quantitative and value parameters.

The winning companies *chose* to offer better value for money to the customers through innovations and to raise their levels of productivity. They offered better conditions and dignity to their employees than their contemporary companies, even though they had the option to behave like other money-making companies in that environment.[5] They looked after the interest of all stakeholders. Most of them aspired to become world-class companies, compete in international markets and become international companies. Some of these companies built world scale plants with state-of-art technology and benchmarked with the best in the world.

They *made the difficult and challenging choices* driven by their aspiration, passion and vision and distinct ideals and values for their policies and operations. For example, companies like Ranbaxy opted for competing in international markets, when easy options for making lots of money were available in the large protected domestic markets. Instead of following the common paradigm of making 'quick money' in the scarcity-creating 'license and permit raj', they chose the challenging option of operating in the most competitive world markets for learning and developing long-term competitiveness to build an international company, or a company with international standards. That is why we have chosen to refer to such companies as 'values-driven enterprises'. Values represent some ideals or norms considered desirable as means or ends in themselves, as opposed to expedient choices for short-term gains.

The founders and their successive chain of leaders of outstanding companies are driven by a passion, aspiration, ambition and vision to do something much greater than merely amassing wealth. There is a distinct cause or *purpose* than purely 'business-to-make-money' that is propelling them. For example, laying the foundation for the industrial development of India, as by the founders of business houses like the Tatas in earlier times, or the dream of building the most respected, world-class organizations offering highest quality services and products internationally as in the case of Infosys, Wipro, Satyam and Sundram Fasteners in the contemporary period.

Similar drives could be noted for building an enterprise which would give the most reliable and efficient products with the best possible technology, offering gainful employment and wealth-sharing business model with all its stakeholders, as in the case of Hero-Honda and Titan. In several aspects akin to this business model is the case of Reliance, with the added orientation to develop and tap large dormant or potential markets in India by building world-scale plants and projects with state-of-art technology.

Some of the outstanding companies with similar orientation are also multinational companies operating in India, or companies launched by foreigners in India who chose to identify themselves with the needs, requirements and aspirations of the country. They operated with strong professional values, creating valued products, wealth and employment, like Hindustan Lever and Larsen & Toubro.

All these distinguished winning companies developed and nurtured an identity, character and culture that gave a *sense of pride* to their employees, and shareholders and inspired *trust and confidence* among the customers and other stakeholders.

> *The common elements in all winning companies are 'the passion to win' in the competitive environment and to build an enterprise as an institution with a distinctive purpose, values, culture and identity. They strive to be known for their high standards in service and quality of products, outstanding performance, and achievements and supremacy in their industry.*

Such a company is an *institution and an enterprise* that tends to survive and continue to grow and develop to higher levels far beyond their founders' lifetime and imagination. Its core characteristics consist of the purpose, values, culture and identity, that seem to get imprinted in its genetic code, as in the case of Tata Sons, TVS, HLL and several other such renowned business houses and companies. These characteristics are passed on from generation to generation. They provide them a co-evolving continuity (i.e., an evolving organization along with the evolving and changing business environment). *Such companies are able to sustain themselves through the rough and tumble of the changing business environment by constantly adapting to and pro-acting upon the environment through changing leadership, strategies, policies and practices to survive and grow, while maintaining the continuity of their core characteristics. Such organizations operate on a markedly different paradigm, as compared to the 'Money-making Commercial Outfits' that follow mainly the 'business-for-profit-only' paradigm.*

FACTORS, CHARACTERISTICS AND PRACTICES THAT DISTINGUISH THE PURPOSEFUL VALUES-DRIVEN ENTERPRISES

Let us now take a look at the patterns of distinct factors, characteristics and practices that are common among the outstanding winning organizations, as noted in the companies that we studied. We noted about twenty to twenty-five characteristics that seemed to recur in most of the organizations studied. Several of these characteristics are well known and familiar and some are not so familiar, or not as much emphasized. A closer and deeper analysis of these factors and characteristics led to the identification of five major clusters on the basis of which we have developed the 5-I framework. We chose to describe these clusters in simple terminology that would be familiar and easily understood by practicing managers. However, the contents of each cluster and their *nuances* are very different from their commonly understood meanings, as will be seen in their elaboration and discussion that follows.

The five clusters of organizational attributes that constitute the 5-I framework and distinguish the outstanding organizations are:

1. ***Inspiring Leadership:*** The energizing, direction-providing and driving force that inspires and mobilizes people's talents and resources.

2. ***Innovative Strategy:*** Conceptualizing innovative business models, distinctive approaches and initiatives for long-term survival and growth.

3. ***Implementation Skills and Process-driven Execution:*** Superior processes, systems, structures, logistics and technology for producing, promoting and delivering products and services and getting results.

4. ***Internal and External 'Win-Win' Relationships:*** Developing network of external and internal relationships, mobilizing resources and creating goodwill.

5. ***Identity – Purpose, Values and Culture:*** The purpose, values and culture that constitute the distinctive identity and character of the organization - its sustaining and aligning core.

When we tried to put the different factors, characteristics and practices under these clusters, we noted that they were highly interactive and overlapping and, therefore, it was not possible to treat them as discrete independent categories that could be placed in separate boxes. They appeared more like interdependent parts of a highly interactive, dynamic, organic system. These clusters appeared more like the five mutually interacting and overlapping circles as shown in Figure 2.1.

It was the interactive, dynamic Configuration of all these key elements that gave the companies a sustainable competitive edge and not merely one or two factors like strategy or core competence.

This dynamic organic system, however, could not be visualized as a closed system. Instead we could see it as an open system that was interacting with and interdependent upon the external business environment. This point will be further discussed as a theoretical construct to explain the larger issues of sustainability in later chapters.

The five major clusters that we identified in the '5-I Framework' as constituting the key elements of the system and their sub-categories, consisting of the factors, characteristics and practices will be described in later chapters. Before we go into the details of these elements, let us take a holistic view of the distinguishing characteristics of the winning companies that have demonstrated sustainable competitive edge.

Figure 2.1: The Five Distinguishing Elements of Purposeful Values-driven Organizations

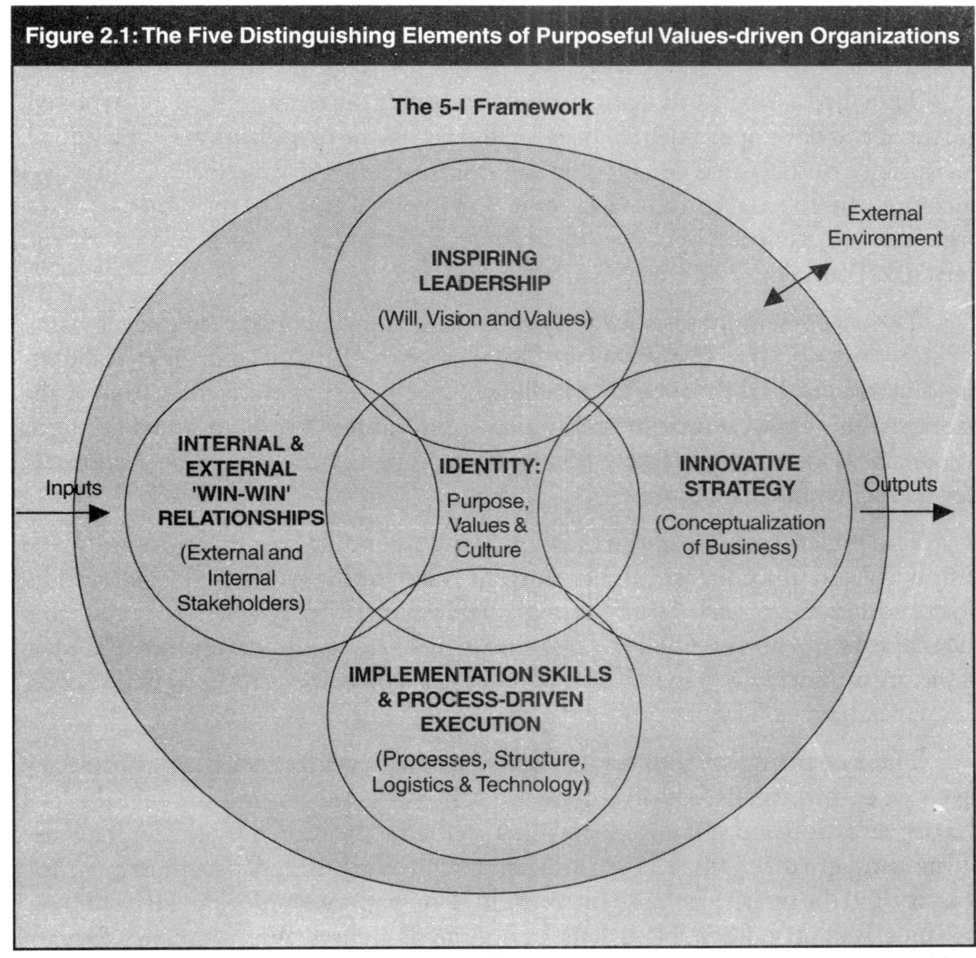

Following is a brief overview of the patterns noted in the five clusters:

Inspiring Leadership

Leadership in outstanding organizations covered in this study that demonstrated sustained outstanding performance and competitive edge was inspiring leadership driven by a passion to win. They were more operationally value-based and principle-centered. They set highly ambitious goals and chose to operate in challenging business environments to enhance their internal competence and develop their competitiveness, as clearly evident in companies like Ranbaxy, Infosys, Titan and Sundram Fasteners.

They had a long-term institution-development orientation. They attracted, nurtured and developed talent and leadership across the organization. They valued, encouraged and created organizational environment for innovation, initiative, entrepreneurship and constant improvement in every aspect of the working of the organization, as noted in companies like Hindustan Lever, Wipro, Satyam and Larsen & Toubro.

They were seldom satisfied with the status quo. They had a long-term vision for the company, anticipated the need for change and initiated changes to take the organization to higher levels of excellence. They were acutely conscious of the proposition that sustainable competitiveness cannot be maintained without sustainable leadership, as could be observed in companies and groups like Hindustan Lever, Eicher and Tata Sons.

The leaders of some of the most outstanding Indian organizations followed simplicity and in some cases almost austerity in their life styles. They believed in, practiced and role-modeled some strongly held values and principles. They followed the metaphor of an extended family in relating to the members and stakeholders of the organizations they founded and/or headed, as in companies like Hero Honda, Titan, Ranbaxy and Infosys.

Their inspiring style of leadership led to the development of extraordinary levels of commitment, involvement and sense of pride among the members of the organization and stakeholders. They seemed to be driven by the larger cause of building great organizations, supremacy in their business or industry in the country and the international arena, as could be seen in companies like Hero Honda, Reliance, Ranbaxy, L&T, HLL, Titan, Sundram Fasteners, Wipro, Infosys, Satyam and business houses like Tata Sons.

The inspiring leaders subsumed their personal glory and gains to the institutional interest of the organizations led by them.

Innovative Strategy

The leadership and management of the winning companies conceived, initiated, evolved and pursued strategic business models that were more innovative, adaptive and pro-active. They were highly focused on creating and delivering value to the customers. They persistently ensured providing superior products and services. They developed innovative and effective strategies for supply chain management, marketing and finance for capturing and sharing value that led to high profitability and growth, as demonstrated by companies like Hero Honda, Reliance, Satyam, Infosys and Titan.

These companies pursued a dynamic focus on selected market segments, products, brands, customer groups, locations and regions. They selectively chose their basis of competition. They initiated strategies of differentiation on various factors like product characteristics, quality, price, access, delivery, service and brand image and moved up the value curve when their products and services got 'commodotized', as done by companies like L&T, Titan, Hero Honda and Infosys.

They converted threats into opportunities and constraints into imaginative business solutions. They perceived opportunities where others saw limitations and barriers. They sensed business opportunities beyond the visible horizon as clearly demonstrated by companies like Reliance.

They kept 'ear to the ground' to detect changes in markets, systematically as well as informally. They obtained feedback and information from customers, consumers and employees. They constantly gathered and analyzed information from various sources about changes in the business environment as practiced in companies like HLL, Eicher, Wipro and all other winning companies.

They sensed and anticipated change earlier than others. They were quick in responding to change and often initiated change ahead of the competition as in the case of HLL and Motorola.

They converted latent needs into demand by innovative business propositions, by offering high quality valued products and services at affordable price, as exemplified by Reliance, Titan and Hero Honda.

They often re-defined the industry and re-invented their organization through multiple transformations in the changing business environment and yet maintained a continuity of their core values, purpose and identity that could be noted in companies like Wipro, Hindustan Lever, L&T and companies managed by Tata Sons.

Some of the outstanding Indian companies chose the internationalization route for competitiveness, or were more internationally oriented in their choice of strategies, policies and management practices, like benchmarking in productivity, quality, cost, technology and scale of operations. Most such companies chose to master and develop technology on their own and avoided dependence on joint ventures, as clearly articulated and practiced by companies like Sundram Fasteners, Eicher, Ranbaxy and Reliance.

A significant notable trend in strategy for developing sustainable competitive edge chosen by the distinguished winning Indian companies is transformation into Indian multinational companies.

Process-Driven Execution

The winning companies are deeply concerned with and acutely aware of the importance and centrality of effective execution[6], implementation, monitoring and measurement of results-outstanding examples of which are companies like Reliance, Infosys, L&T, Hero Honda and Ranbaxy.

They are professionally managed, high performance oriented and process driven. They developed, institutionalized and rigorously followed processes, systems, policies and practices that would ensure highly efficient and time-bound completion of plans, programmes, projects and initiatives. They focused on achieving high levels of productivity, quality, cost reduction and delivery of products and services in their operations as noted in companies like Ranbaxy, Sundram Fasteners, Reliance, Hero Honda, Infosys, Satyam and Hindustan Lever.

They reviewed their structure, systems and processes and modified them from time to time to ensure their effectiveness and nimbleness in responding to the changing requirements, as practiced in companies like Satyam, Wipro, Infosys and Ranbaxy.

They acquired, continuously improved, upgraded, developed and adopted the technology that would give them the best results, as noted in companies like Hero Honda, Eicher, Titan and Sundram Fasteners.

They made special efforts for developing skills and competencies of the staff and for acquiring, utilizing, sharing and developing relevant information and knowledge across the organization, as specially emphasized in companies like Hindustan Lever, Satyam, Wipro, Infosys and Ranbaxy.

The investment in directly related research and development for improvement of existing products and development of new products was seen as the key for survival, growth and competitiveness as clearly evident in companies like Dr. Reddy's Labs and Ranbaxy.

'Win-Win' Relationships

These companies painstakingly built, nurtured and protected their brand equity, goodwill of customers and stakeholders. They cultivated mutually supportive 'win-win' relationship with all their stakeholders of which an outstanding example is Hero Honda.

Their philosophy of business was based on mutuality of interests with their stakeholders. They balanced and protected the interest of their stakeholders and tried to equitably share the gains with them. They did not subvert the interest of other stakeholders for the interest of promoters or controlling owners, as stated and practiced by companies like Titan and Infosys.

The winning companies cultivated excellent relationships with their stakeholders - shareholders, dealers, vendors, customers and employees. They tried to develop positive and supportive relationship with a significant external interfaces like the government and regulatory agencies.

Distinct Identity–Purpose, Values and Culture

The winning companies were clear about their unique purpose and articulated it succinctly in a simple and understandable form. They emphatically followed certain values and business ethics. Interestingly, a strong relationship could be observed in their ethical values and economic value generated by them.

They operated on a principle-centered paradigm and did not compromise on their core values for short-term gains.

They practiced a high degree of professionalism and meritocracy in policies, decision-making and governance. They ensured such orientation through openness in communication, wide discussions and consultative decision making. They thoughtfully developed organization culture, processes and structures that supported these concerns.

They built a strong and positive brand equity for their company and their products, and painstakingly maintained and nurtured it. They cultivated a distinctive institutional identity and promoted a sense of belonging, commitment and pride among its members.

They demonstrated concern for the larger socio-economic and environmental issues of the country, initiated some programmes to deal with a few carefully chosen specific issues directly or through their benevolent foundations. In some cases, they provided thought leadership to deal with such issues. They were more conscious of their Corporate Social Responsibility.

THE 'PURPOSEFUL VALUES-DRIVEN ENTERPRISE'

To sum up, the most important characteristics of winning organizations capable of developing and sustaining competitive edge are: clarity of purpose, adherence to their core values, a distinct identity and passion and vision of their top leadership for supremacy in their spheres of action. Their ability to foresee, inspire and bring about change, initiate innovations, attract the best talent and develop leadership and competence across the organization distinguishes them from ordinary organizations.

Their leadership is highly ambitious and passionate about the supremacy, performance and excellence of their organization as an institution. They ensure the continuity and strengthening of its core identity, values and purpose, subsuming their personal ego and glory to the success and longevity of the organization.

They are proactive, open and receptive to information and feedback from various sources. They visualize and anticipate changes and conceptualize innovative strategies. They are able to implement them courageously, effectively and speedily.

They develop and nurture 'win-win' relationships with all their internal and external stakeholders and follow professionalism, openness and meritocracy in their management and governance.

Such companies co-evolve as open dynamic socio-economic-technical systems with the changing business environment and pro-actively initiate strategies, businesses, products and services that redefine the organization, the industry and the markets.

Such outstanding, dynamic firms are clear and committed to their purpose, are 'values-driven' and value-creating organizations. They are able to develop and sustain a competitive edge to survive and grow in the turbulent and challenging business environment. We have characterized such organizations are 'Purposeful Values-driven Enterprises' (PVEs). They are based and operate on a paradigm that is quite different from the paradigm of 'Money-making Commercial Outfits' (MCOs).

In the following chapters, we shall explain and illustrate the factors, characteristics and practices and their nuances that distinguish such organizations, especially in the Indian context. We will give the observations, insights and information from which we drew our inferences and propositions and developed the conceptual framework given above. We will place before you extracts from interviews that highlight the insights and words of wisdom of some of the most experienced business leaders and professional managers. We will cite examples from written case studies and other published material about these companies and our field observations that may help in substantiating our inferences and propositions. We will give detailed analysis of the performance of the companies selected for this project to critically examine the validity and relevance of the sample.

As explicitly stated earlier, the five clusters of factors characteristics, and practices emerged as overlapping circles shown in Figure 2.1. Therefore, quotes from interviews, or examples of practices to illustrate a particular point from a company, may be repeated in different chapters to support quotes of the holistic complexity of the organization. Such repetition has been done on purpose to explain the inter-related and overlapping patterns in each cluster of the key elements in an organization.

REFERENCES

1. Research Interview with Mr. G.V. Prasad, Executive Vice Chairman & CEO, Dr. Reddy's Laboratories Ltd.
2. Peter F. Drucker, *The Practice of Management*, (New York: Harper & Brothers Publishers, 1954), 77.
3. *ibid*, 62.
4. James C. Collins and Jerry I. Porras, *Built to Last*, (New York: Harper Business, 1997), 55.
5. According to Prof. Ishwar Dayal, a particular behaviour cannot be described as a 'Value' unless the person has and exercises choice for that behaviour. (View expressed by him in a personal discussion with the researchers.)

6 The term 'Execution' to describe the processes of Implementation was developed by Larry Bossidy and Ram Charan, in their book entitled *Execution: The Discipline of Getting Things Done*, (New York: Crown Business, 2002).

CHAPTER THREE

Sustainable Competitive Edge

An Overview of the Key Factors

'The ability to learn faster than the competition may be the only sustainable competitive edge'

ARIE DE GUES (THE LIVING COMPANY)

WHAT IS SUSTAINABLE COMPETITIVE EDGE?

How do business leaders and professional managers view sustainability of organizations?

What could be some key factors leading to sustainability?

A simple way of looking at the notion of 'sustainable competitive edge' is that it is the distinctive ability of an organization to sustain outstanding performance over long spans of time. It is the ability of a company to transcend trade cycles and other factors that lead to corporate demise.

We explored different viewpoints of business leaders and professional managers on this subject and, after considerable discussions, chose the following definition of Sustainable Competitive Edge for the purpose of this research:

> *Sustainable Competitive Edge is the* ***distinctive intrinsic ability, resilience and endurance*** *of an organization to maintain* ***relative superiority in performance and growth,*** *in a competitive and changing business environment over a reasonably* ***long span of time.***
>
> *It is the ability of an organization* ***to transcend trade cycles and other factors that lead to corporate demise and bounce back*** *when everything seems to have been lost.*

It will be noted from this description of sustainability that we have chosen to refer to it as an organization's internal ability to maintain longevity along with superior performance. It is based on an organization's institutional characteristics, competencies, processes and practices that distinguish it from its competitors. These characteristics endow the organization with resilience and endurance to cope with the moves of the competitors and outperform them. They also enable it to overcome the limitations of product life cycles and transcend trade cycles. Organizations endowed with such competitive edge tend to influence the business environment, redefine the industry, go through multiple transformations and reinvent themselves.

In short, sustainable competitive edge gives an organization resilience, adaptability, ability to change and innovate to continue to survive and grow in the changing turbulent business environment. It is manifested in the organization's relative qualitative and quantitative performance over time. However, it would be unrealistic to think of sustainability as an eternal phenomenon.

Although it is difficult to specifically measure sustainable competitive edge, it can be inferred through an organization's performance and growth on the basis of its operational, financial, marketing and other relevant parameters as compared to the competing firms in the same or similar industries over long spans of time. More specifically, it can be measured through profitability and productivity measures, return on assets/capital employed, financial ratios, market capitalization, value creation and other generally accepted criteria of superior performance and growth over extended periods of time.

Let us now examine the different views expressed by leading professional managers and business leaders about sustainable competitive edge in organizations.

From our interviews, study of literature on sustainability and perusal of case studies, it became increasingly evident that to understand the phenomenon of sustainability it would be more relevant to view the *'organizations as living, organic, dynamic entities that are co-evolving with and pro-actively impacting upon the business environment'*. It is a different paradigm than the traditional, mechanistic and somewhat passive discourse of 'strategic fit' between the enterprise and its environment as stated in most strategy textbooks.

The organic view of organization and the metaphor of biology to understand the phenomenon of sustainability were emphasized by Mr. Gopalakrishnan of Tata Sons. Stating his view that organizations follow the laws of biology he said,

"If you have a long tenure, you care little for your succession. Love of posterity is a consequence of the fear of death. As turtles have a very long life, they seem to care little for their offspring."

Regarding the time span and criteria to be considered for measuring sustainability for business organizations, he said: "I would say probably not less than 10 years. If it is more than 20 years, then the lessons are very instructive. So 15 years is a good ball park figure... Some crude measures of sustainability would be improvements in earnings per share, growth and profits, return on capital employed and improvements in productivity."

Regarding the key factors to which one can attribute sustainable competitive advantage, Mr. Gopalakrishnan said, "I think one of the very key factors is how the leadership, and by this I don't mean just the CEO, *but the top group of 8 to 10 persons, see their own term*... In organizations with sustained and sustainable competitive advantage, the top leadership do not think of their regime only, but they think of their regime *as a small part of a relay race*. They see their regime as an the opportunity to hold the baton for one part of a race that is not won by their running well, but by their predecessors having run well and their successors also running well."

For ensuring long-term sustainability of your organization, Mr. Gopalakrishnan advised, "treat your successor like your son". Stressing this point, he said: "Many organizations that do not have sustainable competitive advantage suffer because the moment a person takes over, either deliberately or inadvertently he runs down a few things done in the last lap. When he finishes his lap, he writes a glorious book of what and how wonderfully he did it, making people wonder whether his successor can ever continue it".

It also became clear to us that sustainability cannot be treated as an eternal and absolute phenomenon. It is finite and relative. All that can be done is to understand what can lead to relative longevity and superiority of organizations, their products and services, their profitability and growth. Analyzing the complex phenomenon of sustainable competitiveness, Mr. Subodh Bhargava, former CMD and advisor of Eicher, stated that: "There is hardly a company globally where sustainability is unlimited...There are cycles and from yesterday's 'In Search of Excellence' companies, I suppose eight out of ten do not exist and the same is true in India." Competitiveness, he thought, "Would have to be on different planes. It is not just the cost, it is *the value derived by the customer.* Second, the quality, technology area and the third, reliability, marketing, service, timing – and *all that a customer looks for.* And finally it is the *brand* which comes to signify competitiveness, which is very high priced but still has a sustained customer patronage...this is one definition of competitiveness, there could be some other definitions also... What affects competitiveness are inputs, value addition and output...Whereas inputs and market conditions are affected by external factors, value addition at whatever level, like treasury, manufacturing, supply chain, managing efficiently and *consumers' mindset contributes to competitiveness*...If the consumer is not demanding enough, things will go differently in any market. There is an iterative process of consumers vs competitiveness."

Emphasizing the importance of governance, leadership and ability of management to change as the key factors for sustainability, Mr. Bhargava said: "There is only one word which is common to different aspects of sustainability and competitiveness, that is *Governance* – the quality of governance comes from *leadership*. So the sustainable competitiveness cannot be brought in until the organization has got a sustained high quality of leadership and sustained outlook towards its people. Sustained (positive) outlook towards people does not mean softness. It means motivation, it means skill, it means development, it means training, it means ownership, it means involvement and it means empowerment." Another aspect of good governance, he emphasized, is the concern for the stakeholders: "If the owners are going to continue to short-change other stakeholders in whatever environment, then obviously it is not sustainable." In his opinion, "The most critical dimension of leadership for sustainability is *the ability of the top management to change itself,* and transform their organization to remain competitive. Failure is inevitably on account of two reasons: either the top not changing itself and its not becoming the role model for change; or overdoing some dimension of change with a knowledge gap and attitudinal gap at the top level."

The ability of an organization and its management to change itself and the pace and nature of change that are critical for sustainability were most emphatically mentioned by several persons. An interesting but debatable observation was made by Mr. Gopalakrishnan about the pace of change that the 'challenge of managing radical change is to go at the pace at which people are willing to change. If the change is too fast, they die; if it is too slow, you die.'

Dr. Dinesh, director and co-founder of Infosys projected a different perspective to the issue of sustainability. He viewed it from the system based approach. Explaining this viewpoint, he said: "It is not results alone which count when you talk about sustaining excellence. One time you cannot produce and say I will go down that rail. You should be able to sustain performance. That is where the *system-based models* (like the Malcolm Baldridge model) become important. These models give you benchmark on companies, which are excellent. In a sense that: Where you are on leadership? Where you are on strategic planning? Where you are on customer and market focus? Where you are on process management? Where you are on human resource focus? Where you are on information and analysis? There is an emphasis on the approach to *processes* that you adopt and there is equally an emphasis on the results also... So the approach becomes very important. What these models teach you is the approach and show the results based on that continuously... If you follow the philosophy of such approach in your management and make sure that it is there, then you have won the game."

Based on his rich experience in organizations, a very senior executive of the Reliance Group attributed sustainability to *'Execution'*. Reflecting on his experience deeply, he said: "Honestly, if you were to choose between an extremely well thought out strategy and equally excellent executed piece of work, then between the two it is 'execution' which delivers competitive advantage and not necessarily the strategy. What I have experienced in corporate life is that companies which do well what they think or say they will do, would always score over those who say very right things, but can't get the things done. *Execution is the real focus.* Implementation on the ground is what makes them really succeed.

Sustainability, he added, depends primarily on *institutionalization of processes* that would lead to effective execution and leadership that is concerned with institutionalization of processes. Elaborating this point he said: "I have found a combination of two factors as being on top of all that I have said which keep that potential longevity of a business and gives that competitive advantage on a more sustainable basis. These two are: Process – a whole rigor and whole approach of process orientation...In a business it is the rigor with which processes are identified, documented, inter-process linkages are built and process-centric organizational architecture is enabled, cross-functional and cross-process delivery is ensured. It is the whole process view of the organization, which I think gives the organization a lot of competitive advantage. Successful companies don't shoot from the hip. They don't do things in a cavalier fashion. They do it in a manner that they quickly institutionalize processes that are extremely important to build long-term success. The converse of that is that if you have an orientation to build a heavy process-centred, process-centric, process driven company, you need leadership, which appreciates this... I think the long lasting company will be driven by leaders who are more concerned with institutionalization, therefore, they are internally focused."

The other key elements for sustainability identified were: *Speed, innovation, unique strategy, good execution, coupled with leadership that is concerned with institutionalization of processes.* He added: "The identification of elements that need to be measured for sustainability of a company is a complex task... I am yet to articulate it very clearly in my mind, but the words that come to my mind are *the capability to reinvent itself*... We need to go closer to more absolute standards of measurement of corporate performance. It would essentially lie in *the ability not to die,* ability to re-invent itself. Even if everything is lost, can I put it back?"

Sustainability was attributed to the practice of *'Initiatives'* for long-term improvement for competitiveness in Motorola. Mr. Aqil Busrai[1] explained: "Initiative is an act which a company embarks upon which is applicable globally. It is spread to whichever businesses we are in, or whichever country we operate in. We are a pretty decentralized organization, but when we embark upon what we call an initiative, then that is mandatory for all Motorola operations worldwide. We take this *initiative as a very typical sustainable part; it is not a short-term effort.* One example of such initiative was taken sometime in the early eighties and we called it the *'six-sigma'*... that any thing we do, would not have opportunity for more than three defects in a million... People inside the organization also felt that it was carrying things too far...but then the sustainable part of it at that time was that it was driven by the CEO, like personal ambition, that it is possible to do it. We gave ourselves ten years to come to that level... Second, lot of emphasis was put on processes. The processes put in place to make sure that this thing is not just wishful thinking, but gets carried down into the business plans. And the third part was that there were measurement criteria, what you call a matrix."

Elaborating the process followed for measurement of progress of this initiative, he said: "We took a dipstick thermometer reading periodically across the world to say we are on the track and if so, how far are we going, what is our current level? Is it improving or going down? Is it improving in certain pockets, if so why? Can we replicate the success in other pockets where it is not showing good results? This was a continuous cycle. It is easy to start big plans and even announce it tomorrow as a grand plan, but that fizzles out like fireworks... But where you really pick up is when you say: Are you doing it or not? Are we all doing it or not? And that was a big learning for us, because it did not take ten years to reach six-sigma, it took much less. The results started showing in the year four or the year five. And the results have amazing effect for the people to say: 'Are we really able to achieve this?' The moment you start measuring, something starts happening.

Because if your score is say 4.5 sigma, then you say: 'Hey, I never thought I could be even at 4.5 sigma' and then it goes to 4.75 sigma. It is a tremendous amount of boost to the whole process to say: 'I never realized in the first place that I could do at 4.5, I thought I will be in 2.5 or 3' and then to make it to 4.75 or 4.8 slowly-slowly. It is not magic that you can do overnight. It is the success that gives you a tremendous boost and input in sustaining it. *The theme part is sustaining, not starting. And it must give you an edge at the end of the day over your competitors, or by itself in absolute terms."*

Summarizing the process of six sigma initiative for sustainable competitive edge, he said: "So the moment you have three things in place: One, a very strong desire that this is *applied to the whole organization* irrespective of your background, or your cultural background, or your business background. It must be an initiative, which is uniformly applied. You give sufficient time in the organization for the system to succeed and show the results. Second, it must have a *backing of strong process* where you make a facilitating gesture to make the initiative successful. You don't say: 'just do it'. You have to put a process behind it, put resources behind it, put support behind it and resources should not only be monetary. It can be in terms of facilitating skill. It can be target setting for senior management. So you put *accountability* behind that. So you say that I expect you to do this and to do this you will get this resource or facilitating skill. And third, *you must measure,* not just hope for the best...At the end of the whole thing, when six-sigma started becoming the norm of life, you started measuring everything in six-sigma, including the Human Resource Management practices."

How to judge sustainability? Should it be judged by profitability, or by shareholders' return, or the market share? Or, should we look at brands rather than organizations? From the customer's point of view, would it not be good products? The question was also raised: sustainability to what end? Should one not keep in view benefit to the country?

Raising and responding to some of these questions, Mr. Bhaskar Bhatt of the Titan Watch Co., a subsidiary of the Tata Group, thought that *creation of wealth and sharing it equitably among all its stakeholders* was the essence of sustainability. "This is one principle on which the entire Tata group works. For this purpose, most of the Tata companies", he said, "would include among stakeholders the shareholders, the employees, the people whom we buy from, the people whom we sell through and the most important, of course, are the customers and the community you serve... To sustain creation of wealth, you have to change, so we are adapting ourselves and constantly changing to ensure equitable, not equal, returns to all stakeholders... It is a principle, a philosophy that we have been able to maintain and stand by that principle for the first 15 years certainly. We have a very strong workforce which is extremely satisfied and happy; we have a very satisfied customer base; we have a very satisfied reseller base which is dealers, distributors and franchisees; we have a set of vendors who are very happy to work with us; our shareholders may not be so happy, I mean they would expect probably from a company of the stature of Titan much better returns...So, I would say we have sustained our ability to compete in the marketplace and generate surplus to be able to distribute it equitably among all our stakeholders."

Competitiveness was seen as a sub-set of the organization's need to create wealth by Mr. Bhaskar Bhatt. "Wealth and prosperity is what you should be able to re-invest in. Re-invest in everything for growth. If you have to re-invest, you have to be competitive, because you are operating in a competitive market place.... You create that competitive edge that is a combination of marketing, manufacturing, financing, whatever those are the functional drivers of competitive edge. But overall, at a philosophical level, *you are creating wealth for the nation... I think the greatness of an organization is its ability to change with the times without compromising its principles, without diluting the principles by which it exists, by which it lives every day."*

The complexity of the phenomenon of sustainability and uncertainty of findings on the subject were recognized and voiced by several interviewees and yet they felt that the matter was vital and, therefore, needed exploration. "Our concern was that companies written about in 1980s as excellent don't exist today. So, is there nothing that is conceptually identifiable which will ensure long lasting success for an organization? Like human mortality is a subject of investigation, I think corporate longevity is a subject of curiosity. If we are worried that people die and we must find a 'Sanjeevni' for it, we should also be worried how can we build a company that truly lasts. Would vision alone elevate, or would there be anything else? There is no final answer in my mind, but I think the question is valid", as stated by a highly experienced professional manager.

The premise that there may be some basics for sustainability that would remain eternally relevant is also debatable. Questioning this premise, Mr. Gopalakrishnan said, "I don't believe the same basics stay forever". Explaining this viewpoint, he said: "You see the basic rules of what causes success in business is a magic mantra everybody is constantly looking for, but those basic rules themselves are changing... Clayton Christensen in his book entitled *'Innovator's Dilemma'* points out that if you follow all the management gurus' prescription like being close to the customer, continuous innovation, offer value for money, be low cost, offer simple advertising promotions, build big market share, etc., you do all those things but it still doesn't work. He gives example of the disk drive industry. The answer is that *you are looking at a market and its development and there are lots of changes happening in that market. But the light under which you are looking at that market is also changing.* Now imagine that you are looking at the city of Bangalore under the strobe light[2]. The complexity and the number of scenes you see are going to be many. Cars will look as if they are stationary under a strobe light. Therefore, the ability of the management to know when to ignore the changing light and when to look at the changing light is extremely important.

"When you analyze sustainable advantage and success, you look at long standing companies... You take long lasting companies like in Timber industries, or Steel industry and come to certain conclusions based on what an electronic engineer will say is a 'long life cycle'. That may not be relevant for a very short life cycle like the disc drive industry... The industry is changing, because the world of business is now populated not with animals that live 80 years. Now there are 'organization animals' living only 20-30 years or so... Like in medical research, experiments are now being conducted on animals that live a much shorter life cycle, so the time span from childhood to adolescence to adulthood to death is much smaller. You have to change the frequency and that is why biologists are now conducting experiments on fruit flies that have a total life of 1 or 2 days from childhood to adulthood to death."

We have taken cognizance of this thought-provoking viewpoint and refrained from looking for 'mantras' or universal principles for sustainability. Instead *we have attempted to see patterns that seem to cut across industries with larger and shorter time spans, across the sectors and regions in the country, between old and new industries, having various forms of ownership patterns, hoping that we may discover some common threads that may be relevant to pay attention by leaders and managers.* They are also searching for such common threads that seem to have worked and may work at least in the foreseeable future in the *Indian context.*

Voicing his viewpoint based on his long experience as a consultant and advisor, Prof. S. K. Bhattacharyya of the Warwick Manufacturing Group, Warwick University, also said that: "Management must focus not on mantras, but on the product. Sustainability depends on the product and the key to that is high quality... *Sustainable competitive edge comes from detail, rigor and passion...Leadership, passion and long-term business sense hold the key to sustainability*... It requires true grit, determination and passion... Hard work, passion, *commitment and skill to deliver.*"[3]

The issue of sustainability of organizations is becoming increasingly important in the highly dynamic, globally competitive and unpredictably changing business environment. Keyn Wyn Smith, a visiting professor at the Wharton School of Finance, stated that 'the average age of new enterprises in the USA is 11 months – that is like a very high rate of infant mortality of organizations.' He felt that the development of organizations does not follow a linear path. It moves in a cyclical pattern with ups and downs, but the trend must be upward for long-term growth.[4]

The key points that emerge from this discussion and interviews are that the *organizations may be visualized as living organisms struggling to survive and grow in a changing, turbulent, competitive environment.* Their sustainable competitive edge could be described as their distinctive ability to maintain relatively high levels of performance and growth over long spans of time and their ability to bounce back if they faced severe downturn.

Although sustainability is not an eternal and absolute phenomenon, a span of about ten to fifteen years was considered a reasonable period to study the patterns and factors for this purpose. Interestingly, *a competitive environment and the consumers' mindset to demand better products and services* were also identified as important factors in developing organizational competitiveness and sustainability.

The key to sustainability was attributed to leadership and governance. Leadership, passion and long-term business sense appear to be some of the key elements for sustainability. Sustained high quality leadership, with deep concern for succession, development of leadership across the organization and sustained positive outlook towards people were considered important.

The willingness and ability of the top management to change themselves and their organization were considered the most critical factors for sustainability. The ability of the organization to re-invent itself and to change without diluting the basic principles and values by which it lived were highlighted by most of the interviewees. Emphasizing the importance of change for sustainability, Mr. Suresh Krishna, chairman and managing director of Sundram Fasteners Ltd. (TVS Group), strongly emphasized that the "Companies that don't change are not going to exist. To create an excellent company of the future, it is important to change when no change seems necessary. *The time to change is when no need is felt for change.*"[5]

Among the more specific factors, initiatives for improvement across the organization, like 'six sigma' were cited. Implementation and execution were emphatically mentioned as more important factors for sustainability than merely superior, impressive strategies. For this purpose, institutionalized, streamlined processes and systems for implementation and execution were considered as the key.

A holistic and systems approach of leadership in viewing, diagnosing and solving management problems was considered essential for effectiveness. Managerial problems cannot be compartmentalized into functional areas or other categories. The awareness and ability to deal with the inter-dependence of various elements in the organization and its external environment were identified as important orientations for managerial thinking.

Sustainability of business organizations was seen by some as a subset of creation of wealth for the nation, its equitable distribution among all its stakeholders and value addition through internal processes of the organization. Concern for all stakeholders and not only for owners/investors, was emphasized.

The issue of sustainability has become all the more important in the contemporary turbulent and rapidly changing business environment with increasing globalization, in which the product life cycles have become much shorter and the competition for markets and resources is much more intense.

No 'mantras' could be found for such a complex phenomenon as sustainability. Perhaps the good old wisdom like vision, long-term business sense, attention to details, rigor, true grit, hard work, commitment and skill to deliver, determination and passion account for developing sustainable competitive edge as much as powerful insights developed through research, like the concepts of 'core competence' and 'strategic intent'. Hence the need to find through empirical research a more comprehensive understanding of the key factors, underlying characteristics and explicit practices that account for developing a sustainable competitive edge. That is the endeavor of this research-based study.

In the next chapter we will examine the characteristics and practices that were associated with Inspiring Leadership: The Energizing, Direction-providing and Driving Force that inspires and mobilizes people's talents and resources.

REFERENCES

1. Research Interview with Mr. Aqil Busrai, Director – HR, India & SAARC Countries, Motorola India Ltd.
2. The beamed high speed intermittent light generally used in night clubs.
3. Stated by Mr. S.K. Bhattacharyya, Warwick Manufacturing Group, Warwick University (Advisor to two British prime ministers), at the CII's National Conference held in Delhi in April, 2003.
4. Visiting Professor at the Wharton School of Finance, stated in a personal meeting in New Delhi on 3rd December, 2002.
5. Research Interview with Mr. Suresh Krishna, Chairman and Managing Director, Sundram Fasteners Limited.

CHAPTER FOUR

Inspiring Leadership

The Energizing, Direction Providing and Driving Force

'You must be the change you wish to see in the world'

MAHATMA GANDHI

'The organizations that will truly excel in future will be the ones that discover how to tap people's commitment and capacity to learn at all levels in the organization'

PETER SENGE

INSPIRATIONAL LEADERSHIP STOOD OUT as the most pervasive and central element in the success, longevity and sustainability of organizations. We noted that leadership was like a piece of the hologram of the organization. Just as any small piece cut out of a hologram (the three dimensional picture) reflects the full picture – leadership reflected the characteristics of the entire organization and, at the same time, it influenced the entire configuration of the organization.

We have chosen to utilize the term 'leadership' to refer to the *orientation and behaviour of the persons who were in a position to influence the direction and working of the organization.* We perceived it as a *driving force that determined the direction and destiny of an organization.* It articulates a clear purpose and vision and mobilizes peoples' energies and resources to achieve them.

Inspirational leadership is about change, transformation, improvement and challenging the status quo. One of the distinctive characteristics of the purposeful values-driven organizations is that they institutionalize the process of ensuring inspirational leadership at the helm through thoughtful and farsighted concern for succession planning. This was strongly evident in companies like Hindustan Lever; companies managed by Tata Sons and other professionally managed companies.

Generally, the term 'leadership' is used to refer to the style and behaviour of leaders for providing direction, influencing people, obtaining their commitment, mobilizing their talent and energies to achieve organizational goals. We noted that, in addition to referring to leadership as behaviour and style, many of the interviewees used it to refer to the individuals or collectivity of persons who influenced and inspired people in the organization at different levels, irrespective of the formal position that they were holding.

Some authors have distinguished between leadership and management. In their view leadership is concerned with transformation, change, setting and achieving challenging goals; whereas management is more concerned with running the show, meeting the goals and targets and maintaining organizational performance according to the given parameters. Some of them have contended that most organizations are over-managed and under-led.[1]

For academic purposes, it is useful to make such a distinction between leadership and management and between leadership and formal position of headship. It clarifies the difference in orientation in determining organizational priorities, using power and authority and dealing with people. The readers may be familiar with the view that 'mangers are concerned with doing things right, while leaders are concerned with doing the right things'.[2] However, we found that such distinctions were hard to hold in real life situations. We noted that effective business leaders required both leadership and management skills and, in practice, combined the elements of both. They wielded informal power as well as needed formal authority. Therefore, *we have preferred to utilize the term 'inspirational leadership' as a broader concept in the organizational context that is inclusive of formal headship and managerial skills.* We observed that the inspiring business leaders exercised both power (i.e. informal influence) associated with leadership and *authority* (i.e. formal power) by virtue of their organizational role as top managers. They demonstrated inspirational abilities as well as managerial skills.

Leadership is one of the most complex phenomena. The massive volume of literature on the subject and the different meanings and interpretations given to 'leadership', generally confuse more than clarify it for the practitioner. It is probably one of the most researched areas and yet it remains most enigmatic. Our attempt here is to de-mystify the subject. We will present the insights, views and practices related to inspiring leadership, based on analysis and observations in this research, which seemed to differentiate the outstanding organizations.

Whereas the focal point and source of leadership as a driving force was usually seen to be the person at the top, it was also described as a collective process shared by several persons in key positions, as well as a network of people across the organization. In some companies, the term 'leadership team' was used more often when discussing the role of leadership rather than referring to any one individual leader. Explaining this viewpoint, Mr. Pratik Kumar of Wipro said: "Leadership team, actually it is a fairly broad terminology. When I say leadership team, it refers to whoever is in a position to influence his/her team and people who influence in terms of decision-making of his/her own group. In our sense, it would comprise close to about 100 people across the corporation."

Visualizing leadership as a process of mobilizing people, Mr. Kapur of Hindustan Lever Ltd. said: "The organization's *ability to mobilize* its thousands and millions of employees and your trade partners and your suppliers to execute it relentlessly and vigorously every minute, everywhere in the world is hugely challenging; and that is where the leadership role becomes more important. Because, to lead such large sections of people to act in particular way towards a shared vision and a shared objective, is probably the biggest challenge of all."

Leadership was also described as a holistic and change-oriented process. Mr. Subodh Bhargava stated this viewpoint: "A good leadership is always *holistic and comprehensive.* It doesn't just look at product development, or IT, or accounts, or manpower efficiency, or machine tool efficiency. Good leadership, in a holistic manner, is *continuously watching and changing.* The ability to change, walk the talk and being a role model becomes very important."

Emphasizing the centrality of leadership and the systems approach based on Malcolm Baldridge model for excellence in management followed at Infosys, Dr. Dinesh, its co-founder, stated: "Basically if you look at the issues, which are there at any point in time, they are usually not isolated. The whole business to me is a set of systems. So you can't say I will improve in one area only and improve the results. You have to take a systems approach to the entire thing. So when the seven parts (based on the Malcolm Baldridge model) come together, the synergy it creates is lot more than each individual part executing it separately, that is, management creating that synergy between different parts making sure that the whole complex system is able to work in a unidirectional, aligned way with a set of goals that are there. That becomes very important... *It is really the leadership which makes the difference* that is what gets the highest score. Even if you look at the Baldridge model, 120 points (out of 1000 points) go to leadership. *What kind of dream do you have? What kind of vision do you have? What kind of values do you have? How have you been able to set the goals? How have you have been able to sustain the goals? Do you have a review process for goals being set there and measured there and aligned there?* So that is very important. In fact when the Baldridge guy came, he said that the first thing we look at is leadership, not in terms of human leadership, but leadership as a system, which consists of many different parts. So how that is *setting the direction* for the remaining parts is very, very important."

Seen in the perspective of the discussion and observations given above, it would appear that leadership is not merely a matter of style and behaviour of individuals about which so much has been written and researches have been done. It depends equally, or perhaps more, on the inner motivation, values, beliefs, attitudes, insights, knowledge, skills and outlook of the key persons in the organization, whose intentions, ambition and vision provide the driving force and direction to the organization. Besides, it encompasses the development of processes, systems and cultural norms developed by the leaders in the organization that support certain kind of attitudes and behaviours that ensure setting challenging goals and achieving high levels of performance.

Based on our interviews, study of cases and observations, we noted the following major characteristics and patterns of inspiring leadership that appeared to be instrumental in providing sustainable competitive edge to the organizations:

1. **Pro-active and positive mindset**
2. **Passion and ambition**
3. **Competency building and winning paradigm**
4. **Clear vision and mission**
5. **Institution building and continued outstanding leadership**
6. **Openness, learning and change**
7. **Thorough knowledge, attention to details and holistic view**
8. **People-centric, team based approach, empowerment and commitment**
9. **Simplicity, values and character**

These characteristics of leadership and their inter-relationship is shown in Figure 4.1.

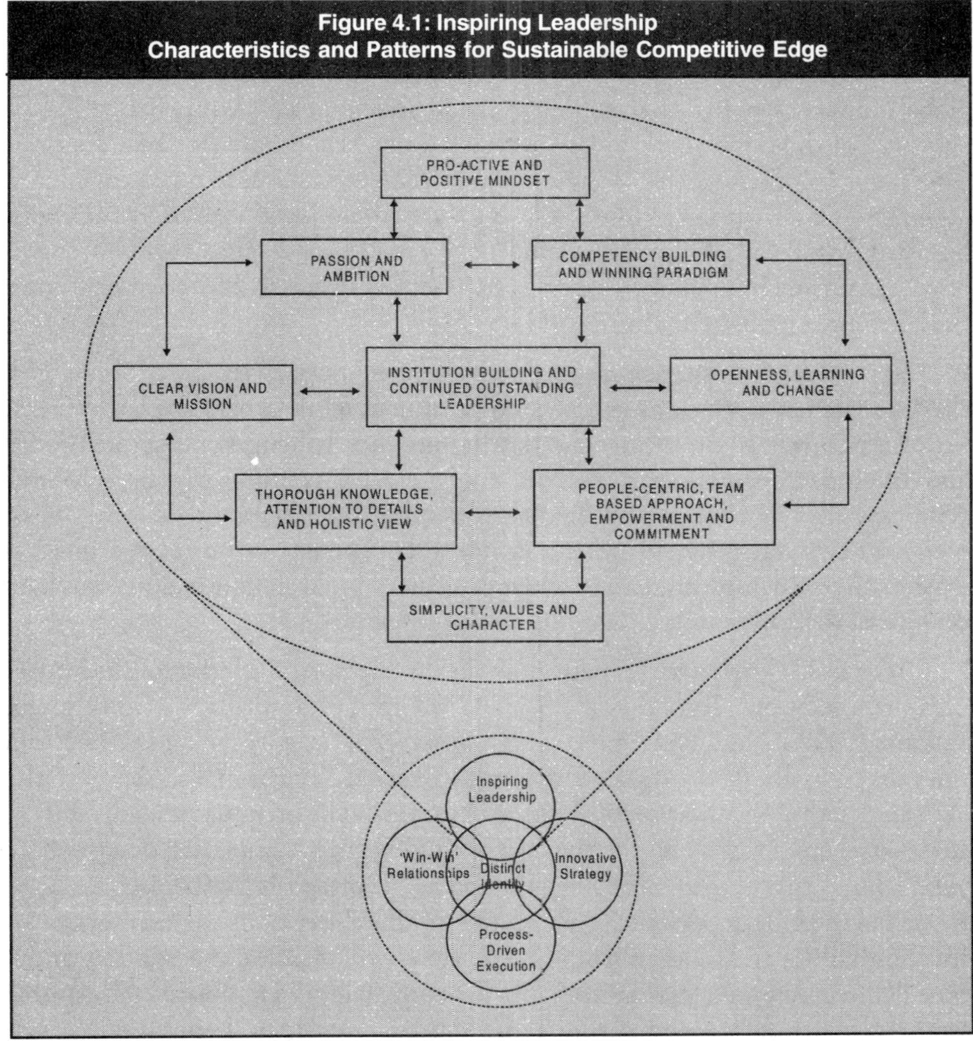

Figure 4.1: Inspiring Leadership
Characteristics and Patterns for Sustainable Competitive Edge

Let us now take a close look at these characteristics and their manifestation in practices as stated or inferred from interviews and observations during our study.

PRO-ACTIVE AND POSITIVE MINDSET

When we were reviewing and analyzing the scripts of the interviews, we were surprised to note that not a single interviewee from the most successful organizations talked about the problems and constraints in the external business environment – the infrastructure bottlenecks, unfavourable government policies and laws and other constraints. Nor did they mention the need for protection from global competition. In fact, in some companies like Ranbaxy, Mr. D.S. Brar, CEO and MD of the company said that protected markets would not help them in developing competitiveness. Therefore, they deliberately chose to operate in highly competitive international markets, so that they may develop global competitiveness. Similarly, Mr. B.M.L. Munjal, the founder of Hero Cycles, described how he refused to take government's quota of imported parts for cycles and decided to manufacture the parts and develop their own vendors.

In most other outstanding companies also, the interviewees talked about how their leaders saw opportunities in the environment while others saw constraints, how they converted the threats and restrictions into challenges and opportunities and developed business against all odds. To give one example, Mr. Brar, MD of Ranbaxy, said: "We did feel that if we keep blaming the policies and the constraints, we won't help ourselves. So we felt that it is still possible to do business. I think, as a company, we demonstrated that it was possible to build an international business despite all the constraints".

We could clearly see this pattern in the description of mindset of the leaders of Reliance, Wipro, Infosys, Tata Sons, Hindustan Graphite, Dr. Reddy's Lab, Satyam, NTPC, Hero Honda and several other well-known companies. They did not complain about the constraints in the external environment, or blame the external factors for their inability to do business. The attitude of leadership in these companies was similar to the 'Mirror and Window' approach described by Jim Collins[3], that is, they set challenging and ambitious goals for themselves. They looked in the mirror, when they failed, to examine the reasons within themselves for their failure and to learn from it. And they looked out of the window at the blue sky to thank their stars when they succeeded. They did not blame the external factors for their failure and attribute their success entirely to themselves.

The leaders of most of the outstanding organizations demonstrated a *proactive approach* rather than a reactive approach in dealing with the environment. They created business opportunities through their understanding of the latent needs of the customers and society and overcame the barriers and constraints through imaginative solutions, mastering technology, creating goodwill and mobilizing talent and resources.

Another distinct characteristic of such leaders was their *positive and optimistic outlook*. They seldom complained or despaired about the government policies and environmental constraints. Instead, they tried to influence and change the policies; and, in some cases, found imaginative ways of dealing with the situation within the legal framework. They were driven by hope and confidence to create a better world to live in, in spite of all odds and constraints. They saw a positive side in every situation. They were the ones who saw the half glass full of water, rather than the empty half of the glass.

They built on their own strengths and the strengths of their organization members, rather than nagging all the time about their weaknesses. They concentrated their attention on developing the competencies of their organization and tapping the opportunities in the domestic and global markets, rather than seeking crutches of protection from the government or grouse about the threats of competition.

Thus, an outstanding characteristic of the leadership of successful and sustainable organizations is a *pro-active, positive and optimistic outlook*. This is similar to what has been described as the Stockdale Paradox by Jim Collins in his book entitled '*Good to Great*'. He has mentioned how Admiral Stockdale survived and helped other prisoners of war in the Vietnamese prisoners of war camp to survive in spite of worst torture, by dint of sheer faith and confidence that in the end they will prevail, while at the same time confronting the most brutal facts of their current reality, whatever they might be.[4] We found similar grit and determination among business leaders like Mr. L.N. Jhunjhunwala and Mr. B.M.L. Munjal, who described the heavy odds against them when they were establishing their organizations. The highly restrictive and hostile government policies towards private industry at that time, the atrocious tax laws, the unwillingness of multinational companies to give technology and other serious constraints in obtaining resources did not deter them. They had enormous self-confidence and found imaginative ways of overcoming the constraints to build and sustain highly competitive organizations. Similar orientation of Mr. Dhirubhai Ambani, the founder of Reliance, is legendary.

PASSION AND AMBITION

Out of all the characteristics noted among the leaders of highly competitive organizations, if we were to choose the most outstanding ones, we would say: passion and ambition.

The leaders of outstanding organizations were driven by passion and ambition to achieve very challenging goals.

They had the will and vision to raise the organization to the highest possible levels of success.

A deep urge for supremacy in their industry or business and a winning paradigm against all odds distinguished the leadership of the outstanding companies.

Passion to win and commitment to ambitious goals provided the energy and the urge for supremacy and led to benchmarking and excelling in competition or comparison with the best.

The winning paradigm provided the challenge and excitement of success against all odds.

Their passion for success and ambitious goals were unlike and distinctly different from the 'marginal growth and survival paradigm' of most other organizations[5].

Passion

Passion stood out as one of the most striking characteristics in the success of outstanding organizations. It was described, in various ways, by most of the interviewees. It could also be observed palpably among the members of such organizations across different levels in the organization.

Our observations of the outstanding companies and considered views of business leaders and professional managers confirm the opinion that *nothing great was ever achieved without passion.*

We have earlier highlighted the view expressed at Dr. Reddy's Labs that *'only companies and leaders who are passionate about what they are doing will be able to create great organizations...* Without passion you cannot create great organizations. You have to be very excited about what you are doing. We believe we are very excited about what we are doing, because we are making a difference in people's lives.'

Passion was identified as the most important factor for sustainability of competitive edge, along with innovation, entrepreneurship, globalization and focus on people.

The success and growth of Reliance is legendary among Indian companies. From very humble beginning a few decades ago, the company has risen to towering heights and dominates several sectors. 'From an initial investment of a mere Rs. 15,000 (less than $2000) in 1958 to start a trading house, followed by setting up of his first tiny manufacturing facility in 1966, Dhirubhai Ambani [its founder chairman and managing director] managed to build up a synthetic yarn, textiles and petrochemicals empire – one which had a market capitalization in excess of Rs. 80 bn (about $2.7bn) in 1994 and was the only Indian entrant in *Business Week's* listing of the fifty largest companies headquartered in developing countries'.[6] The company now dominates the telecom sector also and had market capitalization of Rs. 46,501.24 Crores in 2003.[7]

The successors to Mr. Dhirubhai Ambani, his two sons - Mr. Mukesh Ambani and Mr. Anil Ambani, are equally known for their ambition, dynamism and success as corporate leaders. When asked in an interview about the future of Reliance, Mr. Mukesh Ambani said:[8] "The first thing that drives business is growth. The second thing that drives business is competitiveness. In each one of our businesses, *we are passionate about competitiveness.* At the end of the day, we have a track record where we have outperformed others in virtually every parameter of competitiveness."

Mr. Yogi Sriram of Larsen & Toubro (L&T), while describing the leadership qualities of his company's managing director, said: "Mr. Naik, who leads the business, has - if I may use the term - an *incorrigible passion.* A passion which is so robust and so sustainable that at any point of the day if you ask him, he will gush about a strategic plan concerning L&T, or about vision concerning L&T, or something about the business, or something about building the talent. He is very upbeat in terms of enthusiasm levels, tremendous enthusiasm level and that is perhaps the engine and the fuel, which really leads many people even through very difficult circumstances."

Mr. Rajinder Singh, Former CMD, National Thermal Power Corporation, one of the highest rated public sector organizations in the country, expressed a similar view based on his long personal experience of raising the performance of NTPC to extraordinary levels. He said: "The most important factor in my opinion is the CEO and the passion he has for the organizational purpose. It is like *'junoon'* – an obsession. You think about it all the time, you dream, your entire life revolves around that purpose, that passion."

Mr. Amineedu, vice-president HRD of the Bharat Electronics Corporation (BEL), another distinguished public sector corporation, emphasized a similar opinion based on his experience of building and commissioning a new factory of BEL in record time in a relatively less developed area and against heavy odds: "I believe it is only if you have a passion for excellence, whether you are at the chief executive level, whether you are the director or some other level, that makes a difference and gives you some sort of satisfaction. If some public sector organizations are doing extremely well, it is because their chief executives have that *passion to accept challenges,* no other consideration."

Prof. S. K. Bhattacharyya of the University of Warwick, Advisor to two British Prime Ministers, who has vast experience of consultancy and is well known for helping organizations globally to achieve high levels of excellence, specially in raising their levels of productivity, shared a similar insight when he stated (at the CII's Annual Conference held in Delhi in April 2003): "Rarely has anything great been achieved without passion."[9]

Passion stood out as the most powerful driving force for leading organizations to success. That is why we have chosen the title: 'Passion to Win' for this book.[10]

Commitment for Ambitious Goals and Urge for Supremacy

Leadership in the most successful organizations demonstrated high commitment to ambitious goals, that often appeared far-fetched and to many in the organization as unrealistic and non-achievable. The leaders seemed to be driven by a deep urge for supremacy in the industry and markets. They set for themselves, and the organization, highly challenging goals. They persuaded and inspired the members of the organization to achieve such goals. Even when they were small organizations, they thought like big players in the industry.

Talking about some of these characteristics of leadership in the Satyam company,[11] Dr. U. Balaji said: "I remember when I first joined, our turnover was something like Rupees 7 crores or so. For me to join a 7 crore company was something my colleagues were saying: 'Are you in the right mind?' But I have seen here a certain energy, a certain entrepreneurship. You can see that energy flowing. You can see a purpose. People wanting to do something they are passionate about. So I think a few things, like the ability to think long-term, ability to invest in people, ability to invest in infrastructure, *ability to think big, behave like big* - all these things have created an organization with a structure and processes in such a way that a lot of autonomy is experienced here."

While describing the leadership style of Satyam's founder and managing director, Mr. Ramalinga Raju, Dr. U. Balaji said: "Mr. Raju is a person who doesn't interfere much with people's work, once the vision is set, is negotiated and is worked on. He is very *ambitious.* Though he is very soft spoken, he is *very aggressive in terms of the goals set* and where we want to go... Though we were small, we *always thought big,* thought like a big player – big both in terms of ambition and aspiration. I remember Mr. Raju saying in 1996-97 that we would become 10,000 people by 2000, so people laughed, some people kept quiet – those who had experienced growth from 150 to 1000. But to say that in the next 3 years we will become 10,000 was preposterous. But the fact is that today we are almost 10,000 people... We always behaved like and thought like a big player, for example our investments in the Satyam Learning Centre."

While describing the highly ambitious thinking and urge to excel in the leadership of the Reliance group of companies, Prof. Sumantra Ghoshal and Prof. J. Ramachandran have quoted that: "...these two inheritors of Dhirubhai's mantle (Mukesh and Anil) also claim to be different from the scions of other industrialist families in India. Asked to define how they thought of themselves, Mukesh explained: 'As two bright young Indians without the historical baggage of saying we are a big multinational company, or with a 100-year family history; we have a fire in our belly, *ki kuch karke dikhana hai* ('we have to achieve something'). That is what keeps us driving."[12]

According to H.T. Parked, the then head of ICICI Ltd., who had sanctioned Reliance's first institutional loan, 'Dhirubhai always spoke of international standards and sizes...This commitment to creating world scale capacity, in turn, was based not only on Dhirubhai's ambition to 'do only extraordinary things', but also on specific logic..."As described by S.P. Sapra, *Dhirubhai threw that incrementalist mind set away.*[13]

Mr. Rajinder Singh, former chairman of NTPC, narrated his goal-setting style with a similar approach. Describing his experience of setting a very challenging goal, he said: "I asked our management team how much time would they require to build a new 1000 mega watt thermal power station?[14] They said it will take atleast 55 months to complete it. I asked them to cut it down to 40 months. Some said 'the chairman is mad.' I called all concerned people and said: "You are right. I am mad. It is my *'junoon'* – my obsession and conviction that it can be done. Those who feel it can't be done and are not with me can leave and I will not hold it against them. Others who are willing to take up the challenge may stay back." They all stayed. They asked what is in it for them. I said I will give you three months' salary for each year on meeting the milestones of progress. I paid two crores and saved two hundred fifty crores. The plant was completed in 39 months."

Responding to the question: What was the driving force to take Infosys to such high levels? Mr. Dinesh, director and co-founder of the company, said:

"Basically if you look at the dream we have, the dream is that *we will be a globally respected corporation providing best of solutions,* leveraging technology, which is the best in its class. So you start driving yourself to higher levels of competence, higher levels of benchmark. We are in the world competition area; we are no longer in Indian industry space. An immigrant will always have to prove better than the local. An immigrant who is sometimes better than the local has to drive harder to be even better. The simple reason is that when there is no competition, then you are your competition; so you have to improve... Every human being aspires to be unique. If you were to relate Infosys to a human being, it has its dream through us, then it has to be unique, it has to compete. *It has to be able to show the difference to the clients from the clients' point of view, from the employees' point of view, from the stakeholders' point of view.* So every time you do new things you are improving."

A similar orientation could be noticed in the leadership of Wipro Corporation. Explaining the management's philosophy, Mr. Pratik Kumar, vice president (HRD) said: "We have been very clear in our approach, that is driven largely by a very well articulated belief system that whichever business we enter into, *we should either be among the top three players or not be there at all...Which* means that we will exit out of the business if we are not there among the top three players in that particular segment in a defined number of years. If you notice, though we get spoken of a lot in terms of our success in IT and other areas, there are enough number of examples where we have consciously just walked out of the businesses also. Simply because we felt that the time it is taking for us to make it into a success is much longer. So the first point (that enables us to compete) is in terms of our ability to respond to the environment quickly; and the second is driven by our internal belief, *our desire to be there right on the top.* Why is it important is because it leads to certain kind of other behaviour in the organization and a certain kind of mindset which is very performance driven, which tells you that – look, if you want to actually remain in the business, you have to aptly deliver and you have to deliver it successfully."

Mr. Brij Mohan Lal Munjal, founder and chairman of the Hero Honda Co., which is now the largest motorcycle producing company in the world,[15] described how he set a challenging goal of producing a highly fuel efficient and sturdy motorcycle to suit the requirements of the Indian customer and meet the Indian road conditions as early as the year 1985:[16] "What (kind of motorcycle) India would require was very clear to us. The first model of motorcycle that we brought out in 1985 was not in the Honda stable. It did not exist. It was got designed by ourselves; rather I would say my son was responsible for getting it designed from Honda. Being in the bicycle business, I knew the local conditions throughout the country and the requirements of the customer..."

"I have seen it thoroughly and visited the country and had a complete and detailed knowledge of the road conditions, requirements of load to be carried by people and how they load the vehicle, the conditions of the user's pocket and what he can afford and what would he appreciate most in the motorcycle once he has invested his money in buying the motorcycle. What will be his monthly expenditure on it. And that is what paid us. At that time there was no two-wheeler that was capable of giving more than 40-45 kilometres per litre and was nowhere near or had even heard of a motorcycle that would give 80 km per litre. We said we will bring in a motorcycle with 80 km per litre. Our competitors, the media and the general public...They just laughed and said what are they talking about, they have returned from Japan and are talking like this! We proved it. And now all two-wheeler manufacturers are talking about 82-85-87 kilometres per litre.

At that time also Honda company was offering us a sleek and beautiful looking model, but we said let us first make, and bring in the market, a sturdy looking and real good performing model...And it worked really well and after that we brought many different models, but that model is still demanded in some areas."

From the abovementioned extracts from interviews, it can be clearly seen that the leadership in the outstanding companies had:

- A deeply felt passion to succeed.
- A strong urge for supremacy in their industry.
- They set highly ambitious and challenging goals to achieve them.
- They had the will, commitment, determination and tenacity to achieve such goals.

These are the key characteristics of leadership that make the difference. These were the important factors in their success.

COMPETENCY BUILDING AND WINNING PARADIGM

The leadership in the outstanding companies was distinctively oriented to building competencies for competitiveness and were driven by a 'winning paradigm', i.e. the will and determination to win in tough competition and succeed against all odds.

They sought and chose to operate in a challenging business environment, rather than work in an easy and protected environment that would breed mediocrity.

These points are best illustrated in the business philosophy and approach of the leadership of the Ranbaxy Company. As stated by Mr. D.S. Brar, CEO & managing director of the Ranbaxy Laboratories Ltd.: "We believed that we have to be amongst the leaders in anything we do, so whether it is in India or it is internationally in the area in which we are... whatever examples I have given, I think at the guts the position has emerged from leadership or management which thought in very unconventional ways and (that accounts for) today as a company wherever we are... I will give you 4 or 5 examples. In early eighties we thought that despite the license raj, in which people used to export to get import licenses and, therefore, made huge profits on imports, because it was a protected market. We felt 'No, there is 99 per cent business outside and it would be futile to believe that (such) business is not profitable."

"There was huge business and profit opportunity in a very short time from USSR (now Russia). Our management, our leadership, took a business decision that 'No! If we participate very fully in the USSR market, it will be no different from what we have in this country. It will actually erode our competitive ability in the international markets, so we will come out of one controlled system and fall prey to another controlled system.' So much so that many industry analysts and observers started questioning our wisdom of staying away from USSR and said you are almost impairing the company. But we said: No. We will go to those markets which allow us to test our competitive abilities in line with the best. If it gets turned up, then I think it is a way forward. But going from the Indian controlled economy to USSR state economy type of market would not lead us forward. So we did not go for it."

"We recognized that product patents will come eventually, so to invest ahead in science, technology and innovation was the only way forward. Therefore, as early as 1993 or 1994, when the rest of the industry was saying that we don't want the product patents in India, we, as a company, stood up to say that product patents are good for intellectual capital building in this country and we made investments in drug discovery in 1995 onwards."

"Many people still believe that USA (market) is a very high risk and high reward model and it is very difficult to develop business in USA. But we felt that without (operations in) USA market, there is no international recognition, at least in our industry. You cannot ignore 40 per cent of the (world) market and still say you are an international company."

A similar *winning paradigm* leading to the bold initiatives of Dhirubhai Ambani and his successors in the Reliance Company have led to phenomenal growth and success. A closer scrutiny of almost all leading IT companies like Infosys, Wipro and Satyam also reveals a similar mindset. In Glaxo-SmithKline Beecham it was described as the 'winning attitude'. It was considered as a cornerstone of their philosophy of business leadership and carefully nurtured as a key element in the culture of the organization and among the members of the company.

CLEAR MISSION AND VISION

Another distinctive characteristic of the leadership of outstanding organizations was that they articulated, expressed and shared the organizational purpose and goals in very simple, easily understood and tangible mission and vision statements.

In the outstanding organizations, the wide awareness, commitment and identification with the stated vision and mission and earnest desire to achieve goals consistent with them, was notable. People, even at the lowest levels, could easily describe and identify themselves with their organization's mission and vision. Instead of hanging on the office walls, or on the covers of fancy brochures of the annual reports, the vision and mission statements of the outstanding companies seemed to be inscribed in the hearts and minds of their organization members. Unlike such companies, the leadership and members of most of the organizations are seldom clear about the basic purpose, mission and vision that they are pursuing. When you put such questions to the managers and employees, they usually fumble and look for the written statements made by their top management. One often comes across elaborate vision and mission statements developed with the help of external consultants that are difficult to recall by the employees.

The concepts of purpose, vision and mission are to help the top management and leadership to develop clarity, focus and selectivity in defining the nature and scope of their business and to evolve a distinctive character and identity for their organization. Unfortunately academic writings on these concepts are often ambiguous and complex, that tend to confuse the business leaders and managers.

Mission

Unlike the military parlance in which it means a very specific task, the term 'mission', in the context of business organizations, refers to the basic, distinctive and more enduring purpose for which the organization exists. Mission is the *raison d'être* of the organization, i.e. the generalized purpose or the reason, which justifies the existence of the organization. Each business organization is created with a purpose that is usually broader than merely making money. It exists and survives by satisfying some specific needs of the customers/consumers in the society through products and services; it makes resources productive and, in the process, creates surplus value that makes it profitable and sustainable.

The mission statement is usually a succinct statement of the organization's purpose as perceived and stated by its management. The mission statements usually delineate the scope of operations of the organization in terms of products, services and markets; and the unique character and identity that the organization aspires to achieve. 'A mission statement is a company's statement of purpose. It typically comprises a statement of what the company is trying to achieve and very often defines, in broad terms, the business that it is in. If mission outlines what the company is attempting to achieve at the present time, its vision offers a view of what the enterprise might become.'[17] *'It tells who we are and what we do as well as what we'd like to become.'*[18] Some leaders prefer a narrowly focused mission – specially at the unit level while some define their organization's mission in broader and general terms at the corporate level that enables them to choose wider range of multi-business operations and markets.

The mission statement articulates the response to the classical strategic management question that the stakeholders, employees and the company management like to ask: 'What business are we in?' Simple, clear, but carefully thought mission statement helps in providing rationale and legitimacy to the organization and gives it a clear identity and purpose that help in focussing and mobilizing people's energies and resources for achieving organizational purpose. It also helps in developing strategies, long-term plans and policies. Some companies incorporate and articulate their basic values and policies in the mission and vision statements to express their existing or desired distinctiveness and character.

Vision

Vision refers to a desired, tangible, achievable and, in some cases, vivid image of the future state of the organization. Some companies specify a time frame for achieving such a desired state. If such vision is widely shared and inspiring, it can be a powerful strategic tool for motivating people and taking the organization to great heights. A related well known concept developed by Hamel and Prahalad is 'strategic intent'. They see it as an 'animating dream'. 'A powerful strategic intent is one that encapsulates both the logic of the strategic direction and the animating challenge – the sense of discovery and destiny – that motivates managers and employees alike throughout the organization[19]. It refers to 'leveraging a firm's internal resources, capabilities and core competencies to accomplish the firm's goals in the competitive environment' and outperform the competition.[20]

Mr. G. V. Prasad, CEO of Dr. Reddy's Labs[21], stated the purpose of his organization in very simple words. He said:

We are creating medicines that will lead to people having a healthier life. This is a larger purpose than making profits and once we are passionate about this cause, the profits will follow. *Having a larger purpose is really uplifting,* and makes people passionate about what they are doing. It creates alignment, empowerment, energy and passion for work.

The vision statement of the company has been described as follows:[22]

- Our vision is to become a discovery-led global pharmaceutical company.
- We will achieve this vision by building:
  - A workplace that will attract, energize and help retain the finest talent available;
  - An organizational culture that is relentlessly focussed on the speedy translation of scientific discoveries into innovative products that makes a significant difference in people's lives; and
  - A global marketing organization that understands and responds to the need of the customer.

Mr. B.M.L. Munjal, founder and chairman of the Hero Honda Motors Ltd.[23], emphasized clarity and focus in vision and scope for developing successful business and considered these as the key factors for sustainability. He said:

> Firstly, we have very, very clear vision of what we want to do in life, in career, in business. Don't you think that when we were making bicycles and motorcycles, (other businesses like) the cement plants, the textile mills (and many other business options) would not have come our way? Some people came and said why don't you buy an aeroplane, why don't you run taxis and all that. Most of these things come naturally. You don't have to go and look for them. People come and show your balance sheet and say you have surplus amount, you are doing well, your

profitability is so much, why not get in this business also? But you must have noticed that our focus has been first on bicycles and then on motorcycles and within the engineering industry itself.

We had lot of opportunities in which we could do well. Now it is time that one of my sons has initiated a new business and may be going into IT in a big way. We are doing it, but whatever we can do within the competence, within the available resources, within the available time with us. Not simply taking anything which will hamper our present business. Whenever anybody has started business by taking out money from the present business and taking out time from present functioning, he has neither achieved success in the present business, nor in the new business. We did not let that happen. Focussed attention, focussed goal, very slow growth, very slow movement – we never wanted to jump over things much faster.

The mission statement of the Hero Honda Motors Ltd. is as given below:[24]

We, at Hero Honda, are continuously striving for synergy between technology, systems and human resources to provide products and services that meet the quality, performance and price aspirations of our customers. While doing so, we maintain the highest standards of ethics and societal responsibilities, constantly innovate products and processes and develop teams that keep the momentum going to take the company to excellence in the new millennium.

Mr. D.S. Brar, CEO & managing director of the Ranbaxy Laboratories Ltd, also highlighted a similar emphasis on clarity and delineation of the scope of business in the mission and vision of their company:

Fundamentally *a company must decide what business it is in.* This is one of the core issues: whether many of the business groups in India got distracted because they have multiple businesses? In our company we believed that we have to be amongst the leaders in anything we do, whether it is in India, or it is internationally in the area in which we are. The company must show and demonstrate leadership. It is not possible to do that if you are involved in multiple areas or activities. So, as early as 1994, *we had to decide that in our mission and vision statement the company will stick to the area of pharmaceuticals* and not fritter away its energies into any other related or unrelated areas. And while Dr. Parvinder Singh –

> who was our chairman then – as a private individual had his own independence and freedom to setup businesses which he liked, but as a leader (of our company) he had indicated that he would not like to encumber this company by diversifying into areas in which he felt there was potential. So this company was left to concentrate essentially on pharmaceuticals. So this *key and core focus helped us a lot then in building competitive advantages within the company,* whether it is the area of research and innovation, or our competitive cost structure inside, or in our innovation through our delivery systems technologies that we have.

Ranbaxy chose to operate in the pharmaceutical business in the international markets and to develop its distinctive character and identity as an international company, in spite of heavy odds and high risks, as will be explained later. Describing how this transformation was brought about and how an attempt was made to seek understanding and commitment of each and every employee to such vision of the company, Mr. Brar said:[25]

> One of the leadership challenges, management challenges we had in the Company was how do we sell this concept (of Ranbaxy as an international company) to the whole mass of people (in the organization). There were a lot of skeptics who felt this will not happen. (They thought) how this internationalization or becoming an international company was possible and that too in the pharma field from India - is a very distant kind of thing. Our own employees, managers, supervisors, were very doubtful that we will achieve that. Selling this concept that we can become an international company was difficult, but we did it from 1993 to 1996. It was like a National Anthem which was drummed at every possible occasion, that we will become an international pharmaceuticals company... You know if you start narrating something again and again, you start believing in it...
>
> I was at one of our annual days of our plants at Devas near Indore. About 1500 to 1600 people (employees) including their families had come for the annual day. There were three or four ladies standing there and one had a little child in her lap. So I went up to them and I asked them in Hindi: What motivates you best in this company? What do you look up to in this company? So this lady – I remember her words and I have quoted this in many conferences, even in international conferences – said: *"Hamari davaiyan jo yahan Devas me banengi, woh videsh mein jayengi, aur woh America jaengi"* [The medicines that will be produced here in

> Devas will go to foreign countries, they will go to America]. This is the biggest thing which makes me proud of our efforts. I called our production head, Mr. Bindra and I said that don't sell the message anymore. If a housewife is telling because that is what she is hearing from her husband, then my biggest challenge is how do I sell my Devas manufactured medicines in the US...So that was the level to which this commitment to internationalization was sold to each employee, that no doubt was left that we have to become an international company.

The mission of the Ranbaxy Laboratories Ltd. is as stated below:[26]

> Our mission is to become a Research-based International Pharmaceutical Company.

Talking about the mission and strategy of the Glaxo-SmithKline Beecham Company, Mr. Dwarkanath,[27] said that:

> We are very focused, because we are a Science Based Consumer Health Care Company. We are not here to sell ice cream, if it does not add value to our business. (We are focused on) Nutrition – scientifically, so that anybody will be able to substantiate what we claim and that gives a competitive edge... It is not only products with quality and fame, but also that add value to life. It is stemming from our business mission statement. Our global quest is to improve the quality of human life, to make them live longer, better and happier.

The vision statement of the Hindustan Levers Limited has also been articulated in a simple statement:[28]

> Our vision is to meet everyday needs of people everywhere.
>
> The vision that inspires HLL's 32,400 employees (40,000 including group companies), including about 1,425 managers, is to "meet everyday needs of people everywhere – to anticipate the aspirations of our consumers and customers and to respond creatively and competitively with branded products and services which raise the quality of life." This objective is achieved through the brands that the company markets.

The leadership of Infosys Technologies Ltd. has described the vision of their company in a simple statement in their Annual Report 2002 as:

> Your Company's vision is to be a globally respected corporation that provides best-of-breed business solutions, leveraging technology, delivered by best-in-class people.

The leadership of Wipro Limited does the exercise of vision building from time to time. They prefer to have more specific goals in key areas to make their vision statement more tangible. Following is the vision statement of Wipro Limited as stated in their Annual Report, 2002:

Vision

We had, in the calendar year 2000, formulated our Vision for the year 2004. Our visioning challenge is to make our thinking ambitious and serve as a turbo-charger for the organization. Vision creates an executable dream for us to strive hard towards achieving. The Vision we have set for ourselves is:

Business Leadership: Among the top 10 information technology services companies globally and the No. 1 information technology company in India.

Customer Leadership: The No.1 choice of customers through innovative solutions and six sigma processes.

People Leadership: Among the top 10 most preferred employers globally by creating an environment of empowerment, intellectual challenge and wealth sharing.

Brand Leadership: Wipro brand to be among the five most admired brands in India.

From the above-stated examples, it will be noted that one of the most important roles of leadership is to articulate the purpose, mission and vision of the organization in *the simplest possible terms and to ensure that it is widely shared and understood across the organization.* It may appear to be an easy task, but in reality it is the most difficult and complex task for the top management and business leaders. *Clarity and focus in business purpose, mission and vision are evidently the most critical elements for the success and sustainability of organizations.*

INSTITUTION BUILDING AND CONTINUED OUTSTANDING LEADERSHIP

A distinctive characteristic of leadership in companies with a sustained track record of success was their strong orientation to long-term institution-building of the organization, rather than using the company merely as an instrumentality for seeking opportunistic, short-term gains.

Contd....

They painstakingly developed and nurtured a distinguished and strong institutional identity and brand equity that was a source of cohesiveness and pride to all its stakeholders.

The top management of such companies saw their term like only one part of the relay race in which they were keen about the success of the company and their successor to win the race. The top management was deeply concerned about continuity of high quality institutional leadership and took carefully thought out steps well in advance for succession planning.

They had transformational and visionary leadership that kept organizational survival and development goals above their personal goals. They made special efforts to carefully induct, nurture and develop leadership across the organization to ensure continued high level of performance and growth of the organization.

Institution Building

We see institution building as the essence of far-sighted, visionary leadership that is deeply concerned with the success and sustainability of an organization far beyond their own term. This point is similar to what Collins and Porras have stated in their well known book *'Built to Last'* as the difference between 'time telling' and 'clock building.'[29] In their words, "Having a great idea or being a charismatic visionary leader is 'time telling'; building a company that can prosper far beyond the presence of any single leader and through multiple product life cycles is 'clock building'."[30]

Let us see the examples of long-term institution building orientation and continued outstanding leadership from the interviews and statements about the companies studied.

The long-term institution building outlook, as opposed to short-term opportunistic gains, was a common orientation among the well-known multinational companies as well as the Indian companies. Describing the guiding philosophy and orientation of Glaxo-SmithKline Beecham, Mr. Dwarkanath said: "We have a long heritage. We are not here as a trading organization to make profits just by acquiring and disinvesting, or just do some trading...We don't believe in that."

We have described earlier the case of Ranbaxy company choosing to operate in the tough competitive international markets rather than seeking quick gains in protected economies of India and the USSR keeping in view their long-term institutional development concerns.

Similar concern for long-term institution building could be noted in many of the outstanding Indian companies studied, like Tata Sons, Hindustan Lever, Larsen & Toubro, Hero Honda, Infosys, Wipro, Satyam and several others.

Developing a distinctive identity for the company and its brands and developing a sense of belonging and pride among the stakeholders and employees as a part of the institutional development process was also an important concern of the leadership in these organizations. The way in which the sense of identity, brand image and pride were nurtured among the stakeholders and employees of companies like Infosys, Wipro, Hindustan Lever, Hero Honda, Ranbaxy, Dr. Reddy's Lab., Larsen & Toubro and Titan was notable. It will be elaborated in the chapter on Institutional Identity.

While sharing his thoughts on building the organization and his business philosophy, Mr. B.M.L. Munjal, founder chairman of the Hero Cycles and now chairman of Hero Honda Motors Ltd., which had achieved the status of the world's largest two-wheeler company in 2001,[31] said: "I don't think I am in a position to give a sermon. I am a practitioner myself, but still I would say that we often give up focus in a hurry. It is like going for a specific task and, on the way, getting strayed by thinking: 'let me do this or that also', as there are many distractions on the way, so we lose time and opportunity and don't achieve our goal. Focus must be clear, absolutely clear. Then we should make targets and then to meet the targets we should lay down the steps... As I told you, we could have become very rich long long ago by taking short cuts of import quotas from the government... Back in the fifties, the government decided to give 150 licenses for 5000 bicycles each, by importing some parts and asking licensees to manufacture the rest. We said: No one will make parts for only 5000 bicycles and in all likelihood people getting license and quotas will just sell the parts and make money. We decided right then that we will not be in the list of such 150 licensees. Instead, we applied separately for industry license for manufacturing bicycles... We moved with clear focus in small steps, consolidating each step at a time."

"Do not move up to the next higher step, until you have strongly consolidated the earlier steps... And see to it that whether you are dealing with your seller (the dealer), your buyer (the customer), or your supplier – each is fully satisfied. Look to their satisfaction and then your own requirements. Your dealer is your ambassador. He is 'Hero Honda'. They are proud to add 'Hero Honda' to their name. Have ethical business, value-based business. One who gives up values can never be successful. Be clear about what you consider ethical in the given context..."

"I see to it that if any customer has any complaint, it is redressed the next day... Replace the motorcycle if needed...But ensure a satisfied customer. Have a satisfied dealer, a satisfied supplier and keep your own people (employees) satisfied. You will get satisfaction in doing this and money (i.e. profits), in fact much more money will follow you...If you take care of their economic needs, their sentimental needs and their psychological needs, then you don't need to worry about anything else."

"Right from day one, our idea was: Give full value of money to the customer, without having before you an ambitious profitability factor. Profitability has been always behind us and it has seriously followed us because we have left that behind. Try to satisfy both..."

"There are many stakeholders in one's business. You have to deal with them well and look after their interests...That can only be done if you have kept your requirements behind you. If you always keep your needs primary and give less importance to the needs of others, then you can't do anything. This is the principle that I have followed.

Continued Outstanding Leadership

The orientation for long-term institutional development was actualized and supported by the concern for continued outstanding leadership, succession planning and developing leadership across the organization. As stated earlier in chapter 1 on sustainability, Mr. Gopalakrishnan, executive director of Tata Sons Ltd., had expressed the view that "in an organization with sustained and sustainable competitive advantage, the top leadership do not think of their regime, but they think of their regime as a small part of a relay race." Elaborating this view and illustrating the importance of continued outstanding leadership for developing sustainable competitive edge, he said: "Hindustan Lever is a good example (of such leadership). In the late 60s and early 70s, when I joined Levers, it was a fairly average organization. It was a good organization, but nothing to write home about. Then certain things happened from the early 70s to this date. It is over 30 years which have made it sort of improve its trajectory. And now in the last 15 years people have recognized it as a sustained competitive advantage organization... There are several things that Hindustan Lever leadership did ... part of it is that they run as a leadership race. The emphasis is as much on making sure that there is somebody else to take the baton for the next lap, as on running your own lap well. The emphasis is on ensuring that your interest for the growth of the organization exceeds your emphasis on yourself..."

"In Hindustan Lever, there were leaders like Prakash Tandon, Vasant Rajadhyaksha, T. Thomas, Ashok Ganguly, followed by Susim Datta[32] ...the time span is almost 45 years and time and again Hindustan Lever has been able to produce (outstanding) chairmen. They are all very different people, but each one served his 5 years, 7 years, 10 years in a way that when you stand back and look at it, it looked like pieces in a necklace, where they are all matching. While there must have been individual flaws, at the end of it you see the necklace in its totality. And although the pieces look very different, they all fit together."

"The second thing is that the people, who become CEOs or top managers, like every other human being have their weaknesses and their strengths. They are bound to be competent in marketing, or accounting, or whatever, but they are also likely to have a touch of hubris, arrogance, conscious of their own superior skills... It is that self-confidence that they were radiating that made somebody pick them up as future leaders. Now what can happen to a leader is that once he gets the top job, his infatuation with his own self and own image can take over the real task of his infatuation or his commitment to the organization. That is how people get lost in their own grandeur and then organization can go to seed...Because they want to see their picture in the newspaper, they want to be giving all the lectures, so that they are seen to be the whole reason why the organization exists, rather than the other way round. So the second trait of sustained organizations and their leadership is that top people in the company can constantly demonstrate that their motivations and ambitions for the company exceed their motivations and ambitions for themselves."

"If you look at many great companies and there are many in our history... You go to 50s, 60s, you see the great mercantile companies of Kolkata which used to exist, like the Balmer Laurie Andrew Yule, Martin Burn, Bird & Company, Union Carbide, Dunlop, Bata,.. ICI, ...it could have gone higher... each one has its own story as to why it went down. But in many of them you will find that they had a stint of leadership of somebody who was more obsessed with himself, his grandeur, his money, his wealth, than for the company. And that is why people say – though not fair to all private business houses – but in many business houses people say *'maine paisa lagaya, maine apna capital nikal liya, baaki abhi company chal raha hai'* [I had invested my money in the company. I have taken out my capital, now the company may go on] ...It is a way of saying that I have bailed out, now the company may survive or die is a different matter."

"I regard your mentoring, your concern for the next person to be as successful, if not more successful than you, as one parameter. Your concern during your tenure that your actions are taken more in the interest of the organization than yourself to be a second very important consideration (for developing sustainability in organizations)...I think it comes back to this very difficult thing to define called *Continued Outstanding Leadership."*

The high concern for continued outstanding leadership and succession planning was best illustrated in a personal conversation with Mr. P.L. Tandon in which he said that when he was appointed as chairman of Hindustan Lever and was invited to the headquarters, the first question that was asked from him was: "Mr. Tandon, what would happen to Hindustan Lever if you were knocked down by a bus while crossing a street? How do you propose to take care of that kind of exigency?" Similar concern could be seen in most of the outstanding organizations in one form or the other. In Ranbaxy, the leadership of the company was handed over by Mr. Parvinder Singh to an un-related professional manager, Mr. Brar and not to his sons who were being groomed. Expressing a concern for continuity and succession, Mr. B.M.L. Munjal said, "We have the company organized in such a way that whether I am there tomorrow or not, the company will definitely prosper and progress, much more than what it is today...Everything has been beautifully organized and everything is on paper... and there are capable people in every key position."

The concern shown and investment made for *development of leadership across the organization* by companies like Tata Sons, Infosys and Wipro is notable. Infosys has established a Leadership Institute at Mysore at which Mr. Narayana Murthy and Mr. Dinesh personally conduct sessions, in addition to top ranking faculty and speakers invited from most distinguished institutions. Similarly, at Wipro, special programmes and courses were conducted for development of strategic leadership, sometimes at heavy cost, by inviting the best-known faculty from overseas.

Another aspect of institution building orientation was institutionalizing the *processes for attracting, inducting, training and nurturing the best possible talent and grooming leadership talent from within.* As Mr. Gopalakrishnan said: "The intention to institutionalize the development (of high quality leadership) that organizations adopt is through HR practices. Attracting the right talent, identification of the better talent, grooming the best talent and creating a culture of excellence through *HR practices*... The way to institutionalize the development of leadership across the organization is through robust system of HR processes, but in many companies enough attention is not paid to this aspect."

Describing the emphasis on development of leadership talent from within, Mr. Pratik Kumar, corporate vice-president of Wipro, said: "What we had at Wipro as an organization was a very *strong pool of leadership talent,* which had an ability to scan the market and the environment and the leadership that was willing to bet on it with a reasonable due diligence... Wipro has had a track record of creating leadership for the industry and it is not without design that we entrust a whole lot of responsibility on to the individuals. They run it like independent business. They are entrusted with their own decision-making and they are held accountable as well. They are taught to manage in a tough environment. They are taught to handle businesses by building their own team. So they get groomed as very good leaders... We, as an organization way back in 1970s, used to recruit talent through campus placements from engineering campuses. Mr. Premji himself, till about the 80s and early 90s, used to interview every person who used to get into the organization. Every person getting into the organization he would personally interview... So careful process in terms of selection of right kind of people... led to creating a cadre of leaders over a period of time."

OPENNESS, LEARNING AND CHANGE

Openness, willingness and ability to learn and change were the most important distinguishing characteristics of the leadership of the companies with sustainable competitive edge.

The organizations, whose top leadership operated with a closed mind, were unwilling to obtain and listen to feedback and information about the realities within and outside the organization and did not want to change faced declining performance and deteriorating organizational condition. They had little chance of survival and very often disappeared.

If we were asked to identify only one characteristic of an organization and its leadership that was found to be most critical for sustainability and competitive edge, we would say: It is *their openness, willingness and ability to change.* Organizations whose leadership were not open to information, feedback and learning – and were unwilling or unable to change with the changing business environment-invariably stagnated, declined, withered away and died. This point was very emphatically made by most of the interviewees and demonstrated by the attitudes, values and practices of leaders in the dynamic and successful organizations.

Openness

About openness and transparency and their criticality for building trust, shared vision and empowerment of staff, Mr. Subodh Bhargava said: "Openness and politicking are two opposite things. The organizations, which get into politicking... despite all the technology, keep going down. There is no organization, which has survived politicking. In all Indian family owned third generation businesses this is what is happening..."

"Openness has two advantages: *Firstly,* it conveys direction in creating shared vision, congruency of policies and action; and *secondly,* it inspires people. It has got double benefit. It makes everything convergent, transparent and it is a tremendous confidence building tool. Everyone has got a lot of confidence in it. At Infosys transparency is one of its strengths...

"But transparency is in the process and information. I would say it is not that decision-making should be questioned. It is the information available and sharing those decisions. Each human being would come to his own conclusion, right or wrong. I would never allow transparency to be let through decisions. I will allow transparency of information and on all the information available. Even in Eicher, we have always said union can come and examine the books. They could never say *"ye bonus ke liye to ek balance sheet hai, or asli koi aur balance sheet hai"*. [For bonus this is the balance sheet and for other purposes there is another balance sheet]. We say each and every accounted transaction information is available. You can sit with our accountant and see what you want. *You see, transparency ultimately builds trust. Trust enables shared vision. Trust is an essential pre-condition for empowerment. If I don't trust you, there is no way I will empower you and then decision-making will become slow.* If I don't trust my regional manager in Kanpur, he is not empowered. Then he will be referring to me all the time.

Mr. Brar of Ranbaxy also emphasized and illustrated the value of openness in his organization and also openness in sharing information with their partners, like the suppliers. He said: "If you sit in one of our meetings you will see people tearing each other on issues such as why was it ten days late? They are openly discussed. This data is not hidden. They are not shrouded in any mystery. It is blown out and is openly discussed. Mistakes are not hidden; they are openly displayed so much so that sometimes we find that we are very critical..."

"It is not the old paradigm that if purchase man could deny information to his supplier, he could squeeze him on prices.... That was the old paradigm. Today we have everything open to our suppliers and say: 'well this is what we want, this is our cost structure and this is what we would like from you'. This is total transparency. He is open to everything the company has in terms of what we do and, therefore, he becomes a partner with you..."

Giving an example of how some special type of packing bottles for exporting medicines to the USA were developed in India through the suppliers, he said: "The supplier had full access to our technical capability, knowledge and US FDA regulations. I mean he could not spend that kind of time and effort to gain knowledge of that. We provided it free to him, this kind of technical consultancy. We take a lot of such initiatives."

Mr. Bhaskar Bhatt of Titan, talking about the change-oriented, open and transparent style of leadership of his CEO, said: "He has always driven innovation and a consensus based approach in management style. A very open, very questioning style. What you did yesterday doesn't mean it will help you succeed tomorrow. Questioning this and *reinventing yourself all the time* is something he has taught everybody. What you did during the license period doesn't mean that you will be successful today. So today, the entire drive is to change our business model to suit the tomorrow – whether you look at manufacturing, or marketing, or relationship with your customer, use of IT, or leveraging current technology, the supply chain and bringing down your cost through better working capital management and, of course, operational efficiency issues. But leadership style has been one of giving complete freedom to the operating managers, *open and transparent style,* and a questioning style and at a very fundamental level customer oriented style which is right from CEO downward."

The willingness and ability to change depended primarily on the *attitude of the top management leadership towards openness and learning.* Organizations in which top management was unwilling to obtain and examine internal feedback from various levels in the organization and external feedback from the market and other relevant sources, were bound to get into deep trouble. Such companies were not keeping themselves fully informed and aware of the changes taking place in the business environment, technology, competitors' moves, customer needs and preferences. The rigid, closed-minded and sometimes 'over-confident' and 'egoistic' leaders fell into such trap, often with disastrous consequences for the organization. They seemed to prefer to live in the aura of their past success and glory than to face the harsh realities and change. This phenomenon often happened when the leaders surrounded themselves with 'yes men' and a 'kitchen cabinet' that insulated the leaders from disturbing and unpalatable feedback about feelings of important stakeholders, facts and realities of their organization and the changing business environment.

Competency Trap

A similar phenomenon is the *'competency trap'*. When some organizations become obsessed with their success based on a particular competency, style of functioning and approaches to doing business in particular ways that give them success, they assume that it will work irrespective of changed situations. If they do not have the openness to face the facts and flexibility to change and come up with new strategies, structures, systems, styles and skills, they have little chance of sustaining themselves. The outstanding examples of turnaround and radical change with the changing business environment in IBM, Intel, General Motors and General Electric at the international level and TISCO, Wipro and TVS Motors in India are well known. On the contrary, a large number of companies owned by well-known business houses in India that thrived during the protection days of 'license and permit raj', have declined or disappeared because they could not or did not want to change.

Mr. Gopalakrishnan compared the above-mentioned phenomenon among the organizations to the Icarus Paradox in Greek mythology. He told the story of Icarus, the son of Daedalus. Daedalus was a very innovative person who, along with his son was imprisoned by the king in a jail with high walls but an open sky. Daedalus was very ingenious and fixed wings to the arms of Icarus with wax that enabled Icarus to fly. So Icarus flew and was able to fly higher and higher. So he kept flying high and came so close to the sun that the heat melted the wax joints and Icarus fell down and died. He said: "*Yeh kahani hai* Greek mythology *ki, toh* management is also like that *ki jo aapki strength hai woh yahan tak pahunchati hai, ab aapko* gear shift *karne ka samay jab aata hai toh aap sochte hain joh maine kiya hai wohi theek hai. Isko akde hue log bolte hain, ki beta maine bachpan mein* Mathematics *padha tha aur is ne faraq kiya tha, to tumhe bhi yehi karna chahiye*" ["This is a story from Greek mythology, but management is also like that. Your strength takes you upto a point, but when the time to shift the gear comes, you think what you have been doing so far is the right way. It is like some rigid person saying to his son that 'in my childhood I had studied mathematics, which made a difference, so you should also do that."]

Continuity and Change

It is, however, important to clearly understand that *change and continuity are not mutually exclusive.* Like many other paradoxes in management, both continuity and change are essential and they go together in organizations with long track record of sustainability. This point has been forcefully argued and established by Collins and Porras in their well-known book *'Built to Last'*, as well as in Arie de Gues's book *'The Living Company'*[33]. The ability of an organization to maintain the core in terms of its identity, core values and core purpose, while changing most other elements like strategy, structure, operations, systems and processes, technology, products, markets, etc. in order to cope with or influence its changing business environment, is the key to survival, sustainability and growth.

The key to sustainability is the *fine balance between continuity and change,* and clarity in the minds of leaders what was important to continue and what needed to be changed.

Mr. Subodh Bhargava of Eicher articulated the importance of ability and willingness of the leadership to change as the most central characteristics for sustainability and competitiveness. Based on his long experience of heading a leading engineering company, he said: "As the environment changed – either the input side or the output side–by de-licensing to lowering of the barriers for export, import, or global market access, change was inevitable and the process of change itself had to be led. *So the leadership's greatest (characteristic), the most critical dimension, is to be able to change itself, transform themselves and their organization to remain competitive.* There are no fixed formulae for competitiveness. To my mind what was true five years ago may not be relevant today, because either the target has moved ahead, or somebody has grabbed the target, so they are looking for a new target. So you have to change. And change, once again the totality-of investment patterns, to technology, to processes, to people. And I think it is a question of attitudes and mindset - that (as leader) I am willing to change. People who have failed to change have really not been able to remain competitive and found themselves bought out or extinguished."

The importance of change and how and when to bring about change in organizations for sustainable competitiveness was vividly described by Mr. Suresh Krishna, chairman and managing director of Sundram Fasteners, a company that has got the best supplier of the year award from General Motors continuously for five years which is given only to the best 100 out of the 30,000 suppliers of GM. The company is a 100% supplier of radiator caps to GM and has supplied 50 million caps with not a single cap being defective. The company has also won several other coveted awards. Mr. Krishna categorically stated the point that companies that do not change are not going to exist. He emphasized that *to create an excellent company of the future it is essential to change when no change seems necessary.*

Elaborating his views, experience and philosophy that enabled Sundram Fasteners to achieve its present outstanding stature and competitiveness as a manufacturing company, Mr. Suresh Krishna said: "First of all you have to have a vision. Our vision is that Sundram Fasteners should be one of the best companies in the world. And you must become a multinational company. If everybody else in the western world can do it, why can't you? Second, this vision has to be communicated over and over again until their (i.e. all company employees') vision and your vision completely gets merged. Right from the day go, right from 1966 when we started this company, I was the first employee of this company. So I have now been with the company since it started. I have been talking to my workers at least three times a year at every location, sometimes three, sometimes four times. I tell them everything about the company right from sales to profit and loss, the competition, what happens in the world, with General Motors, TPM, everything that happens in the company – I talk to them. The entire company knows exactly what is happening. So I have now been doing it for 37 years."

"The company has got a very clear goal. People write about the company so they are proud to belong to a company which is written about, which is shown as a role model. You have to sustain that 'role modelship' and so you work harder and say that we cannot let down our company. Everybody likes to be on the winning side, everybody wants to be in the finals and win the finals, so they say that we need to see that this company succeeds. It has also become such an important concern that no unit at any point of time wants to create any kind of problem, because they will say: 'You have spoilt the name of Sundram Fasteners.' That kind of commitment (is on what) the entire Sundram Fasteners is moving. The people part of it is extremely important. First, you have the *vision,* then you have *communication* on top of the agenda, the third part is to *set milestones* for the company. You say that by such and such time we are going to do such and such things. Every milestone you cross, your confidence grows. Be it getting ISO-9000, be it exporting, be it capturing a new territory, getting a TPM Excellence award, or whatever. Every time you cross a milestone, you keep on setting new milestones. And you keep raising the bar. Every time you raise the bar you say now let us jump this. Then you say this is easy, let us raise the bar a little further. Setting milestones is very important. But, more than that what is important is coming through as a winner every time you raise the bar."

"If you have the vision, communication and milestone-setting and you come through as a winner, you have an organization which is tuned to a direction which is bound to succeed. *What I have found most difficult in my entire career is to introduce change when the company is doing well.* People turn around and say what is wrong with this, there is nothing wrong with this, so why should we do this and improve this. Everybody says we are a good company and our financial results show that we are a good company, but the management is not satisfied. What is happening to our chairman? Why is he not satisfied? Why is he all the time saying this is not right, that is not right? Why is he never satisfied? *I always tell them the minute you become satisfied that is your downfall.* You cannot at any point of time become satisfied."

Explaining the philosophy that guided his organization, especially regarding excellence and change, which reflects the unique aspects of Indian culture in organizations, Mr. Suresh Krishna said:

> I always tell them (the employees) that this concept of dharma in Hindu philosophy is doing your job to the best of your abilities. The dharma of a school teacher is to become the best school teacher, not only in his district but also in the world. The dharma of a good musician is to become a most recognized musician in the world. *The dharma of a good businessman is to become the most recognized and successful and most sought after businessman in the world. So we must be that. That is our dharma.* We must fulfill our *dharma* because God has given us so many opportunities. It will be very wrong on our part if we don't utilize these opportunities. God might as well give these to somebody else who might utilize them better. There is also a saying that if you do your dharma properly, it would not only protect you but also protect your future. What it really means is: it will create enough well-being in the society to look after you and your children and grand children. That is what it really means. That is why they say you practice your dharma properly. You have nothing to fear. This is the most difficult challenge when the company is doing well... *I always tell them that one must change when you feel there is no necessity to change,* and it is very important. It's exactly like saying you must exercise when you are healthy. A lot of people say that I am healthy, there is nothing wrong with me, I had gone to the doctor, checked all my parameters, everything is ok, no blood pressure, no cholesterol, nothing.

But that is the time to look after yourself. What is the use of all this if you have a stroke and after that you can't exercise. I always tell them you must change when you are healthy.

Responding to the question about the key factors that enabled Hindustan Lever to maintain its competitiveness, Mr. G. Kapur, executive director–foods, also highlighted the importance of change for its sustainability. He said: "One thing, which I can say is that *the ability of the organization to anticipate change and continuously change itself, is the first thing* which comes to my mind. If I look back, I think one of the huge strengths of HLL, despite being a fairly big company in terms of its scale of operations, is that in our history we have actually been able to bring about a very sharp focus on what was appropriate at that point of time... Now, if you get into the 90s (the first phase of 90s) when the liberalization programme really started and there was more elbowroom for the organizations to operate. I think HLL probably was the fastest in terms of moving into the area of mergers, acquisitions and reorganization to really consolidate itself in the entire FMCG sector and in the areas where we were interested in. Now coming into the late 90s and the early part of this decade when the markets have opened, the markets have become competitive. We are going through a phase where we are becoming very sharply focussed on consumers and brands, because the competitive landscape has changed and, therefore, you cannot operate in an unfocused way both with your consumers, your categories and your brands. I think at this point in time, or at least for the last 2-3 years, we are sharpening our focus around what we believe are our main brands The 30 power brands as we call them and alongside bringing or taking the organization to the consumer in its fullness and becoming very sharply focussed in consumer insights and innovation programmes and so on."

Giving a historical perspective of the development and change of Wipro, which at present is one of the largest IT companies, Mr. Pratik Kumar, corporate vice-president - HR, illustrated the ability of Wipro's leadership to scan the environment, anticipate and quickly respond to change. He said: "Just to give you a background of Wipro, we started our business way back in 1945 and, over a period of time, we have diversified. When we started, it was a consumer care business. In fact Wipro used to be known as Western India Vegetable Oil Products Company and over a period of time we have gone to Infotech – first on the hardware side, then onto software arena. We have gone into medical equipment, engineering products also. But there is a method in terms of how we have grown over a period of time and that has largely come from *our ability to respond to the changing environment quickly, swiftly and in a very thoughtful manner."*

"If you look way back in 1945, India was a largely agrarian economy at that time. There was shortage of edible oil and so we responded by getting into that particular area. The late seventies was the time when political activism led to the exit of many multinational companies and you had IBM, Coke and other MNCs moving out that led to a vacuum. Unlike in the consumer product segments, where you had a lot of Indian brands coming in and then falling on the wayside, in information technology, lots of Indian companies found a space in which to enter and they have been able to consolidate and grow..."

"What we had at Wipro, as an organization, was a very strong pool of leadership talent which had an ability to scan the market and the environment and the leadership which was willing, with reasonable due diligence, to bet on it... Little later, in the mid-eighties information technology boom continued and we found markets growing in terms of specialized needs for software solutions. That is the time we responded actually by spinning off software."

*"I would say, as an organization, we have always been alive to the changing market. And our ability to respond to it quickly and swiftly in a very nimble manner has been one of the reasons why we have been able to adjust to the changing times very quickly...*Even last year, when we went through a down turn, we found that our ability to adjust was far quicker than perhaps the other companies in the sector, whether it was in terms of cost efficiencies, or whether it was in terms of cost takeouts and the rest, we were able to actually adjust to it much quicker and swifter. So that is one of the elements which differentiates us."

Mr. J. Shankar, corporate treasurer of Wipro, added, "... historically, during the last 54-55 years, our growth in profit would be about 23 per cent (annually). Our market capitalization growth also would be somewhere in the region of 20 per cent plus (annually). Twenty per cent plus growth (annually) over twenty, twenty-five years is phenomenal. *This we have been able to achieve by reinventing ourselves through various businesses."*

Describing the change oriented and change supporting attitude of the leadership at Infosys, Mr. S. Sukumar, manager - corporate planning, said: "The attitude and the mindset of the top management regarding change is extremely important. If the top management is not open to change, the processes can easily become meaningless. I would say that one key element which has acted very much in our favour is the attitude and approach of the top management. It not only supports the change, but it also enables these changes to occur, which is extremely important."

Responding to the question how his strong emphasis on being focussed was reconciled with the need to change in the highly dynamic, changing business environment, Mr. B.M.L. Munjal, chairman of Hero Honda said: "It is not that we have a fixed view and our vision has stopped there. The change in my way of looking at things is taking place almost every day, every hour, every minute. Yesterday only I took a (major change) decision in my organization. Earlier I was against too much of automation in my plant, because we don't need blind people in our organization. Now, when I am seeing that employment is getting out of our hand and it is becoming a burden on our total cost, we are re-thinking this matter. Yesterday only I discussed this in my organization and this is a change in our focus (on employment policy). So far, my focus and (policy) was as much employment as we can provide and now (our policy will be to) provide employment, but let it not be a burden on cost, a heavy load on our cost of production, as our cost of production is coming on our head. By focus I did not mean that we (narrow down) to the same technology level, working level, functioning level, dealing level... (It is more about the scope of industry and products that you choose to work on.)"

Leaders as Foreseers and Avid Learners

The leaders of successful companies were described as persons who saw way ahead of their contemporaries. They were described as *'avid learners'*, who were constantly seeking knowledge, information and feedback from various sources and were willing and flexible enough to change, to meet the challenges of the changing times.

These orientations of leaders and companies that survived radical changes in the business environment, were very well described by Mr. Aqil Busrai of Motorola. Giving examples of the leaders of some outstanding companies like Kodak, who foresaw changes in technology and changed over to digital technology, He said: "That's where average companies and good companies get differentiated and that's where good leaders and average leaders get differentiated. *Good leaders see the future.* They don't only have vision; they see the future trend. How hard it is to accept the reality, even if it means closing down their (existing) operations, they accept it. The average leaders keep on hoping that: 'no-no, we will still fight the market.' We will still improve our product, we will still survive; and after some time they just can't manage. The technology goes on a quantum jump shift. Then they lose out on the market."

"These leaders have one common element – *they keep themselves aware of the data and trends and facts more than intuition. They read a lot; they interact a lot. And the second trait is that they are open to challenge themselves.* Whatever they have believed in, they are willing to break that belief after sometime. Some of the pig-headed leaders who say: 'what I have said is right and can never be changed even by myself', have actually brought the company down."

If you see the attitude of some of the good leaders, who are not fickle-minded, they see a trend coming in. They have the data to see that and they want a lot of data. They want a lot of proof and empirical stuff to say: 'really, are we looking at a short-term change, or looking at real change, or looking at cosmetic change?'. If they find that yes, everything around them shows that this change is coming in, then they are willing to break their own mould and say: 'I think I need to change'. Those are the good leaders who change with the time, based on the data and facts and not what their gut feel says and not that they have made a public statement and see to it that 'come hell or water, I'll stick to it'.

"So if you see the trend of these leaders, they are very interactive people. They don't stay in their own field of specialization. They go and read things outside their specialization. They go and interact on things outside their specialization and it applies to anybody. Even a HR guy, a good HR guy talks about technology: what is happening to this? What is happening to that chip and why is it going in this direction? The natural curiosity to have that learning and what is happening around makes them different."

Based on this comprehensive discussion of rich experience-based viewpoints and illustrations, we can state with a high degree of confidence that an outstanding characteristic of the leadership of successful companies that demonstrated sustained competitiveness is their *openness, ability to foresee change and willingness to learn and change.*

THOROUGH KNOWLEDGE, ATTENTION TO DETAILS AND HOLISTIC VIEW

The top management in several of these companies highly emphasized leading by knowing the subject thoroughly.

Contd....

They believed and practiced the dictum that it is essential for the top management to have a thorough understanding of business and intimate knowledge of relevant technology to lead from the front.

They viewed management problems holistically, but considered ensuring attention to details as the key to success.

When we asked Mr. D.V. Kapoor, the first chairman of NTPC, to share his thoughts, based on his vast experience, about the most important factor that led to the successful completion of very large and most challenging projects and making the NTPC such a respected company, he said: "The key is attention to details. If you cannot do it yourself, ensure that somebody does it and then ensure that the detailed plans are implemented as per the schedule."

Mr. B.M.L. Munjal, chairman of Hero Honda, expressed a similar view. He emphasized that unless you have thorough knowledge of business and technology of the industry you are running, you cannot lead from the front. This did not mean close supervision and non-delegation of authority, but a full understanding of the technology and business operations, awareness and overseeing the progress and ensuring attention to details. Emphasizing this viewpoint forcefully, Mr. Munjal said: "I would insist that the quality, the product, the customer relationships, the dealer relationships are *much more important than the strategies which one draws out,* or the plans one draws out. Even if you draw a strategy or a plan, you are drawing the strategies and plan of these things only. Where to get technology? How to implement that technology? How to produce it? Process management and how to reach to the actual consumer? Until you have that strong chain and you have built that chain and you have devoted more attention and time to those things, you can't get good results. That's the little difference between us (i.e., the academics and the practitioners). Sometime people take it in a different way. They say: 'You are the chairman of such a large company, why are you going into such minute details?'."

"We have fully decentralized [operations in the] company. There are individuals who are fully empowered. I don't sign a cheque, my son doesn't sign a cheque, no director signs a cheque at all. It's a completely decentralized company. But in spite of all that [I keep myself fully informed of business plans and technology]. Yesterday I took some people to the plant. When I was explaining, telling them about the equipment, its output, what we feed in, how much output we get and what is the advantage of this machine over the other, they got little perturbed and asked: why should you know all this? I said this is the only difference. You must know what you are talking about."

"Until you know the subject, you cannot lead anybody. If you want to lead somebody, you must know that aspect, that subject fully. You may not have studied that. I have not gone to a business management school and I haven't gone to an engineering college... Once I was buying a very large equipment, a large rolling mill in the early sixties and I was one of the persons sitting around the table for discussions. There were about seven experts sitting around. These were civil engineer, chemical engineer, mechanical engineer, electrical engineer, actual mill designer, a mill manufacturer, etc. They were discussing technical details and it was a treat to talk to all of them. They also felt happy and I also felt very happy that I could understand and discuss the technical details and answer to all those people... If you have to lead a team, if you have a goal, which you want to attain and reach, you must first know it yourself."

This view appears in contradiction to the view held by leaders like Jack Welch who insisted that the top men should concentrate on the broad picture and need not go into details.[34] The contradiction can be reconciled if we keep in view the frame of reference of a single product company vs a multi-product corporation on the one hand and the management by highly knowledgeable professional leaders in the specific businesses and product lines of a company like General Electric on the other hand.

Further, the *need to combine attention to details with a holistic view* of leadership was considered equally important. The holistic view meant looking at the totality of the organization, as well as viewing specific management situations and problems in totality and not fragmented into functional aspects like marketing, finance, operations, or human resource problems in isolation. The analogy of fragmented view was like looking at a problem through a shattered mirror, whereas looking at a problem holistically was like looking through a convex mirror. As Mr. Subodh Bhargava had emphasized, "I would say the bottom-line [for developing sustainable competitive edge] would still be the leadership and the people inside the organization. Also, it's just not any one dimension. *Good leadership is always holistic and comprehensive.* It just doesn't look at product development, or IT, or accounts, or manpower efficiency, or machine tool efficiency. A good leadership is – in a holistic manner – continuously watching and changing. The ability to change, walk the talk and being a role model becomes very important."

PEOPLE-CENTRIC APPROACH, EMPOWERMENT, COMMITMENT AND TEAMWORK

One common thread clearly visible in all outstanding organizations was people-centric approach of leadership that attracted the best talent and created conditions for empowerment, commitment, sense of belonging and ownership *and teamwork* among the people working in the organization. More than on any other resource, they bet on the *talent and commitment of people.*

> *A very high priority was given to search, attract, retain, train, develop and leverage the talent and leadership across these organizations.*
>
> *These organizations genuinely treated the talented people, their empowerment (i.e., trusting them and giving them freedom to act), their development, enthusiasm, commitment and teamwork as the most critical factors for sustaining competitive edge.*
>
> *The style of leadership generally was more informal, open, persuasive and role-modeling, rather than impersonal, rigid, command and control, or bureaucratic. There was, at the same time, no compromise on performance and results.*

Illustrating the emphasis on people as the key to organizational survival and excellence in the Larsen & Toubro Company, Mr. Yogi Sriram described the philosophy of Mr. Larsen, one of the founders of the Company. He said: "Mr. Larsen is a 94-year old patriarch of this family. He goes around, shakes hands with us... and many younger people and senior management people. They are really inspired by him. He is like a walking legend, if I may put it that way. He says and this is to quote him: 'Machines will be there, buildings will be there, but there is nothing if you don't have people.' So that sentence actually epitomizes the entire fabric of this (company's) culture and value system."

Search and Development of Talent

In the IT companies like Infosys and Wipro, as well as in most of the other dynamic companies like HLL, L&T and Tata Group of companies, the leadership emphasized inducting bright young people with high potential for learning, training and developing them and imbibing the work culture of their organization.

Companies like Infosys chose young people on purpose to keep the profile of the organization young and invested heavily in their training and development.

Describing the approach of Infosys for search and development of talent, Mr. Sukumar said: "The organization has focussed on being very young, which means that we recruit people who are brighter than us, who have that potential and fire in their bellies so as to make things happen and openness is naturally there. The average age of the organization is about 26 years... the focus is on keeping the organization young."

"Another aspect (leading to competitiveness of Infosys) is about people focus on high quality people. Our recruitment process is extremely stringent. And in fact, the more important thing, I would say, is the culture that Mr. Narayana Murthy[35] keeps on reinforcing, which is that we need to recruit people who are brighter than us...If you go deeper into human psychology, typically from a security perspective, you would like to have somebody who is not better than you. (But in our company the work is done by) knowledge based groups, so everything depends on how much value you bring to the table as a superior, as a head of the department...So that culture is reinforced and people go ahead and purposefully want to recruit people who are brighter than them."

The rigorous talent search of HLL through campus recruitment programmes from leading institutions all over the country and intensive field based training is well known. Mr. Gopalakrishnan described how HLL emphasized hands on learning from his personal experience at the beginning of his career as a young science graduate when he joined the computer department of HLL. The young trainees were attached to experienced sales people to learn the primary functioning of the company, irrespective of the department in which they joined. They were given the same allowances and facilities as a salesperson would be entitled to. They travelled with them wherever they went to get first hand experience. The experienced senior people did mentoring to develop the desired skills and attitudes and imbibe the organizational values among the young trainees.

A very different approach to searching and mobilizing talent was described by a highly experienced professional manager of one of the most dynamic and leading companies included in this study. He said: "Any contemporary discussion on what gives competitive advantage to companies is not complete without consciously recognizing the role *people* play in it. Now it is in a way a motherhood statement and a platitude to say that people will be the competitive advantage of any company. The question is not whether human resources are really critical, but the question is what kind of human resources? What kind of people? What type of people will give you competitive advantage? Will any person give? The answer is clearly: No!... (If you were to examine these questions)...you probably cannot afford an egalitarian and altruistic perspective that every human being is good and everybody will be able to contribute and everybody is okay, we need to take them and develop them... You probably will come to a more... Differentiated view that there is talent, which is different from non-talent and that companies which want to jump start their capabilities don't have the luxury to bring in anybody and grow them over a period of time. They need to really strategize as to what kind of people they hire? How do they deal with them in a strategic manner? How do they align them with the strategic goals of the organization? So that these very talented resources become productive and actually add to the competitive advantage of the company... Our works done so far in this direction, to my mind, are not yet very adequate, while there is a lot of talk about it."

"The successful companies which achieve long-term success have very different and unpublicized, unrecorded ways of doing these things. Their methods of choosing the right people don't follow a textbook pattern. They don't necessarily follow a method of advertising, recruiting through a lot of interviews and/or doing some track record based selection, or anything like that. They have varieties of methods and one of the popular is, of course, the network of relationships, which are leveraged to get the right people."

"Similarly, the methods of building competitive advantage within the human resources of your company necessarily may not be achieved only through workshops or ...the more (common) HRD kind of approaches, which we are used to....But by very rapidly moving people through a series of tasks, which are critical and hence shadowing them with the top leaders and then picking the best. The top leadership is personally investing in finding out talent, cutting across hierarchy and going to where the talent really lies. It could be in a youngster, could be in a middle manager. It may not have anything to do with the role, title, position; may not have anything to do with pay, perquisites, etc., but it's something to do with what people really do and can achieve. How do you spot it? How do you bring it into the main stream of the company? There's a lot of talent in the company, which gets lost within the maze of its hierarchy, bureaucracy, even in modern firms. I have seen that the competitive companies approach this task very uniquely, not through any normal formula driven approach. They go and think out of the box and do out of the box things. The leadership for this (talent search and development) is taken by the business leader and not by the HR management."

The criticality of high quality talent, especially in the more knowledge based industries like information technology and pharmaceuticals was highly emphasized. In other sectors also, it was felt that high quality expertise must be obtained from whatever source to develop sustainable competitive edge. Eicher obtained services of technical experts from various countries as consultants and advisors for short durations as it was difficult to afford their salaries for long-term positions. Similarly, examples were given by Mr. Jhunjhunwala, of the LNJ Bhilwara Group, of hiring people after their retirement from multinational and foreign companies to develop technology which was otherwise not accessible. In the Ranbaxy Company, key managerial personnel as well as research scientists were hired from different countries where they have their operations.

Articulating the importance of international level managerial and technical expertise to develop sustainable competitive edge in the Indian companies, Mr. Subodh Bhargava said: "Strengthening your team with global managers... who bring the requisite expertise so that our buying for various competencies and skills and all is strong... The global expertise, irrespective of the colour of the skin, or the title of the passport, is something to my mind a key strategy for bringing in the skill and competencies which will enable sustainable competitive edge."

Style of Leadership, Commitment, Teamwork and Empowerment of People

It is generally believed that whereas a certain style of leadership and management that disempowers people and enforces compliance and conformity may obtain short-term results by the use of authority, it may not lead to commitment, sense of ownership and pride in belonging to the organization. These factors, in turn, affect initiative, productivity, creativity, innovativeness, risk taking and entrepreneurship within the organization that are required for developing competitiveness and excellence.

Is it possible to build a great organization when its employees – especially those whose knowledge and expertise is critical for its own growth and growth of the organization – are alienated, demoralized and frustrated because of the style, behaviour and attitude of the key leaders in the organization? What style of leadership is most appropriate for achieving high levels of performance and competitiveness? Such questions have been debated and researched by academics and there are strong beliefs among business leaders and practitioners on such questions. Usually people develop their own personal theories about human motivation and look for evidence to confirm their belief and persist in practicing their tacit theory. They tend to give highly generalized examples to uphold their belief and practice.

Broadly two generalized types of assumptions and beliefs dominate people's thinking: one that subscribes to the view that the leaders have to be tough, demanding, only concerned with results and therefore, should not let feelings and emotions come in their way. The underlying assumptions about people in general and employees in particular being that they inherently dislike work, avoid responsibility, lack initiative, do not have risk taking ability and are not innovative. Therefore, they have to be driven by 'strong leadership'.

The other set of assumptions is the opposite view that people do have inner motivation and, given the right conditions and incentives, like to take up responsibility, enjoy work, have potential for creative and innovative solutions and can take initiative and risk for better performance of the organization. Douglas McGregor had coined the terms theory 'X' and theory 'Y' for these two archetype set of assumptions about human motivation, leading to two distinctly different and almost opposite styles of leader behaviour.[36] Generally people confuse theory X and theory Y as 'hard' and 'soft' theories of leadership and we have heard many managers in organizations, other than those included in this study, say that in Indian conditions only theory X works! *Theory X and theory Y are not hard and soft theories. These are two sets of assumptions or mindsets of leaders about people in general and those whom they lead. These two set of assumptions lead to two broad ways of dealing with and relating to people and the style of leadership practiced by the leaders.*

We often come across managers in organizations (other than the ones included in this study), who believe that the theory 'Y' approach is 'soft', 'academic' and theoretical and not suited to Indian conditions. This, we feel, is a distorted view of the theory 'Y' of McGregor and an over-generalized opinion in dealing with the contemporary organizational situations in India. We shall give examples later in this discussion of such approach being practiced in the most successful and competitive organizations in India.

It is seldom realized that there is a powerful factor called *'self-fulfilling'* prophecy working in all leadership situations. Self-fulfilling prophecy means that we end up creating consequences that we believe in, because of our own behaviour. So when we operate with a 'theory X' mindset, from a sub-conscious belief that people cannot be trusted, they are not creative, do not want to accept responsibility, have no initiative – we treat them as immature, drive them by diktat, do not trust them and do not give them responsibility. They 'over-direct' and 'over-control' them. As a result the people – specially the brighter and more competent ones – who are led like this become alienated, frustrated and demoralized. They do not take initiative, do not take risk and do not utilize their creative potential. They either leave, or become passive and compliant. This further reinforces the mindset of the leader following such practices as his or her belief about people gets confirmed. Then the leader says: 'Didn't I tell you, that people are like that!' So, having got confirmation of his assumptions, he becomes more convinced of his original assumptions and pushes his style harder only to end up, in most cases, with disastrous consequences for the organization. He/she gets caught in a quagmire, rather than come up with creative, imaginative and innovative solutions from within to face the crisis and take up the challenge, that only highly committed, competent and motivated staff can deal with.

We noted that in some organizations that were going into a tailspin because of downturn in the industry, the leaders and managers became more and more convinced of their theory X type beliefs, pushed the employees harder and took more harsh decisions of downsizing, cost cutting, etc., only to find themselves in deeper trouble, incurring greater losses and losing some of their most talented personnel.

The real issue is not 'hard' or 'soft' approach of leadership, but the 'negative' and 'positive' assumptions about people. Such assumptions affect the ability of the leader to diagnose the level of maturity of the people whom he or she attempts to lead, relate to them appropriately, inspire them and help them to grow and utilize their talent most effectively. People who have subconscious negative assumptions about people, as identified in the 'theory X', may not always be 'hard' leaders. They may be quite 'soft' in terms of goal setting and pushing for results. Likewise, those having the positive assumptions about people described as theory 'Y' may not always be 'soft' leaders and in fact have often been found to be very 'tough' in setting highly challenging goals and demanding very high levels of performance.

Having basically positive assumptions about people as identified in theory 'Y' is not contradictory to being tough in expecting and/or demanding the highest levels of performance. This point became clear long ago when concern for task and concern for relationships were seen as not two opposite ends of a continuum, but as two separate dimensions in a 2x2 matrix, in which different combinations of task and relations orientation were possible and were needed according to the requirements of the situation and maturity level of the persons being led. *The effectiveness of the style of leadership was, therefore, found to be a function of situational sensitivity and behavioural flexibility of the leader, with different styles being effective in different situations, depending also on the level of maturity of the persons being led.*[37]

Great deal of research has been done in this area, indicating that human motivation is more complex and employee behaviour and effectiveness of leaders is dependent on the nature of situation, relationship between the leader and the led, level of maturity of employees and many other variables. It is now well established that one style of leadership may not be effective in different situations and with different people. Perceptive situational sensitivity, insightful understanding and empathy of specific employees' motivation and feelings, their level of maturity, socio-cultural context and relationships are important in determining suitability of the style of leadership.

Currently, there is a great deal of interest in the concept of *Emotional Intelligence* - the ability to manage our relationships and ourselves effectively.[38] In the simplest words, it refers to the ability of the leader to empathize with the emotions of the followers, self awareness and ability to manage his/her own feelings and the feelings of others. In their book entitled *'The New Leaders'*, Daniel Goleman and his co-authors state that "The fundamental task of leaders, we argue, is to prime good feeling in those they lead. That occurs when a leader creates *resonance* – a reservoir of positivity that frees the best in people. At its root, then the primal job of leadership is emotional...Conversely, we sound a warning about the power of toxic leadership to poison the emotional climate of a work place."[39] They have identified six leadership styles that effective leaders utilize ranging from visionary to coaching to commanding – as the situations demands.

When the leader has a clear understanding of the changing business environment and has a clear vision of reorienting or reinventing the company, he may have to take tough decisions to cut the flab, move out of the business in which they don't have a chance of being competitive and substitute people whose competencies, skills, attitudes and mindsets have become obsolete and irrelevant to the new requirements. Such leaders usually have quite positive and realistic assumptions and, in fact, bank upon talented people, a network of relationships and contacts and involvement of people across the organization to bring about radical change and turnaround. After taking such tough 'economic' measures, they often resort to 'organizational development' oriented measures.[40] They create a conducive organization climate and work conditions, very positive and well conceived human resource policies and practices, that would generate high degree of involvement, commitment, empowerment, creativity, risk taking and innovativeness to take the organization to a high trajectory of competitiveness and performance. This is what Jack Welch evidently did at GE and Ratan Tata did, in his own way, at Tata Sons, Tisco and Telco.

Let us now look at the people-centric approach and practices of some of the outstanding organizations included in this study.

Mr. B.M.L. Munjal of Hero Honda said categorically about the way how the employees, especially the workers should be, and are, treated in his organization. He said: "So long as you treat your workers like machines, thinking that so many units work in my organization and since they work for so many hours so they can take that much wage or salary, then you cannot distinguish yourself from the others. You will remain one like others. If you have to be different than others, they (employees/workers) have to be part of it (the organization). And when they will become part of it, if you read them, you understand them and they read your organization and they understand your organization and they become one with the others. Once they become a part your organization, then they will put in whatever they have... You have to lead them not only by walking before them, but also by walking with them, in the same language, in the same spirit, in the same fashion, in the same way of working. What you expect from them, the same way you work with them... We never allowed a difference or distinction (between workers, employees and ourselves) in our organization. (*hamne yahan kabhi bhi koi farq ya* distinction *nahin kiya*).

"My cost of production, my per man productivity in bicycles is the highest, in motorcycles it is the highest.... Our workers are the best paid workers (next only to Maruti). In addition they are provided highly subsidized meals, tea, etc... But the productivity of these people is quite high... *I don't pay them from my pocket. It's the company, it's the product, which pays. It is their output, which pays them...* (The key is) to locate the right people to operate the factory and train your worker as much as you can... If you want to lead anybody, you have to lead from within (i.e. from your heart) and not merely by words."

The importance of organization culture in which the people feel free to express their views freely and frankly as a critical factor for innovation and change, a working environment and a gains sharing system that generates a sense of ownership and teamwork was highly emphasized in knowledge intensive industries like information technology and also in most of the other organizations. *A distinct shift in the style of leadership was indicated from the command and control model to much more egalitarian, less hierarchical, informal style, in order to encourage creativity, innovativeness and risk taking.*

This distinctive shift in style of leadership was clearly articulated at Hindustan Lever. Describing this phenomenon, Mr. Kapur said: "We have undergone a very significant change in leadership style in our company... Earlier our leadership style used to be much more autocratic, in the sense that leaders were hero-worshipped and they were distant from the people. They used to have a command structure. There was a very strong sense of discipline, command and control in the organization. That was appropriate for that time, but today the leadership style is very different. The leader is not distant from anyone–he is accessible to every employee in the company. In fact he would reach out to each person on a first name basis. Now, with the leaders, the style is no longer autocratic, it is much more participative. It reflects the confidence to take a lot of criticism, a lot of pointing out of mistakes, a lot of suggestions, a lot of improvements in the board thinking. It is transformed completely. Earlier when you had to meet somebody from the senior management, you had to fix an appointment as an employee. Today that system doesn't exist anymore. Everyone sits with his door open and anyone can walk in and so I have seen a change. I am not ever going to be convinced that this was right or that was right. I believe both were right for the specific situations."

The deep concern of leadership to create most conducive conditions for knowledge workers to learn, grow and contribute is best reflected in the policies, practices and facilities provided by the IT companies. The degree of autonomy, flexibility and encouragement to innovation and entrepreneurship provided to the staff in companies like Infosys, Wipro and Satyam is remarkable.

Infosys has created a university-campus-like environment at their work place and was given the 'Best Employer' award in 2001.[41] They introduced the 'Employee Stock Options' fairly early and most other companies have similar schemes. Mr. Dinesh, co-founder and director of Infosys, explained the people-centric policies and practices at Infosys. He said: "We have a very good human resource system. In our business the key, the only variable and the only asset we have is people. So to manage that very efficiently, we have a very good human resource system... Good healthy competition is thereby creating a very high performance oriented work ethic. The people compete, the rewards are aligned towards that and people are encouraged to compete. There is less hierarchy. There is an open culture in the company."

"Infosys provides the learning opportunity, that's very important... We provide good facility where they (the young bright people) can learn. So we invest quite a lot, 6-7 per cent of our revenue goes towards education and research. And not now, we have been doing it for several years. The second thing is good competition, which is required. We provide that healthy competitive environment. There is less hierarchy, meritocracy is recognized and people who produce results are the ones who will get rewarded. You create different bands of performance and recognize people for the performance that they have produced. The rewards are also based on those bands of excellence that people have produced...Third, employees' stock offer plan is also there, where people who have created wealth for the organization–they also get rewarded."

"We were the first company in 1994 to have produced the first stock offer plan so that is also equally important. As people grow in the organization, first they join you for learning, then they join you because they want to be closely associated with the company. So you have to create that kind of atmosphere also. It means that emotional bonding is very important. Physically everyone can provide the same space...Then the learning also they are able to provide. Therefore, emotionally they have to get attached to the company. We do that through many different ways. One of these is the several cultural events that we organize, where the extended family of Infoscions comes together. They come and visit Infosys...Then another thing is, we also have the campus kind of atmosphere that we have created. It is not like a business place. It is like a learning place... It is like an extended university, so the learning is continuous. We provide that kind of an atmosphere, so the people also don't feel that they are 'working'."

Explaining his viewpoint about people's needs, he said: "People have three hierarchies of needs: (the need for) learning, emotional bonding and financial stability... As they grow in their lives, we, as the organization, have to provide for these needs. And Infosys provides them very well... (The employee turnover in IT industry is very high, but)...Ours has always been about 50-60 per cent less than the industry average. Not just this year or last year, but for the last 10-15 years. We have been adjudged as the best employer among multinationals, not just among Indian companies."

Another example of highly people-centric approach, encouraging innovativeness and entrepreneurship was noted at Satyam Computer Services. Explaining the style of leadership and human resource policies and practices of the company, Dr. U. Balaji,[42] said: "We look at our four values, out of which one of our key values is about people: respecting, trusting and dignity for people – that allows people to perform up to their potential. There is a sense of ownership among the people here. Second, it is an extremely entrepreneurial company, which is quite unlike a very structured, large, defined organization – that is very-very different, because there are set processes and procedures and it is easy to lose decisions in the large structure. Here people behave like entrepreneurs. We have an unwritten, but widely popular joke: it is easy to get forgiveness rather than permission. Also it is very, I would not call permissive, open kind of a culture where it is possible for one to make mistakes. You can always say that the intent was good, I wanted to do this stuff it went wrong. It is not seen as something negative or things like that, that allows people to try new things and experiment and our ability to invent business models which give tremendous amount of flexibility to the customer.

"The openness with which we work and the freedom that people enjoy here that allows people to come in and work with us... that's what allows us to bring in people. And the kind of freedom that they enjoy, you do not believe that you are working in a typical organization, so to speak. There is very little interference except for a review where whatever one has committed, is one delivering them or not. Otherwise it is as if I am running my own company, till such time when corporate finance person asks what happened to the P&L and how do you propose to go about this, etc. At that point of time only I see that I am a part of a larger company, otherwise it is like running my own business. So the autonomy provided is very high..."

"We take trouble in getting a person and then trying to see whether the person resonates with the company's culture and things like that. Once that is done then the person is, by and large, left alone and given a lot of freedom. The growth that the person experiences, both professionally and personally, depends on his own limits. For example, if I want to run a business and build a business, let us say 100 million dollars worth, I just go and make a business plan and present it to them and if they like it then they would go about doing that. Apart from that, we also have formal schemes of building up entrepreneurs internally...We had a programme called STEP, Satyam Technology Entrepreneurship Programme... we have one still continuing. In that, if as an associate [the term used for staff members of the Satyam], I get a bright business idea and I think it is viable, I could present it to a Committee. The Committee could assist and then allow me to be the CEO of that company. The company would give me resources as lending as part of their share, my sweat is my share in that. Unfortunately in India we still don't have a law which allows for sweat equity, but there are some ways of playing around with it, with the mechanics of it. The idea is that I hold a significant stake in the whole thing and if this product or the business that I make becomes a very viable one in a significant way, then I could go public and I become a significant shareholder of that. We have one youngster who is running a business now with around 50 people.... I think ownership comes primarily by asking people to take responsibility and generally we don't push people. We don't micro-manage."

The people-centric approach of some of the outstanding companies is epitomized by the motto of Mr. Narayana Murthy, who says: "Infosys is a company by the people, for the people and of the people". According to him the key to employee involvement in an organization is the sharing of information about business performance, plans, goals and strategies through an effective system of internal communication.

Another very distinctive common thread in the outstanding organizations seems to be a tacit team-based approach at all levels, right from the top down to the lowest levels. Highlighting the importance of teams for the organizations' sustainability, Mr. Gopalakrishnan said: *"None of us is smarter than all of us put together."*

Although it was not as explicitly stated, it seemed to be taken for granted that without effective teams and inter-team cooperation and collaboration, the organization cannot function efficiently or effectively. Organizations in which teamwork was lacking faced enormous interpersonal as well as inter-functional/ inter-departmental problems leading to serious losses in efficiency, effectiveness and achieving their goals, as well as in developing innovative ideas and solutions to improve organizational performance. Various practices were followed to develop teamwork, informal relationships and 'family feeling', which were quite conspicuous in organizations like Infosys, Satyam, Hero Honda and Ranbaxy. Different types of teams were created at different levels, like strategic planning and review teams, cross-functional teams, project teams, quality circles, etc.

The people centric approaches were aimed at developing high levels of commitment, involvement, empowerment, autonomy, flexibility, innovativeness, creativity, risk taking, entrepreneurship, sense of belonging, ownership and pride and teamwork among the people working in and for the organization. But above all, such approaches were aimed at achieving highest possible levels of performance and competitiveness. These companies had a high performance ethic and made no compromises on productivity, quality and meeting challenging standards of performance. The people centric approaches and philosophy of management were institutionalized through carefully developed human resource management and development policies, processes, support systems and practices to which the top management leadership gave a high priority and personal attention. Some of these processes will be described in later chapters.

SIMPLICITY, VALUES AND CHARACTER

The top leadership in several of these organizations maintained conspicuous simplicity and in some cases almost austerity in their life style and dealings with people.

They demonstrated their philosophy and values in their personal and work related behaviour and walked their talk. They generally demonstrated openness, accessibility and contact with organization members and stakeholders.

They spent money where it was most productive, rather than for their personal aggrandizement.

Although the top management leadership maintained a low profile, they demonstrated a high level of equanimity and strong character, values and wisdom. In addition to providing leadership to the organization, they also thought of larger social and economic issues facing the country that were addressed in some specific company policy initiatives and/or through separate initiatives.

These qualities gave them an edge that enabled them to withstand enormous pressures and take farsighted, tough decisions in most difficult situations and for changing and steering the organization through turbulent times.

Their courage, imagination, thoughts, values, actions, conduct and contribution inspired respect in the organization and society.

When we arrived at the office of the chairman of the Hero Honda Motorcycles, the headquarter of the world's largest two wheeler manufacturing company, located on the first floor of a crowded market place and the receptionist in a small glass cubicle informed the chairman about our arrival, Mr. B.M.L. Munjal came down to personally receive us and took us to a committee room. Perhaps sensing our probable disappointment with the size and location of his office, he said: "We put the money where it is most productive."[43]

His striking simplicity and modesty was reflected not only by the modest office from where he worked, but also in his life-style, his values and philosophy of life. He described how he led the company by his personal example and work and deeds and not by words and how the values of personal discipline and hard work were an integral part of his family values, also imbibed by his sons, who had made enormous contribution to the management and development of the company. Describing some of his own and his family values, he said: "In our family, my eldest brother is 82 years old. He is a very religious person. Early every morning he spends some time on his pooja [prayers] etc. We are running several educational institutions. He first goes to all the schools and then he is the first one in the plant. It looks very awkward to say from one's own mouth, my working hours are much more than anyone, any youngster.... Since there are different venues, different places, I want to keep myself fully informed. I want to retain my presence."

"Our youth who are exposed to the western management education about leadership or success, often confine themselves too much to bookish knowledge. They sometimes mind my getting into details and ask: Why do you want to go into that detail? *Usne hi bachaya hua hai.* [Only that attention to details has saved us]."

"I have initiated some very unusual kind of educational programmes for our workers' families. We have a very young workforce, the average age of our factory workers would be around 23 or 24 years. Most of them are newly married, ...so we conduct a course for the workers' wives in batches of 25 ladies. First, they need to realize that they are a person in their own right. They need to know that their husband is working at the right place, doing the right job and that they also need to give support to him.

"Like the programme for their wives, for the workers also, in addition to technical training about the working of machines, etc. they are also made aware how they can develop their character, moral development and health... Similarly, we do programmes for our dealers, who come in batches of about 20 and spend four nights together. They learn a great deal from each other about the best and most effective practices and exchange notes on practical tips...But more than that, instead of giving training to tell how to sell, how to manage money, if you have clarity about yourself, about being a good human being, you will not do anything wrong. *Aap ulte raste nahin chalenge* [You will not go on the wrong path]. This is how we keep developing people.

"Now I am 78. As I told you, my elder brother is 82 and he is as healthy as anybody else. He also goes for a regular morning walk, that makes the children feel that they must also go for the morning walk. That is what you have to do: set an example."

"(The key to success is) Ethical business, values based business. *Values jisne chodi woh kabhi bhi kamyaab nahin ho sakta.* [One, who gives up values, can never succeed in business]. Value based business (is the key). You need to be clear about your values. Sometimes it may happen that what I consider ethical, you may not consider right... you need to be clear about that."

"We believed in these values earlier also, but when we were working out our collaboration with Honda, we discovered some very lovely thoughts and practices, that made us realize how people in the world have progressed. They said, the place where you set up the factory, the water coming out of your waste water treatment plant should not damage an inch of somebody else's land. The smoke that comes out of your factory should not at all damage the environment around. Whomever you appoint as your dealer, take responsibility for his profitability. If he makes money, he earns enough money, he will be your life-long friend. Similarly ensure that your vendor makes money, otherwise he will give you sub-standard goods or go to somebody else. These were exactly the ways we were working."

Mr. Munjal shunned publicity of himself. Once Business India, a leading business magazine, called him and congratulated him that their jury had decided that he will be next 'Business Man of the Year'. Mr. Munjal said, "Thanks, but suppose I say No, I am not accepting it, as I don't deserve it." They said, "No problem. You may or may not agree. The jury has decided your name, so it will be published. According to our system, the photo of the Businessman of the Year is published on the cover of the December issue. We will leave this cover page blank and write down below that Mr. Brij Mohan Lal Munjal has not accepted it".

Mr. Munjal also did not let any distractions sway him from his single-minded focus for developing his business and organization. He was offered chairmanship of several leading business associations, etc., but he refused to take them up, in order to give his full attention to his business. He said:

Aap apne saaye ke peeche bhagoge, saya aage aage jayega; aap roshni ki taraf jaoge, saya aapke peeche aayega" [If you follow your shadow (i.e., false glory), it will run ahead of you; if you have your aim and goal towards light, towards truth, the shadow (i.e. fame and glory) will follow you].

The above stated example is not an isolated case. The simplicity of life-style of Mr. Narayana Murthy is also well known. In one write-up on him it was stated that on Saturdays, his driver has a weekly off day. He is driven by his wife to a bus stop to board a company bus to go to the office. The founders, each worth billions, queue up at food counters with trainees and remain accessible to the lowest. Similarly, the value of using the company money as one would use his own money is emphasized at Wipro. The billionaire, Mr. Azim Premji, would not hesitate to travel by economy class in domestic travel.

The low profile of humility was combined with great ambition for the organization. This was, in some respects, similar to the 'Level 5 Leadership' described by Jim Collins.[44] As stated by him, a Level 5 leader is "an individual who blends extreme personal humility with intense professional will. According to our five-year research study, executives who possess this paradoxical combination of traits are catalysts for the statistically rare event of transforming a good company into a great one."[45] Such leaders were self-disciplined, with compelling modesty and an iron will. They are ambitious for the company and not themselves.[46]

The leaders of outstanding companies also demonstrated high level of *openness and accessibility, tolerance for different views,* and willingness to change their decision if they found merit in the viewpoint of their colleagues or juniors. They chose to follow meritocracy and professionalism rather than their personal preferences and ego. Emphasizing such values enshrined in the culture of Ranbaxy by Dr. Parvinder Singh, Mr. Brar, MD of the company, said: "There is a meritocracy value, which is totally institutionalized in the company. It was a company, which was and which is still owned 32 per cent by a family. But the family's chairman, Dr. Parvinder Singh, was so visionary that there is no family member on the Board today. They will come as they grow. When Dr. Singh was alive, he was the only family member on the Board. I will give you this last example on professionalism of this company and this is one of the values that we cherish in this company. We are open, we are highly critical, we can say what we want in this company and which is denied in many companies. You know we have a system where there is a Policy Committee, which comprises of six people which decides all the policy and strategy of the company and then the Board. All the people who report to the Policy Committee, their annual appraisals and their recommendations for promotions are discussed jointly by the policy committee. If I have eight people reporting to me and the other five have four or five people each, those 30-40 people are reviewed jointly. Then a very collegial view is taken. It is a combined view of everybody and many times it happened that if Dr. Singh, who was a 32 per cent owner of this company, came up with a recommendation, I remember once that he wanted to promote somebody and we shot it down. We said we don't think this guy is justified and you have not taken the right decision and he said I think you're right. Thrice he took back such decisions. He said my colleagues are right, I am taking a more emotionally favoured decision. Now that kind of professionalism runs through this company."

Let us now look at the qualities of character for the top management leadership. Mr. Gopalakrishnan of the Tata Sons very well articulated these. Illustrating the requirement and development of various skills in the managerial career at different levels with the analogy of a tennis player, he explained: "You ask a tennis player what makes an excellent tennis player. In the first 4–5 years of his career he says you must learn your strokes very well: forehand, backhand, volley, overheads, etc. But then everybody has learnt the strokes, by that time you have no special advantage. 50% is technical skills, 25% may be human skills. Let me take the tennis example. There may be technical skills of the game, another 25% may be stamina and another 25% may be mental equanimity, because you should not give up when you are getting your shots wrong. In the middle of your career you are playing with other people who have also mastered all the basic ground rules of the game. What distinguishes you is your stamina. If you can last five sets and the other fellow loses his steam in three sets or four sets, then he has also mastered, he has also gone to meet the trainer, he is also very good. Now you are playing in Wimbledon, the Australian Open, then what distinguishes the finest tennis players in the world is not technical skills, it is not stamina, but *mental skills – equanimity*. I call it *character*. So, when there is a fifth set going on, there is four hundred thousand dollars at stake and you are at a tiebreaker and there is a line call and you get upset with the umpire when a Mike Denness does what he did, does it upset you? I call that equanimity, mental character, whatever you want to call it. What happens is, if I take technical skills, physical skills, stamina and the mental skills, which is equanimity and character, then the ratios change. In the early part of your tennis career, the ratio is sort of 15-30-20. In the second stage of your career it becomes 35-35-30. In the last stage of your career it becomes 25-25-50."

"What makes that crucial difference between being the champion at Wimbledon and being the runner-up is having that mental equanimity, that character. If I take the same metaphor to management, you can learn all these skills: How to do quality control? How to do financial analysis? How to do all these things? The first 10 years of your career are spent in learning all these skills through attending to courses, going to IIM, learning at colleges, all that stuff, but frankly at the end of the 10th year all the good people have learnt the skills reasonably well. Okay then what distinguishes your ability to have the equivalent of what I called physical skills and the stamina, the equivalent of that in management is having the human skills right. You have got the techniques, but do you have the skills to get other people to work? Do people like to work with you? Do they say *bahut apne ko sochta hai, ek tara hai* [He thinks too much of himself, but he is a single performer] it doesn't work. You look at his leadership skills, human relationship, can he lead a team? Can he work with the colleagues? Are these skills available in him and when he has got that also, then you have got 2-3 candidates. They are all trying to be a chairman, managing director of a large company. Then it is character, that when he is pushed to the wall, can he decide what is right and wrong? It's a very difficult decision. What is right and wrong can be a subject of great debate. For example, *'Mantri ji ne yeh kaha hai ispe hum kaise respond karein. Kabhi lagta hai ki yaar yeh thoda sa kar dein toh order mil jaayega, aur iss saal ke profit badh jaayenge, us sthithi mein aap kya karte hain ?'* [The honourable minister has told us, so how do we respond? Sometimes it appears that if we oblige the minister a little bit, we will get the order and our profit for the year will increase. How do you deal with a situation like that?]"

"Just like earlier I said technical skills, physical skills and mental skills in tennis, in management I would say technical skills are learning management and quality control and new product introduction; and the second one I call human skills; and the third one I call skills of character. And for the very senior management, the skills of character are extremely important. That is what distinguishes one great leader from good leaders. There are lots of good leaders, but very few great leaders."

The character and courage to take tough decisions in the most difficult situations, as exemplified above, distinguishes the leadership in outstanding organizations. This characteristic of leadership is similar to what Noel Tichy has described as the leadership 'Edge' in his book *The Leadership Engine,* that he discovered in his interview with Jack Welch. He has described how Jack Welch pointed it out to him: "In the early 1996, my colleague Ram Charan and I were in Welch's office to discuss our ideas about leadership. I was sure that my three-pronged model with ideas, values and energy would be a hit with Welch, so I had eagerly looked forward to rolling it out for him. But it took Jack only a nanosecond to knock me flat. "You forgot something," he told me. *"A leader's got to have edge. Without that, nothing else matters."* Welch started to come alive. His suit jacket already off, the pace of his speech quickens. He gestured with his hands, as if that would bring the words out quicker. "A lot of people have good ideas and good values and they can even energize others. But for some reason they are not able to make the tough calls. That is what separates, for me, whether or not someone can lead a business."[47]

So far we have examined the characteristics of leadership within the organization. As stated in the beginning of this sub-section, the leaders of outstanding organizations also distinguished themselves by their thoughts and actions pertaining to larger socio-economic concerns of national significance, which were in some cases reflected in the company's policies and strategies and in some cases through separate initiatives. For example, as pointed out by Mr. Gopalakrishnan, "HLL's chairman always had an image, which is far beyond just being a chairman of the company. HLL has always been in the forefront of thought leadership in the country, making suggestions, which are within their area of knowledge, like how can the country become self-sufficient in oil-genfacts? Like how retailing can create more jobs in the country? Or, how the trading system in a country of the little shops and the big shops can bring prosperity to the people? And rural marketing. In all these areas where HLL has significant experience, they use that experience to throw light on some facets of national significance."

In the light of our comprehensive discussion, we can state that leadership, with the distinguishing attributes that have been described in detail, emerges as the single most important factor in developing sustainable competitive edge. We will now examine the second cluster of factors, characteristics and practices that have been identified as 'Innovative Strategy'.

REFERENCES

1. John P. Kotter, *Leading Change*, (Boston: Harvard Business School Press, 1996).
2. See the works of Warren G. Bennis.
3. Jim Collins, *Good to Great*, (London: Random House, 2001).
4. *Ibid.*
5. Sumantra Ghoshal, Gita Piramal and Sudeep Budhiraja, *World Class in India* (New Delhi: Penguin Books, 2001)
6. *Ibid*, 192.
7. "BT500 – India's Most Valuable Companies", *Business Today*, November 9, 2003, 53.
8. "Cover Story: The Mind of the Strategist", *Business World*, August 25, 2002, 37.
9. S. Ghoshal – Prof. S.K. Bhattacharya of the University of Warwick at CII's Annual Conference.

10. (The importance of passion in the success of organizations has been recognized by some other authors also. See, for example, James R. Lucas, *The Passionate Organization – Igniting the Fire of Employee Commitment*, AMACOM, New York, 1999)

11. Research Interview with Dr. U. Balaji, Vice President - Satyam Learning Center, Satyam Computer Services Limited.

12. Sumantra Ghoshal, *et al., ibid.*

13. Sumantra Ghoshal, *et al., ibid,* 198.

14. Personal Discussion with Mr. Rajinder Singh, former chairman and managing director, National Thermal Power Corporation Ltd. (NTPC).

15. *business2media*, New Delhi, January 15, 2002.

16. Research Interview with Mr. B.M.L. Munjal, chairman, Hero Honda Motors Limited.

17. Robert M. Grant, *Contemporary Strategy Analysis* (Oxford: Blackwell, 2002), 60.

18. Thomas L.Wheelen, J.D.Hunger, *Strategic Management and Business Policy* (New Jersey: Prentice Hall, 2002), 11.

19. Gerry Johnson and Kevan Scholes, *Exploring Corporate Strategy*, (New Delhi: Prentice Hall of India, 1997), 225.

20. G. Hamel and C.K.Prahalad, *Strategic Intent*, Harvard Business Review, Vol. 67, No. 3 (1989).

21. Research Interview with Mr. G.V. Prasad, executive vice chairman & CEO, Dr. Reddy's Laboratories Ltd.

22. Source: www.drreddys.com.

23. Research Interview with Mr. B.M.L. Munjal, chairman, Hero Honda Motors Limited.

24. Source: www.herohonda.com

25. Research Interview with Mr. D.S. Brar, CEO, Ranbaxy Laboratories Limited.

26. Source: www.ranbaxy.com

27. Research Interview with Mr. P. Dwarkanath, director – HR, GSK Consumer Healthcare Limited.

28. Source: www.hll.com

29. James C. Collins and J.I. Porras, *Built to Last* (New York: Harper Business, 1997).

30. *Ibid*, 23.

31. *business2media*, New Delhi, Jan.15, 2002.

32. Speech given in Mumbai, on 11th December, 2001 by Mr. R. Gopalakrishnan, executive director, Tata Sons Limited at the Bombay Chamber of Commerce and Industry in the Leadership Lecture Series.

33. Aries de Gues, *The Living Company* (London: Nicholas Brealey, 1999).

34. Jeffrey A. Krames, *The Welch Way* (New Delhi: TataMcGraw-Hill).

35. Mr. N.R. Narayana Murthy, chairman of the board, Infosys Technolgies Ltd.

36. Douglas McGregor, *The Human Side of Enterprise* (New York: McGraw-Hill, 1960).

37. P. Hersey and K.H. Blanchard, *Management of Organizational Behaviour: Utilizing Human Resources, 6th Ed.* (Englewood Cliffs, NJ: Prentice Hall, 1993).

38. Daniel Goleman, *Harvard Business Review*, March–April 2000, 80.

39. Daniel Goleman, R. Boyatzis and McKee, *The New Leaders* (London: Little Brown, 2002).

40. Michael Beer and Nitin Nohria, *Harvard Business Review*, May–June 2000.

41. *Outlook*, New Delhi, January 27, 2003.

42. Research Interview with Dr. U. Balaji, vice president – Satyam Learning Center, Satyam Computer Services Limited.

43. Research Interview with Mr. B.M.L. Munjal, chairman, Hero Honda Motors Limited.

44. Jim Collins, *Harvard Business Review*, Jan. 2001.

45. *Ibid*, 68.

46. *Ibid.*

47. Noel M. Tichy, *The Leadership Engine* (New York: Harper-Collins, 2002), 191.

CHAPTER FIVE

Innovative Strategy

Conceptualizing Innovative Business Models, Distinctive Approaches and Initiatives for Competitiveness

---

'Strategy takes shape in the determination to create value for customers'

KENICHI OHMAE

'If you do what you've always done, then you will get what you've always got!'

ANONYMOUS*

IN THE PREVIOUS CHAPTER, we discussed inspiring leadership as the driving force that motivated, aligned and energized the people, mobilized their talent and resources and provided direction and vision to the enterprise. We described the philosophy, characteristics, orientation, styles and practices of leadership of the outstanding organizations that demonstrated a sustainable competitive edge. In this chapter we will focus on the distinguishing features of the strategies of these companies that evidently enabled them to develop and sustain competitive edge.

The term strategy, like many other terms in the field of management, is often used loosely and is defined by different authors and practitioners differently. Before we proceed further to explore this subject, let us clarify the specific meaning that we have associated with the term 'strategy' for the purpose of this study.

We have utilized the term strategy to refer to the unique way in which the leadership of a firm chooses to conceptualize its business, its long-term goals and characteristics of the organization to achieve a competitive edge in relating to its markets, changing business environment and stakeholders for its survival and growth.

---

* Motto in the office of Clyde Fessler at the Harley Davidson Company (Business World, Kolkata, 24 Nov. 2003, p.50)

More specifically, we see strategy as the top management's articulation of the business models to create and capture value from time to time, within the broad framework of its unique philosophy of business and the character of the organization. In the simplest words, strategy can be described as the long-term direction, scope of business and configuration of resources that gives an organization relative advantage in a competitive and changing environment.

The historical, present and planned strategy of a company can be understood by identifying the scope of its existing and proposed business in terms of products, services, customers, markets and regions. It is reflected in the level of performance achieved and the goals and objectives intended to be achieved. In a broader view, it encompasses the policies, norms and standards chosen to achieve the goals, the existing and proposed configuration and mobilization of resources and the choice of the basis of competition that distinguishes the company from its competitors. The strategy reflects the ambition of the organization's leadership and the manner in which they interpret and define its vision and mission. It also shapes these elements, the nature of the company's business and its other institutional characteristics as a dynamic process.

The main questions that we have considered relevant to examine the 'strategy' of organizations in this study are: What are the distinguishing practices, orientations and characteristics of the strategy of the outstanding organizations? What are the key elements in the strategy of these companies? What kinds of strategies are developed and followed by these companies? How are these strategies developed, reviewed and changed? What are the common patterns in developing and choosing strategies that distinguish these organizations from average organizations? And what lessons can be learned about strategy to develop sustainable competitive edge?

The analysis of interviews and other available information examined by us indicated some distinctive orientations and practices related to strategy of the outstanding organizations in the following aspects:

1. **Sensing business opportunities; process driven planning and review.**
2. **Customer-centric value-creating propositions; building brands and innovative business models.**
3. **Internationalization for competitiveness, talent and technology.**
4. **Sustained dynamic focus.**
5. **Basis of competition, moving up the value curve and leveraging competencies.**

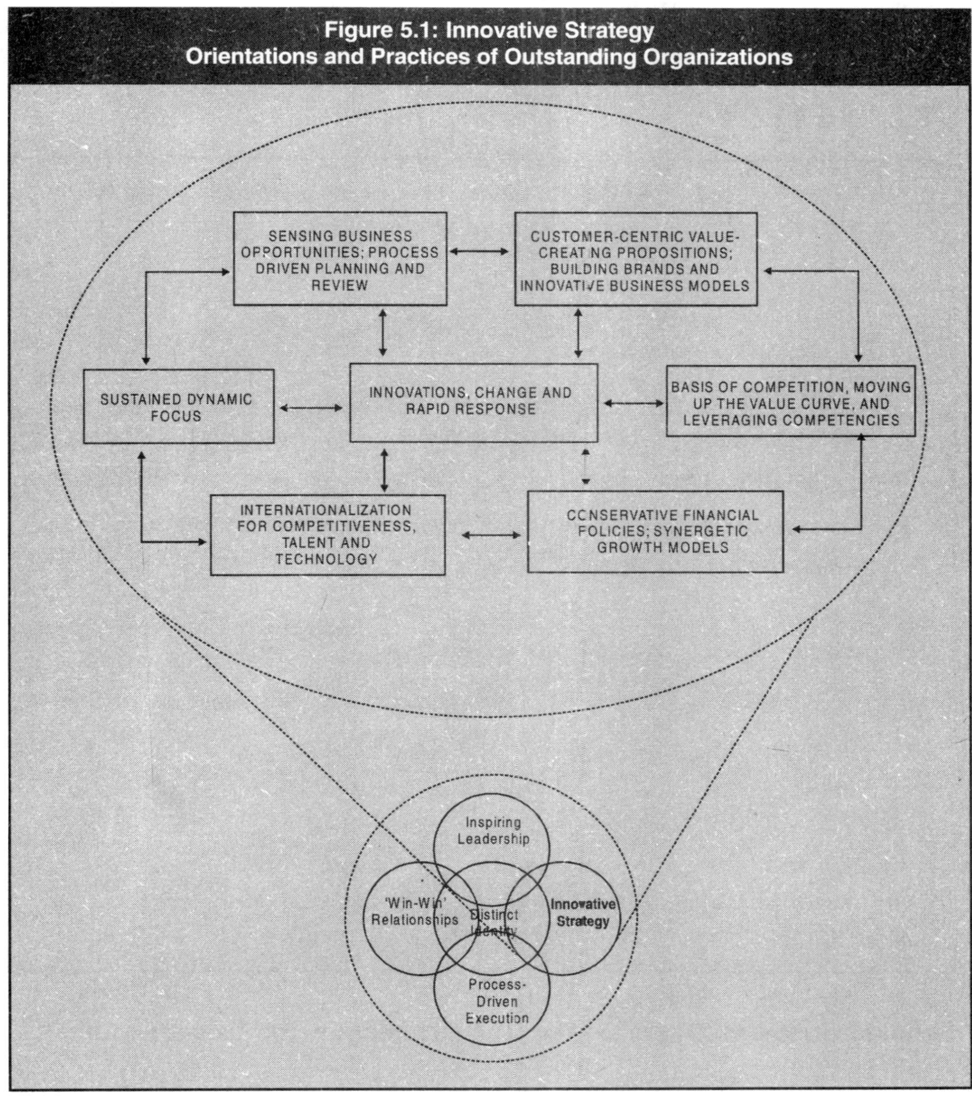

Figure 5.1: Innovative Strategy Orientations and Practices of Outstanding Organizations

6. **Innovations, change and rapid response.**

7. **Conservative financial policies; synergetic growth models.**

The aspects of strategy and their inter-relations are shown in Figure 5.1.

Let us now elaborate these points, examine the empirical basis for identifying the various aspects of strategy stated above and the business philosophy and practices from which we inferred them in our research.

SENSING BUSINESS OPPORTUNITIES; PROCESS DRIVEN PLANNING AND REVIEW

The outstanding companies engaged in active search for new information about markets and technologies from various internal and external sources. They were highly alert about the moves of the competitors.

The management of outstanding companies kept their 'ears to the ground'. They were in close touch with consumers, customers and markets and keenly observed changes and shifts in customer satisfaction, preferences and markets.

In some companies, the entire management was mandated to personally go out to the markets and seek periodic information and feedback from consumers and customers.

They seemed to possess very strong capability to sense new business opportunities and see potential for business where others saw barriers and constraints.

They had the knack of converting latent needs of people into tangible demand by imaginative, innovative business propositions.

They converted the threats and challenges into opportunities for change and growth.

They had institutionalized processes through which they constantly engaged in review of business performance, emerging scenarios and strategic planning. A pre-determined cycle of meetings and workshops of managers and other processes across the organization was followed to scan the changing competitive environment, review the performance and strategy, do strategic and operational planning and communicate it across the organization.

Sensing Business Opportunities and Challenges, Ear to the Ground

The importance of being 'close to customer' has been emphasized in well-known writings and practiced by many companies. But we found some of the outstanding companies in our study going beyond that. They sensed business opportunities where others saw barriers and constraints. They converted the latent needs of people into demand by offering quality products and services at affordable price for the larger masses and high value propositions for the elite. The examples of Reliance, HLL, Wipro, Titan and Hero Honda stand out in this context. In order to sense such opportunities, they kept an 'ear to the ground'.

Highlighting the importance of sensing business opportunities and understanding the needs of the customers and consumers as critical for sustainability, Mr. Bhargava of Eicher emphasized: "Entrepreneurial ability to smell out an opportunity by having your ear to the ground, being close to the customer. You can't identify opportunity out of nowhere or through a desk research. You have to be somewhere there to identify opportunity, which is very risk-taking, entrepreneurial ability... I think listening to the customer in a most impartial objective manner is the thing. What tools are we adopting? Not CRM, it's CSI - Customer Survey Index, employee survey index. And the tools (like listening to the customers and employees) have been left out somewhere, out of our arrogance, or whatever (reasons). We say, Oh! employee is bound to say salary is low. Do we have to work on that dimension? There are many other dimensions the employee tends to be concerned about. Similarly, the customer (has many concerns). And these (obtaining information and feedback) are not being done by internal people. Gallup and IMRP and others are doing it."

He emphatically stated that: *"The learning organization is nothing but has got ears to the ground, listens to the customer and has got what's happening around in changes, changes quicker than competition, the ability to change quicker than competition is one of the key ingredients for sustainable competitive edge."*

The strong emphasis on listening to the consumer through personal contact, in addition to all other means of obtaining information and feedback about the market, was highly conspicuous in companies like Hindustan Lever and Wipro. A senior executive of the ICI told us about his personal experience with Wipro when they were doing some IT related work for their company. He said that while the Wipro project team was working on site in the ICI, one fine morning he was surprised to see that the Chairman of Wipro, Mr. Azim Premji, personally walked in and discussed about the project with several managers of the ICI as well as with the project team members. Similarly, Hindustan Lever has institutionalized the process of personal contact with customer and consumer with all levels and functions of management.

Describing the practice of obtaining feedback from customers and consumers through personal feedback, Mr. Kapur of HLL said, "Being a consumer goods company, the challenge all the time is to become more and more outer directed, than inward looking and the traditional way where the marketeers are at the forefront. And relying on them to provide consumer information to the rest of the organization doesn't work very well. All of us feel the need that all our functions should actually have a direct interface with the consumer and consumer interaction cannot be the sole responsibility of the marketing function, because each aspect of our functioning should be guided by our consumers. Now, that's a big challenge for us. We want our commercial people to be as consumer focussed and engaged directly with the consumers and our customers, as indeed we want the marketeers and the sales people and the market researchers and the research people to be directly interacting with the consumers. That's a big-big priority for us. Otherwise what tends to happen is that large companies tend to become very inward looking because of a successful past or whatever."

"We actually deliberately do things like two mandated days for the entire set of management of the company. Wherever you are, you have to spend half a day talking to the consumer; half a day talking to your customer, which is your stockists or retailers; and another half a day talking to your suppliers. We did that, I think 2-3 months back and we'll again do it. It is non-negotiable. Everyone has to be out there, whether you are in the commercial or in the board of the company, or in any of the branch offices of the company, or a production manager of a factory - no matter where you are - because that's our source of learning. Being a consumer goods company we are forced to be much more responsive to the market place than probably certain other industries, because the speed of change in the market place that we operate in is very fast. The competitive issues keep revolving everyday. You are constantly, proactively or reactively, dealing with competition."

The capability of the leadership of Reliance company for sensing and tapping business opportunities where others see problems and constraints is legendary. From an initial investment of a mere Rs. 15,000 (less than $ 2000) in 1958, to start a trading house, followed by the setting up of the first tiny manufacturing facility in 1966, during the days of highly rigid government controls and licenses for starting and operating industry, it managed to build up a synthetic yarn, textiles and petrochemicals empire and has moved into sectors like oil exploration, power and telecom. Over the years, Reliance plans to tap a market of over 1 billion consumers with an integrated portfolio of energy, telecom, power and financial service. It was rated as India's No. I private sector company with profits close to a billion dollars and sales of $ 13.7 billion. Reliance's turnover is 3 per cent of India's GDP, its exports of Rs. 11,500 crores are 5 per cent of the country's exports and its market cap is roughly 7 per cent of the BSE[1].

So also the leadership of Wipro Corporation, that was originally Western India Vegetable Products Ltd., sensed and tapped business opportunities in fields that were not very obvious or related to their main business, such as lighting, precision engineered hydraulic products, medical diagnostic systems, computers and information technology and is today one of the leading players in the businesses in which it operates[2].

The ability to see the market beyond the domestic boundaries and taking a long-term perspective, characterized many of the organizations included in this study. To illustrate this orientation, the view of Mr. Brar of Ranbaxy that has been mentioned earlier also, deserves attention. He said, "Many companies in our country have taken a very microscopic view of markets in terms of business opportunities...I am speaking in our industry (pharmaceuticals). We are just 1 per cent of the world market as a country. It is difficult for us to believe that 99 per cent of the market being outside, one cannot build a sustainable business there and only rely on the internal market."

Another significant point noted in connection with sensing the customers' needs is thorough first hand understanding and knowledge of the local conditions, requirements and constraints of the customer. Elaborating his experience in this connection, Mr. B.M.L. Munjal said: "(We keep our) eyes and ears open. I think the number of surveys Hero Honda has got done, very few people could have afforded and very few people would have done. Once the survey was conducted of 25,000 contacts of 1-1/2 hour to 2 hours duration each. We had thorough knowledge (of the requirements of the market and customers). We also had the advantage of collaboration with Honda, who had their eyes and years open to the world markets and trends and we had eyes and ears open to the local conditions of India. What India would require, we are very clear. That is how our first model that we launched in 1985 was developed. It was not in the Honda stable. It did not exist. My son and me were responsible for getting it designed from them."

"Having been in the bicycle industry, we have combed the entire country and sitting here when somebody talks about any town, I know where it is and what it is like, say for example where is Sithamadhi, where is Jabalpur, where is Mau. I have seen it thoroughly and visited the country and we had a complete detailed knowledge of the conditions of our roads, the load conditions for use of vehicles, how they carry load on the two-wheelers, what is the condition of the pocket of the customers, how much can they afford as running expenditure. In our conditions the monthly expenditure on running and maintaining the vehicle is the most important factor. That is what paid us most (in developing the products and capturing the markets). At that time also the people at Honda wanted to give us a very sleek and beautiful model, but we said let us first launch a sturdy looking and real good performing product and it worked really well. That model which we launched in 1985 is still demanded in some areas. We made a product, which the customer was looking for and was wanting. We didn't produce a product and thrust it on the market."

Process Driven Planning and Review of Strategy

Some leading thinkers of strategic management have said that strategic plans should be written in pencil, i.e., they should be flexible to respond to the changing situations. We found it operative in most of the organizations studied. We noted that most of the leading companies have well developed and institutionalized review systems and processes. In fact, the professionally managed organizations were highly process driven in planning, implementing, monitoring, reviewing and changing the business strategy from time to time. Explaining the elaborate system of planning and review at Ranbaxy, Mr. Brar stated that: "The review processes are very well outlined. There are five or six committees, which run the business. There is a Pharma business committee, which meets four or five times a year and it is responsible for all business strategies, operations and implementations. It meets for three days every quarter of a year. One day is devoted to operational issues and two days to strategic and other important issues... The major term plan, which was earlier a very figure oriented excersise, is now a more directional, a more qualitative document which is made for 1+4 years. Every year the base year is the budget for next year. Then we extrapolate for four years. That meeting takes place in the month of March/April where the regions come again."

"Then broad, macro - it is not completely blue sky thinking - you know like that may be our products will get useless, or something like a new science will come, its not like that. It is a limited blue sky. What are the new opportunities, new directions, new challenges and new things they see as they sit at that time? This is a broad overview which we update every year. There is a turnover focus, there is a profit focus, productivity focus and employee focus - all that is there. Then new countries, country to be divested or country to be added, all those issues – so that is a major milestone, an annual milestone...Then we have the budget sessions, which start in September and culminate in the month of November. Presently, we are going through that. So, there is a very comprehensive review mechanism and planning mechanism in place in the company. It is very-very comprehensive and this budget excercise starts from the country level."

"Each country does a detailed presentation to the regional director and prior to that there are 6–7 countries, which form the core of our business, which contribute almost 75–80 per cent of our business... They go through a separate management review in the host country prior to the budgets, like I got involved with the US review prior to the budgets of the US came. We were, as a management, in the US for three days to study online what are the issues. That's the kind of review mechanism that is in place, but on a day-to-day basis the countries are quite independent, autonomous... So it is quite a complex operation."

An equally comprehensive and institutionalized system for scanning the environmental changes and emerging business requirements, reviewing the performance and strategic plans from time to time and communicating these with the entire organization was noted in the IT companies. Mr. Pratik Kumar described in detail how the strategic planning process and communication exercise was done at Wipro: "If you look at how we do our planning process in the organization, it gets kicked off sometime around October/November in the year where we have the broad understandings of the market environment-where it is and where it is going, as an input through the individual business units. Around the same time, we have the strategy workshop where the entire leadership - we do not forget about the leadership of even youngsters who are not still in the leadership position, but we think they can contribute, they are brought in. Then we flash out of what we think should be our strategic direction for the company. What are the key areas that we should be focussing on? What are the environmental factors, which are going to affect us? What is the competition going to do? Who are our competitors on a global scale and how do we scale up to be there? So it's a fairly intense 2–3 day kind of workshop, which we typically do it and get facilitated by one of the leading business schools internationally, or some of the management gurus with whom we actually spend time."

"Once that is done, we take it to the next level – the business unit...The business unit level would go down to each of their lines of business, product groups and others. They actually spend time with the next level managers. The next level managers will draw inputs of their teams. So fairly large cross-sections of people are involved in terms of drawing out strategy. And then we have again a convergence process by which we bring everything together on the table and try to see in terms of what are we finally looking at."

"Once we have the strategic plan which is through, we take it to the next level in terms of the working of the operative plan. An operating plan also goes through a similar rigor where again we go through in terms of numbers or in terms of any of the financial parameters, in terms of the kind of investment, which needs to be made. So everything gets decided fairly early by around middle February when everything is closed. And that is the time when we actually go into creating the structure to be able to deliver on that plan. Whatever changes are required in terms of leadership, people, bringing in new people, moving someone to a new role – everything gets frozen by around middle of February and is announced. And people who are supposed to run it next year get into the roles by this time.

"What happens after that is, that the leadership team goes through with the plan with the entire organization of about 14,000 people. This time we used the web cast mode where we talked about the entire plan for the year. We talked about whatever challenges we see. It is a half-a-day kind of a session where the presentation does not take more than 45 minutes. The balance of 2–3 hours would be only question and answers from cross-section of employees globally hooked in and they will be asking all kinds of question. Everyone on the desktop can see and I can actually send in my question that will get relayed and the chairman will be answering and his team of immediate leaders will be seated. So it's an intense 2–3 hours kind of questions where people ask you questions on why certain things are not happening? Why are we not succeeding in certain area? What kind of spending are we doing? Why are we not growing? And there is a consistent uniform message, which goes out to the people that makes them aware of, what is there in the environment? What should they be expecting? What should they be doing?

"It is a good forum for developing our perspective, in terms of setting expectations. So this is done across year after year, every year. It is part of our annual calendar, which again gets followed up. Every quarter the leadership team of the businesses go back to the employees and do it. So communication plays a very important role in setting the right kind of expectations, making the organization alive, remaining to be simple, remaining to be informal, remaining to be prudent in terms of what we do and over a period of time I guess its becomes part of our culture – the way we do our business."

CUSTOMER-CENTRIC VALUE CREATING PROPOSITIONS; BUILDING BRANDS AND INNOVATIVE BUSINESS MODELS

The essence of a successful business strategy is to create value for the customer and consumer. All the other elements and processes of management and organization are merely the means for it. The primary purpose of strategy is to sustain, enhance and capture value in the dynamic, competitive, turbulent and often-unpredictable changing business environment. In this sub-section we will examine how the most successfully sustained organizations created and captured value.

Customer-centric, Innovative, Value Creating Business Propositions

Value to the customer was like the magic mantra to the most successful organizations. Following are some of the patterns that have been noted in this connection:

- *The management in these companies shared a deep concern to provide genuine value to the customer. They tried hard to understand the needs of the customers and developed and delivered products and services that would give them feeling of satisfaction and joy.*
- *They saw productivity and quality improvements and lowering the cost of production and delivery primarily as means of being customer friendly.*
- *They constantly explored and experimented with superior value propositions and business models. They did not get caught up in bureaucratic and traditional mindsets and did not always start with 'a priori' business model. They allowed and explored new business models that would create value for the customer.*

Value to the Customer

The deep concern for providing genuine value to the customer as the cornerstone of business strategy could be noted in most of the outstanding companies. These organizations always came out with products and services in which the buyer perceived the value addition to be very significant. In this sense they were not creating distinguishing characteristics for the sake of creating (referred to in the literature in economics as deliberate obsolescence), but coming out with a genuinely good product or service. To illustrate this point, we may look at the strategy followed by Hero Honda, Titan and Satyam companies.

As stated earlier, both in the case of Hero cycles and Hero Honda motorcycles, the pre-dominant strategy in the formative stages of the company was to provide a product at an affordable price for the mass segment. They developed products that were sturdy, designed to suit the Indian roads and use conditions, highly efficient and dependable, economical to maintain and – in the case of motorcycles – highly fuel efficient, compared to the competition. "Right from day one", said the founder chairman of these companies, Mr. B.M.L. Munjal, "Our idea was to give *full value for money* to the customer, without having before us a very ambitious profitability factor. Profitability has been always behind us and it has followed us so seriously because we have left it behind."

Similarly, analyzing the factors that contributed to the competitive edge of Titan watches in the market place and emphasizing the importance of the product that would give extraordinary value for money to the customer as the most central factor, Mr. Bhaskar Bhatt said: "What contributed to the competitive edge that we have in the market place? There are a number of factors...I should imagine all of them have contributed in equal measure. The first and foremost has been the product that we have offered to the Indian markets and have continued to offer. On the one hand excellent quality at a functional level which has been ensured by a world-class manufacturing facility that we consciously invested in. The other is the styling, which is the look. What goes inside and what is perceived outside – in both we have invested huge amount of time and effort. Our styling is relevant. It was relevant at that time (in the early stage) and it is relevant today."

"We are considered as *innovators* primarily on account of the looks of our products. So product is one (distinct factor) we offer. An array of products which caters to practically every segment, every significant segment of the Indian market. We make watches for children; we make luxury watches – like gold watches at 35,000 rupees. *But we have made sure that we give extraordinary value for money.* Today the example of that is an equivalent watch at any price point would be at least 50 per cent higher in the European market, or in the South American market, or in the American market for equal quality and equal brand – I am not now talking of super premium brands that would sell because of their name."

"We are considered by those who travel abroad that our image is premium but our price is not. They find the prices unbelievable. We have kept it within the reach of the Indian consumers. So, as I said, product in terms of styling and quality, value for money, ensuring that it is within their means. We have to drive our cost down all the time so that you are able to make profit."

The concern to provide value for money to the customer by driving the costs down and improving the productivity and quality was described essential for a customer friendly approach. Mr. Subodh Bhargava of Eicher said: "You can't be a customer friendly company without very efficient, cost effective production."

Another striking example of customer-centric, innovative, value-creating orientation in business strategy could be noted in the Satyam Computer Services Company. Describing such orientation, Dr. U. Balaji said: "It (Satyam) is an extremely entrepreneurial company, which is quite unlike very structured, large, defined organizations. It's very-very different because (in large structured organizations) there are set processes and procedures, in which it is easy to get decision lost in the large structure. Here people behave like entrepreneurs. We have an unwritten but widely popular joke, which says: 'It is easy to get forgiveness rather than permission!'[3] And it is also very – I would not call permissive – but it's a very open kind of a culture, where it is possible for one to make mistake. You can always say that the intent was good. I wanted to do this stuff, it went wrong. That is not seen as something negative or things like that. It allows people to try out new things and experiment.

"*Our ability to invent business models which gives tremendous amount of flexibility to the customer,* is the other thing. That is also a part of our values: we call it 'customer orientation.' Now the typical customer orientation of keeping the customer satisfied, deliveries being good, those are the regular stuff that everybody does. But what we do is: *we always explore and see what kind of values can be created for the customer.* We go beyond the normal call of, say delivering good quality product that is creating value solutions for the customer. For example, if customers want an exclusive development centre for themselves, we would do that. If a customer wants to have a joint venture with us, we explore that."

"So we see a business model as a man-made constraint that can be negotiated. You don't get caught into this control model: 'it has to be invented here and it must be built here. It must be grown here and we must build it' – that is not the model. *The model is to facilitate value for the customer in whatever form.* So the structures, business models, all of them we believe are only to serve that purpose. Whichever gives most priority to the customer we do that. *So we don't start a priori with a certain model of things and don't get caught in that.* We do have our own models of business here. We do offer an array of models, but it is possible that we would create a new one and the amount of flexibility that the business leaders experience and that latitude allows people to try new things."

"Basically Satyam has tried new things, like – for example – we were the first ISP (Internet Service Providers) in the country; and second, we probably are the most complete end-to-end IT solutions provider. While we may have to still fine tune, improve, build, that's an on-going process, but in terms of occupying business spaces we have gone into end-to-end model. For example, we have looked into networking and things of that kind at one level, at infrastructure management on the other side and to management consulting on this side. So we acquired a small company called Saturn from Chennai at that time, that later got merged into the company through which basically we got a group of professionals who are typically looking to consulting based on IT. Any management consulting leveraging IT, that is what this group was focussed on; business process engineering and things of that kind... *Our objective was to give to the customer the maximum value, so that it is a 'one stop shop'* and he doesn't have to shop around ten places to get something done."

Building Brands and Effective Business Models to Capture and Sustain Value

Brand equity was seen as one of the most important factors in sustaining competitive edge.

Building brand equity for their company and products and maintaining it was a key concern in the strategy of the most successful companies. Brand equity also helped them in attracting high caliber talent in India and overseas.

They developed novel and effective business and revenue models to capture the value created by their expertise, products and services.

Building Brand

The criticality of building a brand, sharp customer focus and providing value for money to the customer by driving the costs down, improving the productivity and quality were described as customer friendly approaches that are essential for sustainability of an organization. Mr. Subodh Bhargava of Eicher articulated this viewpoint by saying: "You can't become an excellent technology company without having a very sharp customer focus and you can't be customer friendly without very efficient cost effective production – until you have evolved a brand. But then you have to deliver through that brand whatever that brand does. The designer brand charges you ten times and still you buy that shirt... There's an evolution process, until you have arrived at a brand. Then you take holistic (approach to management) as granted. It is not a conscious outlook and then everybody is working just to retain its brand value or enhance its brand value.

He further emphasized the importance of building brand of the country for survival of its industry in the global markets. He said: "Just as the company builds its brand, the country needs to build a brand. And a country cannot build a brand on technology alone. Country cannot build a brand because it has reached the moon. Its brand has got many other attributes, which the global consumer sees, from reliability to values, to everything else. And reliability reflects quality of governance and sustainability, or stability and everything else. So this is a very macro envelope sort of a thing. I would say it might be relevant from the point of view of any probe on competitiveness, because ultimately it is not where we are, but how we grow better."

Brand building, as a key element in strategy to develop sustainable competitive edge, was equally emphasized by most of the companies. It was also considered as an important means for getting a dominant position in the chosen market segments, as well as for attracting the best talent in the organization. Irrespective of the sector, brand equity was considered as a key element for the long-term success of the product as well as the company. Executives of companies like Titan, Hindustan Lever, Satyam, very specifically stated the importance of brand building as a means of developing sustainable competitive edge. In the case of all other successful companies also the role of strong brand equity in sustainability was quite evident.

Describing Titan's brand building strategy, Mr. Bhaskar Bhatt said: "The second thing, apart from our product, is our brand image, which is giving us a significant competitive edge. We have consciously invested in building an image, which is a very widely known brand today. The imagery of Titan is more of style, elegance, quality and reliability and there is a certain pleasure in wearing a Titan watch. It derives its image from the company's ability to compete in the international arena also. That is, many Indians do feel a sense of pride when they wear a Titan watch. That is what our survey has told us, that when you go abroad, you still wear a Titan watch because you feel it is equal to anything else available elsewhere in the world – not competing with the Rolex's and Omega's of the world – but certainly with the Citizens and Seikos.

"The reality of the situation in India is that we are way ahead the number one brand, way ahead! We have 58 per cent market share. Global brands we are having in this country for the last three years. They have not made a dent in our market share. You know, I am differentiating between the facts and what has led to that. The facts you can verify in any case. But why we have been able to sustain this as I said: One is the product, one is the brand image and the third is our distribution strength. I believe we are one company which understands India and its nuances from the north-eastern corner to the south-western corner pretty well."

Hindustan Lever, which has demonstrated outstanding ability in developing and sustaining brands and probably has one of the largest number of well-known brands in the fast moving consumer goods industry, is now sharpening its focus on select brands. Describing this strategic shift, Mr. G. Kapur said: "We are going through a phase where we are becoming very sharply focussed on consumers and brands because the competitive landscape has changed and, therefore, you cannot operate in an unfocused way with your consumers, your categories and your brands."

"I think at this point in time we are – or at least for the last 2–3 years – we are sharpening our focus around what we believe are our main brands. The 30 power brands as we call them and alongside bringing or taking the organization to the consumer in its fullness and becoming very sharply focussed on consumer insights and innovation programmes.... In a strategic sense I think that is one aspect of both HLL and Unilever because both these companies were large congloramates rather than very sharply focussed FMCG businesses. Over the years, they have become very sharply focussed not only in FMCG businesses but brand businesses. We say that we are a 30-brand company now, or we want to be a 30-brand company in terms of the internal processes and so on."

Effective Business Models and Capturing Value

The innovative and imaginative business and revenue models hold the key to success in creating and capturing value. The outstanding organizations carefully studied the business opportunities in domestic and global markets and came up with quite unconventional models of business. The success of leading IT companies like Infosys, Satyam, HCL and the pharmaceutical companies like Ranbaxy can be attributed considerably to their innovative business models. To illustrate this point, we can take a look at the business model and strategic perspective of the Ranbaxy company. Describing the viewpoint that provided the basis for the business model and internationalization strategy of the Ranbaxy company, Mr. Brar said: "Many companies in our country have taken a very microscopic view of markets and in terms of business opportunities. You are well aware that for decades we have kept our industry immune to international competition, immune to influences of technology and influences of better business and management practices from abroad. And we had a setup here with high tariffs and protected markets for license holders. We, at least at Ranbaxy, believed that all these are extremely counter-productive to innovation and sustainable competitive edge."

"So within the rules of the game that were played in this market, we felt that there was still a sustainable business model which allowed us to function – despite the constraints that the government or the system had imposed. Which was to look at markets more closely and in terms of their business potential, or in their intrinsic evaluation of markets. Rather than looking at odds all the time and that's in line with that thinking we strongly believed."

"We are now observing in our company that USA is becoming our single biggest market, like it does for all businesses. USA in most of the business segments or industry segments constitutes anything between 30 to 40 per cent of the world market in our Industry. They constitute 42 per cent of the world market. So any internationalization would be incomplete if we don't tackle the US market. What is happening is that India was our original big market and what has taken us 25 years to reach a level, the USA will do it in 5 years... We sold our first product under Ranbaxy label in the USA in February 1998. In next year we are facing a situation that USA will overtake India as the single biggest market ... We felt that without USA there is no international recognition here, at least in our industry and you cannot ignore 40 per cent of the market and still say you are an international company. So USA was the key to everything that the business wanted – science, technology, innovation, market competitiveness, quality and sustained competitive advantage."

"What internally we said was that USA and India are on two opposite sides. If we can benchmark US quality and we can benchmark Indian costing, we would have achieved (success) as the rest of the countries will fall in line literally. With the Indian cost structure and the US quality – this is the point that I made to you earlier was a benchmark. How can we blend these two seemingly conflicting issues and I was describing to you that there was a time when the cost went up and then it tapered and now the cost structure is coming down because those markets are paying. *So the Indian cost structure and the US quality – if you can match these two, rest of the countries will fall in between."*

The successful organizations developed novel, innovative and effective revenue models to capture the value created by their knowledge and service and to share it with their stakeholders. For instance, in the case of RIL, the introduction of cell phones to potential users at a very low cash down payment is one such move. Obviously the firm would be able to recover even the cost of handsets reasonably fast. Of course RIL can afford to undertake projects at such a gigantic scale because of their cash position. It would be recalled that the company was able to raise funds from international markets at the most competitive price prevailing at that time and a schedule of repayments, which was to start after a very long period. It would also be recalled that this firm has been responsible for introducing convertible debentures. They identified the needs of the buyers and what presents as an obstacle is studied very carefully and translated into a commercial success.

In a different context, some IT firms used training component as the revenue model. Still, in other cases, it could be the margin on replacement of some important parts, like a cartridge in the case of printers from Hewlett Packard. Thus, it is not essential for the product in its original form to be viable. It could as well be a situation where the real revenue is generated by other related activities. The most glaring example of this would be found in the case of newspapers where the real revenue is generated by billings of advertisements.

In the case of special expertise rendered by any consulting firm, revenue could accrue from new features developed in the product or service. Thus, in the case of technology transfers, the real income may not come from the original transfers of technology but from the contract to make newer or upgraded versions of the technology. It is important to understand how much this factor of capturing value was used by firms covered in this study. The evidence of this was available in the case of IT firms who generated substantial revenues from subsequent assignments. This is very similar to the penetrating pricing policy followed in economics, where one charges a lower price to get entry into the market and uses its credentials to realize the subsidized price offering from subsequent relationships.

Internationalization for Competitiveness, Talent and Technology

Internationalization of organizations and all their operations stands out as the most significant factor for developing sustainable competitive edge in this study.

Most of the outstanding companies deliberately chose internationalization of their operations as a strategy to enhance their competitiveness.

They did not opt for the internationalization of their business for getting government supported benefits of export earnings or earning foreign exchange, but primarily for developing competitiveness and in some industries, for getting a share of the more profitable and larger global markets.

They opted for such strategy for developing world-class competencies, like superior managerial processes and practices, better technology and quality of products, high

Contd....

caliber talent and building brand image. Having acquired such competencies, they leveraged them in the domestic markets.

They aimed at mastering technology and tried to own and develop technology by themselves, in most cases, because it was not easily available or transferred by their foreign collaborators.

Some companies developed world-class technologies either through effective collaborations or in some cases, by hiring the services of expatriate technologists and consultants.

Their primary consideration for internationalization was to develop high quality products, develop world-class organizations and operations and, in some cases, to have world scale plants and operations.

Internationalization for Competitiveness

In addition to the distinctive leadership characteristics that we identified in the last chapter, if we were asked to identify *another most important factor that led to developing sustainable competitiveness in the Indian organizations as indicated by this study, we would say: Internationalization of organization and all its operations,* or exposure to international management, markets, technology, benchmarking and scale in operations.

Four Patterns of Internationalization

We discovered four patterns followed by different companies to enhance their competitiveness through the internationalization route.

- *One* was to *completely transform the company into an international organization,* as in the case of Ranbaxy.
- The *second* was to primarily *operate in the international markets and benchmark all the operations and quality with international standards,* as in IT companies like Infosys.
- The *third* was to *own, develop, internalize and master the technology by obtaining access to international level technology directly and leverage it in domestic and international markets,* as in the case of Titan; or through various means like hiring foreign technologists, experts, consultants, professional managers on long-term or short assignments, as in the case of Eicher and Hindustan Electro-Graphite.

- The *fourth* and relatively rare pattern, was a *highly effective and synergistic collaboration with an outstanding international level company with considerable convergence of values and mutual interests,* as in the case of Hero Honda.

It may be noted that these four patterns are different from the patterns that were common in Indian organizations in the pre-liberalization days. The emphasis, at that time, was on exporting goods to earn foreign exchange. The motivation for exports was seldom to enter the overseas markets, or set up units overseas to tap such markets. Usually, the companies would export to take advantage of incentives for export provided by the government, or to meet export obligations that were allowed to operate in India, or import goods in India.

The four patterns of internationalization that we have identified are emerging as strategies to develop competitiveness. Let us now examine specific examples of these patterns.

Ranbaxy stood out as a company that purposely chose internationalization of the organization as the key strategy for developing competitiveness under the leadership of Dr. Parvinder Singh. Describing this philosophy that continues to guide the strategy and policies of the company, Mr. Brar said: "And I still believe that internationalization of business, which opens up the company to competition, which gives you a distinct ground to test your metal in terms of technology, product offering, services, whatever is very crucial to the business...Then operational effectiveness is the third major (factor), where I believe whether it is supply chain, whether it is productivity, productivity of assets and human capital, it is absolutely essential that we benchmark in line with the best in the world, not only in our industry, but also across the industries to ensure long-term sustainable advantage in a multi-country kind of business. I think operational effectiveness of the company is a fundamental given (for international competitiveness) but most of us, in India at least, do not have an effective supply chain, do not have productivity measures, which are in line with international standards."

"We did feel that if we keep blaming the policies and the constraints, we won't help ourselves. So we felt that it is still possible to do business. I think, as a company, we demonstrated that it was possible to build an international business despite all the constraints."

Most of the outstanding companies chose internationalization of all their operations as means of developing capabilities, superior managerial processes and practices, better quality and technology and high caliber talent for developing a sustainable competitive edge. As stated above, the form of internationalization ranged from complete transformation of the company into an international company on the one end, to internalization of international level technology and management practices through induction of foreign experts or exposure and training of staff on the other end. This was noted in organizations such as Ranbaxy Laboratories, Infosys Technologies, Satyam Computer Services, Wipro Technologies, Titan Industries, BPL Home Appliances and Eicher Motors. All these companies expressed a confidence in their ability to compete with the best at the global level. We have already emphasized the importance attached by Ranbaxy Laboratories to internationalization of its operations. In other cases too, in companies like Titan Industries and BPL Home Appliances, internationalization of operations has also helped them to get a share of global markets and develop their brand equity.

Describing the strategy of the Titan company to enter international markets to develop their competitiveness and brand equity, Mr. Bhaskar Bhatt said: "Very early in the life of Titan we chose to go global and global in the true respect, which is building the brand globally and not merely selling our products. That has brought a huge amount of learning for the Indian market, because we were ahead of most of the others in terms of understanding what competitors are likely to do when they came to the Indian market. Because we were already operating in a middle-eastern theatre as a number three or number two brand in those markets that are very competitive markets. We are in Europe, we are in the far-east, we are in 40 countries as a brand promoting it locally and creating awareness and image. And so this whole global approach is to make the company globally respectable and competitive. It is something which very few people know about."

Similarly, in the case of Satyam, massive investment was made in the training of people to bring about a change of mindset to make it a 'Customer Oriented Global Company'. Explaining this approach, Dr. Balaji stated: "We invest significantly in people's training, for example in the year 1999–2000 we had 4000-odd people in India. We had almost all the 4000 people trained by a set of professors. From the US, seven professors and a few practitioners were invited for a programme called 'COGO, i.e., Customer Oriented Global Organization. ... What happened (historically) was that we started off in India. All said and done, you cannot envision beyond what you can see. While we know we are in other countries and all that, we really don't get a feel of that. And another thing is that the nature of the demand from the customer has changed. In pre 2000, the customer was telling us what needs to be done...Now the customer is saying he has an open piece of land. Tell me what kind of building will be made? These are my needs, or I may not even know my needs. And tell me what value will it create. So it is for us to figure out...And from there to build a value solution for the customer, leveraging IT may be part of IT solution, part of management solution, may be business processes solution and range of things. The customer is expecting value at the end of the day. How is it going to affect my top line or the bottom line – that's what he is asking? So that needed a *mind shift, or a small shift in the mind.* That's how we brought in these professors from the West. We have done it from professors here also."

"We said, if we are global company, then let all of them experience global – whatever it means. Otherwise it will be like a psychological apartheid. Whereas in US they get all the exposure and people here don't get it...So we did this programme for 4000 people including services, that is non-business people – the support services. Everybody went through this, some of them went through a 5-day, programme, some of them went for 2–3 days and some of them for 2-days and others went to one day programme. But the point was that the message was the same...We had a few professors from Harvard come here and do a 3-day programme for us, that was very intensive."

The message is very clear: If Indian firms have to compete with foreign firms, an understanding of their process of thinking and decision making is extremely important and critical. There is no doubt that an understanding of the way of thinking of global companies enables executives of domestic firms to chalk out superior strategies, improve their operations and quality of products, besides helping them in getting a better deal in international negotiations. The companies that have competed in international markets and developed international operations have acquired more confidence. This confidence has given them a self-propelling force to improve upon their performance in the international as well as domestic markets. Internationalization has also helped some companies like BPL Home Appliances to overcome the sluggish demand in India for their products. Besides, it gives them some cost advantage to procure the products made in India. Mr. Bhaskar Bhatt of Titan mentioned that the executives do not have any hesitation in facing competition from foreign companies, having tested themselves in several international markets.

Attracting the Best Talent, Mastering Technology and Quality and Leveraging Competencies

The importance of high quality of human mind is well established in knowledge intense sectors such as IT, pharmaceuticals and others. Firms use alternative ways to get the best brains available globally. This can be judged from the fact that a number of foreign firms have recruited graduates from Management Institutes and Indian Institutes of Technology to get the best brains. Indian firms have also been engaging the best-known people from overseas for improving their domestic and overseas operations. For example, Ranbaxy engaged very senior executives from reputed organizations to help their European region. Similarly, they recruit the best brains for operations in other countries. The CEO of Ranbaxy emphasized: 'Let us not impose Indian management on foreign plants of the company'. The company followed the policy of having an Indian as either the CEO or CFO, nothing beyond that.

As stated earlier also in the earlier chapter on leadership orientation, to get the best talent, Mr. Bhargava of Eicher emphasized the importance of developing sustainable edge through the services of global managers and experts. He said: "The other very important thing for sustainable competitiveness as a tool, to my mind, is strengthening your team with *global managers* who can demand and who bring the requisite expertise, so that our buying for various competencies and skills and all is strong. Otherwise if I go to Ricardos and AVLs, what they give me and couldn't give me, if I am not experienced and my team is not at that level. I can't even buy (the right technology from) them. They will take me for a ride ... It's not an NRI that I am talking about. We should not be worried in their dollar equivalent salaries. I always split between the two. I said, look there is a cost of living, which must be in Indian rupees and there is a retirement, post retirement savings in dollars if you are working in India. I have to enable you a savings of say 10,000 dollars, you must get 10,000 dollars (saving) and get a quality of life. It's not liberal translation of dollars to rupees salary, which many multinationals have done to their own parent organization, that is foolishness. There was a way out, which they haven't done."

"I think the Indian industry very strongly needs not just technology partnerships...Because there are global R&D firms...and others (technology suppliers), we can buy services from them and they can't hold anything back from us either...what they call testing process or experimentation or whatever. If I am a customer of theirs, not a partner, not a joint venture, they can't dictate to me. I dictate to them."

It was also pointed out that in case the companies are not able to afford global managers and experts on full time basis for long tenure, then other alternatives to obtain international expertise have been worked out for shorter duration assignments. Whereas most companies find NRI's more affordable, they have brought experts from different countries depending on the specialized expertise and requirements of business. Mr. Bhargava said: "We got the Germans, Japanese for a couple of years... We brought people from America...I couldn't afford their salaries for a whole year, but I got them for six months, or three months. I got them every 3 months for 2 days or 4 days and to add value to our design of a 20 tonne truck to bring that global knowledge. And what they told us, we were then able to demand (from the technology suppliers), if it was engine related or something else. *The global expertise irrespective of the colour the skin, or the title of the passport, is something to my mind a key strategy for bringing in the skills and competencies which will enable sustainable competitiveness*...And it is not only global managers, but also global technologies."

Describing how small interventions from international management experts could make, significant difference, he gave an example from the garment industry. "...It is amazing how a garment factory, by converting a simple model of (production), not the factory or the sector, he (an international expert) converted each set of 7, 8 machines into a profit centre - just that much - 8 machines were a profit centre. So in a factory of 200 machines, we had 14 profit centres. Now each 8 machines had 12 girls or 10 people and they were told that today you have lost so much, so many rupees and you have gained so many rupees. It is motivating, it is encouraging ownership, because firstly I became my master – that look, as long as you have to produce so much more and then you could use this tool more, that daily profit you will get X amount and of daily losses we will deduct Y amount, if that is what is going to drive this thing. If you are able to create (the sense of) ownership, as (for example, has been done) in Infosys to exploit the opportunity available, you don't need those direct incentives as cash incentives. You build that ownership, a sense of ownership. It's a shared vision."

The emphasis on internationalization helps in improving technology. Most firms have realized that participation in international fares and competition brings to their knowledge latest technology available to foreign firms. It was pointed out that because of fierce competition at global level, most international companies are unwilling to give the latest technology. Therefore, some Indian companies had to use some dubious ways to procure technology. Other companies, such as Reliance, have always believed in procuring the best technology available at the global level and opted for outright purchase of technology. It was felt by companies like Eicher also that buying and owning technology outright was a better option, as it gave flexibility to develop the technology further and did not lead to dependence on the collaborator for technology upgradation and innovation. However, in case of Hero Honda, the collaboration model seems to have worked very well and enabled the company to have what was described as the best in the world technology available, so far. They seemed to have worked out a 'win-win' model of mutual synergy, compatibility of values and interests that is rare to find and sustain.

Internationalization also helps companies in improving the quality of their products. This is because foreign buyers are extremely demanding as regards the quality of the products. The supporting evidence for this assertion comes from the experience of Ranbaxy Laboratories, which did not want to use two qualities of product: one for home demand and another for foreign markets; although it meant a steep rise in costs in the initial stages. Revenues generated by sales in foreign markets covered the high costs. Quality consciousness and timely delivery is encouraged by major sales turnover coming from the foreign markets. This was evidenced in the case of companies in IT sector such as Infosys Technologies, Satyam Computer Services Limited and Wipro Limited. For these companies, quality of product is taken as a prerequisite and not as an added advantage. These companies have followed all the techniques that have been used by efficient foreign companies. These techniques include CMM accreditation, six-sigma and other international quality certifications. Some companies have reached a stage that their major earnings come from foreign sales. These include Ranbaxy Laboratories, Infosys Technologies, etc. In fact the demand from foreign countries enables these companies to take advantage of economies of scale. These improved capabilities and economies of scale are then used to lead in the domestic market. This is like the standard rule followed by companies who use low per unit cost as an advantage to allocate resources towards research and development and investment in the future.

The central point that emerges from this research in respect of technology is that *it is critical to own and master technology.* Different routes have been followed by companies to master technology, such as internationalization of operations, hiring of foreign experts, outright acquisition and upgradation of technology through internal R&D, reverse engineering, collaboration, strategic alliance, joint venture, etc. In all these models, it was important to ensure internalization, ownership and autonomy for developing appropriate technology consistent with the requirements of competitiveness. In fact companies which shook off dependence on foreign collaboration did better in the long run than those that remained dependent on them, as demonstrated by companies like the TVS Motors and Eicher.

The key points regarding development and mastery of technology and internationalization as a means of developing sustainable competitiveness can be best summarized through the views of Mr. Suresh Krishna, chairman and managing director of Sundram Fasteners, a company of the TVS group that has been consistently rated as one of the best suppliers of General Motors for the last several years. He categorically stated that: "I for one personally feel *joint venture companies have got a tremendous disadvantage* that they become very dependent on the parent company, or mainly foreign company to give them technology, to give them systems, to give them these things. *Literally they become, I personally feel, competitively crippled*... The company I run, Sundram Fasteners, from day one when we started in 1966, has never had joint venture partners. We had to struggle on our own in a way... The minute you enter the international market, it is a totally different game altogether. It is like night and day. And after you have a vision of becoming an international company, or if you have a vision of becoming world competitive - for which you need an enormous amount of drive, internal drive – then you can do a lot of things with the company to achieve that goal."

Sustained Dynamic Focus

The outstanding companies chose sharp and sustained focus on selected customer groups, consumer needs, product lines, brands, market segments and markets.

The focused approach was combined with a keen awareness of changes in market and customer preferences, moves of competitors, new and untapped opportunities, technological breakthroughs and changes in regulatory policies.

It was more like maintaining a 'dynamic focus' in the selected domains of business, rather than a static focus. It was like an auto-focus video camera adjusting to a moving target in changing conditions.

At the corporate level, business houses chose multiple foci and floated different companies to tap new business opportunities in the growing and changing business environment.

Identifying the basis of their competitiveness and leveraging resources, accordingly, were constantly pursued to remain ahead of the competition.

Identifying their inherent strengths (core competence) and leveraging them for initiating new businesses, entering new markets, or introducing new products and services were common practices in most of these companies.

The most central point in the views expressed by Hero Honda's founder chairman about the success of their organization for developing sustainability and competitiveness was 'focus'. His emphatic message to entrepreneurs, business leaders and budding professional managers was: "We (should) firstly have a very clear vision, a very-very clear vision of what we want to do in life, in career, in business... Don't you think that during (our long history of success) when we were making bicycles and motorcycles, the cement plants would have come our way, the textile mills would have come our way (and so many other such options)...Focused attention, focused goal and very slow growth, very slow movement – we never wanted to jump over things much faster...Still I would feel that people lose focus and get swayed by other distractions, so the time is lost... and that opportunity is lost. Focus should be very clear. Then we should make targets and plan proper steps to achieve the plan. The word strategy is used so often, without strategy we cannot plan proper steps... Focus, then steps, slowly each step should be consolidated. Until you consolidate the first step strongly, don't move to the next step and see to it that when you are dealing with anybody, whether he is your seller, your buyer, your supplier, he is fully satisfied. Look to his satisfaction first and then to your own requirements."

The M.D. of Ranbaxy, Mr. Brar, expressed similar emphasis on focus in defining the scope of their business that has already been stated earlier also. To recall his view, he had said: "Fundamentally every company must decide what business it is in. This is one of the core issues: whether many of the groups in India have got distracted because they have multiple businesses? In our company we believed that we have to be amongst the leaders in anything we do. So whether it is in India or it is internationally in the area in which we are, the company must show and demonstrate leadership. It is not possible to do that if you are involved in multiple areas or activities. So, as early as 1994, we had to decide in our mission and vision statement that the company will stick to the area of pharmaceuticals and not fritter away its energies into any other related or unrelated business."

The concept of focus is often debated and is not clear to many people because of the issues involved in determining the scope of business on various parameters, like market segments, range of products, regional presence, related and unrelated businesses and their relevance at different levels within a corporation such as the strategic business unit level or the corporate level. Further, there is often lack of clarity about the concept of core competence. The classic view of Robert Katz[4] that one should choose the narrowest possible scope of business consistent with the existing or potential strengths of a particular business unit is one point of view; so is Peter and Waterman's well-known view on 'Stick to the Knitting'. However we know how companies broaden their scope to dominate the market across a wide range of segments as in Titan and also grow through various forms of integration, such as horizontal, vertical, concentric, etc., as in the case of Reliance. They also diversify successfully into related and unrelated areas at the corporate level, like in the case of Wipro.

We found a few points regarding focus that deserve attention. One was that focus meant both attention of management and application of resources to a particularly chosen scope of business. Second was the relationship of the chosen area of diversification to the internal and potential strengths and the ability of the company to leverage its core competence. The third aspect is that a multi-focus approach through different business units was quite viable if the corporation was able to develop leadership, effective organization structure and systems and a basic framework of values and management culture across the organization and its business units, as in the case of Tata Sons and Wipro.

The fourth important point that we noted was that the real life behaviour of companies was more like a 'sustained dynamic focus', rather than a static focus, keeping in view the changing requirements of markets, preferences of customers, changes in technology, etc., as in the case of launching new models of motorcycles for different segments and changing preferences of customers in the case of Hero Honda and in watches in the case of Titan. As pointed out by Dr. Balaji of Satyam, "it was like aiming at a moving target." The focussed approach was combined with keen awareness of changes in market and customer preferences, moves of competitors, new and untapped opportunities, technological break-throughs and regulatory policies. The analogy for this that comes to our mind is that of an auto-focus video camera constantly adjusting its focus at a moving object. The need to be constantly in touch with the environment and to review the strategic focus systematically was elaborated by Mr. Dinesh of Infosys. He said: "I think the key...is to constantly be in touch with your environment, more often than what you would do otherwise. To be more and more customer focussed is very important that you need to do and be agile all the time. That is where the agility that you need comes from the culture that you have created, it comes from the systems and processes that you have developed – so that once you decide and say this is the way you'll go ahead, then you know it happens that way everywhere and you have a feedback system (for review)... Developing those kinds of systems and processes that you can deploy and quickly implement is what you need and creating the culture of an organization which can adapt very quickly with high performance and work ethic is very-very important. *It is all interrelated, which means you have to revisit your strategies more often and make adjustments as and when you need."*

"Broad strategies may not change, but you really have to revisit the underlying tactical strategies that you may have and adjust those things and empower people to take decisions. Everything can't come from the top, because people are reacting to what is happening on the field. So they should be empowered to take decisions to satisfy the customers and be result oriented. Ultimately any idea, strategies about an idea, strategies about an assumption, set of assumptions you are making about your future plans – only history will tell you whether you did the right strategy or not. But you can't wait, so you have to continuously keep watching what is happening. Towards that *an organization, which has a systematic approach to solving its business problems, will have an advantage in the long run.* Because a tweak in one area that you do, if you don't look at what may happen in another area, you forget."

"That is particularly important when an organization grows to a size where you can't (do it yourself). One guy may be able to look at it when it's only a 100, even 200 or 300 people organization. But when the organization becomes bigger, it grows; it has multiple locations where it is operating, complex markets in which it is competing. Unless you take a systematic approach, you will have problem. That is where (systems like) balanced scorecard will try to give you a balance between financial perspective, customer perspective, learning and growth perspective and process perspective. If you translate a strategy into a set of measures, those measures will give you results that you are expecting. The balanced scorecard forces you to take all these four different perspectives not in equal way, but it says: Have you considered all these four aspects, which are integrated, in a sense and their boundaries. It gives you a framework in which you are operating. Models like CMM, ISO-9000 models and to some extent six-sigma – we are using that also. These (systems and techniques) give you the (tools) for converting the strategies into a set of operational goals that you have in delivery, very high quality, reducing the cycle time – all of those things are helped by such models."

It may also be noted here that when companies over-stretched themselves with diffused focus into unrelated businesses, they tended to get into serious problems and lost their leadership position in their main business also, as in the case of BPL. As was pointed out about the problems being faced by the company, which had a leading position in television sets manufacturing industry. It had made lots of money in the protective environment before liberalization. Instead of consolidating its leadership position, being driven by an entrepreneurial vision of expansion and diversification, it diversified - encouraged and promoted by the financial institutions for their own vested interest in putting their money further in the form of debt in the company - and opted for expansion into unrelated diversification, such as telecommunication. They later realized that they had 'bitten much larger than what they could chew', because of the huge license fees and the assumptions with which they went into it, like that there will be only two players in each circle, that were completely changed. Similarly getting into the soft energy, that is the dry battery and alkaline battery production - these investments of hundreds of crores in those businesses which were really not addressing what may be called a support to the core business, was a most dangerous situation that they found themselves in, as described by some very senior managers of the company.

It will be noted from this discussion that the outstanding companies chose sharp and sustained focus on selected customer groups, consumer needs, product lines, brands, market segments and markets. The example of Ranbaxy Laboratories is most clear in respect of its focussed approach. The same characteristic has been demonstrated by Hero Honda, except that they have now started diversifying into attractive businesses such as IT and provision of services, such as payment of bills of electricity, water, etc. In the case of some firms, the same was achieved by having one of the sub-units specializing in that particular sector. For instance in the case of Satyam Computer Services Limited, there would be different units dealing with different businesses. In the case of Wipro Technologies, different businesses are given total autonomy to carry out their activities. Thus, such firms can be simultaneously very focused as well as diversified. There is of course the positive aspect of diversification because recession does not affect all the sectors equally. The focussed approach, on the other hand, allows the organization to develop a very minute understanding of complex issues. In the 90s, the consulting firm McKinsey and Co. had been emphasizing that the organizations should concentrate only on those businesses where they are either number one or number two in the industry. This practice has been followed by General Electric Company, which has attempted to divest out of businesses where it did not command such strengths. In the case of Wipro also the company has decided to create independent units to take advantage of opportunities arising in sectors other than the main business of the company and they also follow the policy of leadership in that business by retaining their position among the top three firms in that business.

BASIS OF COMPETITION, MOVING UP THE VALUE CURVE AND LEVERAGING COMPETENCIES

Identifying the basis of their competitiveness and leveraging resources accordingly were constantly pursued to remain ahead of the competition.

Identifying their inherent strengths (core competence) and leveraging them for initiating new businesses, entering new markets, or introducing new products and services were common practices in most of these companies.

Identifying the Basis of Competitiveness and Moving up the Value Curve

Identification of the basis of competitiveness and leveraging resources and competencies to sharpen the edge to meet the challenges of competition were considered an important key for developing effective strategy by the top management. This subject has been explored in the field of strategic management in considerable depth. From a practitioner's point of view, Mr. Gopalakrishnan very well articulated it. He said: "Coming back to new product introduction and so on, you have to be very clear as a top management group in a company: what is the basis of your competitiveness? Is it cost or is it differentiation? If, for example, I am running a steel company, or I am running a soda ash company, there is no point in trying to do too much on differentiation. I have to be the lowest cost producer. I have to have single-minded focus on driving my costs down. But if I am a software company, or a consumer goods company, or a telephony company, then – of course, I must keep my cost under control – but my single greatest basis of competitiveness is my differentiation compared to my competition. Which could be a new product introduction, giving a new service, better quality of service, better reliability of service and so on. When you get them mixed up, then you have a problem. People who are in steel try to become value added and they get mixed up without getting their costs under control and, conversely, if you are a software company and you are all the time running down the costs, then you would never become a value added player. So I think the ability of the leader to articulate with his top management what is the basis of competition, what is the basis of competitiveness and, therefore, what are the techniques and tools that must be used to enhance the basis of competition have to become very clear."

"Let me take some examples, say from within Tatas. We have Tata Steels, Tata Chemicals, Tata Power. As you know, electricity is electricity. Now, I know you can make better and poorer electricity in terms of continuity of supply, frequency variation, etc. But if you run your generator well, you have your fuel right, you create the same electric power. I am oversimplifying it, but everybody can produce power and we have been doing it for the last hundred years and God willing will continue for the next thousand years. But there is no great skill in it. However, if you produce high cost electric power, like a well-known company has done recently, then you get into a different tangle. So the focus has to be very clear. As compared to that, take the Taj India Hotels. If you reduce the tariff for the room by Rs. 500, that will not get you more business compared to Oberoi. But if you give very caring and personal service in the room and the restaurant, for that kind of service you can earn not only Rs.500, but even Rs.1000 more...you must feel good about it...It is that kind of ability to sort out *what are the key drivers of your growth and profitability,* that will make a lot of difference to the base of your competitiveness."

The issue of choosing between large volume and low cost strategy versus differentiation or 'niche' strategy is critical for strategy. It has been debated and explored considerably in management literature. However, we found that in the companies studied it did not come out as a mutually exclusive either/or proposition. In most companies we found a dynamic situation of changing the combination of the two with relatively more emphasis on one of the two, depending on the stage of maturity in the industry. The situation seems to be that in most industries, as the barriers to entry got lowered and technology and other factors became more easily accessible, the products of the industry got 'commodotized'. Therefore, the leading players had to move up the value curve (sometimes referred to as value chain by some, though that is a different concept)[5]. This is done by moving to higher level of technology and improved or new products through knowledge inputs based on research and development. For example, in steel industry the Tata Iron & Steel Company, having reduced costs and increased productivity substantially during the last several years, is now focusing on product mix with value added specialized products. The same approach can be seen in several other industries, like in pharmaceuticals Ranbaxy Company was strategically moving up the value curve from generics to research based higher value products. The same pattern was noticeable in the IT industry also. All the same, there is no denying that clarity about the basis of competition, market positioning, taking advantage of learning curve and leveraging core competence are very central for strategy to develop and sustain competitive edge.

Similarly, in consumer durables, like the Titan Watch Company, we found coverage of a very wide range of market segments, from relatively low end to high end, through which the company acquired a dominant market position. And yet the clarity about choosing where to place strategic emphasis was extremely important, as explained in the case of Titan by Mr. Bhaskar Bhatt. He said: "I am not saying that you can't succeed in the Indian market. Although nobody other than Titan is making money in the Indian market today. That is one problem. That is an industry problem. But if you were to choose the very high-end like Omega as a brand, Titan has no play in that. It has no product in that segment. Nobody who is wishing to buy an Omega will buy a Titan. They can play in that area and make money. That is a separate business model. You need the Aishwarya Rai's and the Shahrukh Khan's kind of imagery which again Titan is not making the mistake of emulating that. Now they seem to be successful by getting celebrities to endorse their product, so can I also do it? It is not that. *You have to be what you are you know.* You are good at developing product, communicating in a certain manner, distributing in a certain manner, you get better at it, you innovate there. It is not just because somebody is successful doing something else, you can import that to your organization. *Relevance is very important. How well you can do it? You can do some things well, you can't do everything well."*

The strategic move towards higher end of value curve as a long-term strategy for sustainable competitive edge was very clearly articulated by Mr. Yogi Sriram of L&T. Describing the future strategic direction of L&T that demonstrates this approach, he said: "Our strategic future direction is to become an Indian multi-national company. Our route to becoming an Indian multinational company is to move into 'asset-light' businesses, which means businesses which have lesser amount of capital employed, much more human capital – businesses which are knowledge driven. Businesses which use the very rich domain knowledge that is available within L&T."

"The business model that we would like to really see – shall we say emerging – is that we would like to use the domain knowledge that is available within L&T to be transformed into viable commercial propositions. Just to give you an example, we have already started two initiatives which are going very strong. One of them is called the embedded software business division which is located in Mysore. Embedded software is very specialized part of the knowledge driven business. It is the business of the future, because the kind of customers that we would be looking at in the embedded software, the kind of customers we are looking at are those large fortune 500 companies, who are into controls, who are into intelligent systems and there is a range of applications right from white goods, to space, to defense, to nuclear, to switchgear, to metering equipment. Embedded software can be used almost anywhere and we already had the domain knowledge. We had people with that kind of domain knowledge, we just sectioned them off and put them in Mysore and we are treating them now as a separate entity."

"Another good example is our effort for growing e-engineering solutions. E-engineering solutions is a group of engineers who are using very state of the art software, like PRO-E, like KTR, like IDEAS – these are all CAD software and the kind of customer that we would have, and we have, are customers in the US, ancillaries of the automobile industry, space, defense, nuclear – all kinds of users of high technology CAD applications. Now, why I am specifically talking about these two is unlike the other information technology majors in this country, at least, the ones that I can think of, except one of them which is attached to a large group of companies, the rest of them do not have this advantage of strong manufacturing domain support."

"We very clearly want to use that as a business proposition for really growing our top line and bottom line and as you asked to maintain a position and to grow in terms of sustainable competitive advantage and the other issues, of course, not just using domain knowledge like this through the asset-light rule, but also our current businesses. Like, let us say heavy engineering division. We would like to move into high technology areas. We are already into pretty much high in technology areas, but we would like to move aggressively into high technology areas...the areas of the future. The idea is to move away a little bit from the lower end of the value chain and move into the higher end of the value chain. The approach is very similar also in our project management businesses..."

"The other route for us is through joint ventures to get into major higher end of the value chain kind of projects because, for us, higher end of the value chain projects in terms of construction businesses like stadium, airports where high technology is used, unlike roads etc. that would be at the lower end. Therefore, we would like to move our businesses to this high technology route."

"The same applies also in our engineering and construction businesses. We would like to take up projects, refinery projects, projects that are large turnkey projects, whether it is power projects, or whatever, that would really add value to the business in terms of high technology. Very clearly, the first step towards becoming a global multinational is to be extremely aggressive in terms of export."

"We are very-very clear that the future lies in being extremely competitive in terms of response time, in terms of cost, in terms of quality, because while India has a prime lending rate of six and a half per cent, which is the Reserve Bank prime lending rate and 12 or 13 per cent when you talk about lending rates from banks, we are acutely aware of the facts that there are certain Southeast Asian countries which lend at much lower rates like 1.5 or 2 per cent and so on. So there is a big difference and therefore there is a lot of competition. So just saying 'exports' is not enough. You have to be extremely competitive, so in that process we will also increase our reach."

"What we are trying to do is to discover niche markets, discover what is it that India can indigenously produce, rather than aping the multinationals. I want to give you an example of medical electronics. We have big plans. We want to ramp up the medical electronics turnover to something like 80 million US dollars and that would mean growing from a base which is pretty small today. It means a lot of effort to indigenously produce patient monitoring systems, to produce systems which are applicable even in homes in the US. Just to give you a little glimpse of the US market, today in the US market for hospitalization, if one is talking about going to John Hopkins or one of the big hospitals, it is extremely expensive. If one was to have the misfortune of myocardial infarction, the kind of patient monitoring machines that are used there, the kind of rates that are charged are probably more expensive than the most expensive hotels, just to make a comparison. So the tomorrows in the world, especially with the calorie careless Americans, is going to be really having even homes with these patient monitoring systems, may be even in the cars and may be collapsing them into much more smaller machines. Today, if you look at the big multinationals that one can think of, they get their know-how and know-why from abroad. But since we have the domain knowledge, we would like to really indigenously work on that and then discover new markets for that."

Building on Strengths and Leveraging Competencies

Hamel & Prahalad, the authors of most cited article *"Strategic Intent"*[6] emphasized that leveraging your resources is very crucial. In simple words, it is not enough to be good at doing something, but it is essential to use that attribute to maximum advantage. It means that if a firm has acquired some competence, say, 'Six-sigma' by Motorola, it has to be leveraged. This is precisely what Motorola did by giving it out to GE to start with and GE, in its own turn, leveraged it to all its businesses.

Most IT companies and other companies are also making use of this concept of six-sigma. Take another example: if being innovative in financial and business models and effective implementation of projects are some of the inherent strengths of Reliance Industries Limited, it had to make sure that they used these to their maximum potential. So they leveraged them to come out with a new financial instrument known as convertible debentures, initiated the process of purchase of grey yarn from small producers, used the extra competence in project management to complete most projects ahead of schedule. Thus, innovativeness permeated other areas beyond the financial instruments.

Every organization has to find other uses for their core competence. If this is not done, then the effort which has gone into developing that competence may prove to be uneconomical. To give example from the book *'Knowledge Creating Company'* by Nonaka & Takeuchi[7], the investment in most inexpensive but tastier bread making machine would not have justified investment in the same, unless it was replicated and extended in other areas such as rice making machines, yogurt making machines, coffee making machines, etc. Similarly Canon with its competence in flat screen did not stop at the point of flat screen technology for the TV set, but extended it to the computers, palm tops and other uses. One could multiply the examples, but the simple fact remains that unless one finds opportunities to leverage the competence enjoyed by any organization for multiple uses, being small or large, it is not the most effective use of such a competence. One could cite the example of Microsoft aggressively entering into various new markets to get the volumes to justify investment in developing softwares for operating systems. One could see the glimpse of this in the case of Ranbaxy Laboratories wherein it is making an attempt to introduce two new drugs every year. This is because of it having reached some level of competence in the area of basic research. Similarly, we have already noted above how the L&T is planning to leverage its technical competencies.

INNOVATION, CHANGE AND RAPID RESPONSE

Innovation, change and rapid response were the most distinctive characteristics of the strategies chosen by the outstanding companies.

They initiated, valued, supported and institutionalized innovation in products, processes and all other aspects of management.

Contd....

Strong emphasis on Research and Development suited to their requirements was considered as the key to their survival and competitiveness.

They constantly reviewed their strategy, assessed the need for change and demonstrated remarkable nimbleness in responding to the changing market and business requirements, adapting, anticipating and pro-actively initiating change.

They did not become complacent with success. They foresaw the need for change far ahead of others and initiated change when they were doing very well and apparently did not need any change.

Quick and rapid response to change, anticipating and initiating change enabled them to maintain their strategic superiority.

Most companies saw speed in all aspects of business operations as a competitive edge while, at the same time, most of them chose to move up by consolidating and building on their competence slowly and steadily.

They put in extraordinary disciplined effort to meet demanding time deadlines for initiating and implementing new strategies, projects, product launches, quality and service improvement initiatives.

Innovation and R&D

The dynamism of the outstanding companies in terms of innovation, change and rapid response was very evident and palpable. These orientations permeated the strategic thinking and actions of the outstanding companies irrespective of the industry in which they were operating. The pharmaceutical and IT industries were most emphatic in identifying innovation and research and development as the keys for sustainable competitive edge. The statement of Dr. G.V. Prasad is most explicit in this connection. He said: "As far as Dr. Reddy's Lab goes, I would put out three factors which give us sustainable competitive advantage. The first factor is innovation and entrepreneurship. The second factor is globalization. And the third factor is people..."

"Innovation is something we really drive strongly across all businesses in our organization. We look at what is the cutting edge in terms of technology, in terms of business practices, in terms of how we can create value by combining various disciplines of knowledge. Really, innovation is one of the biggest strengths we at Dr. Reddy's bring to the business. Then we couple it with entrepreneurship: how to create opportunities to realize value from this innovation. So we combine entrepreneurship

and innovation. That is one reason why I put both of them into one bucket. We use, we drive innovation towards cutting edge, then we use entrepreneurship to realize the value created out of this innovation. Then we need to look at where the best value for these opportunities can be created, (for that) we globalized. So we have really focused on the most important countries in the world for value creation and globalized our operations. So we scaled our innovation and entrepreneurship by globalizing the operation."

"You see, the very fact that if you look at our chairman, he symbolizes the innovation. He really leads the research effort. So there is a high premium placed on innovation in the organization. And continuously by setting the culture to recognize and reward innovation and value innovation in people, we have created an environment where innovation is at a premium, where people like to innovate, want to innovate, because that is their claim to fame. So right from the chairman's level the most senior person in the organization, when he gives a signal that innovation is important, research is important, there is an energy in the organization towards innovation. So I think sponsorship from the top is what is the key to create the environment for innovation."

"Innovation in our company is not limited to science or technology. It is across businesses, it is across business practices, across human resources, management, business, business development, regulatory – everywhere. So the ability to innovate and combine various disciplines to create value is what gives us sustainable competitive advantage. When I am saying innovation, *innovation in science is very critical. But innovation in every sphere is important.*"

"There are so many innovations that Dr. Reddy's Lab has done. If you look at the research side, we are the first company in India to develop molecules and have licensed them out in terms of new chemical entities for new therapies. We are also the first company to launch many bulk actives in this country. We also have the largest portfolio of products for the US in terms of our bulk actives. We were the first company to get 180-day exclusivity for engineering which is really a combination of development, legal innovation, innovation and regulatory affairs, combining various disciplines. We also are very innovative in our own application of information technology. For example, we were the first company to put ERP for our size of a company in this country. We use information technology extensively, we link all our vendor stores, corporate purchasing system through the web so we are quick to adapt to innovation. Also, the other thing which we do very well is on the people side. We quickly move on any innovative human resource practice and spread that across the organization. Those kind of things keep us at the cutting edge of the innovation...For example, we recognize that talent is very important. So we hire from anywhere in the world, we create the right working environment for them, we are flexible enough to bring people into this country through various means."

Mr. Brar of Ranbaxy expressed similar emphasis on innovation and R&D. He said: "I can only say that in our industry, which is a knowledge based industry, recognition of innovation has been the competitive edge which will take the company forward for this crucial process of sustainability. *Ours is an industry which derives its whole foundation on research and innovation.* While Ranbaxy is itself a generic (drugs) company - which means that we market drugs which were discovered elsewhere and have patent protection in the markets round the world - we believe that though generics is an excellent business, without innovation and R&D sustainable advantage cannot be maintained for the long-term. Many companies in our country have taken a very microscopic view of markets and in terms of business opportunities. You are well aware that for decades we have kept our industry immune to international competition, immune to influences of technology and influences of better business and management practices from abroad. And we had a setup here with high tariffs and protected markets for license holders. We, at least at Ranbaxy, believed that all these are extremely counter-productive to innovation and sustainable competitive edge. So, within the rules of the game that were played in this market, we felt that there was still a sustainable business model which allowed us to function despite the constraints that the government or the system had imposed and which was to look at markets more closely and in terms of their business potential or in their intrinsic evaluations, rather than looking at odds all the time."

The importance of mastering technology has already been enunciated above in the sub-section on internationalization. Here we would like to restate and emphasize the importance of internal research and development as a means of competitiveness. R&D has been a relatively neglected area in Indian industries. Very often, R&D was done by companies for getting tax benefits, because of government's policy of providing more than 100% tax benefits for R&D. In most companies R&D was considered a marginal activity, as technology was provided by joint ventures. Whatever R&D was done was also confined to 'know how' and not 'know why'. This led to dependence and lack of development of internal competence and competitiveness in Indian organizations to face competition when liberalization and international competition began to hit the Indian companies. Very few companies were farsighted to obtain and develop technology through *technical collaborations* (not joint ventures with financial and management control of the foreign company), outright acquisition of technology and hiring foreign experts to master and develop their own technology.

Most of the companies included in this study followed the pattern of mastering and developing technology internally through high emphasis on relevant focused research and development of technology suited to their specific requirements. The importance of R&D is being recognized now even by small and medium sized companies. "Nimbleness in R&D is the key to sustainability... Reducing the time between development of an idea and converting it into a marketable product makes all the difference in competitiveness", said Mr. Bharat Tandon, a young first generation entrepreneur who had built a successful dynamic enterprise called Vetcare in Bangalore.

Almost all the organizations included in this study placed a great emphasis on innovativeness. In Wipro, it was described as 'fierce openness to new ideas.' In Satyam, we were told about numerous innovations and pioneering ideas like creating a 'little India experiment' 30 miles off the customer's location in USA as a pre-cursor to developing the off-shore software development model. They developed and tried several innovative business models to give to the customer the maximum value, like integrating IT and management consulting and creating a 'one stop shop', so that 'he doesn't have to shop around ten different places to get something done.'

Most of the multinational companies like Motorola invested heavily in R&D. They consider innovation and R&D as the most critical factor for developing and sustaining competitive edge. Outstanding companies do not wait for the changes in market and technology for their response. They anticipate and initiate innovation through R&D. The orientation was well illustrated by Motorola. "We are a technology industry", said Mr. Aqil Busrai. "Obsolescence is much faster in this industry. The way we tackle it is like many other companies: a lot of research and development, because this is like running on a treadmill. If you are stationary, you will fall. If you run, you might not go far, but you have to run. That running is keeping a very close watch on where the market is, like what technology changes we can initiate rather than follow. I mean if you have read recently in the papers we have come out with what is called Arsenicgelium, which is a process applied on silicon now that makes the chip transmit data at the speed of light. It is not commercially out yet, but the whole concept – just imagine the concept. Take today's chip on a silicon, which works on a pretty high speed 2g, 2.5g, 3g. We are talking about 3g already. Then you look at that in the context of Arsenicgelium, which says it will transmit data at the speed of light – your whole way of communicating 5–10 years down the line would have changed. Now the sustainable part comes out of investing into that research, rather than saying we have got a very good product and let us now keep on selling this, because then it is only till the competitor comes up with a better product.

"The sustainable part comes in investing a good part of your energy into saying this product is good, but okay it is already there. Now let me see what other things I can do and not just improving, not again marginal improving or tweaking we are talking about. Again taking a quantum jump. I'll give you another example: if you look at Kodak, when George Fischer took over Kodak, his priority at that time – if you remember Fortune interview – that he will go into research on film-less camera. That was in 1994. At that time, digital camera were not even in the market. Prototypes had come in. NASA was using it, but it was not commercially available. Actually he was selling his complete stock in trade of Kodak, which was started as a film company, a camera company. But obviously he saw that this will be only up to a X number of years. That my company will have a product which the people will buy."

"Today Kodak has, because of the strategy, branched out in digital camera and does not feel the pinch of being obsolete like the Remington Rands of the world who got wiped out when the typewriters became obsolete. They did not anticipate that their product would ever become obsolete. Who thought typewriter would ever get obsolete. I mean my parents would never have thought that this typewriter would become obsolete. Today I have a typewriter in my home. My daughter found it the other day and she said, 'What is this?'. She can't believe that people actually used to insert paper and type. So looking at what changes are coming and anticipating that change is part of sustainable strategy. And that's where average companies and good companies get differentiated. And that's where good leaders and average leaders get differentiated."

"Good leaders see the future. They don't only have vision. They see the future trend. What reality is? How hard it is to accept the reality, even if it means closing down the operation, they accept it. The average leaders keep on hoping: no-no we will still fight the market. We'll still improve our product. We'll still survive. And after some time they just can't manage. When the technology goes on a quantum jump shift, then they lose out on the market."

The importance of innovation, not only in products or services but also across the entire value chain, was identified in several organizations as one the most significant differentiating factors for developing and maintaining sustainable competitive edge. A senior professional manager in a highly dynamic Indian company articulated this point by stating: "If everybody is doing something new (like IT enabled services), so we should also be doing it–is not going to make companies competitively very advantageous. In fact, there is more reason why the future players would be more niche players - players who take a position around their offerings and build a certain uniqueness to it. And, therefore, they are distinguished. They are distinct and their offering can command a price that their margin can lead to a profit. The strategy of the future would be a strategy for the niche, for that commanding niche, which is not running a rat race with others. That will lead to a lot of other things, for example the *ability to innovate around offerings* will be the one, which will distinguish the successful from the not so successful ones. *This innovation is not a product innovation alone. This innovation is an innovation throughout the value chain.* On the extreme end, the ability to innovate into how do you educate your customer, make him appreciate values which he has not seen before. Two: how do you deliver the product to the customer by innovating the processes and you can go up the value chain throughout? How do you position the product and how do you do the offering? To summarize these what is the unique strategy that distinguishes you from the mass, is the second important piece for a competitive advantage. The third, is the ability to innovate from the concept to the finish, everywhere, each piece of that value chain, so that, that uniqueness is actually implemented. *It's possible to do it only through innovation.*"

Innovation, not only in products but also in several other areas, was noted in many companies. Some of the examples of innovations in the distribution channel that developed into a core strength for the company were noted in case of HLL, Hero Honda and Titan. Let us examine Titan's distribution channel for this purpose. Describing the uniqueness of Titan's distribution channel, Mr. Bhaskar Bhatt said: "In distribution network I must tell you that we have qualitatively very different kind of network compared to most of the other companies. We have many classes of stores, at the top of the heap is our World of Titan Exclusive Store. The role of that store is to project the image of the company and yet be profitable. And then we have a next rung of stores, which are multi-brand stores, but which are controlled by us, are called 'Timezone'- they are the top-end retailers of the country but they come under a chain called Timezone. And then there are 7000 outlets. At the top there are only 250 outlets, which barely contribute 35 per cent of the volume of the business, but they contribute hugely to the image of the company."

"Timezone also keeps competitors' brands but by contract – this is a very different contract, it is a very unique to Titan and the watch industry. In fact initiated by Titan, an innovation in distribution...We said that if we could have a relationship with top 250 watch outlets in this country, (then we will have outlets) wherein over a long period of time they will be selling more of our products than competitors' product. You cannot do it merely by increasing their marginal profitability. You have to work with them, understanding that they are multi-brand dealers. They will never be exclusive. So we have a contract with them wherein they are permitted to sell brands, which are specified by us – including the big brands, including Citizen and Timex, etc. We actually build traffic to those Timezone stores for all watches, but the conversion is mainly to our brand. It is a high risk, high return strategy."

"We ensure that the counter space given to Titan is 60 per cent of the total space. That's the only thing internal in the contract, rest is free to do what he wants, except that he has to sell only those brands which are specified in the contract, which is done through a process. What we do also in this is that we ensure high returns to him from cooperative buying we do with 130 Timezone stores. Every competitor has to come to Timezone. We offer instant access to brands across the country, so they can talk to one (source). So when Citizen comes (and discovers that) Timezones sell over a million watches, one and a half million watches, we said: okay there is that network who sell one and a half million watches. If you have to access this network, you can negotiate with this chain but through us. You will have to give them higher discounts. You have to ensure that they are promoted. We say we save your cost, because you don't have to go about accessing these 130 fellows and individually signing them on. So everybody benefits, the brands benefit, but for the company it is high-risk high return proposition. There is nothing in the contract to say that he must sell so many Titan watches."

"At least for the last 5 years our market share there has been higher. So they (Timezone retail watch stores) see in this a cooperative (model). They feel literally that this company has brought that customer to my store and they are strongly backing us on our side... Now what we do is the positioning of the store as a trusted watch shop. We do a thorough check on the antecedents of the manufacturer: What quality product he is bringing? Will he give service? It is before he can access them, so the rif-raff brands are not permitted on this. All the positioning is the 'trusted watch shop', so the customer can blindly buy a watch in this outlet."

It is worthy of noting specially that the *very unique way of working in the market place that Titan has developed with its business associates has given it a definite competitive advantage,* any individual part of which cannot be replicated by the competitors. As emphasized by Mr. Bhatt further, "Many have failed in trying to do this, which is what convinces me about this business of completing the loop within the organization, the chain of processes, the chain that links all processes together makes the organization unbeatable. No part of the chain can be simply taken out and replicated. Timex, Westar, the Swatch group, Citizen – these four organizations I have known who have tried to take bits and pieces of ours (but could not succeed)...It is a complete process: the way we manage our business associates, the way we train our people, the manner in which we conduct ourselves, I mean our supply chain process. It has taken us years to build it and we still have got many more years to go to perfect it, but from an external view point – that which is visible – seems to be easy to replicate and therefore succeed, but it is not so."

Institutionalization of Innovation

Whereas innovation is recognized as an important factor in the success of any enterprise very few companies have developed adequate processes, systems and culture to encourage creative thinking and convert creative ideas into profitable business propositions, commercially successful products, or better and viable solutions for business problems. The important difference between creativity and innovation is often not appreciated. All creative ideas do not become innovations. Innovation is a far more complex process, as it requires enormous effort and investment to convert a creative idea into a tangible commercial product, service, or a workable solution. We found innovation as a pervasive phenomenon in most of the successful organizations included in this research. In fact it was an important differentiater between outstanding and average organizations. However, there were only few organizations that institutionalized the process of developing innovations in a systematic and thorough manner. We would like to cite the practices for institutionalization of innovation from HLL and Wipro, as they have developed fairly sophisticated systems and processes for this purpose.

Explaining the system and process for developing an idea into a commercial product, Mr. G. Kapur of HLL said: "We have a very structured and, in a sense, a very demanding, *innovation process* in the company. It's a well-structured, well-organized process, which is well articulated. It is very strongly enforced around the company and it is such that it allows for very lateral and creative execution. But the framework is the same for every one. For example, we believe that – and it is commonly shared – it is on everyone's computer and things have to be updated every day, etc. We have, what is called 'innovation funnel' where the mouth of the funnel is fairly wide and is the funnel that captures all the ideas. There is an attempt to ensure that the ideas come from all possible sources and there is a formal process for creating ideas in the funnel. It gets a bit narrow because you screen the ideas and move them into a more rigorous evaluation phase. At each stage there is a gate and the idea cannot move beyond that gate unless the defying gatekeeper approves it based on some rigorous assessment. From the idea to the ideas which will be pursued and resources allocated to and then to a stage where you say that through a structured market research the potential of the idea is demonstrated, upto which it gets into a test market. And then into a roll out and then into an international roll out, depending on the idea."

"This funnel, and each stage of the funnel, is clearly articulated with processes and systems and gatekeepers at every stage, who formally approve things forward. This is entirely audited, meaning it is as important as the commercial controls in the company. So there is a very strong focus on consumer led innovation. Therefore, the research and technology part of it will depend on the consumer insight, rather than the other way around. We don't really say that let us do a lot of research and technology and see if it finds relevance for the consumer and let us try its need. If there is consumer idea which requires a research and technology, then of course – depending on the opportunity etc. it will be allocated that resource. But till the time we articulate the consumer end of it and the business end of it, the corporation is not going to commit any research and technology resource..."

"There are three processes in the company, which operate in parallel. One is of course what I described as the consumer, starting from the consumer and that forces you to sort out all these issues because when you start with the consumer, the price at which you sell is a very important issue there. Therefore, that process forces you to look at the value of the offering to the consumer and does not allow you to do cost plus pricing. In fact the specific thing... the thought process is that we have to sell at a so and so price. Everything, which comes from manufacturing and distribution and so on are within our control. So, let us be extremely innovative today to match the challenged cost, rather than add up all the cost that we incur.

The second strength of the company is in its (probably) leading edge expertise in supply chain management. That is a leading edge of expertise.... I am not aware of any company in the world, which does supply chain as well as HLL. The third expertise for us, I would believe, is our system of commercial controls and measurement that is a very strong and rigorous process of the company. Therefore, while at the marketing end we encourage people to be highly speculative in seeing connections, seeing patterns and so on and so forth, but when it comes to committing resource, everything has to go through a very rigorous commercial evaluation. This is just to ensure that at every stage the potential size of the business is what attracts resources and not really the glamour or attractiveness of an idea per say because every idea has to ultimately be attractive for the organization... There is always a huge tension between encouraging the people to be speculative, creative, consumer sensitive and yet at the same time applying all the commercial rigors, all the commercial evaluation, before we commit big time resource behind ideas. Now, that's a tension that we manage all the times and it's not easy...."

"Now 5 per cent (success rate) is not good enough, because the cost of failure is becoming very-very punishing with each passing time. Now you have to become better. The old belief that 50 per cent of advertising money will work – we don't know which 50 per cent and the success rate of 5 per cent is good enough, etc. They are all going out of the window now, because organizations which are only that successful will not be able to survive, or at least they may not be able to meet the expectations of the shareholders. If you have one failure in a year in terms of a big national launch, you lose 40–50 crores."

“oWe found somewhat similar and more elaborate systems and processes for institutionalizing innovation in Wipro. The head of the innovation initiative team[8] of Wipro described to us how innovation was viewed and what processes were developed to initiate, capture and convert new ideas into innovation: "I would say innovation for us is a growth engine. We will look at it through 'innovation initiative', where in our service business normally the time does not permit us to look into several aspects. But this initiative would help us look at growth opportunities and then do work up-front before even the technology really emerges as a standard."

"One of the things that we articulated in our promised segment was the innovative solution that we are committing to the customers up-front. That led us to think what are we doing. It is easy to put something as a promise statement, but we need to quantify it and then say what we are exactly doing to make that happen."

"What innovation means to one organization will not be same to another organization. We went about studying how the best organizations across the world do. What do they do? What are the academicians talking about? And that was the time when it was just about beginning. I can tell you the difference, because in the year 2000 the amount of material that was available on innovation and the amount that is available today, there is a huge difference. As seen in six sigma, when we started, hardly anything was available on the subject. Similar situation existed regarding innovation. I was one of the first members in this particular team who did this study."

"What we did was, we went about studying western class organizations such as 3M, Home Depot, Nike, etc. We went and talked to professors at Harvard and every university known for work on this subject. And we had half a day meetings with at least top ten consultants who are focused only in the areas of consulting – not the general consulting organizations, but doing very specific work in this area. We went and met them and understood the whole thing and one of the objectives was to look for somebody who could handhold us, end to end, in this journey, like how we got Motorola University to help us to kick-start the six sigma initiative. But it came as a surprise that each organization was pursuing things in a way that was right for that culture and their needs. There is no generic framework that you can take it and apply to your organization and make it work. What we did was, we came back and that was the time we got this rude shock. We went around for a month and then felt that let us identify somebody who can help us and at the end of it we said there is nobody. Everybody is talking differently, so we have got to create our own thing."

"It was a big challenge and, once we came back, we also were doing our vision exercise at that time and then we could clearly look at our vision exercise and align the innovation initiative to match with that particular vision. That timing was perfect, so what we have done is the whole innovation initiative... We learnt from all these meetings that only when innovation is valued by the customer it will give returns, because there are several organizations which talk to us in terms of innovation being led by R&D and the research not being really in sync with what the market really wants. Much of the research keeps happening in its side and the marketing and the customer want something else. And if you are not able to marry these two, then it is bound to fail. What we did was – we defined what innovation is for us? The way we have defined innovation is *'Innovation is implementation of a new idea resulting in a marketable product or service'.*"

"It means that for us innovation is not just coming up with an idea because in many places innovation is linked directly to creativity. You have to do some programmes on creativity and then finally what comes out of it? There is no organizational mechanism to convert this in a very formal way. So many of the things are lost and over a period of time it loses its steam. For us innovation is not just coming up with an idea. It is the implementation of the idea which is the more difficult part. It is not just implementation for the sake of implementation. It has also got to do with customer needs. We defined our innovation process out of all the learnings that we have and we created our own innovation process document, which is a gate process and clearly structured like other roles. What are the responsibilities of each of the players? What is going to be the process with which the ideas will come taken forward. What is the organization mechanism that will get supported?"

"Then we have got this classical gate process, which many organizations follow for different things, where we take the idea from conception to commercialization in a very structured way. It may appear contradictory to some people, saying that: innovation and structure, innovation and discipline - what are you talking about? Is it not going to be a hurdle for this whole innovation? But we are clearly distinguishing the process of coming up with an idea which requires a lot of freedom, etc. After you have come up with an idea, how does the organization take some of those ideas into commercialization part? It has to be a highly disciplined process, it has to be highly structured. We have linked these two parts. How an idea is accepted is one part; and after acceptance how you take it to commercialization is the trickier part that many organizations have failed (to develop) in the past. We have concentrated on this. So initially when the idea is born, the best guide to judge the idea is the idea generator himself. We have created a kind of a questionnaire, which the idea generator himself applies to that particular idea that he has come up with. And unless he clears certain marks, he will not even bring it to the council...We have chosen some four areas in which we would like to have ideas coming in for us to really take it to commercialization...Once the ideas have undergone self-evaluation, then each of these themes has a business manager. The business managers are full-time dedicated and very-very senior people who are heading these themes. They will be the people who will evaluate the ideas first and then get it to the innovation council for funding. The innovation council is functioning according to an approach like our VC (Venture Capital), and would evaluate the proposals in the same way. Ultimately all ideas have to be evaluated with the market... and one critical element that we have got in each process, each gate of the process, is that ideas have to get some kind of commitment from the customer or from the market."

"Another important element of innovation process/discipline is that in any innovation idea there are a lot of uncertainties and more the uncertainties the more important it is to have a very methodical project management process in place, where you are able to identify upfront: what are all the bottlenecks you are likely to face? What are the risks that you have got? What are all the disruptive technologies that can come and take away the benefits of all the work that you have done and for all these risks that you identify up-front you need to prepare the risk mitigation plan....The project management process has ensured that."

"Last year was the first year (of the innovation initiative). Year 2001–2002 was the first full year of innovation and we have been able to not only make success out of the projects that we have taken, we have broken even and we have started realizing, generating revenues for the organization in one year's time. People felt that innovation and whatever we are doing doesn't match, but it is now validated. Wherever we go and talk outside, people are appreciating. Yes, this is what is the real work of innovation and not what is often talked as creativity part of the thing, which is most frivolous in many organizations; or it is taken up in a very serious way but with no organizational mechanism backing it up, so whatever happens loses its way."

In order to encourage new ideas and innovations, some incentives in the form of reward and recognition system were developed in Wipro, so that people will actually be tempted to post an idea. For example, from the time the Innovation Council clears an idea till the time of 18 months gets over, whatever revenue comes, one per cent of the top line – not the bottom line – irrespective of whether the organization makes profit or not, goes to the idea generator. The core team shares three per cent of the revenue in the first 18 months. Although the idea plays an important role, the core team does a lot of work. The idea generator may be a part of the core team also, so he gets a double benefit, as he gets part of the 3 per cent revenue shared by the core team members. Another thing is that Wipro has an Innovation Intranet. The Innovation Intranet collected some 256 ideas in 2001. The organization has high commitment to the innovation initiative and the CPO of Wipro Technologies heads it. At the corporate office, the corporate vice president drives the initiative and this gets reviewed in every board meeting. The progress on the innovation initiative during the last quarter gets reviewed.

It may be emphasized here that organizations that value innovation not only create a reward system and other supportive processes and systems to promote innovations, they also create a culture of openness to new ideas, openness in communication and tolerance of differences, as we will explain later in the chapter on values and culture.

Change

The centrality and criticality of change for sustainability of organizations can be hardly over-emphasized. We have already discussed the willingness, ability and orientation of leadership to change as one of the most important factors that was noted as the key-differentiating characteristic in organizations having sustainable competitive edge. Illustrating how change management is the key to sustaining competitive edge, Mr. Subodh Bhargava of Eicher stressed the point by stating that: "Indian companies who have been changing well in time...have revived because of the basic ability of the *leadership and change management.* Companies (like TVS and Bajaj in the two-wheeler industry) have revived sharply. That is what I would call competitive sustainability, where you are able to come back...Let us say the impulse for change has come only because of threat to survive by and large. There are very few farsighted and proactive companies; and many, many today, I would not know the numbers, but several thousands, that would have moved in the direction of wanting to bring about a change – some successfully and some not so successfully. And the failure is invariably on account of two: either the top not changing itself – its not becoming the role model; or secondly, just overdoing some dimension of change (without having a holistic view)...There is a knowledge gap and attitudinal gap. But the attitudinal gap is only at the top, which matters. If the top – number one – wants to change, the second tier has to change and the third tier and so on, for, the entire organization must change."

In the same vein, identifying change as the key factor for sustainability, Mr. G. Kapur of HLL said: "The ability of the organization to anticipate change and continuously change itself is probably the first thing which comes to my mind. Because if I look back, I think that has been one of the huge strengths of HLL. Despite being a company which is fairly big in terms of its scales and operations, in our history, we have actually been able to bring about a very sharp focus (through change) on what was appropriate at that point of time."

In this section we would like to briefly describe the patterns of change noted in strategic thinking and formulating strategy, that had a direct bearing on the sustainability and competitiveness of organizations.

Three distinct patterns could be noted in orientation to change among the organizations: the *reactive style,* the *adaptive style* and the *proactive style.*

The Reactive Style

This was the style of change followed by the organizations in their strategy when the market, technology and regulatory requirements changed substantially and the organization was practically 'forced' to change for survival. This was usually done after the other organizations and competitors had changed and there was little option but to change to keep pace with others. The past success of a certain type of strategy and mode of working, emotional commitment of the key leaders or promoters to certain plants, products, or businesses made them stick to their past and persist with the illusory hope that somehow things will improve. Often they justified their existing strategy to themselves, and those who differed, by the assumption that external changes are temporary, or that their customers will stick to them. Some would blame the government, the competition and others for their continuing decline and subconsciously hope for some miracle to happen to bail them out in the face of the challenge of change.

The leadership and management of organizations that followed the reactive change style would persist with a outmoded mindset in spite of visible declining indicators of performance, clearly proving the theory of behavioural scientists that the habitual modes of thinking and behaviour are very 'hard wired' and, therefore, not easy to change. When the situation would become untenable and threaten their survival, they would gingerly make marginal changes, or have knee jerk reactions like cutting costs, tightening controls, blaming and sacking some individuals whom they would consider responsible for the failures. Some would try to venture out into unrelated businesses that seem lucrative without a thorough assessment of their core competencies and strengths, or hire external consultants to solve their problems without deeply reflecting on their own mindset and the nature and magnitude of external change. The reactive approach to strategic change is usually too late and too little and very few organizations survive that follow such an approach.

We noted several examples of reactive change in organizations that had been highly successful in the protected environment and developed business models suited to that situation. They developed in-house facilities to ensure continuity of supply of all parts and components in the manufacturing industry; built large inventories to ensure no stock-outs and stoppage of production because of import restrictions, poor infra-structure and other bottlenecks and uncertainties in the supply lines, etc. They found themselves burdened with heavy overheads, under-utilized facilities, excessive redundant manpower and inflexible operations when competition in the market from domestic and multinational firms increased. The profit margins became thin as cheaper imported goods or cheaper products manufactured in the unorganized sector began to flood the markets. Similar – and in most cases worse – situation existed in many public sector organizations that were burdened with excessive centralized control of government bureaucracy, stifling red tape, agonizingly arbitrary and slow decision making, archaic rules based on pervasive mistrust, absence of professional management and interference by politicians with no accountability for results.

The Adaptive Style

The second pattern can be described as the adaptive style. This style of change is more like coping with the changes in the business environment. There is greater openness, flexibility and responsiveness in such organizations to external changes. They see the 'writing on the wall' and the management engages in reflective exercises to review their strategy, realistically examine their strengths and weaknesses, the opportunities and threats in the business environment. They initiate carefully considered changes in strategy and operations to meet the challenges of change in markets, technology, regulatory requirements, moves of competitors and other external or internal changing realities. This approach and style of change is relatively more effective than the reactive style and usually enables the organizations to survive, but does not necessarily ensure sustained competitive advantage.

The Proactive Style

This is the most forward looking style which was conspicuous among the outstanding organizations. The approach in this was to foresee the future through various means, such as strategic workshops and meetings in which strategic review and scenario building was done to anticipate and foresee change and develop different strategies to develop competitiveness. As described above, there were institutionalized practices for holding such meetings and workshops of top management in which unit heads, regional heads, functional heads and several other key members participated along with the key members of top management. The orientation of management was not only to anticipate and prepare for change, but *to initiate and proactively create change* by developing new technologies, launching new products and services, new business models, or re-defining the industry and re-inventing the organization. Such initiatives transformed organizations and set out new rules of the game for the industry. We have already cited the examples of such change initiatives by Kodak in changing over to digital imaging, Motorola's initiative of six sigma and cutting-edge research. There are many such examples among the well-known multinational companies.

Among the Indian companies included in this study, there was evidence of movement from adaptive approach to the pro-active approach to change in the most dynamic organizations. Proactive approach to change was clearly evident as the cornerstone of strategy for developing and sustaining competitiveness by companies like Ranbaxy, Reliance, Titan, HLL, Infosys, Satyam, Wipro and Sundram Fasteners. We have already quoted above how Ranbaxy chose to become an international research based pharmaceutical company and function like a multinational company in all aspects. And how it has purposely moved towards higher ends of the value curve – drug discovery in pharmaceuticals – and operate in highly competitive world markets, when it could have comfortably made considerable profits in protected markets. Similarly, we have stated above how HLL anticipated change in the various phases of change in the Indian economy and swiftly changed and consolidated its position in key product lines through acquisitions and mergers in the FMCG sector to tap vast opportunities in the liberalized business environment in India. Reliance is too well-known for sensing vast business opportunities in diverse sectors ranging from textiles, petrochemicals, power and energy to telecom by converting latent needs into demand through its highly innovative business and finance models, world–class technology, world scale operations and excellent track record in project implementation. In the case of Titan, it was stated that, "What you did well yesterday doesn't mean it will help you succeed tomorrow. Questioning this and reinventing yourself all the time is the key...today the entire drive is to change our business model to suit the tomorrow, whether you look at manufacturing, or marketing, or relationship with your customer, or for example IT, or leveraging current technology, the supply chain, bringing down the costs through better working capital management... and of course operational efficiency related issues".

Wipro's proactive approach was described as its 'ability to respond to the changing environment quickly, swiftly, in a nimble and a very thoughtful manner', that has enabled it to adjust to the changing times very quickly. It has been constantly reinventing itself through tapping new opportunities in various businesses that enabled it to move from the edible oil business to several high technology businesses including a key position in IT.

Describing Wipro's approach to deal with the issues of change and uncertain future, Mr. Pratik Kumar said: "It is difficult to predict the future, but as we say internally, the only surety is that future is going to descend on us. People who are able to see earlier than others are the ones who are able to work on it quickly and be able to reorient change, gear themselves up to meet the challenges of future better...We do this exercise very regularly, where we talk about articulating a vision for ourselves, we map ourselves over a scenario of about 3–5 years in terms of where we would like to go? What is our aspiration and what is our vision? And what will it take for us to get there? Whether the existing business model will survive, whether our growth needs are to be met only through organic means? What are the challenges which we are going to see in going further, in terms of getting into new areas, getting into new geographies?.... Now these are challenges and we have to identify, therefore, what should be our market strategy? What should be our people strategy? Will that be enough? Then there is a good possibility of getting into a scenario of mergers and acquisitions. If you get into those scenarios, it comes along with its own set of challenges. You talk about a different cultural context, a team which is culturally alien to you. How do you go about assimilating it? How do you go about working along with them? So these are some issues that we map. Currently we have a very well articulated vision for ourselves, that by the year 2004 we want to be among the top 10 software services companies in the world.'

Mr. T. Dasgupta, corporate vice-president and CIO of Wipro added to this view by stating the futuristic vision of the chairman and vice-chairman of the company relating to IT: "These are the people who are actually very enthusiastic about IT and who have the vision to see integration across time zones, across continents, between different cultures that is not possible without IT. First there has to be the global feel, so what is global feel? Global feel means that simple things across continents become paperless, so that is step one. So as we digitize, we actually drive out paper... What we first set about to do is to setup a global culture, a totally global culture in terms of IT, which is benchmarked with the best companies in the world. We don't actually benchmark ourselves with an Indian company. As such we benchmark ourselves with any global company, so if you have to walk into a Cisco, or any other company in Europe, what are the systems you would find? And do we have those systems and those kinds of processes in India? The answer is Yes. This whole thing about the benchmarks, the first thing is don't think like you are a $300-400 million company. Think in terms of systems that will be comparable to the large companies like the GEs and the Ciscos.

A similar pro-active and dynamic orientation and a highly systematic way of dealing with the issues related to change can be noted in Infosys. Talking about meeting the challenges of the future, Dr. Dinesh stated: "I think the key to address the challenges of the future is to constantly be in touch with your environment, more often than what you would do otherwise. To be more and more customer focused is very important. That you need to do and be agile all the time. That is where the agility that you need comes from the culture that you have created, comes from the systems and processes that you have developed. So that once you decide and say this is the way you'll go ahead, then you know it happens that way everywhere and you have a feedback system... Developing those kinds of systems and processes that you can deploy and quickly implement what you need. And creating a culture of an organization which can adapt very quickly with high performance and work ethic is very, very important."

"It is all inter-related, which means that you have to revisit your strategies more often and make adjustments as and when you need. Broad strategies may not change. But you really have to revisit the underlying tactical strategies that you may have and adjust those things and empower people to take decisions. Everything can't come from the top, because people are reacting to what is happening on the field. So they should be empowered to take decisions to satisfy the customers and be result-oriented."

In order to ensure change in strategy, the need to challenge all deep rooted assumptions and focus on keeping the organization young by inducting and grooming bright young people with 'fire in the belly' were highlighted in IT companies like Infosys, Wipro and Satyam. Further, the orientations and practices like looking at problems as opportunities, communicating with and involving people across the organization in strategy development to ensure effective implementation, emphasis on high performance culture through systems and processes and the importance of institutionalizing change were emphasized in most of the winning organizations.

The adaptive and pro-active and futuristic change orientation were not only confined to the organizations in the IT, pharmaceutical and FMCG industries. As mentioned earlier, companies in the engineering industry like L&T, Telco, Eicher and TVS also strongly demonstrated such orientation, as has been discussed in the earlier chapter.

Mr. Suresh Krishna, chairman of Sundram Fasteners, very well epitomized the proactive approach to change for achieving high levels of competitiveness and excellence and how Indian companies can achieve it. He said: "I personally feel that Indian companies can choose to become very, very quality conscious company in India, which itself is becoming more and more competitive. That is one level of competitive quality orientation. If you want to raise the bar further, then you must go to the lion's den – go international. And then manage international logistics, international quality, international manufacturing – that is the next step.

"The *first step* is, as they say in TPM (Total Productivity Management), you must become better than what you were say 5 years ago, the *second step* is you must be as good as the best manufacturing company in the world; the *third step* is everybody must try to catch up with you – everybody in the world. Like Toyota Motor Company, that today is the model of efficiency for all automobile companies in the world."

"There are *three steps to achieving excellence. One* is you must become better than what you were; *second,* you should be as good as the best in the world; third is you are the best in the world and everybody is trying to catch up with you – everybody benchmarks against you. But, if you want to do that, then you have to become efficient. There is no way you can sit at home and do this, because then you will only become the biggest frog in a small pond."

We would like to emphasize the view that proactive style of change is a different paradigm from benchmarking with the best. As was pointed out in some of the most dynamic companies in this study, they did not confine themselves to or were satisfied with merely benchmarking with the best and follow the best-known practices. They aimed at excelling the best companies and going beyond. They challenged all the existing assumptions and demonstrated 'fierce openness to new ideas'. They initiated change when no change seemed necessary, as they were already doing exceedingly well. They never seemed to be satisfied with what they had achieved and never rested on their laurels. They did not only foresee and prepare for the change; in fact they created a changed future by their highly innovative, passionate and entrepreneurial spirit.

Rapid Response

Speed in all aspects of business was seen by most of the successful companies as an extremely important element in competitive edge, though in a few companies the importance of moving up by consolidating and building on their competence slowly and steadily was also emphasized, as in the case of Hero Honda. Quick and rapid response to changed business environment enabled the highly competitive companies in maintaining their strategic superiority. They put in extraordinary disciplined effort to meet demanding time deadlines for initiating and implementing new strategies, projects, product launches, quality and service improvement initiatives.

Speed, as one of the key elements in superior strategy and its implementation, is becoming a crucial factor in the contemporary and rapidly changing business environment. Product life cycles are getting shortened, market and technology changes are very swift and even the regulatory environment is not stable or predictable in the domestic as well as global economy. We are living in the age of turbulent change, uncertainty and discontinuity, in which only the most quick to respond will be able to survive. "What India has learnt, to my mind, over the last 10 years in Indian industry, is that changes are inevitable and constant and therefore the organization has to remain in that flux or constant flux of learning – for what you use the word learning organization. The learning organization is nothing but has got ears to the ground, listens to the customer and has got what is happening around in changes – changes quicker than competition. *The ability to change quicker than competition is one of the key ingredients for sustainable competitive edge*", observed Mr. Subodh Bhargava. Mr. Kapur of HLL sounded a similar note: "Being a consumer goods company, we are forced to be much more responsive to the market place than probably certain other industries because the speed of change in the market place that we operate in is very fast and the competitive issues keep revolving every day. You are constantly, proactively, or reactively dealing with competition."

We found that change was forcing organizations in almost all industries to learn to respond rapidly, with clear, imaginative and thoughtfully developed strategy, combined with skillful and effective implementation, or face extinction. This was very well articulated by a highly placed manager[9], who said: "I think a very distinguishing feature for successful players is what I would call speed. The business environment in which we stand today... actually we are standing on quick sands: quick sands of technology, quick sands of customer preference, quicksands of regulation – both international regulation and national regulation. Every business is impinged by any of these things any where – by way of tariff structure, laws of the land, duty structure, the guarantees involved in terms of getting investment or using investment, or share holding in each area.

'There are tremendously important roles the governments are playing in all countries, both the developed and the developing. They are constantly changing technology with a new Intel chip. Every month you have a new capability to process. Technology in every field is changing quite constantly. What this is creating as an imperative is that *businesses, which have speed, speed to strategize, speed to develop the action plan, speed to implement, speed to go to the market, speed to cope and fight with the changing technology and regulation and keep pace with it and run ahead of it are businesses which will be competitive.* It has tremendous implications on how businesses are done... Businesses are really on a run, much unlike before. Pace has entirely changed. There is no time now for very iterative ways of doing things. You need to get it right the first time, which is a very difficult balance to maintain, because quality processes, getting something right for the first time needs a lot of iteration. At the same time, you need a lot of speed. Those who manage to blend these two would be the ones that will succeed."

"The other important advantage or quality of a competitive player – somebody who is able to out-compete others is because of his speed, because of his innovation, because of his uniqueness of the strategy or the idea and above all the ability to execute with finesse, with excellence, with operational detail. These seem to be the kind of distinguishing features you would commonly hear as competitive advantage."

Reliance Industries Limited is known for its outstanding record of completing projects ahead of time and they have repeatedly demonstrated that it is possible to do so. In fact it is possible to work out very stringent project completion targets by splitting the projects into various activities and sub-activities. The success of this process has been shown when their plant in Gujarat was inundated and damaged by the cyclone. The executives of Reliance Industries Limited suggested to their higher management foreign experts called for the purpose should be asked to go because the time frame which they were suggesting was much more than what the internal team of Reliance estimated and they completed the job accordingly. It has also been done in the case of Bhilwara group of Industries where they could commission a power plant in less than the time indicated by a foreign consultant. The well-known global company, ABB, has also always believed in attempting to complete projects before their schedule, as that can result in substantial gain to the organization and may affect the profitability more than what can be achieved by other measures to reduce costs.

Being conscious of the importance of speed and rapid response for success and profitability, the highly competitive companies put in extraordinary disciplined effort to meet demanding deadlines, to initiate and implement new strategies and projects, product launches, quality and service improvement initiatives.

In fact, rapid response and speed appeared to be the new *mantra* for survival in the competitive environment that was also mentioned by all leading companies in the IT sector like Infosys, Wipro and Satyam. These companies worked meticulously on cutting down the cycle time. Some firms in other sectors even went to the extent of stating that strategy formulation is not that crucial, as the real critical differentiator is the speed with which a firm responds to the changed environment. Speed becomes a competitive advantage because normally companies do not factor in the cost of delays in decision making and implementation. The companies that are conscious of this do not hesitate to put in extra resources for expediting completion of projects. Similarly, the first mover advantage generally gives substantial benefits in new product launches.

CONSERVATIVE FINANCIAL POLICIES; SYNERGETIC GROWTH MODELS

Most of the companies with sustained high performance followed generally conservative financial policies that helped them to generate and accumulate resources internally.

Their enormous internal resources gave them flexibility for taking new initiatives, start new ventures and have a long-term growth perspective, but also made some of them vulnerable to take-overs.

They generally maintained low financial leverage in debt-equity ratio.

Conservative and Innovative Financial Policies: Internal Resource Generation and Low Financial Leverage

Most of the companies covered in the study and those which demonstrated sustainable competitive edge had used the system of internal resources for development and growth. These companies, therefore, demonstrated low levels of debt to equity ratio. Examples of cash rich companies would be HLL, Larsen & Toubro and many others. It is true that some firms have stretched themselves a bit too much and yet have done well. Barring such examples, it is prudent cash policy which has been observed to be the strength of a large number of companies. In academic literature, excess cash reserves are considered to be only a mixed advantage, because it involves losing on interest which can be earned by the firm. Use of a retained resource is acknowledged to be an inexpensive source of funding. However, potential firms who are on the lookout for acquiring companies would be vigilant enough to see such a potential amongst these firms. Therefore, these firms will have to not only demonstrate an ability to use their resources, but also ensure that they do not become victims of being taken over by the vigilant acquirers of firms. This fact has been recognized in academic literature in the work of Marris: *"The Optimal Rate of Growth of Firms"*. In some sense it is a truism that if you over-spend for future by allocating resources, the firm would stand to lose; and if it under-spends for future, it would once again be worse off. It is difficult for us to pinpoint what exactly is that level of right balance of investments in present vis-a-vis investment in future.

Most of the firms that pursued very conservative financial policies enjoyed immense cash reserves at their disposal. A large number of them operated at very low level of debt to equity ratio. The best example of this is to be found in the case of Bajaj Automobiles, but the same is true for other companies as well. Most IT firms have a low ratio of debt to equity. For example, Wipro has very low ratio of debt to equity and is known for its very conservative financial policies. Managers are advised to use company money with the same parsimony as they would use their own money when they have to travel for official work. However, it was pointed out by some senior managers of the company that 'we have a fairly good sense in terms of where to spend our money. So it is not that we do not like to spend money, but we have a great clarity in terms of where we do it. For example, if it means organizing a strategic workshop on leadership, which may cost us 100,000 dollars, we'll do it because we think it is an important investment.'

It is equally true in the manufacturing sector of two-wheelers. Both Hero Honda Motors and Bajaj Auto Ltd have a very low ratio of debt to equity. Low leverage, however, could be an outcome of the cost of investments incurred in these sectors. For example, IT sector hardly requires any investment in fixed capital whereas in the case of automobiles (two-wheeler sector) the cost of fixed assets is high, but not prohibitively large. We may mention that academicians have addressed this problem and have come up with what constitutes an ideal level of leverage. This point deserves special attention because if having a low debt to equity ratio is desirable (assorted with superior profitability), it does not mean that not borrowing any money is the most desired act. In fact, as mentioned earlier, this ratio could be influenced by the sector to which the given product and service belong and equally much by other factors, such as the state of capital market, etc. If the capital market is very buoyant, it is easy to obtain funds from the capital market at a very low cost of capital. On the other hand, if the capital market is sluggish, the firm will have to procure funds through the sale of bonds and debentures.

The access to internal resources enabled these firms to try out new products and services and even to venture into new areas. HLL has been able to acquire a number of companies because of the ready availability of cash. Besides allowing flexibility in experimenting with newer ideas and sectors, it enables firms to acquire attractive companies in related or unrelated businesses as well. It also helps these firms to hold on for longer periods before new proposals become viable. The entry of HLL into the frozen desserts sector was partly an outcome of its cash richness, which enabled it to be in this sector, without generating profits in the initial few years. Such an alternative, obviously, would not be available to cash-deficient companies. In fact, financial institutions insisting on timely repayment of loans and interest aggravate the problem of cash deficient companies. This could force such companies to make sales of their assets in a hurry, resulting in a low level of realizable value for the same. This was definitely true for Arvind mills when it had to sell off its assets in non-core businesses to make payment of the installments of loans and interest. It is said that the same was true of Mallya group of United Breweries.

Companies which over-stretched themselves through high debt often got into serious financial difficulties. We have already referred the case of BPL earlier in which, at the corporate level, the entrepreneurs diversified into unrelated areas like telecom and soft energy and made huge investments through debt. The financial institutions also evidently encouraged such expansion for their own business interest. The result has been that BPL has a huge debt burden and with changed regulations in telecom and changes in business scenario, it was facing a serious financial crunch and problems in debt servicing.

Being a cash rich company is, however, not without some risks associated with the possibility of potential takeover by shrewd investors as stated earlier. This suggests that there is some point of most desirable level of cash availability and other liquid assets. Any move of going beyond this level would attract a possible threat of takeover by vigilant companies. This once again strengthens the theoretical work by Marris on the optimal growth rate of a firm. What do these assertions mean to practitioners: the usual common sense that you need to be cash rich, but at the same time not being so rich that some outsiders may be tempted to acquire such companies. Also, that you cannot afford to ignore the accountability of cash and other liquid assets. Any failing on this count would result in the process of mounting interest rates, sale of assets under distress, recovery of lower value for the assets – once again forcing such firms to sell their assets in larger volume.

Another point to be noted here is that some of the outstanding companies came up with highly imaginative and innovative financial policies and practices. Several companies included in this study demonstrated ingenuity and innovativeness in mobilizing and utilizing funds that kept their cost of capital and inventories low, fund flow well managed and financial health in good shape. When the rates of interest in the country were very high, companies like Reliance came up with instruments like convertible debentures, ADRs, etc. They also developed innovative revenue models to ensure better cash flow and management of funds. Companies like Hero Honda and HLL have managed to keep the cost of their working capital and inventories very low. Hero Company was following the JIT (Just-in-Time) inventory system even before their collaboration with Honda Motors. HLL's biggest businesses operate with a negative working capital supply chain, despite working in a fairly complex environment in terms of being poorly connected and spread over long distances. This is a very unique capability and expertise that the company has developed which gives it a strong competitive edge.

Synergetic Growth Models

The highly competitive companies followed pro-active as well as adaptive strategies in dealing with the changing market requirements and tapping new business opportunities. They chose synergetic growth models for which they utilized both organic (internal growth) as well as inorganic (mergers and acquisitions) approaches for growth and development.

In order to remain competitive, organizations cannot remain static. In the contemporary highly competitive environment in which technology and market changes are very rapid, they have no option but to be dynamic, growth and development oriented. The organizations that we studied were constantly pursuing opportunities by developing strategies for growth and development. Their market capitalization and rating in the industry was also judged largely by their growth and development on various parameters.

Growth and development are different and it is important to be clear about the difference between the two. *Growth is mostly quantitative, whereas development is qualitative.* Growth may be measured in terms of number of units of the same products sold, sales revenue, number of employees, branches, production units and sales outlets and profits, etc. Development is to be judged in terms of qualitative improvements, such as product development and new products launched, innovations in processes, systems and business models, development of competencies and qualitative improvement in inducting personnel in the organization, higher levels of quality, productivity, value creation and overall excellence in the organization. Probably both growth and development are required for sustaining competitiveness, but one without the other may not be sufficient.

In the biological world, excessive growth of the same kind of cells can cause cancer and often leads to problems in organizations like the 'behemoth syndrome'. That is why evolution of species requires mutation and development of more specialized organs and cells in biological entities. Mutation is believed to be a chief agent in evolution, since by such changes new species are believed to evolve; inability to mutate in a changing environment may lead to extinction of a species[10]. Development through qualitative change, therefore, like mutation, is more critical for survival of organizations and their maintaining a sustainable competitive edge.

The organic and inorganic modes of growth are well-known among organizations. The organic mode, based on growth and development from within and generally through internal resources, was evident in companies like Hero Honda, Eicher, Titan and Sundram Fasteners. These companies obtained technology through technical collaborations, or other arrangements that have been described earlier. They chose a focused strategy in their industry and mastered and developed technology through their own efforts, instead of getting into joint ventures. Hero Honda's collaboration mode is a rare, highly successful exception, which is rooted in the similarity of business values of Hero and Honda companies and the win-win philosophy of its founder Mr. B.M.L. Munjal.

Some companies, like Wipro, followed the organic model for diversification into other related and unrelated industries also. Wipro obtained, absorbed, mastered and developed technology mostly through in-house R&D in several of its businesses with the help of carefully chosen international companies, without getting into joint ventures, except in the case of GE Medical Systems, with whom they entered into such arrangement after considerable deliberations. It embarked on a strategy of entering into technological and/or marketing tie-ups with international companies. It, however, stayed away from any overall alliance with a single company. As stated by Mr. Ashok Soota, 'The last thing I want to do is surrender my independence.'[11]

So, in a nutshell, it can be inferred that Wipro as an organization has always been alive to the changing market situation and its ability to respond to change quickly and swiftly in a very nimble manner has been one of the reasons why it has been able to adjust to the changing times very quickly.

Indian companies that wanted to develop sustainable competitive edge generally chose to be internationally competitive and developed their competencies without opting for joint venture mode in which they would be giving up their managerial and financial control. This was very strongly emphasized and articulated by Mr. Suresh Krishna of Sundram Fasteners, as partly quoted earlier also: "I for one personally feel joint venture companies have got a tremendous disadvantage, that they become very dependent on the parent company or mainly foreign company to give them technology, to give them systems, to give them these things. Literally they become, I personally feel, competitively cripple. One, the dependency is too great; second, because the foreign companies also have an interest to protect the geographical turf, they don't help you to export from India. They have come mostly to capture the Indian market and there is no real interest for them to help you export, or help you earn foreign exchange..."

"The company I run, Sundram Fasteners, from day one when we started in 1966, has never had a joint venture partner. We have had to struggle on our own, in a way...All the technical improvements and R&D relating to radiator caps are done by Sundram Fasteners Ltd."

"When you become international and I have said this very often, that only 100 per cent Indian companies can become multinational company – Indian multi national company. *If you have a joint venture partner, you can never become a multinational company...You are always dependent and how can a joint venture company become an Indian MNC? It's an oxymoron statement. We have always felt right from the beginning that we have to remain 100 per cent Indian. We cannot have a joint venture partner; we cannot have collaboration, because that will defeat our entire purpose.* Eventually, my vision for Sundram Fasteners is: 'We must become an international, multinational manufacturing company". In order to do that, first of all you have to strengthen your home base, because home base has to be very-very strong."

"In 1985 we had taken a decision that we can't always depend on the domestic market...The minute you enter the international market it is a totally different game altogether. It's like night and day. And if you have a vision of becoming an international company, or if you have a vision of becoming a world competitive company, for which you need an enormous amount of drive – internal drive–then you can do a lot of things with the company to achieve that goal. But the companies, which feel that I don't have the wherewithal, I don't have the energy to do all these things, they will continue to operate in the Indian economy. They might not become internationally competitive. I have nothing against them per se. I want you to understand one thing: You take American companies. 90 per cent of the American companies are America based, they don't export and they don't go out of the country. But America itself is extremely competitive. The internal market pressures in America are so great that any time they want to get out of the country, they can compete anywhere in the world. But India is not like that. We have got two sets of companies: one set of companies which excel in India – which is not very competitive, but is becoming competitive over a period of time. You take Motorcycles, for example, or televisions/refrigerators/cell-phones. Then there is the other set of companies which, despite the protected market, have gone out and sought to compete in the international market."

"We felt that we were not growing fast enough. We felt that our company was bogging up and down with the Indian economy, which had some good years and some bad years, depending upon the monsoon. It was probably very ambitious. I wanted the company to grow faster than the Indian economy. The only way to do that was to go out of the country and try and do something. It was very hard because nobody had heard of India. India did not have a place in the world market; the Indian capability is being recognized only now in the last 6–7 years, thanks to IT, thanks to pharmaceuticals and now slowly because of manufacturing. Before that, people didn't even know that India existed as a manufacturing base. It really did not exist, because we did not have a manufacturing base which was quality conscious. Let us face it. So, we went out. It was very, very hard, because first of all you have to establish your credibility that you are not a fly-by-night operator. For a guy who is sitting 10,000 miles away, for him in India everybody is the same.

But constant chipping and getting things organized here, I think slowly, very slowly, we were able to capture the market over a period of time."

The emphasis of the Indian companies on procuring technology as against collaboration was most pronounced in the case of Reliance Industries Ltd. also, who have mentioned that they did not believe in collaboration. In other cases too the experience with foreign collaboration has not been very encouraging. The reasons for unsatisfactory outcome of collaborations could be very many, but some of the important factors that led to discard and subsequent termination of collaboration has been the incompatibility of objectives for collaboration. Foreign companies saw it as a transition strategy to get a foothold into attractive potential Indian market.

There have been many cases of incompatibility of financial strength such that after a year or so of collaboration, the foreign firm insisted upon expansion of business requiring further introduction of finances. This was beyond the ability of the Indian partner and finally resulted in the Indian partner selling its interest in the joint venture. Unequal financial strength has another implication. For example, for a large multinational organization, the earnings from the joint venture with an Indian company could be like 'pocket money', whereas for the Indian firm it could be bread and butter. This was the actual case of Infosys Technologies collaboration with a marketing organization in the US, as narrated by Mr. Dinesh of Infosys: "We grew from about 7 people to about 300–400 people in the first 10 years. Of course, our focus was always on maintaining customer satisfaction, making sure that if he is happy, you get more references from him. But we were really dependent on someone else to do the selling for us, having a company in the US, which used to sell ERP packages and we were customizing that package and selling. And then we realized in 1987 or so, that we are ready to grow, but that other company is not able to grow as much."

"Then we went in with a joint venture with a US company. We would bring in the project management expertise, technical expertise – all that is required for developing software solutions – and we thought our joint venture partner would bring the marketing and customer base and there would be a good mix of elements with a joint venture. That lasted for about 3–4 years and really we realized that in a joint venture both the partners have to bring value. If they don't, then the joint venture wouldn't succeed. From the customer point of view you have to bring in value. We were bringing value, but they were just bringing the customers. There was no other value addition. And also they were a management consulting firm, so they were about a 120–125 million dollars turnover company. In the eighties, we hardly had a few million dollars turnover. In that process, this was their pocket money and for us this was bread and butter. *You should never go with someone whose life is not dependent on the business* – that is one lesson. We learnt that very quickly.

"We wanted to grow but they were not growing, because for them something else was bringing their bread and butter, not this. We said we would own the customer directly. *And very importantly, in business, as far as possible for your core competency that you bring in, the customer should know what you are bringing and ideally it should be direct with you.* Our dream was: Yes, we will go through that and see how we can become a consulting type of company. The synergy between the two companies would be there, but that never happened. And then, around 1990–91 when liberalization started in India, we realized that we could have bigger gains, bigger dreams of making sure that we can set up our own operations outside of India. You can get money and the government was also realizing that the exports could bring in revenues for them and with that dream and opening up of (the economy) we went public in 1994 in India and raised money."

Some companies such as Eicher Motors always believed in procuring technology, rather than having a joint venture. In technology intense sectors it is always proving better to own your technology rather than depending upon others. Therefore, Eicher Motors did try to obtain technology and managed to overcome the constraints faced when some component of the technology was held back. Similar problem was faced by HEG Ltd, when it procured technology from France. Of course HEG Ltd. did manage by recruiting the retired engineers of the French company.

Many companies included in this study chose inorganic means of growth and development through acquisitions and mergers also. Companies like HLL, Reliance, Satyam, Infosys and Ranbaxy acquired companies overseas as well as in India. However, the important factor in their acquisitions was not merely growth for the sake of growth, but consolidation; access to markets, technology and expertise; and in a few cases, scale and market dominance. The acquisitions and mergers process is now being widely utilized for various purposes, such as consolidation, backward and forward integration; selective (usually related) diversification; enhancing geographical and overall coverage for market leadership; obtaining complementary resources, talent and expertise; and entering international markets. The disinvestment policy of the government has also opened opportunities for acquisitions, that has led to several large acquisitions by family owned/managed business groups like Tatas, Birlas and Reliance.

As is well-known, during the pre-liberalization period before nineties in which India's economic system and markets were highly government controlled, the system of licenses, permits and quotas helped some companies in cornering markets and licenses. There was no incentive for companies to become competitive. By and large the development of industries and markets was fragmented. 'When the liberalization programme started in the 90s, there was more elbowroom for the organizations to operate. 'HLL was one of the fastest in terms of moving into the area of mergers, acquisitions and reorganization to consolidate itself in the entire FMCG sector and in the areas where we were interested,' as Mr. G. Kapur pointed out, 'Therefore, we saw the merger of Brooke Bond Lipton and then of Brooke Bond Lipton with HLL and then finally Bond with HLL to create one HLL. Similarly we saw acquisitions of companies like Tomco, Lakme and quite a few others, because that was the opportunity and the appropriateness at that point in time. Now coming in to the late 90s and the early part of this decade when the markets have opened, the markets have become competitive. We are going through a phase where we are becoming very sharply focussed on consumers and brands, because the competitive landscape has changed and, therefore, you cannot operate in an unfocused way, both with your consumers, your categories and your brands.'

In order to develop and grow to enhance business spaces in related areas, some companies acquired other companies with specialized expertise in industries like IT and pharmaceuticals. For example, in case of Satyam, as explained by Dr. Balaji: 'We probably are the most complete, let us say, end to end IT solutions provider. While we may have to still fine tune, improve, build – that is an on going process. But in terms of occupying business spaces we have gone into end-to-end model. For example, we have looked into networking and things of that kind at one level; at infrastructure management at the other side; and to management consulting on this side. So starting from this position, we acquired a company called Saturn around that time, a small company from Chennai that later got merged into the company. Basically we got a group of professionals who were typically looking to consult, but based on IT – any management consulting leveraging IT. That is what this group was focussed on. So this company was acquired and we added wealth to it. So, if you see our objective was to give to the customer the maximum value, so that it is one stop shop and he doesn't have to shop around 10 places to get something done. So that was also thinking big.'

As stated earlier, Ranbaxy chose the internationalization route for its growth and development. It also utilized the strategic alliances, joint venture and acquisitions mode to enter into overseas markets to acquire understanding of the nature and working of the international markets, as well as to develop technical and managerial expertise to overcome the difficulties faced in developing itself as an international company. As described by Mr. Brar: "I think some of the areas in which we faced difficulties were: the Indian image in our industry was quite poor. At least today India is being linked up with knowledge based industries like IT and pharmaceuticals. The image of Indian industry, when we started venturing out, was very poor. So the Indian image and the ability of the Indian industry in pharmaceuticals industry – which was dubbed as a copy-cat or pirate industry, which pirated technologies and copied whatever was discovered – was very much there. And then the usual issues of poor quality, inconsistent quality, erratic supplies, delivery, business practices not ethical enough – all those images were what we had to fight. There were no shortcuts to that.

"We had to consistently demonstrate that we were able to overcome some of the odds that were against us. *One of the countries which taught us a lot of lessons was Malaysia, that was our second joint venture outside India in the early 80s* when we were a very inexperienced company in conducting international business. But Malaysia was like a small test market which had a very open policy. They allowed to import anything from anywhere and it was a country which demanded a lot of excellence and quality in line with the developed countries' standards. At the end it was tolerant to an extent: that it did not write you off at the slightest failure. So we had a lot of problems in adjusting to an Indian company venturing out, looking at a very small but very sophisticated market. So whether it was production, or it was quality, or it was allocating capacity for domestic versus export markets – all these were the smaller issues. But I think the mindset issues (were more serious): why should you service a small export market, the CFO would argue? Why would you service a small export market or at marginal cost to develop an international market, when there was a lucrative profitable business in a tariff protected domestic market? So these were the conflicts. Why would you lose the productive capacity for a small market? But there were many issues central to the culture of productivity. How to produce two different standards? (One for the domestic and one for international markets). In the initial years we were saying: exports versus India. But sometime down the line we said: No, we will have only one standard."

"That had another repercussion on us: the domestic market is a very tightly price controlling form of market and our overall cost of production rose in our own plants to comply with foreign guidelines, or regulatory agencies, in countries like USA, UK, Australia, South Africa, or Germany. These are very tough regulatory agencies in order to qualify for production of finished products. From here to those countries the regulatory standards are so tough that we had to upgrade almost everything: quality assurance, quality control, manufacturing equipment, people, which increased the cost of production very substantially. And we became unproductive vis-à-vis the Indian cost structure, because our domestic market was not able to bear that traffic of higher overheads. *But we decided that if we had to develop an international business, we cannot have two qualities in the same plant and that quality definitely being higher, substantially higher, we had to lift the Indian quality to the same level.* That was quite a costly experience, which bloated the structure of cost throughout the company."

"We first took the knock in our bottom-line straightaway. We said this is a knock that we have to take in the larger interest of the company. As export volumes pick-up from the overseas markets, this cost structure will become in-line and they will start bearing more and more overheads. Indian market at that time, which was 80 to 85 per cent of the total market, was bearing that cost structure. So 15 per cent was putting that pressure. So we said: As the 15 per cent became 50 per cent and beyond, this cost will even out and they will start bearing more overheads which is happening now. We had a budget presentation and our regional director who came in from London said: 'Do you know that the Europe, CIS and Africa market is contributing the maximum to your overhead recovery and much more than the Indian per unit recovery?' And he gave statistics that for the same product, how he is paying more. Also progressively we felt outsourcing for Indian market within India was a solution. So while plant capacities filled up with export orders as they came, rather than expanding capacity, we said the Indian production can be outsourced. Therefore we got double cost advantage: outsourcing only for India in line with the Indian cost structure from a third party we gained and also we released capacity for export markets more and more and the cost structure started becoming more and more even, but we went through a lot of pain."

Our discussion about the different modalities of growth and development models points to some important learnings for the Indian companies. Evidently, most of the companies chose a focused business strategy to stay close to their core competence and strengths, except a few well-known business groups. Such business groups had developed a high level of managerial, financial, entrepreneurial and leadership skills at the corporate level that they leveraged to diversify mostly into related and, in few cases unrelated, areas with a multi-business, multi-focus approach that were integrated through well articulated vision, values and passion.

We have identified the 'strategic leadership thought process' based on our observations and analysis of the orientation, processes and actions initiated by the top management to conceptualize, operate and develop the business enterprise with a sustainable competitive edge. Figure 5.2 shows the various elements in such strategic thought processes.

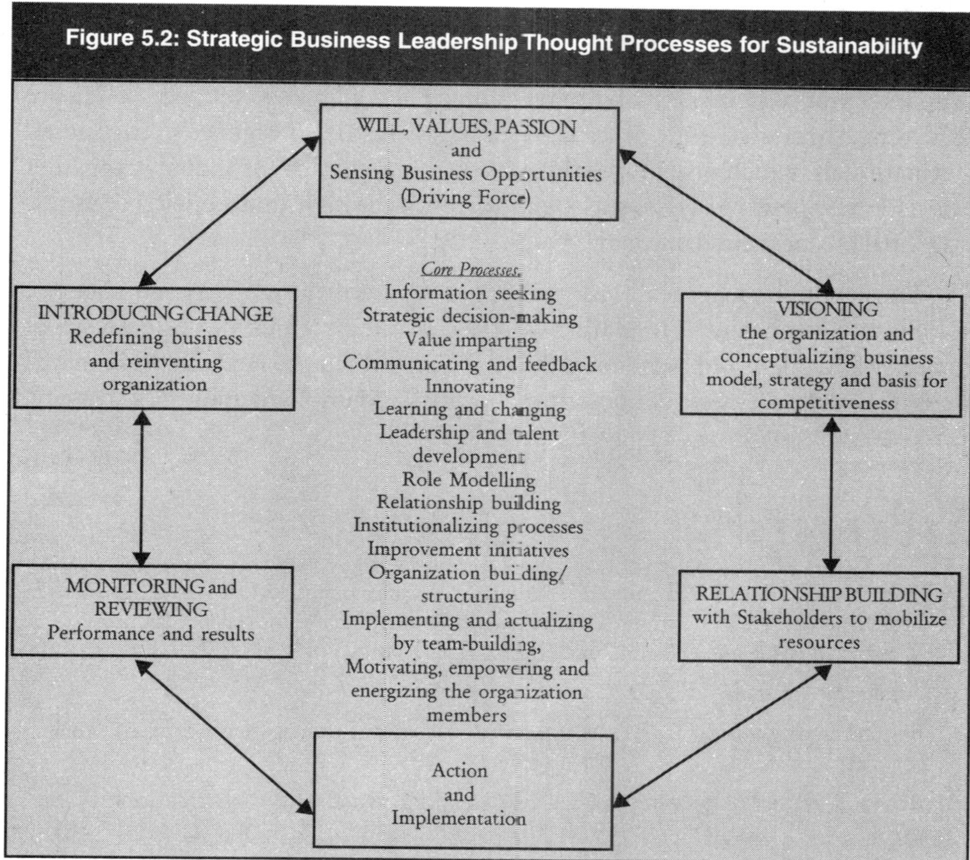

Figure 5.2: Strategic Business Leadership Thought Processes for Sustainability

It is quite clear from the above illustrations that most outstanding companies chose to avoid joint ventures and preferred different modes of alliances and other alternatives to obtain, master and develop technology on their own. They did not give up their ownership, autonomy and managerial control for growth and development.

They chose various synergetic growth models, that were organic as well as in-organic, but their primary consideration was synergy, developing competencies, value creation, consolidation and market dominance. They envisioned and pursued internationalization as one of the main routes for their growth and developing competitiveness, in spite of heavy odds against them. They chose high risk, high return strategies. They benchmarked with the best companies in the world in respect of quality, productivity, technology, R&D, managerial, organizational and people-related processes and practices. Some chose global scale and world-class technologies even though they largely operated in the domestic markets.

The overriding passion of the most admired, successful and competitive companies was to become globally recognized and admired companies. We are witnessing, through the model of these companies, the emergence of the Indian multinationals, which probably is the most viable approach for Indian companies to develop competitive edge to survive and grow in the highly challenging domestic and global business environment.

The key to the success of these companies was, however, not merely superior conceptualization and articulation of their strategies, but the effectiveness, efficiency and quality of implementation. Therefore, in the next chapter we will discuss the various aspects of operations, logistics and implementation of strategy, that constitute the 'Process Driven Execution'.

REFERENCES

1. Sumantra Ghoshal, G. Piramal, and S. Budhiraja, "Reliance Industries Ltd: Growth as a Way of Life", in *World Class in India* (New Delhi: Penguin Books, 2002); and "Reliance Industries: The Winner" in *Business Today*, Delhi, June 22, 2003 Special Issue, Vol. 12, No.12.
2. Sumantra Ghoshal, et al., *ibid. "Wipro Corporation: Balancing the Future"*.
3. Research Interview with Dr. U. Balaji, vice president – Satyam Learning Center, Satyam Computer Services Limited.
4. Robert L. Katz, *Management of the Total Enterprise*, (Englewood Cliffs N.J: Prentice Hall, Inc., 1970).
5. Sumantra Ghoshal, et.al., *Managing Radical Change*, (New Delhi: Viking, 2000), 168–172 for explanation and illustration of the concept of Value Curve. Often managers use the term Value Chain to refer to this idea, which is different, and is based on Porter's concept of Value Chain Analysis in which primary and support activities that lead to value creation are differentiated).
6. G. Hamel and C.K. Prahalad, "Strategic Intent", *Harvard Business Review*, May–June 1989, 63–76.
7. I. Nonaka and H. Takeuchi, *The Knowledge Creating Company: How Japanese Companies Create the Dynamics of Innovation*, (New York: Oxford University Press, 1995).
8. Research Interview with Mr. L. Ramnath, corporate manager – innovation and mission: quality, Wipro Limited.
9. Research interview with senior executive of Reliance Industries Limited.
10. *The Columbia Viking Desk Encyclopedia*, 2nd Edition, (New York: The Viking Press, 1960), 906.
11. Sumantra Ghoshal, et al., *World Class in India*, (New Delhi, Penguin, 2002), 409.

CHAPTER SIX

Process-Driven Execution

'Many people regard execution as detail work that's beneath the dignity of a business leader. That's wrong. To the contrary, it's a leader's most important job'

LARRY BOSSIDY AND RAM CHARAN
(EXECUTION - THE DISCIPLINE OF GETTING THINGS DONE)

IN THE LAST CHAPTER, we discussed the role of strategy in providing long lasting competitive advantage to firms. In this chapter, we will discuss the role of implementation of strategy to keep organizations in excellent shape over a long period. Highly experienced executives as well as business leaders who were interviewed for this research emphasized that implementation of strategy was more important than strategy formulation. They went on to mention that there might not be any significant difference in the strategies followed by well-established companies. Mr. Kapur of HLL[1], for instance, mentioned that the strategy of his company might not be different from that of Procter & Gamble and Coca-Cola in the USA. What is, however, important is the ability of HLL' to implement various courses of action in an effective manner involving thousands of employees. To put the importance of execution in Mr. Kapur's words:

> Outstanding execution has become a very big issue around the world. While I have spent over the last 10 years, people were very much attracted towards strategy and so on. What everyone has realized that without outstanding execution it is all worth nothing and what they have even realized is that getting the right strategy is easy but getting the outstanding execution is very difficult.

Similar views were expressed by a very senior executive of Reliance group[2] who mentioned that out of the two, strategy and implementation of strategy, if he had to choose one, based on his experience in the industry, he felt that it is effectiveness and speed in the implementation of strategy that is more important than strategy formulation. To put it in the executive's own words: "Honestly ... if you were to choose between an extremely well thought out strategy and equally excellently executed piece of work, then between the two it is 'execution', which delivers competitive advantage and not the strategy necessarily. What I have experienced in corporate life is that companies, which do well, what they think or say they will do would always score over those who say very right things but can't get the things done. Execution is the real focus. Implementation – what it does on the ground - in these companies, is therefore, which makes them really succeed. We have people, who have a fine blend either within themselves, or its complementary management teams, or as management process, which allows the complementarity to evolve across the organization. They have ultimately achieved in any of the three ways a certain unique blend between what I call thought and action, between strategy and execution. This is the real test. The amount of preparation – take any industry into account–before you launch a product, or before you offer a service commercially to your customers, or decide on a price. For it you need to do a tremendous amount of preparation behind it in terms of:

- How do you do it?
- International benchmarking, how do you configure your service?
- How do you understand the market?
- How do you segment it?
- How do you position it?
- How do you brand it?
- How do you advertise it?
- How do you deliver it?

Every step of it needs to be planned."

The book titled Execution: *The Discipline of Getting Things Done* by Larry Bossidy and Ram Charan[3] has influenced the thinking of a large number of senior executives and the above mentioned executives could have been influenced too. This book provides the rationale as to why, when everything else is in tune with the best of practices, the chosen strategy still might not work in some companies.

No doubt implementation of strategy is important, but we wish to emphasize that success in implementation would not achieve the desired results if the strategy chosen in the first place is not right. It is also true that, on the surface, a number of companies may appear to be having same/similar strategies, but a more penetrating analysis would highlight the fact that there are significant differences in their strategies: some companies could stick to just one main business, while others could achieve the same through the mechanism of subsidiary companies, concentrating on different businesses. In our view, these two are very different and need to be distinguished. The example of the first one is Ranbaxy Laboratories Ltd., while the example of the second i.e., focused strategy through subsidiary of the same company is practised by the Satyam Group, Wipro Ltd., and many others. It is obvious that managing different businesses is very different from managing similar businesses such as pharmaceuticals though it is possible to further classify pharmaceuticals into sub-businesses such as drug discovery system, drug delivery system, etc.

Also, there is a need to draw a distinction between action-oriented plan for implementation of strategy from different components of implementation of strategy[4]. For instance, in the former case it is translating the strategy into various elements, whereas in the second case it amounts to a review and discussion of different components of strategy such as organization structure, processes such as supply chain management, vendors' development, benchmarking, etc. To give an example of the first interpretation, it may be the strategy of a firm to focus on the quality of product as manifested in superior packaging and looks. A translation of this would include conversion of this into specific actions. These could include appointment of special executives to promote improvement in the looks of the product, obtaining views of the users to suggest improvements in the looks, benchmarking of different parameters along with a time frame within which these are to be achieved. For example, improvement in the appearance of the product could be expected to achieve an additional 5% share of the market. The action plan, on the other hand, would provide the time-frame within which various activities are to be completed and the assessment of the outcome recorded.

Our study revealed the following key elements in the process of execution and implementation that gave these organizations a distinct competitive edge.

1. **Institutionalized processes and systems**
2. **Attention to details**
3. **Search for talent through social networking**
4. **Operational efficiency**
5. **Benchmarking with the best organizations**
6. **Conspicuous institutional practices in key areas**

7. **Mastery, ownership and development of technology**
8. **New technologies**
9. **Less hierarchical, adaptive, flexible and evolving structures**
10. **Coordination mechanisms**

These elements and their relationships are shown in Figure 6.1.

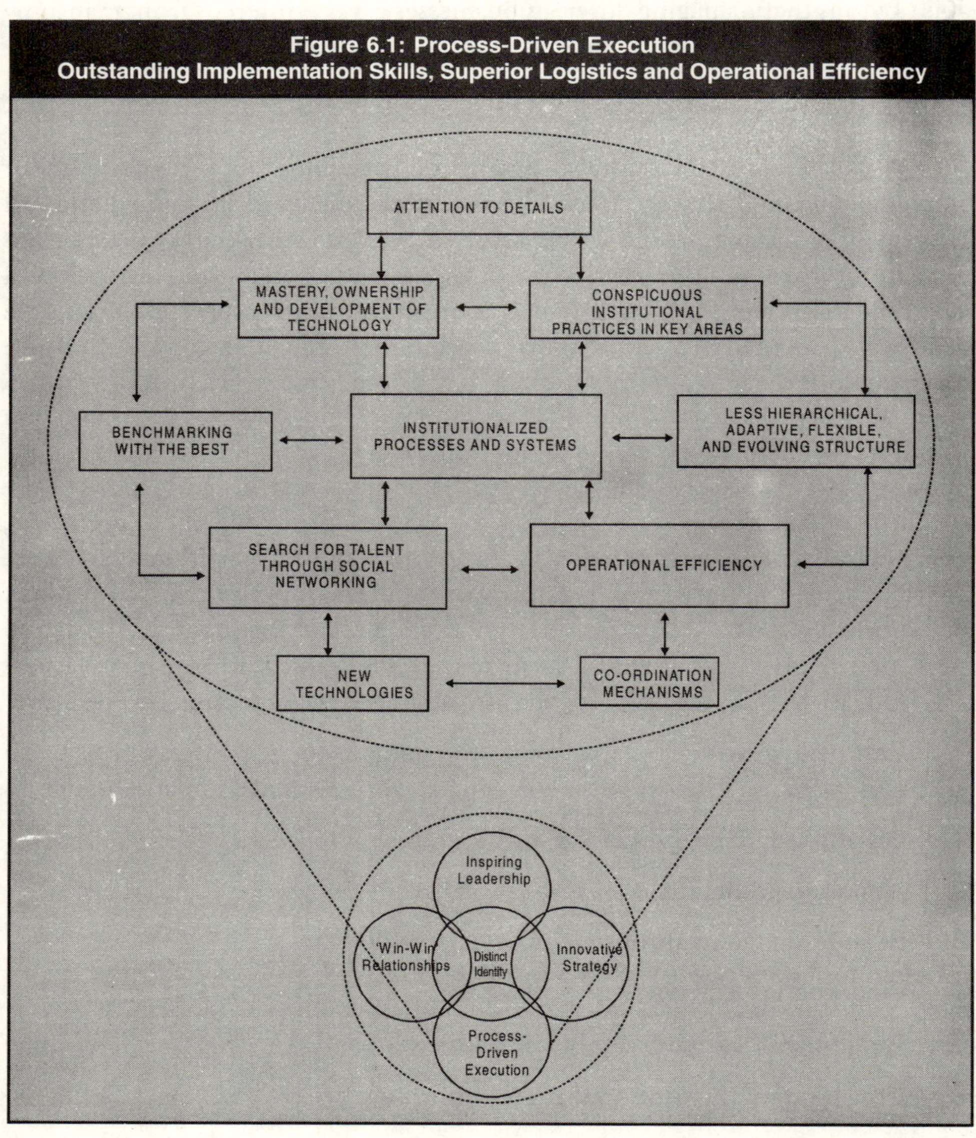

Figure 6.1: Process-Driven Execution
Outstanding Implementation Skills, Superior Logistics and Operational Efficiency

The best manifestation of the processes of decision-making, including organizational structure, is to be found in the case of Ranbaxy Laboratories and is given below[5].

There are five committees which run the business at Ranbaxy. These are:

1. Pharma Business Committee
2. New Product Selection Committee
3. Project Review Committee at the Regional Level and National Project Committee
4. Pharma Operations Committee and
5. Technology Management Committee.

The Pharma Business Committee meets four or five times a year and is responsible for all business strategies and operations and their implementation. It meets for three days every quarter of a year where one day is devoted to operational issues and two days to strategic and other important issues. Every time there is a new subject either in terms of therapeutic area or a country, it is discussed threadbare.

The New Product Selection Committee is under the corporate office and decides what a global product is. It selects the product and relevant technologies for implementation.

Project Review Committee, at the regional level, is multi-disciplinary and involves manufacturing, technology, marketing and medical regulation. It is responsible for deciding how to commercialize a product with speed in the market after it has been cleared for a country or a region. It meets every month while the NPC (National Projects Committee) meets once in four months.

Pharma Operations Committee only concerns itself with operations relating to business, such as logistics, vendor development, input sourcing. This is different from the committees which are responsible for identifying strategy for the company or identifying new markets for the company, etc.

The company has other major milestones to attain in a year such as the medium-term plans. The major term plan (MTP), which was earlier a very figure oriented exercise, is now a more directional, a more qualitative document, which is made for 1+4 years. Every year the base year is the budget for the next year. The 2002 MTP has 2002 budget as the base extrapolation is done for four years - 3,4,5,6. The meeting takes place in the month of March/April. It considers broad macro factors such as: what are the new opportunities, new directions, new challenges and new things that they can see as they sit at that time. It focuses on turnover, profit, employees and productivity. There is a discussion on new countries, country to be divested or country to be added.

Technology Management Committee manages all the technology functions of the company including environmental concerns. Latest advances in technologies are examined to see how to cut time in the development of a new drug, how to get it faster to the market, how to use IT in technology. In-house versus outsourcing challenges are also discussed three to four times a year.

The budget exercise for the company starts in September and culminates in the month of November. Each country where Ranbaxy has a base does a detailed presentation to the regional director. Prior to the budget exercise, the 6-7 countries, which form the core of Ranbaxy's business and contribute almost 75-80 per cent of the business, go through a separate management review in the host country.

The processes are equally well-defined in the case of Infosys Technologies Ltd. As Mr. Dinesh of Infosys Technologies[6] put it: 'Any firm employing 10,000 people or more can't manage employees and their needs manually. To execute that in an excellent manner, the key is the culture of recognizing merit. Then systems and processes to make sure that it is getting done in a very consistent way. We use balanced scorecard to implement and bring an alignment between the different goals that are there for the organization and move it towards one set of goals that all persons are contributing'.

According to him people join Infosys Technologies Ltd., in the beginning, in the early stage of their career, because they want to learn. Infosys provides them with that learning opportunity and spends 6-7 per cent of revenue on education and research. Another consideration is good competition, which is required and is provided through a healthy competitive environment. There is less of hierarchy. People who produce results are rewarded. Different bands of performance are created and people are recognized for their performance. The third element is 'employees stock offer plan'. The idea behind this plan is to ensure that people who have created wealth for the organization are rewarded. The company was the first, in 1994, to have introduced the first stock offer plan. Thus the company seems to be meeting the three needs of its employees very well, which are:

- Need for learning

- Emotional bonding and
- Financial security.

As a result, the attrition rate in Infosys Technologies has always been about 50-60 per cent less than the industry average over the last 10-15 years. The company has been adjudged as the best employer among multinationals and not just among Indian companies. The company recognizes that in the information technology sector, what is constant is change. Every six months the technology is changing and this consequently changes their customer's business. The company is said to be providing to its customer competitive advantage in his business through information technology by offering solutions. This requires that its employees have to learn quicker than its customers. That is achieved through knowledge management systems processes which encapsulate the knowledge.

Such processes are equally well defined in Satyam Computers[7].

Every year, business plan exercise starts in January and the process ends by February, the financial year begins. They have built multiple indices such as 'internal customer satisfaction survey' and 'assessment by external customers'.

They have two measurements: one, ECSM (External Customer Satisfaction Measurement) for external customers, and two, ICSM (Internal Customer Satisfaction Measurement) for internal customers to assess the strategic support units. They also have ISSM: Internal Surprise Satisfaction Measurement. For example how far business units were supportive in providing faculty members from business units to act as resource persons for training programmes. The quality department facilitates all internal surveys. They also have an index called Associate Delight Index based on three parameters. These are AIC where A stands for Associate, I stands for Investor and C stands for Customer. For each one of these there are measurements. For the training department, the customers are internal so ICSM is used. For other departments external survey measurement is applied. In any case, the emphasis is on measurement.

We have described the processes used in some successful organizations in the above paragraphs. These put a special challenge to the top management to ensure that these meetings are not treated as routine affairs and get the attention they deserve. It is true that frequent meetings keep the channels of communication open but could be a wasted effort if the meetings are not taken seriously. In this sense, the real challenge is on the top management to ensure that meetings are well managed both in terms of time and contributions emerging out of the deliberations of the meeting. In fact most successful organizations do ensure that they are in a position to get the views of the youngest of their members. For instance, younger executives are encouraged to express their views on various issues in the meetings at Motorola India. Though it may be a bit out of place to mention, the CEO's of learning organizations spend a lot of time in seeking information from different sources. The portion on learning organization would provide a more detailed account of such organizations.

It is interesting to note that organizations have become very flexible as regards their organization structure. For instance Unilevers, the parent company of HLL, reviews its organization–structure every three years. Other organizations are equally flexible[8].

As Mr. Kapur of HLL said: 'the process of organization structure can never be a one-time exercise. It is an on going exercise which will never finish because there is no one structure which will always be appropriate. Given the business objective of this year, we have to have the structure which is appropriate but that context will constantly be changing. Accordingly, the structure will have to be flexible enough to take the shape of the new requirement. The earlier belief that we will have an organization like this for the next 10 years is no more valid as an idea'. Organization-structuring is a constant job. For example, Unilever undertakes organization-restructuring almost every three years. They change the organization totally because they are also grappling with different issues such as global versus local, international brands versus local brands and so on. The weightage cannot be fixed forever. They are constantly changing the weightage depending on the market situation and they constantly keep evolving the structure.

EMPHASIS ON DETAILS

Most successful organizations are very particular about details and do not just gloss over various alternatives. To be more specific, CEOs of such organizations make it a point to know the technical details of various issues under discussion. The most appropriate example of this is given by Hero Honda Motors. In this case the CEO, even though not a technologist by training, understands the finer points of the technology under consideration. To put it in his own words[9]:

> You must know what you are talking about. Until you know the subject you cannot lead anybody. If you have to lead somebody you must know that aspect and that subject fully.

The knack for going into details could run counter to the perspective of the top management. This was well supported by the statement of Jack Welch of GE who mentioned that he would not be in a position to explain the technicalities, which go into the making of an aircraft engine. It is recognized that the CEOs could, and should, depend upon their specialists for detailed information, but it is essential for the CEO to understand the basics of the technology involved, the alternatives etc. In particular, emphasis has to be laid on asking critical questions in assessing the financial soundness, viability and the robustness of different alternatives. Bossidy and Ram Charan in their book titled 'Execution' have emphasized this in the chapter on 'How to Conduct a Strategy Review'[10]. It is mentioned that the review meetings are not expected to be just superficial and exchange of pleasantries but should focus on asking critical issues on which the success of the strategy depends. For example, it may be very nice to consider that a company could increase its total market share by increasing its market share in Germany by 10%. But unless this idea is supported by more detailed information as to how it is going to be achieved, the strategy does not serve any purpose. For example, continuing with the example, if it is also true that in Germany the strongest competitor of the given company is also present and it is the hometown of that company, then snatching the market share from the strongest competitor in its hometown may be extremely difficult to achieve. Details are important, but how much details ought to be gone into is a matter of judgment, which every organization will have to resolve on its own. One would not expect the CEO to become and have the same skills which are expected at the junior most level employee who does unskilled or semi-skilled jobs. Any undue weightage given to knowing very many things could lead to losing the perspective of policy formulations. However, policy formulation cannot be devoid of the understanding of activities to be carried out.

HUNT FOR TALENT THROUGH SOCIAL NETWORKING

In any learning organization operating in a knowledge intense sector, choosing the right people is the most critical element of success. In fact companies compete with each other to get the best minds available in various institutes of higher learning. Along with the formal process of identifying talent and its recruitment runs a parallel process of identifying competent people through social interaction. It could be meeting such people in different workshops, discussions, both national and international, besides such names being suggested by known persons. It is emphasized that the second category, that of a parallel system of identifying talent, is more crucial[11]. In a different context, we were told that the R.P. Goenka's group specialized in identifying people and getting their concurrence by offering them a package determined by the person to be recruited[12]. There are anecdotes indicating that the CEO asked potential executives to fill in an amount in the space provided as the pay package acceptable to them. This shows the meticulousness with which such individuals must have been identified. It also shows that the CEO has so much faith in the competence of the potential executive that no amount is considered to be unreasonable. Different individuals have different contacts (social networks) which provide the list of potential executives for the organization. An effective chief executive is able to convince such executives to join the organization.

OPERATIONAL EFFICIENCY

These organizations, often obsessively laid high emphasis on operational efficiency, productivity, total quality assurance, reduced or zero inventory, constant improvement in design, materials technology and manufacturing process. The extent of operational efficiency can be gauged from the example of Hero Honda. The company was in a position to obtain inputs at the lowest cost because of prompt payment. They would get components four times a day and the payment of the same would be made without undue delay. In this sense, the organization was practicing the technique of 'just in time' even before the concept became popular with the Japanese companies and was acclaimed by academicians in management institutions. The organization devised ways of creating their own ancillary units wherein great faith was put in the competence of youngsters. This faith has been vindicated and Hero Honda has been able to register the lowest cost of production[13]. As Mr. B.M.L. Munjal, chairman of Hero Honda, said: "We have heard the technique named 'Just-in-Time' during the last ten years or so, but we have been practising the same for the last 50 years."

According to Mr. Munjal, it is the responsibility of the company to look after the interests of its suppliers as well as vendors. Emphasizing the same, he mentioned:

> If you can manage your own things why can't you manage your own supplier? Why can't you manage your vendor? If he understands you

and he understands your language, then he understands that his existence is along with you. He makes money, he earns enough money. It's your responsibility that he makes enough money. If he does not make enough money, he will start giving you substandard goods. He will leave you and go somewhere else.

Satyam Computers have devised an unique way to remain cost competitive wherein the internal departments have notionally a possibility of buying the service from outside. To put it in Dr. U. Balaji of Satyam Computer's words[14]: "As an organization we are organized into horizontals and verticals. Horizontals are focused on technology and verticals on domains. If you look at that each unit head behaves as if he runs the business, including supporting units like HR, training centres and corporate services. Every month we have P&L, we sell our services. Our services are benchmarked against services from outside quality wise, cost wise, responsiveness wise while they have no choice except to buy from us. There is, from time to time, a review which tells us whether it was some customers' complaint, saying I can buy the same programme outside at, lets say, half the price. Why are you charging me this kind of money? We have to really examine as to why is it costing us so much money. To figure out where is the means of making it of value to the customers, we can't say that we are your seller, so buy from us– at whatever price buy from us. This is another way of creating entrepreneurship everywhere in the company".

Let us consider the case of emphasis on productivity, which has been emphasized, in a different context, earlier. The emphasis on productivity, in the case of multinationals, is already well-established. An organization like Hero Honda Motors decided to introduce more recent equipment so as to improve their level of productivity. This meant that they had to change their policy of employing as large a number of workers as possible in order to introduce automation and be cost competitive. Ranbaxy Laboratories had very specific plans of improving its level of productivity and so it decided to benchmark with global standards of productivity and found, as stated by Mr. Brar, that 'Research-based international pharmaceutical companies had huge sales per employee of $450,000 plus because of patent-protection. On the other side were extremely low priced genetic companies producing generics where the average productivity was as low as $15,000 to $ 20,000 per employee and we were at a level of $48,000 $ to $49000 at that time. Now we are close to $85,000 in 4 years. In the next 2 or 3 years we are going to be around $125,000.'[15]

The importance attached to total quality assurance could be seen from the fact that organizations such as Hero Honda believed in replacing the component even in those cases where they doubted the genuine nature of complaint. The chairman mentioned that when so many machines are being used it is possible that there could be some flaws somewhere. Besides, contradicting a customer, even when he or she is wrong, is likely to impair the image of the company.

Most firms have realized that introducing improvements in design is of utmost importance. This is despite the fact that the given model of the product may be very profitable. In this sense the firms are following a policy of creating deliberate obsolescence. This zeal to introduce new designs obviously extends to introducing new materials. One of the multinationals in FMCG sector has been responsible for substituting an inexpensive input in place of the existing one. In fact the organization tried with different variants of the combination of the existing input with the new combination. The focus on cost reduction is so pronounced that all the time the firms are on the lookout for introducing inexpensive inputs. The use of computer-aided design has resulted in the introduction of very many different shapes, colours and metals used in the design of product. In a highly competitive environment, the crux of the matter is cost competitiveness and whatever can achieve the same is being attempted.

BENCHMARKING WITH THE BEST

As mentioned earlier, some firms do not want to compare their performance with domestic firms and were eager to compete with the best at the global level. It could be informative to know that the catchword nowadays is not 'best practices' but 'next practices' indicating that it is the very best in the future which is being aimed at and not the best in the present context[16]. It is highly conjectural as well as speculative to think in terms of best practices of tomorrow and so it remains to be seen as to how the concept of next practices is going to be operationalized. It is quite possible that this idea may end up like the concept of core competence which was extremely appealing, to start with, and got the attention of the practitioners but could not live up to the expectations. Of course, it is difficult to operationalized any factor which deals with the future. But who knows, that's where the solution to the problem may lie and this specific attribute may be the chief differentiator between the good and not so good firms. One could hazard a guess about the next practices through the process of extrapolation or through the process of seeking views of experts. No doubt the technique of scenario building also provides a possible solution to the problem.

INSTITUTIONALIZED PROCESSES AND SYSTEMS

These firms develop superior, streamlined and rigorously followed institutionalized processes. For example, Ranbaxy Laboratories has a well drawn process of making decisions. The company has been divided into various committees, such as, the drug delivery committee, financial committee, committee for introduction of new drugs, etc. The time for meeting of these committee is predetermined and is rigorously followed. For example, anything relating to the dispute regarding a patent would be taken up by the regulatory committee, which is looking after drug registration. One could see a similar process in force at Infosys Technologies and Wipro Limited also. In other cases too there is extreme clarity regarding whom to look to in case of any doubt or problem. For example, in the case of Wipro Ltd, each employee is supposed to be available on e-mail in any part of the world[17]. These mails have to be responded as soon as possible. The company recognized the fact that being available for customer service, 24-hours-a-day, could have its special challenges. For example, the persons who take the call from countries such as Germany, France etc. should be in a position to understand French and German language. This shows that it may be a good idea to extend the company's operation to other countries but it brings with it its own special challenges. If the company claims that incoming calls would be kept waiting for no more than a specified duration, it introduces challenges of its own. To put it in the words of Mr. Dasgupta of Wipro Ltd.:

> you should be able to do your job from anywhere. It should not be important for you to come into office, unless you really had a meeting or something like that.
>
> In fact, at the end of a conversation, I would sometimes say, 'just send me a mail next time, because I am very regular with my mails. I make it a point to turn it around very fast. All mails are cleaned within say the next 8-10 hours definitely. If I get a mail from anywhere before the office opens in US the person would definitely get the response, that's a promise.

The processes and systems in these organizations were constantly upgraded to be in line with the best practices, the aim being to ensure better communication, information sharing, decision-making and coordination. As mentioned elsewhere, Wipro Limited went around various reputed institutes in USA to find out how to introduce a technique like six-sigma in its ideal form. This, in itself, demonstrates that companies are all the time on the lookout for improving their own benchmarks and are not content with what has been achieved in the past. The example of Wipro Limited, given in the previous paragraph, indicates that every executive would be in touch with others. Such a process ensures that the communication process is all the time active. This also implies that the company subscribes to the view that sharing information with others is the best way of involving them. In other companies, such as Eicher Motors, workers can access information about the financial position of the companies.

It is true that if individuals are told about factors on which they are going to be judged, the performance tends to improve. The CEO of Infosys Technologies has been so emphatic about laying down targets that he suggested targets to be laid in respect of projects of the government[18]. In a nutshell, such a philosophy believes in clarity regarding expectation and targets against which the performance of individuals would be measured. In cases where the tenure of the given decision maker may end sooner, it is preferable to specify targets which fall within the tenure of the given incumbent. If a project is likely to take three years for its completion whereas the term of the present incumbent is going to expire in a year's time, it is advisable to identify the stage upto which the project will reach within a year coinciding with the term of the present incumbent. Such a process ensures that the usual excuses that such and such decision was taken prior to present incumbent taking up assignments do not hold.

Another very interesting story narrated by the ex-CEO of Eicher Motors is one in which a very small company decided to divide its different knitting machines into profit centres[19]. At the end of the day the CEO would tell the employees working on these machines as to how much profit has been earned by the given sector. It was reported that employees felt so enthusiastic about the entire process that they were thrilled to know about the profit generated during the day or loss suffered.

It is obvious that when firms have a number of projects running concurrently, it is essential that the organization have information about the stage of completion of each of these projects because the resources released by some project team could be used in other projects. The possibility of use of inputs on different projects emphasizes the need for having a matrix form of organization structure. In a different context, Hamel and Prahalad emphasize the quality of coordination as one of the core competences in the case of global organizations. The success of such an organization depends upon its superior ability to coordinate businesses globally. It may come as a surprise that most small and medium firms do not have access to reliable information about the stage of completion of different projects and resources which are employed in different projects with additional information on the time by which these are going to be released. The introduction of enterprise resource planning has addressed this problem to a significant extent and yet organizations have to restructure to meet their special requirements.

The processes and systems being followed in these organizations ensured efficiency, consistency and quality in performance and alignment of activities and goals across functions, regions and various levels of the organization. It is an acknowledged fact that most organizations which do not have reliable information on availability of cash and inventory do not perform up to their potential. Standardization of procedures and processes ensures that there is consistency and the desired results are achieved. If every situation were to be treated in a different manner, it would be extremely difficult to predict the final outcome.

CONSPICUOUS INSTITUTIONAL PRACTICES IN KEY AREAS

These superior processes were specifically conspicuous in managing and developing human resources. The same was true in reviewing, analyzing and evolving strategies. The budgeting exercise is amenable to standardization and has been attempted in these organizations which also place great importance on performance management. As mentioned elsewhere, splitting the task into activities and sub-activities and associating specific targets at each point leads to improved efficiency. This was reported in the examples cited from Reliance Industries Limited and Hindustan Electro Graphite[20].

> The chairman emeritus of HEG remarked that 'when we (HEG) took the Canadian firm as consultants, I asked them "if you were doing this (project) in Canada how long will it take?" They said one year. Then why do you specify five years for us? The consultants mentioned that it is due to difference in work culture. I said nothing doing. You just prepare

the bar chart giving the details of time required for completing each activity and a comparative figure for the same with the work culture of Canada. We thought that we would take it as a challenge. We got motivated and we completed the project in two years and five months. Part of this understanding comes from exposure to dealing with foreigners. If I take my international exposure we are by now more than 50 years old.

We are sure that other companies are following similar practices. Various companies have used techniques like balanced scorecard for this purpose. These processes were distinctively effective in monitoring the progress of different projects.

Superior logistics, novel and efficient supply chain, upstream activities connected with the supply of inputs and downstream products made from the outputs have been contributing factors towards the performance of these organizations. These firms have devised unique supply chains both upstream and downstream for this purpose. In fact, most of these organizations meet annually at some leisurely place to chalk out the future course of action of the organization. Their logistics, vendor development, selective outsourcing, distribution channels give them substantial cost benefit. The outstanding distribution network, as developed by Titan, is noteworthy. It has been described in detail in chapter 5.

These organizations also demonstrated flexibility to change. But it is widely recognized that flexibility to change is not enough unless the organization knows as to what is the change required. In this context market information, competitive advantage and ability to concentrate on their major value creation functions gets significant attention. It is obvious that the market can provide information on what an organization should be doing and what the organization should not be doing. Qualitative information on these factors provides sanctity of its own but the manner in which the same has been acquired is equally crucial. For instance, which vendor is to be pulled up would be a sound decision if reliable information of their performances were available.

MASTERY, OWNERSHIP AND DEVELOPMENT OF TECHNOLOGY

Most of these process-driven firms demonstrated an understanding of technology underlying various product and services. They made a special effort to internalize the same. Their competence extended to their ability to improve and upgrade the technology. This is one area in which most Indian firms unlike the outstanding companies included in this research have not done very well. The highly competitive organizations demonstrated competence to internalize technology. It was found to be true in the case of Hero Honda Motors. Hindustan Electro Graphites also made an attempt to understand the technology and tried to fill the gaps in its own competence through recruitment of employees who retired from the transferors of technology. The most significant case is that of Reliance Industries Limited which has always believed in procuring technology rather than entering into some collaboration. In fact, they have always believed in obtaining the latest and the most efficient technology. In contrast are the companies which have not made any significant attempt to internalize technology. These include organizations such as Maruti Udyog Limited and, to a limited extent, this could be true of Hero Honda Motors too.

In contrast with the observations of the previous paragraph, there are companies which have developed world-class in-house R&D centres. The names of Ranbaxy Laboratories and Dr. Reddy's Lab come immediately to one's mind. In the IT sector too, Wipro Limited has been making an attempt to be in a position to apply the most sought after infrastructure to develop the most comprehensive software. Some of these firms also chose to obtain technology to be able to make necessary changes in the technology obtained. Such freedom would not be available if the contract was of technology collaboration.

NEW TECHNOLOGIES

These process-driven organizations also identified the power of new technologies like in IT and computer based systems and processes and incorporated these in their working to improve productivity and quality of work. It may be interesting to note that the ex-CEO of Eicher Motors mentioned that Indian IT industry has committed the same mistake of over-dependence on international market. In contrast, the firms from the old economy depended on the captive domestic market. The only difference relates to the fact that they have depended on foreign markets while other manufacturing sectors paid most attention to domestic markets. The point is very simple - The Indian IT firms develop modules of various software which are integrated by the foreign firms, and then sold to the other Indian firms with very high margins. In such a system, foreign firms appropriate most of the margins while Indian firms carry out lower-ranked jobs. Of course, organizations, like Infosys Technologies and Wipro Limited, have recognized this and are making an attempt to move up in the value chain. The real margins lie in designing the architecture of some of these softwares rather than in developing various modules and sub-modules.

LESS HIERARCHICAL, ADAPTIVE, FLEXIBLE AND EVOLVING STRUCTURE

All these organizations preferred somewhat lateral organization structure with few intermediate ladders. Such an organization structure is most appropriate where the speed in implementing the decision is crucial. Also, in knowledge based sectors such as IT and pharmaceuticals, it is important to maintain less formal relationships.

Most of the companies reviewed, evolved and adapted their structure to suit new requirements and some of these companies do it on a regular basis. For example, HLL has adopted a procedure by which an organization structure would be valid for 3 years with a possibility of introducing some change in the intermediate stage too. To put it in the words of Mr. Kapur of HLL:

> The earlier belief that we will have an organization like this for the next 10 years is no more valid as an idea. Also, the organization-structuring is a constant job. For example, if you look at Unilever, Unilever does organization-restructuring almost every 3 years; it changes the organization totally.

These companies have become more flexible, open and adaptive in their approach. It may be a difficult decision because having access to the time of senior executive could mean that the time is not available for more urgent needs. As against this, the advantage is that senior executives get access to information first hand without having to obtain it through various other individuals along with some element of distortion/noise entering into the information obtained.

COORDINATION MECHANISM

The organizations are able to coordinate activities in a manner by having teams working on various task forces, having representation of employees from other disciplines. This ensures that one gets a different perspective to a problem/issue being discussed. If all members of task force have same or similar background there might not be possibility of getting some new insights. The academic literature also suggests that a difference (diversity) in the age profile and professional profile results in superior quality of decisions made. This is definitely true for the decisions made at the higher level.

At the operational level, these companies ensured that there is swift communication, information flow, responsive decision making and quick problem solving. There may be some degree of disagreement as to the utility of making decisions in a hurry. No one would doubt the importance of looking at the various facets of a decision but there may not be any point in continuing the decision over a prolonged period of time. In every possible decision, there is the need to exercise judgment, which includes the decision and the speed with which it has to be made. It is obvious that in critical situations one cannot enjoy the freedom to continue to discuss about the problem but in more usual cases this has to be followed. Of course there could be different views on what constitutes a critical or an urgent situation. Even though it is possible to quantify such situations, at times it is preferable to leave it to the judgment of individual decision makers. If everything could be programmed, there may not be any need to have the decision makers. The robots and the machines would be able to decide the ideal course of action. It's a fairly well known preposition that what distinguishes a more competent executive from others is the ability to decide fast in the wake of alternatives available under the given situation. This has a very strong message for small and medium firms, i.e., you could understand the decisions which were made by some well-known qualified executives and yet, in the final analysis, the decision will have to be contextual because all situations may not be identical though these could be similar.

The discussion in this chapter has focused on the criticality of effective implementation, which, as we found in this research, was based on institutionalized processes for execution in the Purposeful Values-driven Enterprises. Such organizations did not follow ad-hocism in implementation. They had developed highly streamlined processes, systems and structures for getting results, and yet, they were not rigid or bureaucratic in their operations. They reviewed their structures, systems and processes, from time to time and modified them to suit the changing and emergent requirements.

Further, it became quite evident that execution of the strategy and implementation of projects through superior and efficient processes is far more critical in the contemporary and emerging highly competitive environment, than just evolving a superior strategy that may never get implemented. In fact speed of response through highly efficient execution gives a company strategic superiority in the competitive environment.

In order to develop efficient and effective operations and implementation, organizations have to depend on a network of suppliers, vendors, distributors, etc. in the increasingly network based organizations. The trend towards outsourcing of less central activities and concentrating on greater value addition activities is increasing the importance of networking with service providers. All these factors require development of effective relationships with other organizations, in addition to the usual inter-dependence of organizations on their stakeholders, with whom effective relations are important for the survival and growth of enterprise.

In the next chapter, we will discuss the 'Win-Win Relationships' paradigm that the Purposeful Values-driven Enterprises follow with their network partners and the internal and external stakeholders.

REFERENCES

1. Research Interview with Mr. Gunender Kapur, executive director – foods, HLL.
2. Research interview with the senior executive of Reliance Industries Limited.
3. Larry Bossidy and Ram Sharan, *Execution: The Discipline of Getting Things Done*, (New York: Crown Business, 2002).
4. Jauch, L.R. Gupta and Glueck W.F., *Business Policy and Strategic Analysis* (New Delhi: Frank Bros. and Company, 2003).
5. Research interview with Mr. D.S. Brar, CEO, Ranbaxy Laboratories Limited.
6. Research interview with Mr. K. Dinesh, director HR, Infosys Technologies Limited.
7. Research interview with Dr. U. Balaji, vice-president – Satyam Learning Centre, Satyam Computer Services Limited.
8. Research interview with Mr. G. Kapur, executive director – Foods, HLL.
9. Research interview with Mr. B.M.L. Munjal, chairman, Hero Honda Motors Ltd.
10. Larry Bossidy and Ramcharan, *ibid.*
11. Research interview with senior executive of Reliance Industries Limited.
12. Narrated by a very senior executive of RPG.
13. Research interview with Mr. B.M.L. Munjal, chairman, Hero Honda Motors Limited.
14. Research interview with Dr. U. Balaji, vice-president – Satyam Learning Centre, Satyam Computer Services Ltd.

15. Research interview with Mr. D.S. Brar, CEO, Ranbaxy Laboratories Ltd.
16. Prof. C.K. Prahalad during the course of his speech in Mumbai, 2003. He reiterated the same in his lecture entitled 'The Future of Competition' at Tenth Partnership Summit held at Hyderabad, 13th January 2004.
17. Research interview with Mr. Tamal Dasgupta, corporate vice-president & chief information officer, Wipro Technologies.
18. Address by Mr. Narayana Murthy, Tata Memorial Lecture 2002.
19. Research interview with Mr. Subodh Bhargava, former chairman, Eicher.
20. Research interview with Mr. L.N. Jhunjhunwala, Chairman Emeritus, L.N.J. Bhilwara Group.

CHAPTER SEVEN

'Win-Win' Relationships

'It is easier to discover a deficiency in individuals, in states, and in Providence, than to see their real import and value'

GEORG HEGEL

IN THE EARLIER CHAPTERS, we have discussed the factors, characteristics and practices identified in leadership, strategy, implementation processes, logistics and operations responsible for developing sustainable competitive edge. These are the aspects which are elaborately covered in most of the books on strategic management and leadership and are extensively based on researches, writings, concepts and frameworks developed during the last several decades. During our interviews in successful enterprises, we noted one more distinct cluster of managerial concerns and practices that has evidently not been given as much emphasis as it deserves. We have chosen to describe this cluster as 'Win-Win Relationships' that covers the external and internal relationships of an organization. It focuses on the concerns, styles, practices and the underlying philosophy of the top management to build, maintain and nurture good relationships with various external and internal stakeholders of the organization. These companies also develop a mutually supportive and synergetic network of relationships with many other organizations, institutions, persons and entities in society.

We found some of the most distinguished interviewees deeply concerned about building and maintaining mutually supportive, synergetic and satisfying relationships with various stakeholders and other relevant organizations, institutions and persons. They emphasized that the survival, growth and sustainability of the enterprise critically depended on such relationships. Surprisingly, we did not find a separate section or chapter on this subject in any of the leading textbooks on strategic management, business policy, or leadership; although there was mention and discussion of some aspects of relationships as part of other topics in the texts. There has been a greater attention, in recent times, in management literature on customer relations and earlier on industrial relations and employee relations. Considerable attention is being given to the issues of governance, transparency and accountability and larger social and environmental concerns. Attention is also being given to the supply chain and relations with vendors and distributors and other stakeholders; but the discussion seems to be more confined to the technical and economic aspects of the supply chain and stakeholders' interests and less on the relational dimension. Further, little attention is given to the underlying paradigm of such relationships that may be critical to the success or failure of the enterprise.

Arie de Gues, in his well known book *The Living Company* has, however, recognized and emphasized the importance of relationships for the survival and longevity of organizations. Responding to the question raised by himself: what gave companies the ability to change and survive instead of staring blindly at threat and opportunity, he has stated: '...it depended on all four distinctions of a living company: its adaptiveness to the outside world (learning), its character and identity (persona), its relationships with people and institutions inside and around itself (ecology) [emphasis ours] and the way it developed over time (evolution). We could see that the most accessible of these capabilities and the one which often came first, was learning. The long-lived companies were sensitive to their community and their environment. This sensitivity was not soft or driven by social responsibility, it was driven by the living company's self-interest.'[1]

Our research also points to the criticality of external and internal relationships of an organization. Following are the main points that emerged from the study that we shall elaborate further.

1. **'Win-Win' paradigm of external and internal relationships**
2. **Functional relationship with relevant business and societal entities**
3. **Concern for interest of all stakeholders**
4. **Sensitivity to the community and environmental issues**
5. **'Extended Family' like relationship with the key stakeholders**

These elements and their inter-relation are shown in Figure 7.1.

Let us now examine these propositions in the light of the interviews and other empirical evidence based on this study.

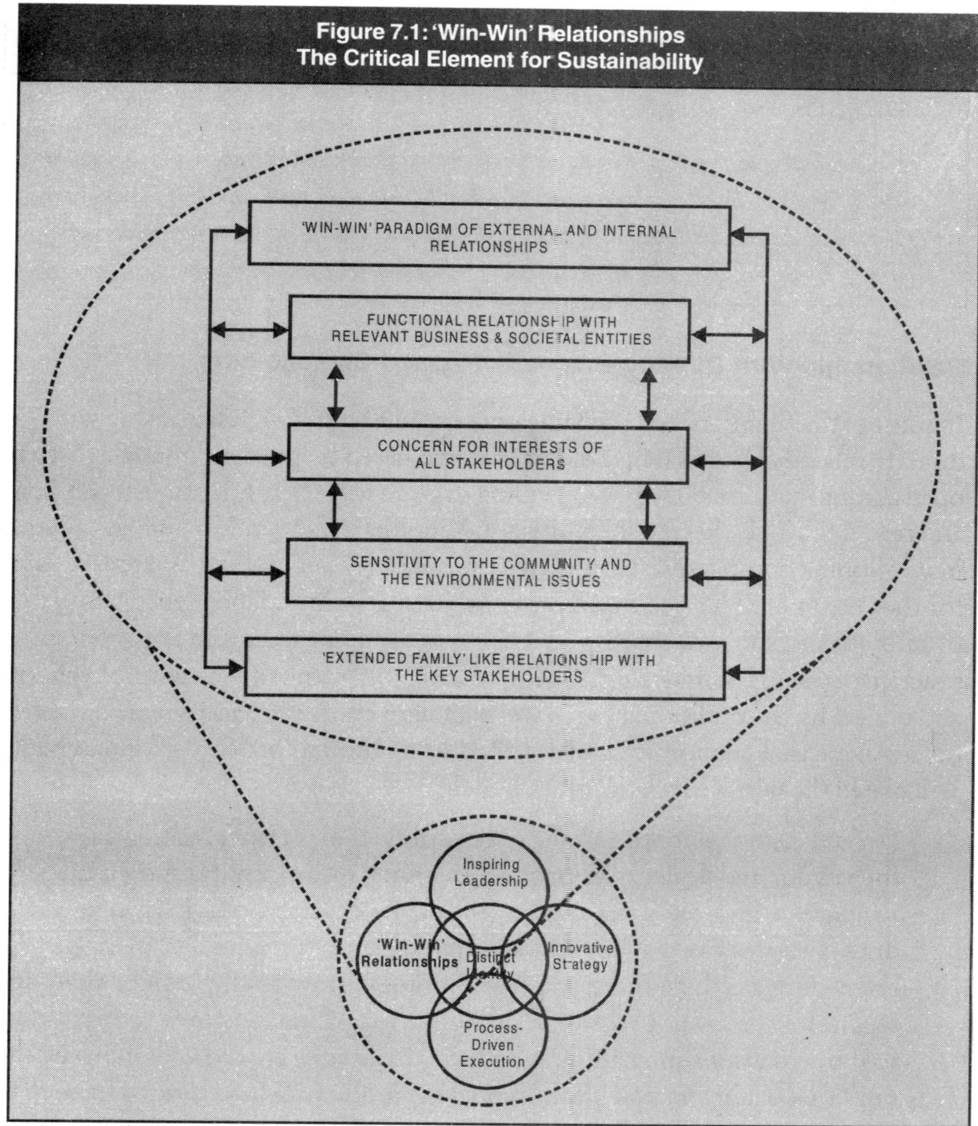

Figure 7.1: 'Win-Win' Relationships
The Critical Element for Sustainability

'WIN-WIN' PARADIGM OF EXTERNAL AND INTERNAL RELATIONSHIPS

The most distinctive characteristic of the relationships of these companies was a mutual trust and mutual gains based 'Win-Win' paradigm in relationship with the suppliers, distributors, customers, employees, shareholders and other stakeholders.

Contd....

Such a relationship was painstakingly developed and religiously guarded by prudent monitoring, sometimes summarily removing those who violated the norms, or did not come upto expected standards.

There was also evidence of positive attitude for mutually sharing the gains consistent with 'Win-Win' mindset, with a deep concern to safeguard and equitably balance the interests of different stakeholders and not only the benefit of the shareholders and controlling owners/promoters.

Relationship With Directly Business Related Stakeholders

In most of the highly rated companies, we noted a 'win-win' relationship with the directly related external stakeholders that was based on prudent mutual trust and open communications. They were willing to share helpful information, technology and resources. They helped their direct stakeholders, like vendors and distributors in developing competence to improve productivity and quality and create value for the customer. This was based on an awareness of interdependence, mutuality of interest and spirit of sharing gains. It was different from the fairly common practice of pitting vendors against each other, squeezing the margins of vendors and dealers by the traditional 'win-lose' paradigm bargaining and operating purely on a contractual economic model. Mr. B.M.L. Munjal of Hero Honda vividly articulated the win-win relationship model:

> I would insist that for the product, the quality, the customer relationships, the vendor and dealer relationships are much more important than the strategies which one draws out, or the plans one draws out. Even if you draw a strategy or a plan, you are drawing the strategies and plans of these things only. Where to get technology, how to implement that technology, how to produce it, process management and how to reach to the actual consumer? Until you have that strong chain and you have built that chain and you have devoted more attention and time to these things (you cannot achieve competitiveness). That is the little difference between us (i.e., the academicians and practitioners).

Elaborating this viewpoint, he said: "we were already practising some things that we noted in the philosophy of Honda, like the view that 'the source from where you are going to get money, ensure that they (the dealers) are better off... *Jisko dealer banao uski profitability ka zimma tum lo.* [The person whom you select as dealer, take responsibility for his profitability]. If he makes money, he earns enough money, *woh sari umer tumhare saath as friend banke rahega* [he will remain with you as a friend all his life]. Similarly treat the vendors (from whom you acquire materials and components.) This was exactly the way we were working. *Jis vendor se maal lete ho uski profitability ki zimmedari tumhari* [the vendor from whom you buy goods, his profitability is your responsibility]. Ensure that he makes enough money. If he will not make enough money, he will start giving you substandard goods. Or he will leave you and go somewhere else. *Hamare yahan itna khoobsurat vendor system hai* [we have such a beautiful vendor system] I have my doubts if anybody else here has that type of system...We saw to it that their profitability is assured. We gave them technology, we gave them tools – whatever required.

"Similarly, while selecting dealers, we spent quite a lot of time. Sometimes politicians became angry with us when we did not give dealership to the person recommended by them. We told them that it did not fit him. By pleasing you one day, I would destroy all my dealership system...We selected the right people, sorted out some. They were handled rightly. And then we make sure that they make enough money. These are certain factors which help us."

We have already described earlier a similar philosophy and practice that was followed by Ranbaxy for developing their vendors, with whom they shared technical information, provided technology and helped them to produce international quality capsules and bottles for the U.S. market instead of importing them. Mr. Brar emphasized:

> We believe, to a very considerable extent, in networking: that growth through business partners – whether it is the competitors, or it is suppliers – they are part of our business. *It is not the old paradigm that was there, that purchase man could deny information to his supplier but to squeeze him on prices. That was the old paradigm. Today we have everything open to our suppliers and say well this is what we want, this is our cost structure, this is what we would like from you and there is total transparency.* He is open to everything of the company, in terms of what we do. He becomes a partner with you.

A close relationship with the dealer network based on a mutual benefit approach was also noticed in the case of Titan and HLL. Both these companies had highly imaginative models of distribution network that have been discussed earlier also. They not only ensured profitability but also developed a strong relationship with their dealers and other 'partners' in the distribution network. This gave them a formidable competitive advantage. The novel and innovative distribution network and relationship with the dealers, painstakingly developed by Titan, was mentioned earlier and may be partly re-stated here to give an example of the win-win relationship model with the dealers and competitors: 'In distribution network I must tell you that *we have qualitatively a very different kind of network compared to most of the other companies.* We have many classes of stores. At the top of the heap is our 'World of Titan Exclusive Store', the role of that store is to project the image of the company and yet be profitable. And then we have a next rung of stores, which are multi-brand stores, but which are controlled by us, called 'Timezone'. ...*You cannot do it (i.e., develop effective relationships with dealers) merely by increasing their marginal profitability. You have to work with them,* understanding that they are multi-brand dealers. They will never be exclusive. So we have a contract with them wherein they are permitted to sell brands, which are specified by us, including the big brands, including Citizen and Timex, etc...*We ensure high returns to him from cooperative buying.* Every competitor has to come to Timezone. We offer instant access to brands across the country. So they can talk to one source.... *So everybody benefits* – the brands benefit, but for the company it is high-risk high-return (strategy). There is nothing in the contract to say that he must sell so many Titan watches...At least for the last 5 years our market share there has been higher. They (the dealers) see benefits in this cooperative (approach). They feel literally that this company has brought the customers to my store and they are strongly backing us on our side."

The above examples and statements indicate that these companies developed and nurtured a mutual trust-based relationship with a win-win paradigm with the vendors and dealers. In some cases, like in Hero Honda, they went out of the way to maintain a helpful and supportive relationship with them, even beyond the business relationship, such as helping some dealers in financial crisis unrelated to Hero Honda dealership. However, this did not mean that the company was soft and complacent towards dealers and vendors - tolerating poor performance and quality standards. In fact, it was clearly mentioned that in case any dealer or vendor did not meet the required standards of performance and quality, or violated the expected norms of business ethics, the company had ruthlessly removed him. Therefore, it may be said that they followed the policy of *prudent trust* keeping in mind enlightened self-interest and not blind trust in dealings with their business partners.

Relationship with Internal Stakeholders

The organizations whose leadership and business philosophy was based on the win-win paradigm in relation to the external stakeholders also demonstrated a similar approach in their relationships with the internal stakeholders. They treated their employees, at the operating and various technical and managerial levels and other personnel internally associated with the enterprise, as integral parts of the organization. They considered their talent, interest, satisfaction, morale, sense of belonging and pride, empowerment, development, career advancement, creativity, innovativeness and entrepreneurship as the most important factors for the growth, development, profitability and sustainability of the enterprise. We have already described earlier the people-centric policies and practices of these companies.

Many companies included in this research were highly rated among the best employers or best places to work in several studies and surveys conducted by well-known business magazines. In some more 'knowledge-based' companies, they were not called employees, like at Satyam they were called 'associates'. Even in the older and highly rated companies in the traditional industries, the attitude towards employees was to treat them as partners. As we have quoted Mr. Munjal earlier:

> So long as you treat the worker like a machine that he has worked for so many hours and produced so many units and so he can take away so much wages you cannot distinguish yourself from others (i.e., other companies). You will remain one like others. If you have to be different than others, they (the employees) have to be part of it and they will become part of it if you read them, you understand them and they read your organization and they understand your organization and they become one with it. When you will make them a part of the organization, they will put in whatever they have. They will put in much more than they can.
>
> My per man productivity in bicycle industry is the highest, in the motorcycles it is the highest. Still I pay my each worker among the highest wages. In our Daruhera plant, a worker gets about 25,000 rupees. He gets his full meal for only two rupees per day, in which he gets morning tea with something, he gets lunch and is free to take as much food as he wants and he gets evening tea with some snacks. He is the best paid man. Maruti pays much more, after that I think in the whole of *India he is among the best paid workers. But the productivity of those people is quite high,*

quite high. I don't pay them from my pocket. It is the company, it is the product which pays, it is their output which pays them.

The leadership and top management in such companies demonstrated a deep concern for creating a sense of belonging and 'ownership'- both financial and psychological, among the employees at all levels through various people-centric management practices and devices like performance related incentives, compensation system and stock options. They followed policies and practices that enhanced mutual trust and open communication with employees and sought to align them and their interests with the organization rather than alienating them. The same paradigm was followed in dealing with their organized representative bodies like the workers' unions and staff associations that led to harmonious and constructive industrial relations, as was explained by Mr. V. Amineedu of the Bharat Electronics Ltd. (BEL), a public sector organization. He gave numerous examples of a very constructive and collaborative relationship between the management and unions that had led to high levels of performance, quality improvement and creative solutions that led to the overall development of the BEL. As stated by him: "In fact we had discussions with our trade union leaders also (for meeting the challenges of change and competition). They are very much willing (to learn and cooperate). They say: let us have some workshops, let us work together to find better ways of what can be done...The trade union leaders are always with you contrary to outsiders...I think one of the reasons is that they can see that the threat to the company is impinging on them much more than on any executives. You see, executives generally feel: okay – if not this company I'll go to some other company, but a non- executive (employee) never feels like that. In reality he (executive) may not leave, but mentally he has such a feeling. But non-executive trade union leaders – they know very clearly (that they have little or no options). In fact, in all these discussions, their first concern is how to make the company vibrant – that is their first motivation. Then, of course, any trade union manager has to bring in some welfare measures, otherwise he won't exist."

"Our trade union 'managers' are very good. To give you an example of the training aspects, when I was heading our Kotdwar unit, the entire trade union leaders' group of 12-15 people were sent to MDI Gurgaon. And recently also, COD (Centre for Organization Development, Hyderabad) was organizing some programme. We have sent 5-6 people and Dr. Maheshwari (Director of COD) was telling: if you had not told anybody, they would not know whether they were trade union leaders. I mean they were talking so meaningfully. It is very important that they get to feel from the rock bottom (that they are) very useful and we have a very structured way of doing it. We have what we call as Joint Standing Council meetings, typically three to four times in a year. We call all the trade union leaders from all the units, one or two from each unit. We discuss the progress of the company: what are the achievements we have made and what are the issues – and it is a structured way in which it happens. And similarly we have apex joint meetings for officers. That also happens around three times a year...I was a technical person, of course I was heading a unit, so I knew how to deal with the people. They come and talk to me like friends. They never considered a barrier – like to be careful, don't talk much, you know, nothing of that kind – no barriers whatsoever."

In contrast with companies that base their relationships on the win-win paradigm, the companies that followed the win-lose paradigm with their stakeholders had opposite results. The consequences of following a win-lose paradigm were lack of mutual trust, absence of openness in communication and shared problem solving; it led to little effort to enhance productivity, efficiency and innovativeness. It did not create wealth through genuine customer value and increase in the size of markets. The owners made short-term gains at the cost of other stakeholders but created ill-will among them - be it customers, employees, vendors and dealers, shareholders or the community. So long as the company had a better bargaining power and the stakeholders had no options and depended on the company, the relationship continued despite discontent. The higher bargaining power of the employers was countered by legal protection to other stakeholders like total security of employed workers and militant trade unions, leading to continuation of exploitative win-lose model of relationships on the part of whoever had the higher bargaining power. No wonder the pre-liberalization phase of Indian industry was full of turbulent industrial relations and strife, scarcities, licenses and quotas, poor productivity and efficiency and ultimately exploitation of the customer. There was hardly any incentive for entrepreneurship and creating products and services of high quality and making organizations competitive.

The dominant pattern of relationship between the employers and employees in companies following the win-lose paradigm was 'master-servant' - a legacy from the feudal past. Business and creation of wealth was suspect and people trusted the government to regulate prices, quality and availability of products, leading to all kinds of distortions in the operation of the market forces and creation of inefficient monopolies. Business firms, which operated on the short-sighted 'commercial' outlook of making quick gains by hook or crook, reinforced the mistrust of public in the business community and led to more stringent controls and running of the economy by the government. That is how the 'license and permit raj' survived through licenses, permits and quotas to govern the markets and the use of legal machinery to regulate industrial relations. The overall consequence was that instead of creation of wealth through innovative, productive, efficient and competitive enterprises the country had highly protected inefficient companies that could hardly be competitive and sustainable when the heat of competition, specially global competition, was turned on with the onset of the process of liberalization, privatization and globalization and WTO requirements.

Even in the pre-liberalization phase, there were business houses and companies that did not operate on the short-sighted 'commercial' outlook of making quick gains by exploiting market inefficiencies. They were established and led by visionaries who had the 'industrial' outlook of establishing enterprises that would make human and other resources productive, utilize and develop modern technology, produce and sell high quality products and services, create wealth and employment for themselves as well as the other stakeholders and the country. Because they operated from the win-win paradigm, they did not see an inherent conflict of interest between different stakeholders and saw the point that only by following a mutually collaborative, open, supportive and 'prudent trust' based approach, more wealth can be created and shared by all equitably.

Therefore, when such companies faced problems and conflicts, they found creative, innovative and productive solutions through discussion, dialogue and, when necessary, the assertion and use of their authority, keeping in view the super-ordinate goal of long-term survival, growth and profitability of the enterprise. Their approach was not a 'soft' or weak approach. We would like to re-state the point made by Mr. Subodh Bhargava in this regard:

> The sustainable competitiveness cannot be brought in until the organization has got a sustained high quality of leadership and sustained (positive) outlook towards its people. Such outlook towards its people does not mean softness. It means motivation, it means skills, it means development, it means training, it means ownership, it means involvement, it means empowerment and all that. And governance, of course. I mean if owners are going to continue to short-change other stakeholders in whatever environment – then obviously it is not sustainable.

FUNCTIONAL RELATIONSHIP WITH RELEVANT BUSINESS AND SOCIETAL ENTITIES

Relationship with Other Stakeholders

Another important and noteworthy point is that the 'win-win paradigm', in admired enterprises, was not confined only to the relationship with vendors and dealers. It was the basic paradigm in relating to all other external stakeholders like customers, financiers, logistics providers, strategic allies, technology providers, joint-venture partners, shareholders, community and even the competitors. An example of this is the statement of Mr. Brar who said "we believe, to a very considerable extent, in networking–whether it is the competitors or it is suppliers – they are our business partners." Similarly, Mr. Munjal recalled a much earlier occasion when a competitor attempted to show down Hero Honda's product by publicizing a comparative statement of the features of their product in the newspapers. 'When that statement came to the table of my son, who having young blood, also immediately made a counter statement', remembered Mr. Munjal, 'I took the statement, tore it off and threw it away. I said, Son, tomorrow they will issue a second statement and then third and then fourth statement. If you keep giving counter statements, the fifth statement will also come. It is better you keep quiet. At best they will give one more statement. Your performance should speak, not this paper. And how many people will read the paper. It is not necessary that your customer reads that paper. You try to prove from the product – your product should speak! Similarly some other competitors engage in competitive advertising, like once along with my marketing team I had gone to Lucknow. Perhaps our competitors knew this, so they had given an ad in Hindi with the heading: *'dekhte hein kisme kitna dum hai'* [let us see who is the stronger one!]. We did not take even a second to bother about it. We spent several hours with our dealers and fully prepared them with emphasis on the product. We keep our focus and emphasis on the product and product performance, heavy emphasis on education and relationships.'

The top management of the most admired companies highlighted the importance of maintaining cordial and supportive relationships not only with the stakeholders identified in textbooks, but also with other influential and interdependent institutions and individuals in the society and a genuine concern for the larger community and environmental issues to safeguard the long-term interest of the organization and business. Sharing his insights based on long experience of running his business against all odds in the highly restrictive and controlled business environment as well as in the emerging fiercely competitive liberal environment and yet making it a highly successful and one of the most admired companies, Mr. Munjal said: "In fact a very important role in the success of our companies was that we could get the best of the technology company: Honda. There is no one better than Honda in the world in two-wheeler technology. In the four-wheeler technology also, in India, nobody can match very well with them. Then good man management, money management, materials management, customer relationship, like CRM etc. – the words that are being talked about today. We have been hearing the term 'JIT' (Just-in-Time) for the last ten years, we have been practicing it for the last fifty years. In our cycle factory, during the last forty years, we never saw more than two to four days' materials inventory and that too for items coming from other cities. Otherwise from the local suppliers the incoming material would come at 8 am, 11 am, 3 pm and 5 pm and is utilized the same day. Similarly, here in Hero Honda Auto company our material comes three or four times a day and by the evening it is all finished."

"If you can manage your own things, why can't you manage your own supplier, why can't you manage your vendor. If he is on the same plateau, he understands you, he understands your language, he understands that his existence is along with you. That was the biggest strength which we possessed why Honda decided in our favour. Name any big house in this country who hadn't talked to Honda. Yet they decided in our favour. They went into details and they studied (and found that) it was exactly the same way of working like we work here, as they were working there. In fact it was a beautiful coincidence that in the year when they came here, for some reason, I placed before them our company's brochure and they placed their company's brochure and the mission statement of their company was by its side. Except for the difference of a few words here and there because of the Japanese language, otherwise it was exactly the same (as ours). Right from day one, the idea was to give full value of the money to the customer, without having before you a very ambitious profitability factor. Profitability has been always behind us and it has followed us so seriously because we have left that behind. Try to satisfy both."

"There are many stakeholders in one's business... You cannot imagine, the stakeholders mentioned in your books are very few. You would have never written in the books that the message of the deputy commissioner will come, or that message of the labour commisssioner's person will come. I just now received a letter from the Deputy Industry Centre that I came to your office and your staff did not talk to me properly, beyond that you have to deal with many many variety of people... It is possible to handle such things if you have kept your requirements behind you. If you always keep your needs as primary and to the needs of others give them less importance then you can't do anything. If you have kept on giving importance to the needs of the other's first (you will be successful)."

"This was also my personal philosophy, but when we were having a dialogue with Hero Honda, they had stated some very beautiful things, which we had already implemented and were part of our life. On hearing such statements from them we realized how some people in the world have made progress. They said: 'Wherever you establish a factory, ensure that the water coming out of the waste-water treatment plant should not at all spoil an inch of anybody's land. The smoke that comes out of your factory should not at all spoil the environment'."

Such experience-based, pragmatic assessment of the socio-economic-political-technological realities, blended with a 'win-win' business philosophy towards the internal and external stakeholders, as well as with the other interdependent societal interfaces is very different from the conventional self-centered commercial outlook generally attributed to businessmen. We noted a fairly similar outlook among other leading companies towards external stakeholders. The top management of these companies cultivated and maintained a cordial, constructive and healthy relationship with the external stakeholders and other important persons and institutions in business and society.

CONCERN FOR INTERESTS OF ALL STAKEHOLDERS

Equitable Sharing of Gains with the Key Stakeholders

The relationship with *other key stakeholders* like the shareholders and other resource providers, like the financiers, also worked better if it was based on the win-win paradigm. Companies in which the controlling owners look after only their own interest and do lip-service to other stakeholders, are not sustainable. It is not unusual to find companies in which the controlling owners care little for the interest of all shareholders and others who have invested their funds and savings with them. They often try to satisfy them only by making hollow promises and just giving token gifts and packages of sweets at the annual general meetings. They focus on protecting their own gains, instead of enhancing the competence and competitiveness of the company and improving profitability of the business to give a good return to all shareholders and investors on their investment and protecting and enhancing the worth of their equity.

On the other hand, companies that follow the philosophy of protecting the interests and sharing the gains equitably with all other stakeholders demonstrate a high level of resilience and ability to survive. This viewpoint was held and shared by many companies included in the study. Mr. Bhaskar Bhatt of Titan articulated an example of this philosophy:

> We are adapting ourselves, but constantly changing to *ensure equitable returns to all stakeholders.* That is one principle on which the entire Tata group works and I suppose most companies would. All stakeholders include shareholders, employees, the people whom we buy from, the people whom we sell through and, of course, the most important: that is the customer; and the community that you serve. Equitable, but not equal – which is, at certain points, we have done well with our factory employees. We pay them the best salaries in that area, wages in that area, which was a conscious decision we took that we would improve the quality of life of our employees. Now, to an extent, it may have come out of the shareholders' pocket. We could have probably paid them, but it is a principle, a philosophy. We have been able to maintain that principle and stand by that, live by that principle for the first 15 years certainly. We have a very strong work force, which is extremely satisfied and happy. We have a very satisfied customer base, we have a very satisfied reseller base: which is our distributors, dealers and franchisees. We have a set of vendors who are very happy to work with us. Our shareholders may not be so happy – I mean they would expect probably from a company of the stature of Titan, much better returns. We have been profitable from year one, so they probably expect better returns. So I would say we have sustained our ability to compete in the market place and generate surplus to be able to distribute it equitably among all our stakeholders.
>
> Competitiveness is a subset of the need for an organization to create wealth. You should be able to create wealth and prosperity. You should be able to reinvest, in everything – reinvest for growth. You should

grow. Now, if you have to create wealth, you have to be competitive, because you are operating in the market place. And how you create that competitive edge is a combination of marketing, manufacturing, financing - whatever, those are the functional drivers of competitive edge. *But overall, at a philosophical level, you are creating wealth for the nation. If you have to be able to do that, then you have to have a competitive position.*

Reliance's extraordinary efforts to ensure good returns and high market valuation for the benefit of the shareholders is well known. We noted a similar concern among most of the leading companies included in the study.

The underlying 'win-win' paradigm of external and internal relationships and the philosophy of equitable sharing of gains with them was noted by us in most of the outstanding companies like Ranbaxy, Tata Sons, HLL, Wipro, Infosys and, with shades of difference, in almost all the other companies included in this study. The companies that deviated from the win-win paradigm fell into the trap of win-lose paradigm and started short-changing their stakeholders thus ending up with difficulties.

SENSITIVITY TO THE COMMUNITY AND ENVIRONMENTAL ISSUES

As we know, the corporate world is in turmoil all over the globe because of corporate governance issues triggered by events like the Enron meltdown. Similarly, problems keep arising because of lack of sensitivity on the part of companies to the community and environmental issues that damage the goodwill of the community towards the business world in general and the concerned company in particular. The fundamental point is that business enterprises exist as economic organs of society and unless they establish a mutually supportive and beneficial relationship – rather than a predatory relationship – with the society and the natural environment that supports the society, their existence is not sustainable - if not in the short run, certainly not in the long run. This point was well recognized and understood by the companies that demonstrated sustainability over long spans of time.

Some examples of sensitivity of the company to the community and environmental issues and its belief and practice of certain positive values for this purpose have already been given above, as in the case of Hero Honda to protect the environment around its factories. As stated earlier in the context of leadership,

Mr. Gopalakrishnan, citing the case of Hindustan Lever, gave a more vivid example of concern for the larger community and national issues. He said:

> HLL has always been in the forefront of thought leadership in the country, making suggestions which are within their area of knowledge: like how can the country become self-sufficient in oil-genfacts, like how retailing can create more jobs in the country, or how the trading system in the country of the little shops and the big shops can bring prosperity to the people. You know, these are all the areas where HLL has significant experience, like rural marketing. And they use that experience to throw light on some facets of national significance. So those are very positive things.

Mr. Gunender Kapur expressed similar views about HLL's orientation in relating to the larger issues and basic values that guide the company:

> Ours (HLL) is a company which is fairly big in terms of its scales and operations. In our history we have actually been able to bring about a very sharp focus on what was appropriate at that point of time. For example, in the late 70s and the early 80s, when the competitive issues were significantly lesser and the licensing issues were significantly more, there was a very sharp focus within the company on creating huge distribution efficiencies. At that point in time the name of the game was distribution. The name of the game was reaching every shop in the country and ensuring equitable distribution, engaging the *government into our thoughts and our proposals, which could create a positive benefit for the society and for the company.* The entire starting of the Integrated Rural Development Programme, the entire focus on research and technology to cut down the country's import bill and then link it into the company's business. So that was indeed the entire set of focus and I think through the decade, we really probed efficiencies in manufacturing, efficiencies in distribution, research capabilities and technology capabilities, specifically aimed at finding local substitutes for imports – import substitution. Now, if you get into the 90s (the first phase of 90s) when the liberalization programme really started and there was more elbow room for the organizations to operate, I think HLL probably was the fastest in terms of moving into the area of mergers, acquisitions and reorganization to really consolidate itself in the entire FMCG sector and in the areas where we were interested in.

The subject of corporate governance has acquired great importance in recent times. The quality of corporate governance has a direct bearing on the stakeholders, community and environment, as well as on the sustainability of the enterprise itself. Underlying the quality of governance is the basic paradigm of relationships that we have been discussing in this section. Articulating the significance of such a paradigm for corporate governance, Mr. Subodh Bhargava said:

> "If you say: competitiveness, sustainability – if you take these parameters, there is only one word which is common in all three (input, value addition and output, that lead to creation of value for the customer and sustainability of competitiveness): i.e., governance, *quality of governance.* Governance, to my mind, comes from leadership. So sustainable competitiveness cannot be brought in until the organization has got a sustained high quality of leadership and sustained outlook towards its people. And such outlook towards its people does not mean softness – it means motivation, it means skills, it means development, it means training, it means ownership, it means involvement, it means empowerment and all that. And governance, of course."

Emphasizing the importance of taking care of stakeholders' interest, he said:

> I mean *if owners are going to continue to short-change other stakeholders in whatever environment, then obviously it is not sustainable.* On the other side, if the leadership of the country is not going to invest and do the right things on infrastructure and to other policies, the unit level or industry level or country level competitiveness will not come. Just as the company builds its brand, the country needs to build a brand. And country cannot build a brand on technology alone. Country cannot build a brand because it has reached the moon. Its brand has got many other attributes which the global consumer sees: from reliability, to values, to everything else. And reliability reflects quality of governance and sustainability, or stability and whatever – everything else. So this is a very macro envelope sort of thing.

There is a growing realization in the corporate sector of the need to pro-actively take initiative in societal and environmental issues that develop goodwill for them in the community, as well as protect the environment and improve the quality of life and well being of the people in the community. Such a realization is indicative of the awareness that the business organization survives in a web of interdependent, healthy and mutually supportive relationships with a host of stakeholders outside and inside the organization. If these relationships are based on a 'win-win' paradigm, they lead to a more sustainable wealth creating and sharing, *generative* model of business enterprise in relation to its total environment; and if it is based on a tacit 'win-lose' model of short sighted zero-sum paradigm, it becomes *predatory* in nature and is difficult to sustain in the long run.

'EXTENDED FAMILY' LIKE RELATIONSHIP WITH THE KEY STAKEHOLDERS

The underlying ethos of relationships with the key stakeholders in most of the outstanding organizations appeared like an 'extended family' that included the employees, suppliers, distributors and shareholders.

One of the most striking features that we noted in most of the outstanding Indian organizations in the study was the 'extended family' ethos in the philosophy and style of management. Extended family ethos means that the top management viewed the organization and its members as part of an extended family, they related to them as if they were members of the family. They used the language, actions and other behavioural cues that reflected a family relationship and environment and utilized the family metaphor on collective occasions. The key point in this ethos was to feel, think and act as a member of the family, keeping in mind that the interest of the family is uppermost and not as paid employees who work merely for remuneration. Relationships in an ideal family are based on love, care, respect and giving; unlike the contractual relationship of bargaining and taking out the maximum from the other party in the deal. Being a country with one of the oldest living civilizations with very strong family traditions, it is not surprising that the family ethos becomes a paradigm of relationships in the work organization also.

If we were to identify the generalized unique character of the 'Indian management', as compared to the dominantly individualistic competitive Western management and Japanese collectivist consensual management, we would say that Indian management is family based and *karta* (head of the joint family - authority figure) dependent.

The 'family feeling' was reinforced on many collective occasions such as annual days, training programmes, informal get-togethers, etc. in which the chairman down to the shop-floor workers participate along with their families. The key members of the top management would participate in the weddings and other family related events of joy and sorrow of the employees, dealers and vendors. They would know many of them personally and by name. They would help them financially and in other possible ways in difficult situations just as they would help their own family members. Some elderly managers would address the young employees as members of family like: *beta, bhaiya, behen, beti* ['son', 'brother', 'sister', 'daughter'] and the younger persons would address the elders as: 'uncle', or *dada* ['elder brother']. In some cases they would utilize the local dialect of the employees, depending on the place they come from, to develop a rapport and affinity with them. In some traditional organizations, the members of such 'extended family' - including dealers, vendors and employees-would go the extent of showing regard and respect to the authority figures and elders on special occasions by symbolically bowing and touching their feet or knees, specially the very senior persons like the founder chairman. The following narrative from the founder chairman of Hero Honda illustrates such ethos.

> *Hum yahan bade different course karate rahte hain logon ko, jaise Adventure and Attitudes.* [we conduct various kinds of courses here for people like our dealers, such as adventure and attitudes]. It has nothing to do with marketing, nothing to do with dealer trend. Many dealers had come and I don't miss an opportunity where there are 10 or 20 dealers of the company. I go and meet them personally...My younger brother, who takes care of the bicycle plant – there he has dealers in thousands – but he would be knowing most of the dealer's friends and most of the dealer's families by name and would have been attending marriages in those families and would have been with them in time of griefs, time of dire necessity and help them in case of need.
>
> I have initiated some very unusual kind of educational programmes for our workers' families. We have a very young work force, the average age of our factory workers would be around 23 or 24 years. Most of them are newly married, ...so we conduct a course for the workers' wives in batches of 25 ladies. First, they need to realize that they are a person in their own right. They need to know that their husband is working at the right place, doing the right job and that they also need to give support to him. They must also acquire knowledge for their personal development. Then a few lectures on house keeping, stitching, etc. are also given.

Some sessions on meditation are also held. It is, three-day programme organized by my daughter in law, but I go myself to address them. She takes care of this education centre and the hospital, Raman Munjal Vidya Mandir and Raman Munjal Hospital, built in memory of my son who died at a young age and, who within a short span of his life, made remarkable contributions to the development of our factories and the vendor network, for which he encouraged about 20 of his classmates and friends who were members of a club founded by him, to set up factories. Each one of them is a successful businessman today.

Like the programme for their wives, for the workers also, in addition to technical training about the working of machines, etc. they are also made aware how they can develop their character, moral development and health... Similarly, we do programmes for our dealers, who come in batches of about 20 and spend four nights together. They learn a great deal from each other about the best and most effective practices and exchange notes on practical tips...but more than that, instead of giving training to tell how to sell, how to manage money, if you have clarity about yourself, about being a good human being, you will not do anything wrong. *Aap Ulte raste nahin chalenge* [You will not go on the wrong path]. This is how we keep developing people.

Consistent with the joint family ethos of Indian culture, often the head of some of the traditional organizations is treated like the karta [elder head of the joint family]. The respect and deference shown to him is sometimes unbelievable to people coming from other countries. Mr. Munjal narrated one of his personal experiences that dramatically demonstrates such ethos:

Pichle do saal pehle ek Honda ke president aaye. Hamne Ashoka hotel ke hall mein piche function rakha tha. Bada sa launch karna tha product ko, toh saare dealers aaye hue the. All over India meet bhi saath rakhi thi, toh saare aaye hue the. Sabko unhone lobby mein khada kar diya. Udhar andhera kiya hua tha ki jab president aur Brij Mohan saab aayenge, aur jab woh andar aayenge to achanak lights kholenge. Aap unke peeche aayenge. 11 baje ka time tha, puray 10 baj ke 55 minute par mein aur president gate par aa gaye Ashoka ke, jahaan hall se andar ghuse and you will be shocked to know that hum 11.25 minute tak hum uss gate tak nahin pahunch paye. Each dealer wanted to touch your feet, ghutne ko haath lagana, aur woh president moo dekhta hi rah gaya. Bola hum bhi aisa karte hain, but I am astonished to see that kahin joh dealer aatvi row mein depth mein khada hai woh bhi haath lagana chahta hai, tab jaake aage jaane dega. Toh 11.25 minute per hum andar pahunche. Balki jab koi haath lagana chahta hai toh mein do kadam peeche bhagta hoon and I have never, never allowed (people to touch my feet). Maine apni bahurani ko bhi nahin kaha ki paer chhoo. But it happens, woh feeling andar se aati hai. But to create that environment, you have to create that image for yourself. Agar aapki image mein khud hi woh surakh hai dikhave se toh koi bhi nahin karega; ek dafa kar dega, do dafa kar dega, andar se nahin karega. Andar se toh jab aapne uski economic care kar li, aapne uski sentimental aur psychological care kar li, baaki koi zaroorat nahin hai.

Hamare kai saare dealer hain unke naam ke saath likha jaane laga hai jaise Om Prakash Singh Badal, unke naam ke saath likha jaane lag gaya hai 'Mr. Baldevraj Hero Honda'. And Hero Honda ke ek dealer ne Hero Honda ke doosre dealer ke ladke ladkiyon ki shaadiyan aapas mein kareen, itni close relationship ho gayi hai.

[About two years ago, the President of Honda came here. We had arranged the function in Ashoka Hotel. We had to do a major product launch, therefore all the dealers had come. We also had the all India meet alongwith it, so all of them were there. All the dealers had been assembled in the lobby and lights were put off. The lights were to be put on to give a surprise when the President of Honda would enter and I was to follow him. The time for the function was 11 am and the President of Honda and I arrived at the gate of the lobby sharp at 10.55 am. You will be shocked to know that when we entered the gate, we could not reach the hall until 11.25 am. Each dealer wanted to touch your feet, or touch the knee. The President was astonished. He said: we also have similar events, but I am astonished to see that the dealer who is standing deep in the eighth row wants to touch you and would not let you proceed until he touches you. I have never, never allowed people to touch my feet. Rather when somebody wants his hands to touch, I withdraw back. I did not even ask my daughter-in-law to touch the feet. But it happens. It comes from within. But to create that environment, you have to create that image for yourself. If there are gaps in you image by false pretensions, then nobody will do it; he may do it once, he may do it twice, but he will not do it from his inner feeling. From one's internal feeling he will do so if you have taken care of his economic need, cared for his sentimental and psychological need - then you need not do anything else.

> There are many of our dealers who have added the surname of Hero Honda to their name. Just as there is the name like 'Prakash Singh Badal', so they will write their name like 'Mr. Baldeveraj Hero Honda'. And some dealers have even married their sons and daughters with those of their fellow dealers - such close relationships have developed among them.]

A somewhat westernized version of family ethos was also evident in the relatively new Indian organizations like Infosys. Members of the organization called themselves Infoscions and would often meet each other in family like get-togethers and take great pride in belonging to the family of Infoscions. Similar get-togethers and a family like atmosphere on similar occasions was described in companies like Satyam and Ranbaxy.

In organizations where the extended-family paradigm was genuinely and sincerely practised by the top management and leaders across the organization, it worked very well in creating a sense of belonging, pride, involvement, ownership and commitment to the organization among the employees and other members related to the organization. If, however, the family metaphor was used as a facade behind which the owner family pursued primarily its own self interest – without caring for the interest of the other stakeholders-it backfired and led to alienation, hostility and frustration among the employees and other stakeholders, leading to decline and fall of the organization.

Relationships Within the Members of the Business Family

Another set of relationships that are most sensitive and critical for the sustainability of the business enterprise is among the key family members in the family-owned business enterprises. A healthy win-win paradigm based relationship among them provided great strength to the organizations managed by them, as can be noted from the cases cited above. Contrarily, many renowned and successful business enterprises have suffered heavily when the relationships among the key members became strained and disruptive. In this connection, Mr. Subodh Bhargava made some highly perceptive observations: "Let me share another theory of mine: Managing family business is actually a function of managing the family. The problem is managing the family; it is never managing the family business. So people need solutions to managing the family. More problems have risen in managing the family."

"Where the family has not had an issue of managing itself, the decisions are by and large positive: there is synergy, energy, it goes up. But family, apart from emotions and sentiments, brings in immense biases...You know the standard theory is that the first generation creates, like Dhirubhai Ambani did and the second generation builds -which Mukesh and Anil and similar others are doing. The third one causes the decline and the fourth one disintegrates. And if they don't do that, the industry will. Before disintegration they start the divide. If you look at ...any family, this model is true. The third generation decline is inevitable because of the number of layers, plus complacency of the third generation. The third generation, youngsters, tend to be spoiled. Second one still takes up the challenge. The first one had the enterprise. Third ones fight amongst themselves. And second one – all the gains, that becomes the problem. Family problem always comes and trust always gets betrayed either on account of plenty, or on account of too many. Fourth generation then breaks up. (In some well known business families) instead of allowing disintegration, they have done neat and clean divisions and now they are all on their own. And they have to labour, each one on their own now. I would say separating businesses into different families is a better solution then to try keep it together artificially, with all the other problems that arise. And this comes to role clarity; this comes to quality of leadership; this comes to single command. If, in the family, there are multiple commands, there is lack of trust. Because if everyone has access to the till, then who took out the silver – nobody knows. And the people down the line exploit; the professionals exploit family differences to the greatest extent for their personal benefit and personal space they create. They play one against the other."

"There are some family owners who are more professional than anyone else, more knowledgeable and are able to bring in that courage and boldness to take decisions minus the emotions and sentiments...And it has got that greatest advantage of enterprise, vision, drive. The family ownership is a good thing to my mind, rather than a baseless ownership. But then the handicaps are many, apart from the quality of management, the growth – unless the business is growing you are unable to take opportunities. Personal wealth as equity stakes is limited, ultimately. How much would you want to do it. Others are growing faster because they have got thousand people giving their wealth into this. So there are pros and cons. I don't think there is an absolute answer – this or that. Both models are workable."

"In India, firstly, professional management is working under some ownership. There is some promoter who calls the shots. He has the privilege of sacking professionals. Actually the greatest problem of business in India is that we don't have an exit policy for the owners and we need one as well for the blue collar workers. The second dimension is that in US, or in mature economies, mature corporate structures, boards have sacked chief executives, or they indict others much more liberally than what we have done. In India we have the lifetime protective employment."

As can be noted in the above analysis, the real issue in family relationships is mutual trust and basic paradigm: whether it is win-win, or win-lose. The family enterprise begins with relationships based on win-win paradigm. With the passage of time and change of generations, the interests of different descendents and members begin to clash as soon as they tacitly perceive the business from a win-lose perspective. And a zero-sum view of business leads to a narrow and limited view of the opportunities, leading to serious conflicts and differences, if the problem is not structurally resolved as suggested above.

To sum up, the key to sustainability of business organizations is not only leadership, strategy and execution, but also the quality of its external and internal relationships. If these relationships are based on win-win paradigm, prudent trust, equitable sharing of gains, safeguarding interest of all stakeholders and sensitivity to the societal and environmental issues, then the long-term enlightened self-interest of the enterprise is safeguarded. The business enterprise becomes a value and wealth-creating organ of the society that enhances the opportunities and well being of the people and development of the society, rather than a predatory organism that siphons off wealth and destroys the resources.

Having examined the four important clusters of characteristics, viz. Inspiring Leadership, Innovative Strategy, Process-driven Execution and 'Win-Win' Relationships, that are shown as peripheral circles in the figure depicting the model of the Purposeful Values-driven Enterprise, we will now examine its core: the Distinct Identity - Purpose, Values and Culture, in the next chapter.

REFERENCE

1. Arie de Gues, *The Living Company,* (London: Nicholas Brealey Publishing, 1999), 32.

CHAPTER EIGHT

Distinct Identity

Purpose, Values and Culture

'Visionary companies display a powerful drive for progress that enables them to change and adapt without compromising their cherished core ideals'

JAMES C. COLLINS AND JERRY I. PORRAS
(BUILT TO LAST)

SO FAR WE HAVE examined key factors like Inspirational Leadership, Innovative Strategies, Process Based Execution and Win-Win Relationships, with all stakeholders and the specific characteristics and practices that were observed and identified to be associated with these factors. These can be visualized graphically as the four *outer circles* of the dynamic evolving organizations, as shown in the Figure 8.1. They keep changing and need to be constantly re-defined and re-invented to initiate and cope with the changing, and increasingly turbulent, business environment. The fifth factor that sets apart the outstanding organizations is the cluster of characteristics represented by the *circle at the core,* as shown in Figure 8.1. We have chosen to describe it as Identity, Purpose, Values and Culture – abbreviated as **Distinct Identity.**

Distinct Identity is the relatively more stable and enduring part of the organization that is essential for maintaining its continuity and sustainability. It is more like the roots of a tree and the genetic code of the cells in the living organisms. This is the cluster of characteristics, philosophy and practices that endows the organization with a unique purpose and character. It provides a common rallying point that bestows cohesiveness, belongingness, a sense pride and purpose and a set of values and culture that pervades the entire organization. It is the binding force that holds the organization together and maintains its continuity.

The key elements that are associated with distinct identity are the principles, values, purpose and culture. These are like core elements that permeate and influence the entire organization. These are unique to each enterprise, yet there are some common threads in these elements that make some organizations outstanding and endow them with a sustainable competitive edge.

Figure 8.1: The Five Distinguishing Elements of Purposeful Values-driven Organizations

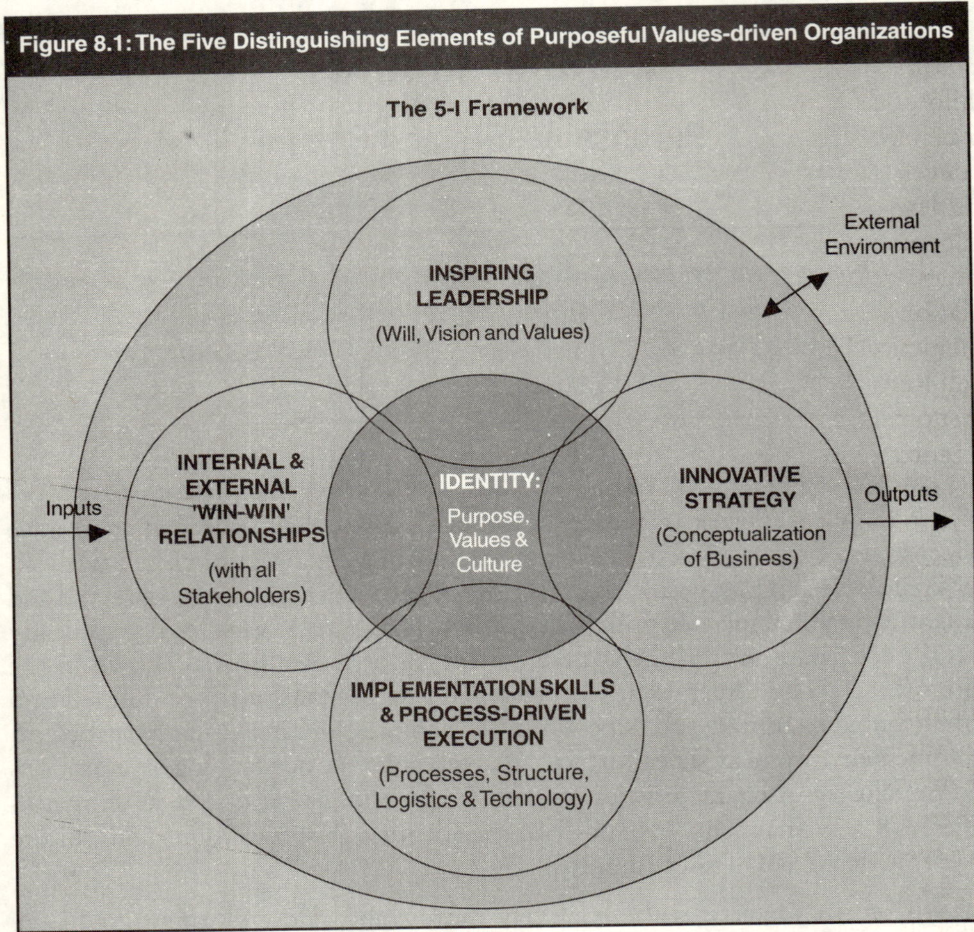

They determine the nature of governance, choices in selection and removal of key personnel; policies, strategies, practices and relationships that, in turn determine the performance and sustainability of the organization in the long run. They are like the roots, the foundation – depending on what metaphor one may prefer to choose. In some organizations these were clearly articulated, stated and explicitly 'taught'. In many others these were not so explicit, yet deeply ingrained, practiced and learned by all members through experience. They are passed on from generation to generation through various processes like selection of key personnel and successors, mentoring, training, socialization, reward and recognition and constant mention of the values and purpose through various forms of communication to ensure their continuity. *These key elements, together, provide the 'genetic code' of the enterprise.*

The passion and commitment to achieve success in business by building an enterprise is formulated and expressed through a core purpose; the ethical practices, philosophy and ideals that the founders deeply cherish are reflected in the guiding principles and core values[1]. As the enterprise grows over time with these elements, it develops a distinctive character, culture and identity. They seem to determine the development of unique competencies and motivation in the enterprise that maintain its continuity. These are manifested and articulated in the forms of shared values, visions, mission statements, policies, practices, strategies, structures, relationships, processes and operations that dynamically evolve over time in close interaction with the changing business environment. Collins and Porras, in their well-known work, *Built to Last* cited earlier have very well articulated the phenomenon of a continuing core and the changing peripheral aspects in visionary organizations[2]. We also noted this phenomenon in the organizations studied in this research and specially in those organizations which had registered sustained growth over a long period of time. *The sustainability of an organization, therefore, can be described as a function of a unique combination of continuity and change. The enterprise has a stable, aligning and continuing core and at the same time a changing and evolving periphery, which together ensure its sustainability in the changing business environment.*

The intriguing aspect of these four key elements at the core of an organization (identity, purpose, values and culture) is that they have seeds of life as well as destruction inherent in them. So long as the values, purpose, culture and identity of an enterprise are consistent in spirit with the basic principles that are close to the ethical foundations of social existence and politico-legal regulatory environment in a specific context, and they are practiced authentically and consistently, they act as a powerful life force. However, in many companies and institutions these are reduced to the rigid outer shell, like ritualistic slogans, consisting of hollow big words contrary to their meaning in actual practice. These are then used as decorative statements on office walls, company documents and in public speeches.

In some cases, the owners and those who are in key positions, to satisfy their baser instincts like retaining power at any cost, accumulating personal wealth at the cost of the enterprise and boosting their own ego superseding the larger interest of the organization, also use these as a cover. In such situations the stated values, purpose and culture become meaningless and can create rigidities like false pride, counter-productive cultural practices, archaic controls, obsolete procedures and practices and inconsistencies between the stated purpose and goals pursued, that may become dysfunctional. These, then, become barriers to feedback, learning and change, adaptability and innovativeness.

The organization, thus, becomes a rigid and closed system that loses touch with the changing business environment, which leads to its decline and destruction. It becomes victim of *'competency trap'* and/or *'culture trap'*, i.e., the belief that its existing competencies and ways of doing business, that have given it success in the past, will continue to lead it to success in the future also. That is how we find many well-known business houses going downhill and also come across catastrophes like that of Enron. No wonder there is so much talk these days of business ethics, values and corporate governance.

Before we elaborate and illustrate these factors, it is necessary to be clear about terms like principles, values, ethical conduct, culture, purpose and identity. These terms are often loosely used and convey different meanings to different people, in different contexts at different times. We would like to briefly explain the meanings that we are intending to convey through these terms here.

We are using the term 'principles' more or less with the same meaning as Stephen Covey, when he stated that 'there are *principles* that govern human effectiveness - natural laws in the human dimension that are just as real, just as unchanging and unarguably "there" as laws such as gravity are in the physical dimension... They are natural laws that cannot be broken.'[3]

The term 'value' represents 'a quality desirable as a means or as an end in itself'[4]; and also as the 'ideals, customs, institutions, etc. that arouse an emotional response for or against them, in a given society, or a given person.'[5] The term *shared values* is used quite frequently in management literature. It may be used to refer to the "basic norms and ideals that guide people's behaviours in the firm and form the underpinning of a firm's corporate culture".[6]

The term 'ethical' refers here to 'the rules or standards for right conduct or practice, especially the standards of a profession'[7]. The gist of all theories of ethics, according to some thinkers, is: 'When you are confronted with the problem of deciding what is right, or wrong conduct, ask yourself this question: Is this conduct or behaviour in the best interest of society? If yes, the conduct is good, otherwise, bad.'

We are utilizing the term 'culture' to refer to shared assumptions, beliefs, values, norms and patterns of behaviour of a group of people. Culture, therefore, refers to the *shared* norms and practices of a group of people. Hofstede's definition of culture may also be relevant for this purpose. He has defined culture as

"Collective programming of the mind which distinguishes the members of one group from another. Culture is to a human collectivity what personality is to an individual"[8]. It would be relevant here to specifically state the meaning of *corporate culture*; which can be defined as "the system of unwritten rules that guide how people perform and interrelate with one another" in an organization[9].

We have used these terms to describe some of the key characteristics of an organization. We visualize these characteristics in the form of concentric circles and a kind of hierarchy of centrality in the context of an organization. At the core, there appear to be the inherent and implicit basic principles that are reflected in the 'business philosophy', 'core values' and 'core purpose' of the company. In addition, we have noted the strong sense of *identity* of the organization as an important factor at the core. The other layers of circles represent the manifest and explicit distinct culture and characteristics based on the shared values, visions, policies, practices and goals. In order to remain profitable and sustainable in the dynamic and changing business environment, its changing leadership develops new strategies, business models, structures, styles of functioning, specific objectives, relationships and processes consistent with its core purpose, core values and distinct identity. Thus the enterprise evolves over time, maintaining the continuity of its identity combined with change.

The 'genetic code' of an enterprise is evidently in the choices and the nature of these key elements that are driven by the ambition, passion, purpose, vision and values of the founders – the entrepreneur and his/her close associates. They initiate and nurture it in its formative years with their collective imagination, passion and competence and, over time, these characteristics endow it with a distinctive culture and identity, that seems to sustain it. Their successors, other leaders and people who join the enterprise and identify themselves with and who are committed to it, carry it forward. While maintaining its basic identity and character, they give new interpretations, visions, direction and competencies to the enterprise with changing times. This could be clearly noted in companies like Tata Sons, TVS group, Larsen & Toubro, Hindustan Levers, Wipro and similar older organizations. It is also evidently emerging in the new companies included in this research like Infosys, Ranbaxy, Satyam, Hero Honda, Dr. Reddy's Labs., Sundram Fasteners, Titan and Reliance.

Those companies that were either not founded on such key elements-like sound principles, clearly identified core values, core purpose and business philosophy-or when their leadership lost the passion for the principles, values and purpose that had won the trust and confidence of the customers and stakeholders, they began to face problems. With time, they deviated far from such core characteristics and competencies; they became insensitive to external changes and non-receptive to internal and external feedback. They failed to learn, innovate and acquire new competencies and develop a new culture. They were not able to anticipate and initiate changes with time in the personnel, governance, policies, strategies, structures, processes, relationships and practices that were essential to cope and deal with the changing business environment. Such organizations tended to decline and usually disappeared.

This happened, particularly, when the top person became obsessed with the aggrandizement of his self image that superseded the real task and commitment to the development of the organization, as pointed out by one of the eminent persons interviewed. It was pointed out by him that "If you look at many great companies and there are many in our history, for reasons I am not mentioning all their names. You go to 1950s-60s, you see the great mercantile companies of Calcutta which used to exist like Balmer Lawrie, Andrew Yule, Martin Burn, Bird and Company, Union Carbide, Dunlop and the names like that. Each one has its own story as to why it went down....but in many of them you will find that they had a stint of leadership of somebody who was more obsessed with himself, his grandeur, his wealth, his money than for the company. And that is why people say, though it may not be fair to all private business houses, but in many business houses people say: *ki maine paisa lagaya, maine apna capital nikal liya, aur baaki abhi company chal raha hai.* [I had invested my capital in the company and I have made my money. However, the company is going on.] You have heard that expression, I am sure. It is a way of saying: I have bailed out, now whether the company survives or dies is a different matter."[10]

Let us now examine and illustrate the above-mentioned points relating to the core cluster that we have described as 'Distinct Identity: Purpose, Values and Culture', in the light of information, views and observations obtained in this research.

The key elements that have been noted in this central cluster are:

1. **Principles-centered paradigm**
2. **Distinctive framework of values, purpose and identity**
3. **High performance culture and global mindset**

4. Transparency and professionalism in corporate governance

5. Concern for broader societal issues and environment

A figurative presentation of these elements and their relationship are shown in Figure 8.2.

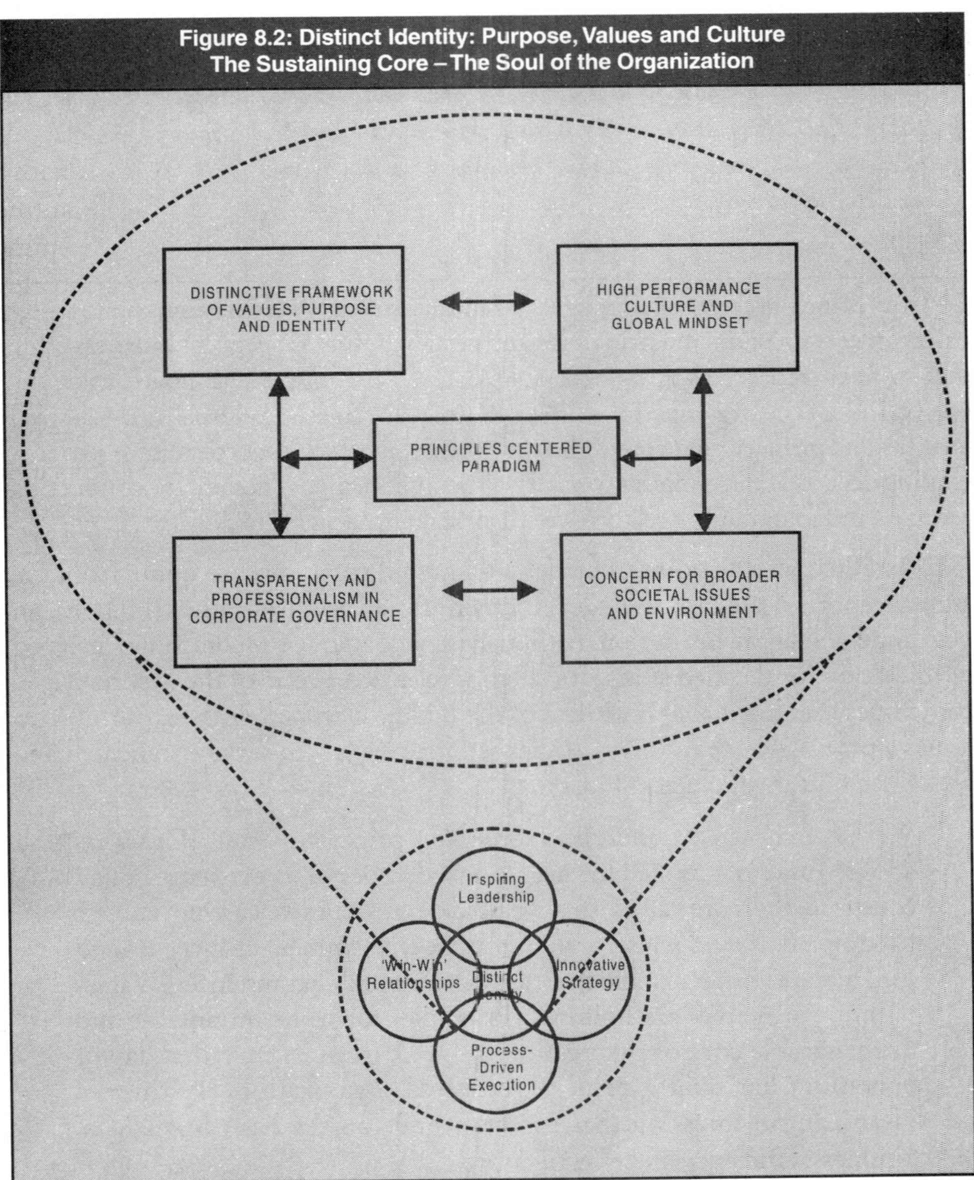

Figure 8.2: Distinct Identity: Purpose, Values and Culture The Sustaining Core – The Soul of the Organization

PRINCIPLES-CENTERED PARADIGM

> *A principles-centered paradigm, reflected in strongly held, rigorously practiced and, in some cases, explicitly articulated, values and business philosophy for doing business in a unique and ethical way was stated, emphasized and practiced in almost all outstanding organizations.*
>
> *Some of the cornerstones of stated business ethics were: integrity, no 'under the table' business, honouring commitments, meeting delivery schedules to internal and external customers, maintaining specifications and quality standards and giving full value for money to the customer.*
>
> *Ethical business was considered profitable business.*

By 'principle-centered paradigm' we mean a strongly held business philosophy based on certain enduring principles and certain defined aspects of business ethic that were considered as non-negotiable. These were like the foundations or the core values of the organization. These values were treated as ideals, most desired qualities and primary guidelines. They provided the criteria for determining policies, making decisions and choices - specially difficult decisions generally for conducting business and maintaining relations with all stakeholders.

To illustrate the point of principle-centered paradigm, we quote from the annual report of the Housing Development Finance Corporation (HDFC), an outstanding financial institution. Although it is not among the companies included in this study for detailed study, it is highly regarded as one of the best managed companies that has made the dream of the middle class people in India to own a house a practicable proposition. It has set unprecedented service standards and re-defined housing finance in India[11]:

> We have chosen to underline some key principles that HDFC has adopted and maintained for nearly two decades of its existence. They constitute the 'core values' that we hold dear - values that are not subject to compromise and reinterpretation as the environment changes around us. They are immutable and true through time and circumstances...Values without principles are hollow... Principles form the immutable and unchangeable core of right action. HDFC, from its very first day of operation, has built a principle-centered organization. By this we mean...an organization that has been built on the basis of fairness, kindness, efficiency and effectiveness.

A similar paradigm could be noted in the business philosophy of several organizations included in this research. To illustrate similar viewpoints, we quote below the views of some business leaders who explicitly stated and emphasized the importance of principles, values and business ethics for sustainability and success of organizations based on their personal experience, conviction and demonstrated success.

Summing up his life-long experience of building from scratch to the world's largest two wheeler company and one of India's most highly admired companies, the founder chairman of Hero Honda, Mr. B.M.L. Munjal, emphatically said:

> (The key to success is) ethical business, values based business. *Values jisne chodi woh kabhi bhi kamyaab nahin ho sakta.* [One who gives up values, can never succeed in business]. Value based business (is the key). You need to be clear about your values. Sometimes it may happen that what I consider ethical, you may not consider so...you need to be clear about that.... *Hum ne aaj tak kabhi under the table business apne nazdik nahin aane di...log kehte hain ki na, ho nahin sakta ji. Sab kuch ho sakta hai, aisi baat nahin, if you are serious and work with sincerity.* [We have never allowed under the table business to come near us...People say: how is it possible? They say it cannot be true. But we say from our experience that it is possible (to achieve success in business ethically), if you are serious and work with sincerity.
>
> Right from day one, our idea was to give full value of money to the customer, without having before us a very ambitious profitability factor. Profitability has been always behind us and it has followed us so seriously because we have left that behind. Try to satisfy your stakeholders...there are many stakeholders in one's business...but that can happen only if you have kept your own requirements behind you. If you always only care for your own needs as primary and give less importance to others' needs, then you can't do anything.

Mr. D.S. Brar, who has been instrumental in making Ranbaxy India's first truly multinational company and one of the most dynamic companies in the pharmaceutical industry, stated the importance of values and business ethics for his organization:

> There are such core values, which the company has. Quality is fundamental to our business. Quality is uncompromisable, so also,

> customer service. *We must provide products and customer service of the highest quality. This is what then ethics and integrity (means to us).* Ethics and Integrity – not in terms of loyalty, honesty (as spoken in general terms and are givens) with which often we get confused. But ethics and integrity more in the form of that we should be. Employees who are open to challenging the system constitute it. And it is our ethical duty to challenge the system – that (kind of) ethics (we want). Not that I am honest, so therefore I am ethical, or I will not steal from the company – those are given. Anyone who does (violate such ethical principles), he is out. Those are different issues. Like if I am invoicing a consignment but the goods are going 10 days later, then you are violating the organizational value of providing customer service, of providing (expected) high quality. That is the kind of ethical integrity that we want in our employees.
>
> And it is not that we don't have problems. But if you sit in one of our meetings you will see people tearing each other on issues like why was the consignment ten days late. These are openly discussed. This data is not hidden. These (kinds of information) are not shrouded in any mystery. It is blown out and is openly discussed. *Mistakes are not hidden.* They are openly displayed. So much so that sometimes we find that we are very critical. So that is what I mean by ethics in our organization.

It may be noted here that ethics and integrity in business and organization was described in terms of providing the highest quality products and service to the customers, honouring commitments inside the organization as well as to the customers, openness in sharing data and mistakes and challenging the system.

Sharing his thoughts on the importance of core values as one of the key factors that give Hindustan Lever the kind of distinctiveness and sustainability, Mr. G. Kapur said:

> And another thing, which I would pick up is *a very strong value system in the company which is completely non-negotiable, specifically in the area of integrity and business ethics,* and so on. So these are some of the things that come to my mind very often: One is for looking at the outside world, constantly looking at the change and the changing. The second is more internal: to say that *our value systems are extremely important for us.* And those really are the frameworks for our decision-making. So no decision can actually be inconsistent with this. So that is where we make our choices. And a very strong belief that to deal with the ever changing world, one thing which has to remain constant is the best quality talent that we attract into HLL.

Sharing his experiences of having faced some of the most difficult situations in ensuring sustainability of NTPC, for which tough decisions had to be taken against the wishes of powerful political bosses like discontinuing electricity supply to the states that had not paid huge accumulated amounts payable to NTPC, sometimes running into hundreds of crores of rupees, Mr. Rajinder Singh, its former chairman said: "Another factor (for taking essential tough decisions and ensuring sustainability of the public sector enterprises) is *integrity, i.e.,* to do what you say, come what may, like honouring the commitment of some benefits that you make to your people for achieving challenging goals... If one is contented with what one has (i.e., with his financial and material means to satisfy his needs), he has tremendous moral authority and courage to take the toughest decisions against all odds and pressures that one may sometimes be subjected to in the public sector organizations."

We came across many similar observations and statements in several companies like Sundram Fasteners, Wipro, Infosys, which indicated a firm commitment to certain principles and values that characterized them. Such principles-centered paradigm of values and business philosophy constituted their character, identity and the way of doing their business.

The key point that emerges from this discussion is that providing genuine value to the customer and earning credibility, confidence and trust of the stakeholders is the key to the survival of any business organization. These can be achieved only through clearly understood principles, disciplined adherence to sound values and ethical business practices.

Peter Drucker had probably identified the most fundamental principle of business, when he had stated that: "There is only one definition of business purpose: to create a customer."[12] It is such an obvious statement that it usually gets lost in the search for developing sophisticated theories and techniques of business. But real life business experiences and researches, again and again, bring this important principle of business to the limelight. Companies usually discover it the hard way that the key to survival in business is to win the 'trust and confidence of the stakeholders and the customers'. They realize that it can be obtained only by offering the customers the best possible products and service, which they consider true value for money and give them the best possible satisfaction. They know that such trust and confidence can be won only through ethical and fair dealings with them. In short, the key to success in business is to recognize and follow the principle that ethical business is good business.

DISTINCTIVE FRAMEWORK OF VALUES, PURPOSE AND IDENTITY

At the core of the company were its institutional identity, a well-defined purpose and a distinct culture with some deeply ingrained shared values. These provided the broad and stable framework for articulating and interpreting more specifically the mission, vision and scope of business, that were reviewed and redefined by its leadership from time to time keeping in view the changing business environment.

The members of the organizations felt a sense of belongingness, pride in the identity, culture and purpose of their company that endowed it with cohesiveness and longevity.

Most of the companies consciously cultivated the organization culture of open communications, teamwork and high performance.

The continuity of identity and culture were reinforced through persistent emphasis, articulation and personal examples set by the organization leaders.

Their continuity was maintained through a careful selection and induction of staff, training and mentoring.

The reward system also enhanced the sense of commitment and ownership (psychological, as well as financial in some cases) among the members of the organization.

A close scrutiny of all distinguished organizations reveals that each company or business house has a distinctive framework of values, purpose and identity based on its own unique business philosophy and some basic ethical principles that constitute its core values. Some companies are known for explicitly stating and rigorously following, their distinctive values framework while others may follow them implicitly and not state them explicitly. Their commitment to such deeply held values, with a clearly defined and practiced business and work ethic and an organizational culture based on such values differentiated them from ordinary companies. Let us examine the business philosophy and practices of some leading business houses to identify such a framework.

The Tata group is well known for its value based philosophy of management. Mr. J. N. Tata founded the group with the purpose of developing the foundation for industrialization of India through the iron and steel industry. As has often been reported in the business press, 'Tatas represent values like honesty, fairness, reliability, technological innovation and, above all, Indian-ness'. The name 'Tata' has become a brand equity for trust, reliability, quality and equitable returns to stakeholders. Tata Sons, as a business group, have been able to develop a mutually respectful relationship with their associated companies as well as the government. The chairman visits the major businesses once or twice a year, spending time in factories, market places and with the management of companies. They believe in the welfare of their employees, attracting and nurturing the best talent in the organization and generally give promotions from within, consistent with a traditional view of valuing the 'home grown jasmine'. Their view is that the non-executive chairman is not responsible for short-term profits and, therefore, helps in the proper functioning of the board and the CEO, provides leadership for better corporate governance and long-term direction of the enterprise. As is well known, the Tata group has diversified into a wide range of industries spanning steel, automobiles, watches, to IT and Telecom. It has transformed many of its companies, which are competing successfully in the Indian and the international markets.

The Tata Group have developed the Tata Business Excellence Model (TBEM) that was introduced in 1999 which every company associated with the group has to follow. It is a flexible model under which the group companies have to improve their systems and processes. It is based on the Malcom-Baldridge model of quality excellence. The important point about TBEM is that companies are judged not just on the basis of profitability or turnover but on a wider set of parameters: leadership, strategic planning, customer and market focus, information and analysis, process management, human resource development and business results. Each criterion has points attached to it with all the seven totalling 1,000. The implementation of the model has helped the Tata group companies to become more market and customer focused. The eventual aim of each company is to reach a score of 600 over the next five-years period[13]. The model is based on some important guiding principles and values that are consistent with the philosophy of the Tata Group. The operational aspects of its values framework could be observed in several companies of the group.

Hindustan Levers is another outstanding company that is known for its values based professional management and ethical business philosophy. We have earlier referred to the very strong value system in the company, which is considered completely non-negotiable, specifically in the areas of integrity and business ethics. The company's philosophy of attracting, training and nurturing the best talent for leadership, identification with the country's changing requirements and thought leadership in finding solutions for them, is well known, as was also stated by one of the eminent interviewees[14]:

> HLL has always made itself attractive to young people to join. HLL's chairman always had an image, which is far beyond just being a chairman of the company. HLL has always been in the forefront of thought leadership in the country, making suggestions which are within their area of knowledge.... And they use that experience to throw light on some facets of national significance."

HLL's branded products in the FMCG sector are household generic names across the country. It has consistently performed well and ranked among the top companies in India.

Larsen & Toubro (L&T) is also an outstanding, professionally managed Indian company in the engineering industry. It is a relatively old organization that has diversified in industries like construction and cement manufacturing. Its success and competitiveness is attributed to its *'very strong value systems and extremely strong merit oriented culture'*. The company has concentrated on good indigenous management and good indigenous manufacturing. It has operated with 'an intent to be up to world-class standard in Indian circumstances'. Further, the secret of success of the company was attributed to attracting and nurturing the best talent in the country. "The company is able to retain such talent because of 'decency - the way we deal with people. When you really need the company, it stands up and is with you. For example, the kind of medical benefits we have in the company. That is why we call ourselves as a caring company. We don't let down people. We may not be the best of flamboyant kind of paymasters, but I think what we provide as its substitute is the caring, learning and professional culture."[15]

Let us take a look at the framework of values and purpose of Infosys and some other relatively new leading Indian companies in the IT and pharmaceutical sectors that have built brand equity for India and changed the image of India and Indian products in world markets. In some ways such companies have done for India what Sony and Toyota did for Japan.

Infosys, one of the best known Indian IT companies, has received numerous awards and commendations for its outstanding performance and is known for its distinct purpose and values. The driving spirit, the purpose of the founders – the seven like-minded but not alike software professionals who came together under the leadership of Mr. Narayana Murthy in 1981 – was to build a most respected 'world-class company'[16]. The company has got lots of accolades and appreciation from its customers and business press. It has often been recognized and appreciated for its distinctive values, integrity, commitment to add value to clients and technology intelligence that differentiates it from many other companies. A lot has been written about the values and culture that drive Infosys. It has been declared as one of India's most admired companies and the country's best employer several times and has won almost every corporate governance and business ethics award in India and Asia. The key element identified for this distinction is 'the unconditional trust that every employee - from the receptionist to the management trainee to the mid-level manager - has in the top management. Everyone believes what the top management says. And everyone is suffused with a quiet pride in the organization and its achievements.'[17]

The employees, who have been with Infosys for a long time, talk, with great admiration, about the values, ethics and conduct of the seven founders, led by Mr. N.R. Narayana Murthy who is talked of as a legend. It was said that they followed ideals like dignity of labour by taking turns to clean their office premises including the toilets during the formative years. The original office building has been retained like a monument in the ultra-modern and beautifully maintained new campus of Infosys in Bangalore that has every facility from most advanced research laboratories, training centre and library to all varieties of food service canteens, putting range, tennis courts, jogging track, indoor games, gyms, swimming pool, shopping and banking facilities and is more like a university campus than a corporate headquarter. The company combines such concern for employees with a very high performance culture and has been able to inculcate a sense of pride among 'Infoscions', the term that employees of the company identify with as being members of the Infosys family. (The term 'scion' that connotes descendant of a noble family has been added purposefully).

Even now, when the company has acquired such a high stature and dizzying growth, the simplicity, accessibility, modesty and egalitarian approach of Mr. Narayana Murthy in dealing with all staff at the lowest level is exemplary. He and other members of top management, stand in the same queue as the young trainees for lunch in the canteens. 'Infosys has always been run by its founders with a fanatical belief in doing things right: we shall not bribe, we shall pay our taxes, we shall share our wealth with all our employees. And this value system has percolated down the hierarchy, since the founders have visibly lived by their principles. Indeed, in the midst of all the bloodbath in the IT sector, Infosys firmly announced that it would not sack anyone.'[18] Mr. Dinesh, director and co-founder, mentioned that the firm followed Mr. Narayana Murthy's motto, that "it was a company by the people, for the people and of the people".

As described earlier, Infosys extends all possible concern, care and facilities for the well-being and convenience of its employees to enable them to give their best to the company. This has kept morale and loyalty of the employees quite high and ensured that India's best and brightest continue to work for Infosys (the attrition rate was a low 7.6% in 2002), although it is not the best paymaster[19]. *At the same time the company has a very high result-oriented, performance management and measurement based culture.* The company is known for its rigorous and highly developed, but flexible and efficient, systems and processes that enable it to deliver 100 per cent each and every time. In fact the company is known to make candid, and usually conservative promises, but exceeds its promises with results.

Wipro is another outstanding company that has received many awards and high ratings by consultancy firms and agencies at the national and Asia Pacific region.[20] Although the company was started in 1946-47, primarily in the edible oil hydrogenation industry, it was adept at identifying business opportunities and niches. It diversified into several other industries like hydraulics and fluid power, lighting, bio-medical equipment, toilet soaps, healthcare products, etc. It was in the eighties that it first entered the computers hardware industry and later in the software industry. In 1994-95, Wipro InfoTech and Wipro Systems were merged with Wipro Ltd. and by 1997-98 software services had become the predominant business of Wipro. The company has re-articulated its vision from time to time, re-defined, re-structured and transformed itself several times under the chairmanship of Mr. Azim Premji, but it has consistently maintained its values framework.

Wipro is being driven by the intent of becoming an Indian MNC/global company and the objective 'to anticipate and meet the needs of customers and fully utilize the potential of every employee'. Its senior executives described it as a company driven by the desire to be on top, to be the industry leader in every industry in which it operates and grow above the industry average. It aims at being ahead of its nearest competitors in industry by a couple of years – which was believed to 'lead to certain behaviours and mindset' necessary for developing competitiveness. It benchmarks itself with the best companies in world in the related industries and wants to think and act like global companies, such as GE and CISCO. It believes that *'most problems of competitiveness and survival in Indian organizations were quality related.'* Therefore, it laid a very high emphasis on quality and 'Mission Quality' was directly under the chairman's office. It has seriously pursued quality initiatives like CMM, PCMM, six sigma, etc.

Its senior executives described Wipro as a 'value led company'. They attributed "the sustained success of the company to being a 'value led' company and the kind of cultural context which we have set for the employees in which they have seen an opportunity to contribute and get rewarded."[21] The company has developed the framework of values that they call 'Wipro Values: What makes us true Wiproites'. Each employee, who joins Wipro, is given the document containing these values and they are emphasized during induction as well as discussed in the training programmes and strictly followed in practice and performance reviews. As pointed out by some senior executives in Wipro, 'we are fanatical in terms of how we do our business and being able to be held accountable against those key values'.

Following are the four key values articulated in this document:

- ***Human Values:*** We respect the unique needs of customers and employees. We are sensitive to their differing needs in our interactions with them.
- ***Integrity:*** We deliver what we commit. With honesty, fairness, reliability and uprightness in whatever we do.
- ***Innovative Solutions:*** We consistently offer novel and superior solutions to satisfy the needs of the customer.
- ***Value for Money:*** Delivering higher value to the customer through continuous improvement in quality, cost and speed.

Some other dominant values that were emphasized at Wipro were simplicity, informality and *'fierce openness to new ideas'*. It was stated that despite their successes, the company was always run like a fairly simple and humble organization in which one would never find any kind of flashiness in the system. So also there was great emphasis on prudence in spending the company money and executives at all levels were to follow the kind of norms in travel and stay in hotels as they would do with their personal money. The reason given for such an approach was to have a certain congruence between an individual's own belief system and the organization belief system. At the same time, they were willing to spend heavily on training, knowledge and expertise development and did not hesitate in paying high fees to top level experts invited from overseas to conduct programmes for the development of their employees.

According to the Chairman of Wipro, Mr. Azim Premji, "Values not only help in achieving success, but also make success enduring and lasting... They provide internal discipline and help weather the storms and serve as anchors in a sea of turbulence of changes... Values transmit trust. Trust is not only at the heart of leadership but forms the essence of relationships." He has emphasized six values for himself which act as guiding principles in the management of his business[22]:

1. Honesty and integrity (that leads to transparency and respect)
2. Hard work and smart work
3. Self confidence (has to be an intrinsic part of our approach in demanding what is due for our merit and ability...nobody can make us feel inferior without our consent)
4. Humility (people with highest self-confidence have the highest humility, because they have nothing to prove to themselves)
5. Persistence (nothing is ever achieved in one go)
6. Passion (giving your hundred per cent in whatever you take up, no matter how small or unimportant).

There are several legendary stories of Wipro management sticking to their values of honesty and integrity against many odds and, at times, paying a heavy price because of their insistence on following ethical practices. For example, in one of their plants they incurred heavy cost for generating electricity by using diesel generators for a long time because they refused to bribe the officers of the public utility service to expedite the electricity supply connection.

The three important goals of the company were stated to be: customer satisfaction, employee satisfaction and financial performance. The strong values orientation combined with a high level of efficiency and effectiveness in utilizing its resources offers clues to its purpose of creating wealth through ethical means by providing the best possible quality products and services.

Satyam Computer Services, led by the soft-spoken Mr. Ramalinga Raju, is known for always thinking big and setting very aggressive goals. The company has defined itself as the 'Customer Oriented Global Organization' (COGO). It has been described as a highly entrepreneurial company that had developed a special programme to encourage 'intrapreneurship', called 'STEP' that provides venture capital to the employees (called associates) to launch a commercially viable idea.

The company is driven by purpose, passion and energy. It has many firsts to its credit including being credited by some of its senior executives for *phenomenal speed of response.*

The senior executives of the company identified four distinctive key values at Satyam that have enabled it to achieve a high level of success and competitiveness. One of the key values is respecting and trusting people and dignity for people that allows them to perform up to their potential. The company creates conditions to provide considerable autonomy, freedom and a sense of ownership among the employees. The second value is that it is *an extremely entrepreneurial company.* There is an unwritten popular joke in the company that: 'It is easy to get forgiveness rather than permission'. The third value is an *atypical customer orientation to invent business models that would give tremendous amount of flexibility to customers.* As spelled out, it meant: 'we always explore and see what kind of values can be created for the customer and we go beyond the normal call of delivering good quality product - instead the approach is to create value solutions for the customer. For example, if a customer wants exclusive development center for themselves, we would do that. If a customer wants to relate to us like a big player – big both in terms of ambition and aspiration – have a joint venture with us, we explore that'. The fourth value is *to always think big*[23].

The company believes in investing heavily in building world-class facilities (like the Satyam Learning Centre) for attracting the best talent from overseas as well as from within the country and to inspire confidence among the customers. The company, like the other leading IT companies, gives a high priority to the best possible training across the entire organization, development of talent and knowledge management.

Dr. Reddy's Labs (DRL) has acquired a distinguished position as one of the leading pharmaceutical companies. Describing the core purpose and core values of the company, Mr. G.V. Prasad (executive vice-chairman & CEO) said: "As an institution where we have been successful, we have generated profits by also doing good. We create a certain feeling in our organization that we are working for an organization which cares for people... If you look at our purpose, or *core purpose of Dr. Reddy's, is to help people lead healthier life.* While I don't completely as a person, as an individual believe that there is a social purpose for organizations, I think the first and the foremost social purpose for an organization is to be successful, to generate surplus, to generate profits, of course all in an ethical and honest way. That's a minimum boundary condition. But once you are on sound (ground), you can contribute to the society, your employees can contribute to the society, your shareholders can contribute to the society. So I think wealth creation should be the first primary driver of our organization in an ethical and honest way."

Mr. Prasad identified three key factors that, in his opinion have contributed towards a sustainable competitive advantage at DRL. These are: innovation and entrepreneurship; globalization; and the talent and commitment of people. Explaining these points he said: "We drive innovation towards cutting edge. Then use entrepreneurship to realize the value created out of this innovation. Then we need to look at where the best value for these opportunities can be created. Then we globalize. So we have really focused on the most important countries in the world for value creation and globalized our operations. So we scaled our innovation and entrepreneurship by globalizing the operation. And finally, we feel people are the key to sustainable competitive advantage. To be able to compete continuously, renew the innovation and entrepreneurship, we need a pool of highly talented people. So the third pillar on which we drive the organization is the people talent. So we combine innovation and entrepreneurship and globalization, with our people power to really become sustainably strong as an organization."

Emphasizing the importance of passion, he added: "You have to be excited about what you are doing and we believe we are very excited about what we are doing, because we are making a difference in people's lives. *We are creating medicines which will lead to people having healthier life. This is a larger purpose than making profits. And once we are true to this cause, we are passionate about this cause, the profits will follow. So having a larger purpose is really uplifting and makes people passionate about what they are doing."*

The TVS Group is another outstanding Indian business group which has created a distinct identity for itself and its companies on the basis of high quality of manufacturing and demonstrating self-reliance in mastering and developing technology. One of its core values is high quality in manufacturing. Sundram Fasteners, one of its well-known companies, is one of the few companies in India to get the TPM Excellence award. It has been supplying radiator caps to General Motors in USA for the last 9 years and during these 9 years not a single objection or defect in any radiator cap has been reposted. They have supplied over 50 million radiator caps and got the Best Supplier of the Year award from General Motors, year after year.

Describing how quality had become almost 'genetically coded' in the various companies of the TVS group, Mr. Suresh Krishna, chairman and managing director of Sundram Fasteners, explained:

> Quality has been in TVS from the day go. The company started in 1912. We are now in the 90th year of the company's existence. *We have always stood for quality. Quality has been a basic fundamental building block for all TVS group companies, in my time, my father's time, my grandfather's time.* People have always said that ... we used to repair cars, we used to run workshops. We used to be dealers for General Motors in pre-independence era. We used to do a lot of repair work. So people used to say if you take it to TVS, you can trust TVS. They'll do a good job, if you take it outside, you don't know what's going to happen. Right from the day go, we used to run a city bus service in Madurai city, where people used to say that we can set the watch by the time the TVS bus comes to the bus stops. We were running 300 buses in the city and so every bus, every route, every bus stop, it had to come to the bus stop on time. And people used to say: 'it is the 3.55 p.m. bus' and could set their watch by it. This kind of quality levels. *It was built in the philosophical foundation for the entire TVS group.* Anybody who got trained (with us became conscious of quality and punctuality). Even I have seen my father talk about it ever since my school days in Madurai. I grew up in Madurai. I came to Madras only in 1962. It becomes a fundamental part of your psyche...Why is an Indian an Indian? Indians have a way of life. You cannot really put it in words exactly what makes an Indian, an Indian. You have to be born in India, or lived in India for a sufficiently long time and interacted with people. The same way what makes the TVS group quality conscious is something that has right from the beginning, sort of, has happened...

While explaining the reasons that in his view gave Sundram Fasteners a competitive advantage, he said: "First of all you have to have a vision, *the vision is that Sundram Fasteners should be one of the best companies in the world and we must become a multinational company.* If everybody else in the Western world can do it why can't you? If you have the vision, communication and milestone setting and coming through as a winner, you have an organization, which is tuned to the right direction..."

He emphasized the role of communication with workers to ensure high level of information, motivation, morale, sense of belonging and pride in the company as an extremely important factor. "In order to do that (i.e., to achieve high levels of quality, efficiency and productivity) first of all you have to strengthen your home base. The home base has to be very, very strong. One of the tremendous advantages that we have had is a very good productive labour right from day one. Since we started in 1966, we have not had a single day of industrial breakdown. We haven't had a single strike, nothing at all in any of our plants. We have got five plants now, one in Madras, one in Bangalore, one in Madurai, one in Pondicherry and one in Hyderabad. None of these plants has ever experienced any labour unrest, nothing at all. We have never gone to court on a labour dispute. The people have always been willing, because we look after not only their well being in terms of salaries and wages, but I personally feel salaries and wages is only a minor product of the entire productivity programme. I think *communication is to me very very important...*"

"Right from the day go, right from 1966 when we started this company, I was the first employee of this company, so I have now been with the company since it started. I have been talking to my workers at least 3 times a year at every location. Sometimes 3, sometimes 4 times. I tell them everything about the company: right from sales to profit and loss, the competition, what is happening in the world, with General Motors, TPM, everything that happens in the company. The entire company knows exactly what is happening. So I have been now doing it for 37 years.

"When you talk like that and they keep on seeing what I say is good for them, the company is growing and not only they are benefiting but their children are also benefiting, because a lot of retired people's children are working in the company. We also give a lot of scholarships for the children's education. We give computer training, all kinds of things like free medical care. They know that the company literally looks after the evolution of the entire family."

"The company has got a very clear goal. People write about the company, so they are proud to belong to a company which is written about, which is shown as a role model. You have to sustain that 'role model-ship' and so you work harder and say that we cannot let down our company. Everybody likes to be on a winning side, everybody wants to be in the finals and win the finals, so they say that we need to see that this company grows.... It has also become such an important matter that no unit at any point of time wants to create any kind of problem, because they will say you have spoilt the name of Sundram Fasteners. That kind of commitment is moving the entire Sundram Fasteners."

Explaining his philosophy of constantly striving for excellence and setting stretch goals for the organization, Mr. Suresh Krishna said:

> What I have found most difficult in my entire career is when the company is doing well, people turned around and say what is wrong with this? There is nothing wrong with this so why should we do this and improve this? Everybody says we are a good company and our financial results show that we are a good company, but the management is not satisfied. What is happening to our chairman? Why is he not satisfied? Why is he all the time saying this is not right, that is not right? He says we don't know what is wrong with the chairman? Why is he never satisfied? *I always tell them the minute you become satisfied that is your downfall. You cannot at any point of time become satisfied. I always tell them that this concept of dharma in Hindu philosophy is doing your job to the best of your abilities.*
>
> The dharma of a schoolteacher is to become the best schoolteacher, not only in his district but also in the world. The dharma of a good musician is to become a most recognized musician in the world. *The dharma of a good businessman is to become the most recognized and successful and most sought after businessman in the world. So we must be that. That is our dharma....*
>
> We must fulfill our *dharma,* because God has given us so many opportunities. It will be very wrong on our part if we don't utilize such opportunities. God might as well give them to somebody else, who might well utilize them. There is also a saying that if you do your *dharma* properly, it would not only protect you but also protect your future. What it really means is it'll create enough well-being in society to look after you and your children and grand children. That is what it really means. That is why they say if you practice your dharma properly...you have nothing to fear.
>
> This is the most difficult challenge (i.e., to change) when the company is doing well...I always tell them that one must change when you feel there is no necessity to change and its very important. It's exactly like saying that you must exercise when you are healthy.
>
> There are three steps to achieving excellence. *One is:* you must become better than what you were; *second,* you should be as good as the best in the world; *third* is you are the best in the world and everybody is trying

to catch up with you. Everybody benchmarks against you. But, if you want to do that, then you have to become efficient. There is no way you can sit at home and do this because you will only become the biggest frog in a small pond. Let me put it that way.

We can infer from these statements that two of the *core values* followed at Sundram Fasteners company are: high quality in manufacturing; and constant endeavour for improvement and change for excellence. And the *core purpose* that is driving the company is to become an Indian multinational company that would be one of the best in the world. The *distinct identity* of the company as being one of the best suppliers to GM in the highly competitive and tough international market is a source of pride and inspiration to the management and all employees of the company.

As illustrated in the case of Sundram Fasteners, as well as in the cases of other organizations discussed earlier in this chapter, *the distinct framework of values, purpose and identity provides the foundation, the binding and aligning force to the company to maintain and develop a sustainable competitive edge.*

Some distinguished companies displayed their character and identity by succinctly stating their character, purpose and values in their logo, like: Infosys - 'Powered by Intellect, Driven by Values'; SmithKline Beecham - 'Consumer Healthcare'; Wipro - 'Applying Thought';

The most important common values, noted across the organizations studied, were aimed at winning the trust and respect of customers and stakeholders through ethical and fair dealings. As stated earlier, such organizations were ***'Purposeful, Values- Driven Enterprises'*** *that created and shared economic value by fair means, following ethical and professional business values.*

HIGH PERFORMANCE CULTURE AND GLOBAL MINDSET

The organizations studied by us endorsed organization cultures that seemed to combine high performance orientation with high care and concern for the employees, customers and stakeholders. They demonstrated a strong orientation towards learning and change, growth and competitiveness, quality and productivity, innovation and entrepreneurship, openness and informality. The patterns of culture observed were more professional and egalitarian, with a high level of openness and the emerging competitive global mindset was evident in most of them.

As stated by one eminent professional manager, the culture of such professional organizations was unlike the traditional 'sethji' culture 'that you cannot disagree with the authority'. Another eminent professional manager emphasized: 'What we are saying is: it is the leadership, essentially, which creates the kind of conditions in the organization to generate all the kinds of aspects including innovativeness, including quality, customer services, ...and there are a lot of facets (that are being talked and written about) these days....such aspects are critical in our context also....But that may be the nucleus to build around, without that nothing may happen and that, to my mind, again *derives from organization values, culture of the organization,* where people feel involved, are free and frank, are able to share work as a team and innovate, create. They are not crucified. They are given a space for innovation, which some management may think is a waste of money, waste of time.'[24]

The professional and egalitarian approach in managing people was even more evident in industries like pharmaceuticals and IT. In a leading pharmaceutical company, Dr. Reddy's Labs., it was emphasized that:

> Creating an environment which is not control oriented, hierarchical and oppressive, the work place should be energizing, empowering and motivate the people to give their best. So *the whole organizational culture should be devoid of politics, devoid of control command systems, things like that.* There should be discipline, discipline is not something we give up and discipline is something, which is different from control and command.
>
> We also, as a management, set an example in terms of how to manage our teams and hopefully that cascades down to the organization and sets the right setting for the talent to perform. So one is the recruitment process, then the whole work atmosphere – how you manage it.
>
> Then the third is developmental opportunities. So people who are good performers should be able to move faster than the others. People who have delivered well should be able to work anywhere in the world, should have opportunities to work in various cultures, learn from different cultures, for which we provide a lot of those opportunities. So our success itself has created that kind of career path opportunities for talent. So we manage talent at various levels, like recruitment, on the job

development, developmental opportunities, fast track of programmes, high reward system, variable pay, etc. Like these there are number of other HR *initiatives* which support the leveraging of talent...

We spend a significant amount of our resources in *continuing education.* We also send our people to various management programmes across the world. We have a guy going for an entrepreneurship programme at Stanford at senior managerial level. I myself attend a lot of programmes. I just came back from a programme at the ISB. We are continuously looking outside. We also have some regular training programmes, as well as participation in global management schools, as well as seminars. We continuously keep the *knowledge flow* going through the organization. We also place a premium on knowledge, so we have several signals by which we communicate this. We give everybody a 50 per cent off on any qualification they get, on any degree they get we cover 50 per cent of the cost. In the case of certain specialized programmes we fund the entire cost. For example, anybody from our company who is selected to the programme of ISB (Indian School of Business) we pay everything and we also pay him the salary during that period which he is away. We pay the fees and we also pay the salary. One year off fully paid and then cover his cost, when he comes back we give him a better position. The only commitment he has to make is that he has to stay with us for three years.'[25]

Culture refers to the widely shared and enduring characteristics of an organization. As we have discussed earlier, it is like collective programming of the minds of people. It consists of the shared assumptions, beliefs, values, norms and patterns of behaviour of the people in an organization. It manifests itself as a system of unwritten rules that guide how people think, perform and inter-relate with one another in the organization. Organization culture is not easily changed and is an extremely important factor in determining the sustainability and competitiveness of the organization.

The subject of organizational culture has been discussed, researched and written about a great deal in management literature. Our purpose here is not to get into an academic debate on the subject, but to look for significant patterns in the cultures of organizations, which are a part of our research that seemed to lead to their success and competitiveness.

Obviously, there is nothing like a single culture that could be said to be ideal for different organizations. Organization culture is something in which the formula of 'one size fits all' does not apply. On the contrary, it is the uniqueness of an organization's culture that gives it distinctiveness and supremacy over the mediocre and run of the mill organizations. However, there seem to be some common patterns and orientations in the cultures of successful and competitive organizations that lead to higher levels of efficiency, productivity, quality, innovativeness, profitability and growth over long spans of time leading to their sustainability. Our search was for such patterns.

One important discovery that we made after this research was that the outstanding organizations have evidently learnt the art of managing contradictions and paradoxes, such as the paradoxes of change and continuity; high performance and high care; development and control; entrepreneurship and professionalism; teamwork and individual initiative; short-term and long-term; passion and humility; professional governance and self interest. Here we wish to draw attention to some distinctive organization culture orientations that were observed in most of the highly successful companies.

The key areas in which the management policies and practices led to the emergence of a distinct organizational culture that enabled high performance and organizational effectiveness were: creating conditions for attracting the best talent and getting the best out of people; training, development, knowledge enhancement and sharing and leadership development across the organization; customer satisfaction and feedback; innovation and R&D; cost, quality and productivity; marketing and financial performance; business and work ethics, openness in communication, meritocracy and professionalism in decision-making; clarifying and sticking to core values and core purpose of the organization. These focal areas were given concentrated time and attention by the top leadership and management and, over time, the consistent policies and practices that were followed became deeply embedded and institutionalized as patterns of culture unique to the organization.

One significant pattern that could be observed was that the outstanding organizations oriented all their policies, strategies, systems and practices to *attract and develop the best talent and create conditions to get the best out of their people.* It was explicitly stated and clearly practiced by organizations like HLL, Tata Sons, Wipro, Infosys and L&T , but was evidently practiced in different forms by almost all the highly rated organizations that were studied. Therefore, the culture in such organizations valued talent and supported the development and utilization of the talent, in different forms, styles and institutionalized practices. The search and development of talent was not only left to the human resource department which, of course, played an important role in it but it was a matter of high priority and personal concern for the top management.

A related pattern was the emphasis on developing *leadership and succession planning across the organization* through various institutionalized processes and practices. We have cited earlier how HLL has developed a culture that emphasizes leadership development across the organization and has institutionalized practices like mentoring and coaching in addition to training, job rotation, sophisticated appraisal systems, etc. Infosys has a dedicated leadership training institute in Mysore, in addition to its large technical training facilities for new entrants.

An emerging global *mindset* to benchmark with the best in the world, operate in highly competitive international markets and adopt best practices for high quality and productivity was noted in many organizations like Ranbaxy, Dr. Reddy's Labs, Sundram Fasteners, Reliance, Hero Honda, Infosys, Satyam and Wipro. We have earlier cited examples of global mindset from other companies. Here we cite the case of Dr. Reddy's Labs.:

> See in 1993 itself we established our presence in the US through a US office. Then we scaled our presence in what we consider the most important markets to operate. Thus we have a presence in US, we have a presence in Europe, we have a presence in Russia, we have a presence in China, so these were the major markets that Dr. Reddy's feels it needs direct presence. And hence we globalized, so that we can take full advantage of the entrepreneurship opportunities in all these countries. We use our innovation to create value, we use entrepreneurship to realize that value and globalization to scale that value.
>
> We have also globalized our research activity. We have a research centre in Atlanta. We have manufacturing facilities in China and Russia, but largely we believe that India has many-many advantages in terms of manufacturing and research. So our core manufacturing assets and R&D assets will be in India. We will go to other countries where required, where it will create a competitive advantage[26].

Similarly a growing emphasis on *innovation, entrepreneurship, R&D was notable* especially in the pharmaceutical and IT companies. We have earlier described how companies like Satyam developed these values in IT industry. It was equally emphasized in the pharmaceutical companies. For example, in Dr. Reddy's Labs it was explained that: "The very fact that if you look at our chairman, he symbolizes innovation. He really leads the research effort, so there is a high premium placed on innovation in the organization and continuously by setting the culture to recognize and reward innovation and value innovation in people. We have created an environment where innovation is at a premium, where people like to innovate because that is their claim to fame. So, when right from the chairman's level – the most senior person in the organization – a signal is given that innovation is important, research is important, there is an energy in the organization towards research and innovation. The sponsorship from the top is the key to create an environment for innovation ..."

"Entrepreneur is a guy who sees what is needed by a customer and who sees what capabilities you have and matches them so we have entrepreneurship at the top level, senior level, middle level, at a sales level. So *entrepreneurship is embedded as a culture.* More than the entrepreneur driving the organization, it is entrepreneurship that is driving the organization at various levels. See the thing is we don't believe in quickly converting into finance. We don't believe that works. But in a culture, which recognizes entrepreneurship, there is always, of course, the pay that is linked to performance. There is a variable bonus plan, there are stock options and things like that. But we don't tightly link – if you do X you get Y. That's not the culture we have. *We have a spirit where entrepreneurship is celebrated, recognized and hence there is a culture where people want to become entrepreneurs.*"

"Quality is almost minimum standards today to compete in a global environment. No question, that is not even a point which we consider as competitive advantage. It is almost like ticket to play, so *we need to be on the cutting edge of the content.* We always are – being in the business of pharmaceuticals (quality conscious). Quality is a very-very important aspect. Quality and order fulfillment and delivery – all those are minimum conditions they enable you to play in this market, but to win you really have to go much beyond that[27]."

Based on the foregoing discussion, we can infer that the organization culture of business houses and companies that were highly successful and demonstrated competitive edge that were studied in this research indicated some or most of the following emphases and orientations.

High Performance and High Care: People-centric Culture

1. *Talent and Leadership Development*

    - Attracting, developing and effectively utilizing the best talent.
    - Leadership development and succession planning across the organization.

2. *High Performance and Result Orientation*

    - Strong customer orientation.
    - Strong emphasis on performance measurement and management.
    - Result oriented work ethic.

3. *Teamwork and Participative/Consultative Decision Making*

    - Emphasis on consultative decision-making, working through teams and well designed processes across the organization.
    - High level of communication and information sharing across the organization.
    - Egalitarian, less hierarchical and informal relationship with employees.

4. *Empowering, Risk taking and Tolerance for Mistakes*

    - Empowering, flexible and freedom giving work practices combined with discipline, monitoring and reviewing performance.
    - Support for risk taking and tolerance of mistakes.

Openness, Learning and Change Orientation

1. *Openness, Feedback, Learning and Change*

    - Soliciting customers' and employees' feedback.
    - High level of openness in communication across the organization.
    - Openness to new ideas and encouraging innovations. (In some cases fierce openness to new ideas and critique in matters affecting organizational performance.)
    - Emphasis on learning, training, education and development through various means across the organization and, in some industries, institutionalized knowledge development

- Continual review of strategy, markets, changing technology and business environment combined with willingness, ability and initiative for change and renewal. (Creative insecurity through 'work outs' in some organizations like L&T).

Competitive Global Mindset

1. *Growth, Innovativeness and Entrepreneurship: Global Mindset*
   - Seeking opportunities for growth in international and domestic markets and competing with world-class technology. Global mindset.
   - Development of competence by benchmarking with the best in the world and operating in competitive international markets.
   - High priority to innovation and entrepreneurship.
2. *Quality, Productivity and Constant Improvement in Technology*
   - Focus on constant improvement for high quality, high productivity and high performance. Strong quality initiatives closely monitored from the top.
   - Mastering and developing technology and constant endeavour for improvement through R&D.

Meritocracy and Professionalism

1. *Meritocracy, Professionalism and Business Ethics*
   - Meritocracy in selections, rewards, promotions and career advancement.
   - Professional approach in planning, decision-making, monitoring and performance review.
   - High emphasis on values-based policies and practices, professional integrity and business ethics.

Family Like Relationships and Simplicity in Style of Leaders

1. *Family Like Relationships, Belonging and Pride*
   - Extended family like relationships, supportive and caring environment across the organization and with direct stakeholders.

- Supportive and caring human resource policies and practices combined with demanding expectations.
- Sense of ownership and pride in belonging to the organization among employees and stakeholders.

2. *Simplicity and Modesty in Style and Prudent Resource Utilization*

- Simplicity, modesty and almost austerity in personal life-style by top leaders.
- Emphasis on prudent resource utilization and expenditure of company funds.
- Efficient working capital and inventory management practices.
- Innovative resource mobilization.
- Conservative financial policies for debt-equity ratio and internal resource generation.

The point to be noted here is that although the characteristics listed above were practiced in many other organizations in parts also, they did not necessarily become internalized in their organization culture. Whereas in the outstanding organizations such characteristics and practices were manifested in their value system. These had become an integral part of their culture, which was persistently practiced and passed on to the new entrants in the organization through various learning and training processes and enabled them to sustain their competitiveness.

TRANSPARENCY AND PROFESSIONALISM IN CORPORATE GOVERNANCE

In an earlier chapter entitled 'What is Sustainable Competitive Edge?', one of the main points made was about the importance of corporate governance. As Mr. Subodh Bhargava of Eicher had said: "If you say competitiveness, sustainability – if you take (all) the parameters, there is only one word which is common in all... *Governance, the quality of governance.* That governance, to my mind, comes from leadership. So sustainable competitiveness cannot be brought in until the organization has got a sustained high quality of leadership and sustained outlook towards its people and towards its people does not mean softness – it means motivation, it means skills, it means development, it means training, it means ownership, it means involvement, it means empowerment and all that and governance, of course. I mean *if owners are going to continue to short-change other stake holders in whatever environment, then obviously it is not sustainable'.*

The criticality of corporate governance has come to the forefront after a major shakeup in the corporate world by the collapse of companies like Enron. The issues pertaining to the quality of corporate governance are being debated almost all over the industrialized world. Governments in various countries, including India, are reviewing their laws and rules to ensure better quality of corporate governance. There is too much at stake for the business world, economies and various stakeholders in the quality of corporate governance. And yet, this is a subject which often takes a back seat in the education and training of business leaders and professional managers.

The most important factors noted for the quality of corporate governance in this study were *transparency, professionalism and meritocracy.*

The companies that are most respected and valued are known for the highest level of transparency. Mr. Narayana Murthy, the chairman of Infosys (which is one of the most valued and respected companies of India), had emphatically told the shareholders in the company's general meeting: "The company would continue to make decisions and forecasts based on a fair assessment of market realities and customer expectations and not necessarily on financial markets' expectations... The company believes in following the *highest degree of transparency and openness* with you".[28] Such forthright candidness about the projections of profitability of the company sometimes led to have a fall in share prices and lowered the market capitalization of the company substantially, but the company has consistently maintained its policy of transparency and openness. Similarly, the rating agency, CRISIL, gave the highest rating to Hero Honda and HDFC for corporate governance and value creation (GVC), based on their assessment of creating wealth for their shareholders while adopting sound corporate governance practices, in which transparency was one of the key factors.[29]

Professionalism and meritocracy are the other key factors that determine the quality of corporate governance.

An example of high degree of professionalism and meritocracy as a guiding principle and the openness of top leadership to listen to the views of responsible managers for the best interest of the company, is evident in the case of Ranbaxy company. Explaining how the company persistently follows the values of professionalism and meritocracy, Mr. Brar said:

> "It is very difficult and the values are constantly repudiated and we say fine, they will be as long as human beings are there, but we carry on.

And then there is *meritocracy value, which is totally enshrined in the company.* It was a company, which was still owned 32 per cent by a family, but the family's chairman Dr. Parvinder Singh was so visionary that there is no family member in the board today (i.e., at the time of interview). They will come as they grow up. When Dr. Singh was alive, he was the only family member in the board.

I will give you this last example of *professionalism* of this company and this is the one of the values that we cherish in this company. We are open. We are highly critical. We can say what we want in this company and this is denied in many companies. We have a system where there is a policy committee which is comprising 6 people, which decides all the policy and strategy of the company. And then there is the PPC on top, the Policy committee and then the Board. All the people who report to the policy committee, their annual appraisals and their recommendations, increases in the compensation, are discussed jointly by the Policy committee. So if I have eight people reporting to me and the other five have 4-4 or 5-5 people, those 30-40 people are reviewed jointly. And then a very collegial view is taken. It is a combined view of everybody and many times it happened that if Dr. Parvinder Singh, who was a 32 per cent owner of this company, came up with a recommendation, it could be challenged. I remember once that he wanted to promote somebody and we shot it down. We said we don't think this guy is justified and you have not taken right decision. And he said: "I think you're right". And thrice he took back such decisions. He said: "My colleagues are right, I am taking a more emotionally favored decision". Now that kind of professionalism runs through this company.

CONCERN FOR BROADER SOCIETAL ISSUES AND ENVIRONMENT

Corporate Social Sensitivity and Concerns

Several outstanding companies and their top leaders demonstrated concern, sensitivity and thought leadership in finding solutions for society's selected economic, social and environmental issues; such as environmental friendly technologies, enhancing productivity of critical sectors and corporate social responsibility.

We have already discussed, in the chapter on Internal and External Relationships, the orientation and concern of the winning companies to safeguard the interests of the stakeholders, matters relating to environmental protection issues and broader social issues. We wish to re-emphasize these points here, as they were also evident in the values framework of such companies and were clearly reflected in their policies and practices.

In the case of Hero Honda, as we have mentioned in the context of leadership and relationships, the chairman said: the place where you set up the factory, the water coming out of your waste-water treatment plant should not damage an inch of somebody else's land. The smoke that comes out of your factory should not at all damage the environment around."

Similarly, in the case of Ranbaxy, Mr. Brar stated: "And then there is *concern for environment and safety*. And again, in our situation, we don't feel that environment safety and health is an expedience. If it (the regulatory requirement) does not come to India, so we can manage it. It is a very high concern for us being in this industry. And again here it is not an issue that we can make, (like) we can be very PR friendly with certain environment health officials and therefore we can run the so called 'approved plant'. It is genuinely going to the technologies that the company has been pioneering – by bringing in *environment friendly technologies,* to make sure that our plants our compliant. Then, of course, shareholders' wealth. That ultimately – at the end of the day – it is all shareholders' wealth. If we can't appreciate that, then we are not good for anything. And also we believe in, to a very considerable extent, in networking the growth through business partners – whether it is the competitors, or it is the suppliers – they are part of our business. It is not old paradigm that was there. If purchase man could deny information to his supplier to squeeze him on prices – that was the old paradigm. Today we have everything open to our suppliers and say: well this is what we want, this is our cost structure and this is what we would like from you. And there is total transparency. He is open to everything of the company in terms of what we do and he becomes a partner with you."

In the case of Tata group of companies, it was emphasized that: 'the greatness of an organization is its ability to change with the times without leaving its principles, without diluting the principles by which it exists, by which it lives everyday. The second (point) is that we take into account some other parameters, which reflect more of *social concerns, equitable distribution not equal distribution to all stakeholders...* There is a process of Balance Scorecard Approach to this and that approach ensures that equitable attention is certainly paid to all stakeholders. In fact all Tata group companies now follow the Tata Business Excellence model, process of managing their companies, which ensures the criteria. It is customer-driven; everything, the whole organization is customer-driven, but it ensures returns to all stakeholders.'

So also in almost all other companies studied, there was notable emphasis on corporate social responsibility and safeguarding interests of all stakeholders. This is consistent with the emerging 'Stakeholder Theory' of corporate management. As stated by Freeman and Reed: 'longitudinal research from Canada indicates that the ethical implications of adopting a stakeholder framework have led to a positive impact on the corporate social performance of the participating corporations. The findings led to a proposition being advanced for empirical testing that when a corporation is unable to continue as a going concern, it will be shown that one or more of the primary stakeholder groups has withdrawn from participation in that corporate system. Findings revealed a significant correlation between sustainability of companies and their policies towards stakeholders.'[30]

Many other companies that have made a mark by their success and have been highly rated for their competitiveness, demonstrate concern for Corporate Social Responsibility (CSR) which is pursued by such companies not merely as an altruistic philosophy, but as an enlightened self-interest. An example of such orientation is the statement of the vice-chairman & MD of Mahindra & Mahindra, a distinguished and dynamic automobile company: 'Corporate Social Responsibility is a very important part of our corporate values but it's not entirely altruistic. Much of what a company does by way of CSR reaps dividend in the form of earning the trust and respect of the consumer and this enhances value for all stakeholders.'[31]

The important point to be noted here is that the outstanding companies that we have described as 'Purposeful Values-driven Enterprises' pursued the concerns stated above not only to maintain mutually rewarding relationships with the stakeholders as described in the chapter on 'Win-Win' Relationships for enlightened self interest but there were also clear indications that many of these companies acted in such matters from a certain value framework with a 'social conscience' that was different from the generally believed business values paradigm.

The leaders of such organizations felt that, apart from the question of enlightened self-interest, they cannot be indifferent to the wider socio-economic and environmental issues and they owe a responsibility towards the wider society and economy of which they are a part. Therefore, they took up such causes either directly through corporate policies, plans and actions, or indirectly through philanthropic foundations established by them as in the case of Infosys, Wipro, Tatas, Dr. Reddy, etc. In other words, they saw the business enterprise as an important organ of society for creating value, wealth and employment, which is interdependent on other societal institutions. They seemed to realize that business enterprise is not only an instrument for enriching businessmen; it can be a highly productive and creative institution for the sustenance, growth and development of the economy and society as well as for the benefit of its stakeholders, if it works with a certain purpose and on the basis of certain values that are mutually beneficial to the enterprise as well as to the society.

The findings and inferences that we have discussed are based on our analysis of interviews, observations and information obtained from published sources about the 19 companies selected for this research. The question arises about the validity of the sample in terms of representing organizations that have demonstrated sustainable competitive edge. For this purpose a comprehensive and critical analysis of the performance of the companies in relation to their respective industries was done. The next chapter is devoted to a 'Critical Analysis of Performance and Sustainability' of the companies studied.

REFERENCES

1. For elaboration of the concepts of 'core purpose' and 'core values', see James C. Collins and Jerry I. Porras, *Built to Last* (New York: Harper Collins, 1997).
2. *ibid.*
3. Stephen Covey, *The 7 Habits of Highly Effective People*, (London: Simon & Shuster, 1992) 32,33.
4. *The Random House Dictionary of the English Language* (India: Allied Publishers Pvt. Ltd., 1969, Reprinted 1977).
5. *ibid.*
6. Robert A. Pitts & David Lei, *Strategic Management* (Singapore: South Western College Publishing, 2003).
7. *Ibid.*
8. G. Hofstede, *Culture's Consequences*, (Beverly Hills: Calif. Sage, 1980).
9. Robert A. Pitts & David Lei, *op. cit.*, 416.
10. Research interview with Mr. R. Gopalakrishnan, executive director, Tata Sons Limited.
11. Sumantra Ghoshal *et.al.*, *World Class in India,* op. cit., (2002), 600.
12. Peter F. Drucker, *The Practice of Management*, (New York: Harper & Brothers Publishers, 1954), 37.

13. The Strategist, *Business Standard*, 13th February, 2001.
14. Research interview with Mr. R. Gopalakrishnan, executive director of Tata Sons, who was formerly with Hindustan Levers.
15. Research interview with Mr. Yogi Sriram, vice president, corporate HR and personnel, Larsen & Toubro Limited.
16. Research interview with Dr. K. Dinesh, co-founder and member of the board, Infosys Technologies Ltd.
17. *Outlook,* New Delhi, January 27, 2003
18. *ibid.*
19. *ibid.*
20. The Hewitt Survey, covering 204 companies in Asia Pacific, which aims to identify the combination of factors that allow financially successful companies to consistently produce good leaders. Five Indian companies were in the list of 10 Top Companies for Leaders in Asia Pacific. Wipro was at No.1, followed by Tata Steel, ICICI Bank in the fifth place, Larsen & Toubro next, and ITC at number nine. APAC markets included were Australia, China, Hongkong, India, Japan, Korea and Singapore. *The Economic Times*, New Delhi, Dec. 4, 2003, 4.
21. Research interview with Mr. Pratik Kumar, corporate vice-president - human resources, Wipro Limited.
22. *Business Standard*, November 4, 2002.
23. Research interview with Dr. U. Balaji, vice president – Satyam Learning Center, Satyam Computer Services Ltd.
24. Research interview with Mr. Subodh Bhargava, former chairman, Eicher Motors Limited.
25. Research interview with Mr. G.V. Prasad, executive vice-chairman and CEO of Dr. Reddy's Laboratories Ltd.
26. *ibid.*
27. *ibid.*
28. *Business Standard*, June 16, 2003.
29. *Business Standard*, Jan. 3, 2003.
30. R.E. Freeman and D. Reed, 'Stockholders and Stakeholders: A new perspective on corporate governance' in C. Hinzinga (Ed.) *Corporate Governance: A Definitive Exploration of the Issues,* (Los Angeles, UCLA, Extension Press, 1983).
31. *Indian Management,* December 2001, 128.

CHAPTER NINE

The Firm as a Living System and the Emerging Modern Indian Corporation (EMIC)

'Seeing a company as a living being means that it is capable of regenerating itself, of continuity as an identifiable entity beyond its present members'

PETER M. SENGE

THE FIRM AS A LIVING, SOCIO-ECONOMIC-TECHNICAL OPEN SYSTEM

In this chapter we will attempt to modify and build the theory of organization based on the framework of analysis, patterns and insights that have been described in the earlier chapters. The main framework of analysis that we have developed in this study is shown in Figure 9.1 and is reproduced below in order to relate it to the theory of organization.

The open systems view of organization is now well accepted in contemporary writings and research on organizations. It is to be distinguished from the earlier mechanistic models of organization. The socio-technical aspects of organization have also been widely researched. A deeper and more holistic analysis of the firm as an entity reveals that it can be viewed as a living, Socio-Economic-Technical Open System that takes the inputs of resources from its external environment and converts them into outputs that create value for the society in which it is embedded (See Figure 9.2).

Figure 9.1: The Five Distinguishing Elements of Purposeful Values-driven Organizations

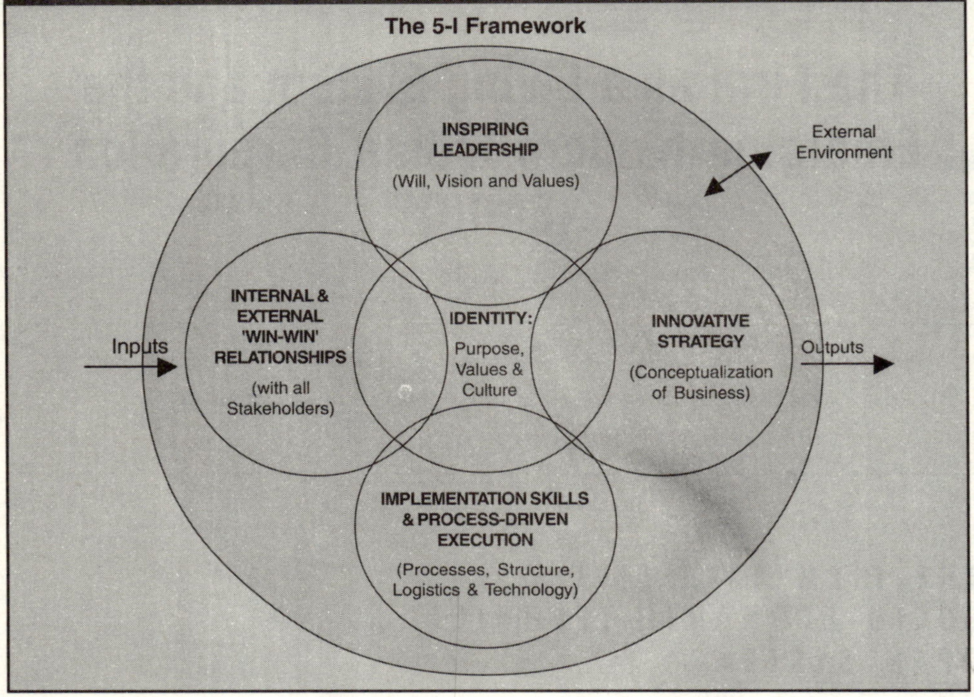

The 5-I Framework
INSPIRING LEADERSHIP
(Will, Vision and Values)
External Environment
INTERNAL & EXTERNAL 'WIN-WIN' RELATIONSHIPS
(with all Stakeholders)
Inputs
IDENTITY:
Purpose, Values & Culture
INNOVATIVE STRATEGY
(Conceptualization of Business)
Outputs
IMPLEMENTATION SKILLS & PROCESS-DRIVEN EXECUTION
(Processes, Structure, Logistics & Technology)

THE FIRM AS AN ORGANIC, CO-EVOLVING, OPEN, SOCIO-ECONOMIC-TECHNICAL SYSTEM

Figure 9.2: Purposeful, Values-driven Enterprise

Identity, Values, Culture &Purpose
Social
Changing External Business Environment, Technology and Markets
Inputs
Technical
Economic
Outputs (leading to Economic value and wealth creation)

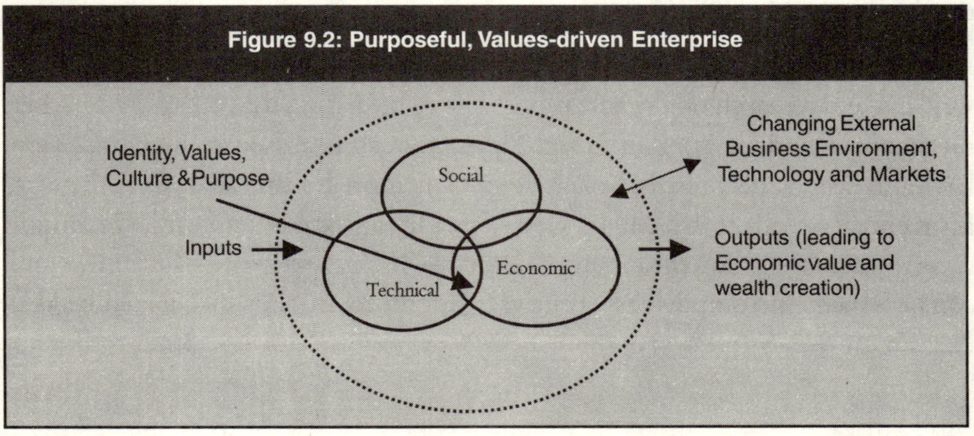

In this model, we are explicitly emphasizing the *organic* nature of organization, adding the *economic* dimension in the socio-technical model and also bringing in the phenomenon of *co-evolution* in the theory of organization, in order to make it more comprehensive, holistic and representative of the empirical reality of the organizations. It is in contrast with the other view of a firm that is subsumed in the philosophy and practice by its ownership/leadership, as well as in the economic theory of firm, that the firm is merely a mechanical instrumentality for profit maximization. It is this underlying paradigm, which in our view distinguishes the Purposeful Values-driven Enterprises (PVEs) from the Money-making Commercial Outfits (MCOs), as explained in detail in Chapter 2.

This model emphasizes the need for managing, developing and constantly improving all the four major dimensions (Social, Economic, Technical and Identity – with distinct values and purpose) of an enterprise on sound lines. Weakness or failure in any of these dimensions can lead to ineffectiveness and decline of the firm.

We visualize the open systems model of organization as an organic, living institution driven by **leadership with passion to win,** which enables it to develop and sustain competitive edge. It is a dynamic entity, closely related to and co-evolving with its changing environment.

The primary purpose of the firm, as visualized in this model, is to create wealth by generating economic value through better products, services and solutions for its customers and consumers and share the benefits with its stakeholders. It develops and utilizes resources innovatively and productively through which it creates value that leads to higher profitability and growth and creates wealth. If the firm performs these functions with a socially desirable and constructive purpose and a strong belief and practice of some positive values and principles for doing business, it inspires trust, confidence and respect of the customers and stakeholders that make it sustainable.

The sustainable firm, therefore, is a value and wealth-creating, living and growing organism that is embedded in its socio-economic milieu and co-evolves with the changing business environment. *The firm cannot be sustainable, in the long run, as a predatory mechanism to siphon off monopoly gains,* or rent-seeking behaviour, that exploits its customers and employees, because it cannot create genuine value that is based on trust and satisfaction of its customers and other stakeholders. That is why the inefficient firms that thrived in the artificially created market system during the 'license and permit raj' in India and exploited the customers and other stakeholders, are disappearing with the heat of competition of open markets.

The sustainable firm is a Purposeful Values-driven Enterprise as discussed in detail in the earlier chapters. It creates economic value through a principle-centered, values-driven paradigm, benefiting the customers and consumers, as well as the other stakeholders of the firm in a fair and generally equitable manner. It is based on a totally different paradigm, contrasted with the common perception of the firm as a profit-seeking mechanism, only to maximize the benefit for the controlling owners, managers and shareholders.

Social, Economic, Technical and Identity Dimensions of the Firm

Let us now describe what we mean by the Social, Economic, Technical and Identity dimensions of a firm as shown in this model.

The **Social dimension** of the organization consists of the *people* and their orientation in aspects like leadership, motivation, attitudes, relationships and all the complex **human** dimensions of the enterprise. It is manifested more explicitly in the clusters of characteristics that we have identified under Leadership, Relationships and Identity (values, culture, etc). It has to do more with the 'softer' variables in the working of the organization and is somewhat similar to the 'people, processes and purpose' aspect of organization as identified by some authors like Sumantra Ghoshal.

The **Economic dimension** consists of the *financial and material resources,* their allocation and utilization; procurement, marketing and other elements directly related to transactions that affect costs and profits. It manifests itself more explicitly in budgets, plans, costing, output and revenue measurements; working capital and inventories; and other aspects that determine market values, returns and profitability of the enterprise.

The **Technical dimension** consists of *technology,* knowledge, competencies and techniques utilized for processing inputs into outputs. Technical aspects include not only technologies, but also systems and processes that determine efficiency, outputs, productivity and quality. The technical and economic dimensions manifest themselves more explicitly in the clusters identified by us as Strategy and Execution. These are somewhat similar to the so-called 'harder' variables of the working of organizations, classified by some authors as 'strategy, structure and systems'

There are also overlapping areas at the interfaces of social, technical and economic dimensions of the organization. The interface of human and technical elements is called 'socio-technical' aspect of the system. Such interfaces and overlaps are also between the economic and technical aspects, as well as social and economic aspects. Thus there are **'socio-technical', 'techno-economic' and 'socio-economic' interfaces** in the organization as may be seen in the Figure 9.2. Examples of these interfaces are:

- ***Socio-technical:*** the work group and technology interface (or simpler interface like man-machine interaction).
- ***Techno-economic:*** capital-intensive technology and its implications on costs, outputs and quality.
- ***Socio-economic:*** compensation system and its implications on employee motivation, morale and outputs.

The firm's efficiency, productivity, quality and quantity of outputs and innovativeness are a function of all these variables, in addition to the variables identified in the main clusters.

In addition to the explicit social, economic and technical aspects of the firm, we have focused attention on the **central core of the organization,** consisting of a strong and distinctive sense of **identity,** deeply embedded **values** and **culture,** and clearly articulated and persistently pursued **purpose** of the organization, as shown in the space where all the three dimensions of the organization overlap at the centre of the figure.

The functional relevance of this model of organization is that it draws attention to the four major aspects of the organization and indicates the criticality of paying attention to all four of them. The outstanding organizations maintain a fine balance in all the four aspects and ensure constant improvement in each one of them to evolve to higher levels of growth and excellence.

In other words, the outstanding organizations pay attention to the social and human aspects by creating conditions that lead to attracting the best talent, keeping it highly motivated, committed and functioning as a team, that sets challenging goals and achieves them. The examples of such characteristics have been given in detail in the earlier chapters and the examples of Infosys, HLL and Hero Honda are a few among the many described in the text.

The outstanding companies have sharp economic management skills, reflected in superior operational, financial and marketing policies and practices that lead to cost effectiveness, high revenues, returns and financial health of the organization. The examples of companies like Wipro, Reliance and Titan given in the earlier chapters demonstrate these skills very strongly.

The technical dimension is attended to very carefully by the outstanding organizations by constantly updating and mastering the technology; and reviewing, streamlining and improving the structure, systems and processes. The examples of Ranbaxy, Eicher and Sundram Fasteners given in detail in the text exemplify these skills very explicitly.

The core of identity, values, culture and purpose has been explained in detail in chapter 8. The attention to this sustaining core is a primary concern of leaders in the outstanding organizations. They articulate, emphasize, role model and educate the members of organization in these aspects like drumbeat. The strength of this core and attention paid to it differentiates the outstanding organizations from the ordinary organizations and is one of the key elements in their sustainability over long spans of time. Examples of business houses like Tata Sons and companies like HLL, Larsen & Toubro, Infosys and Wipro make this point clear.

THE OPEN, ORGANIC, CO-EVOLVING NATURE OF ORGANIZATIONS

The **'open'** aspect of the organization as a system is its openness to information, interaction and relationship with its external environment. As we have explained in detail in the chapter on strategy, the outstanding organizations constantly seek information about changes, new developments, opportunities and challenges in the market, technology and other aspects of business environment. They keep ear to the ground and pro-actively seek feedback from the customers and employees. They cultivate and nurture mutually supportive relationships with the external and internal stakeholders.

It is the openness, willingness and ability to change in these organizations that enables them to be **'organic'**, living systems that survive, adapt, cope with and initiate change proactively. Such organizations continue to grow. It is the key to their sustainable competitiveness. On the contrary, the organizations that function as closed 'in-organic' or mechanistic systems, do not remain in touch with the changes in the internal and external environment. They are not sensitive and proactive in dealing with the imperatives of change. They tend to lose out, decline and die.

The **'co-evolving'** aspect of the organization as a system refers to it growing and changing with the changes in the dynamic environment, while maintaining the continuity of its essential core purpose, values and identity. The companies included in this research clearly demonstrated their constant evolution with the changing environment. Old companies like Tata Sons, L&T, as well as relatively new companies like Wipro, Satyam, Dr. Reddy's Labs, Ranbaxy, were constantly evolving in many dimensions, moving up the value chain and becoming increasingly international in their orientation. A close observation of these companies helped us to identify the phenomenon of the emergence of the Modern Indian Corporation.

THE EMERGING MODERN INDIAN CORPORATION (EMIC)

A Purposeful Values-driven Enterprise with a unique combination of Indian Culture, Western Style and Techniques and Japanese Practices

This research study has revealed the emergence of a new form of business firms in India with the changing business environment, which has some unique characteristics. Such firms are able to successfully compete in the domestic as well as international markets and therefore, seem to be endowed with a sustainable competitive edge. We have chosen to describe such a firm as the **'Emerging Modern Indian Corporation' (EMIC).**

The Emerging Modern Indian Corporation is a unique combination of Indian culture, Western style and techniques of management and Japanese practices for productivity and quality improvement. Such outstanding Indian companies are distinctively Purposeful Values-driven Enterprises as described in this research study. Companies like Sundram Fasteners, Hero Honda and Titan in the 'old' industries and Infosys, Wipro, Satyam, Ranbaxy and Dr. Reddy's in the 'new' industries are some examples of such firms (if they stick to the purpose, principles and values that have developed their character and stature so far).

The uniqueness of the Emerging Modern Indian Corporation seems to be that it has an extended Indian family like caring and 'win-win' relationship with its employees and stakeholders. Their leaders use the metaphor of family in dealing with the employees and other stakeholders. They maintain personal touch and close family-like relationship with them and participate in their occasions of rejoicing as well as sorrow. Their personal lifestyle is usually very simple, guided by middle-class values and is almost austere in some cases.

The EMIC has western style professionalism, meritocracy, openness and egalitarianism and modern management techniques. It also utilizes many western originated processes and techniques like strategic analysis, performance management, balanced scorecards, six sigma, etc.

In addition, the EMICs intensively utilize Japanese practices for improving quality and productivity, like total productivity management, kaizan, kan ban, Just-in-time inventory system (JIT), quality circles, etc. The EMICs have effectively blended these three different streams (Indian, Western and Japanese) of management philosophy, organizational culture, management techniques and practices, while maintaining their Indian identity and key values.

The most striking aspect of the EMICs is their **passion to win,** operate internationally and eventually become Indian multinational/transnational corporations. There is strong evidence of a shift in the mindset of the leadership of such companies. They demonstrate a growing confidence and willingness to compete in the global arena, unlike their earlier counterparts who had a domestic mindset, seeking sheltered markets to avoid competition. Not only the companies in the relatively new IT and Pharmaceutical industries like Infosys, Wipro and Ranbaxy are setting such examples, but companies in the traditional industries like engineering, automobile components and metals like TISCO, TELCO, TVS Group, Bharat Forge, A.V. Birla Group, are also spreading their wings internationally.

Interestingly, most of the business leaders and entrepreneurs who have built the EMICs have a great **passion to win and a global mindset** to build world-class organizations. They dare to dream big and have the tenacity to make their dreams come true, yet they are generally extremely modest and simple in their life style, like Mr. N.R.Narayana Murthy, Mr. Azim Premji and Mr. B.M.L.Munjal. This appears to be a unique Indian cultural trait that distinguishes them from their western counterparts.

The EMICs create and deliver genuine value to the customers, thereby creating and sharing wealth, safeguarding the interests of all stakeholders. They anticipate change and quickly respond to the changing business environment by their willingness and ability to change. They adapt as well as proact by innovative business strategies.

These enterprises are managed through highly efficient and nimble processes, structures and systems across the value chain and supply chain. Their processes, structures and systems are continually reviewed and improved to ensure highest levels of productivity and quality. Their productivity, cost and quality parameters are benchmarked with the best in the world. Some of them are aiming at becoming benchmarks for other organizations across the world.

They combine continuity and change. They stick to their core values, business philosophy and core purpose; and yet they continue to transform, evolve, redefine and reinvent themselves to cope with and influence the changing business environment. They develop a strong identity, learning and competency building egalitarian, team-oriented culture, a sense of pride and belonging among the employees and stakeholders.

They create an internal environment that attracts and nurtures the best talent, innovation, constant improvement, empowerment, risk-taking, entrepreneurship and leadership across the organization. They keep their 'ears to the ground', obtain and absorb enormous information from the environment, encourage openness, high level of communication and feedback from the employees and customers.

They follow conservative and innovative financial policies and generally grow organically as well as inorganically, usually through internal resource generation.

The most distinctive aspect of their strategy is to take **the route of internationalization,** or world-class quality and scale in their operations for developing their competence and competitiveness. There is a growing trend now of acquiring companies overseas to develop international operations and acquire international stature and expertise. The Emerging Modern Indian Corporations are increasingly becoming multinational and global.

Such enterprises strive hard to win and maintain the confidence, trust and respect of the customers and stakeholders by practicing high levels of transparency, professionalism and meritocracy in their governance. They are sensitive and caring towards larger socio-economic and environmental issues and aim at good corporate citizenship.

Such Purposeful, Value-creating, Values-driven Enterprises are more than organizations. They are socio-economic-technical *institutions* that continue to co-evolve with the changing business environment and are able to sustain themselves and retain their competitive edge over long spans of time.

The Emerging Modern Indian Corporation is the Purposeful Values-driven Enterprise that is shaping the industrial destiny and international brand equity of India. It is creating role models that will enable the Indian Corporations to become world-class professionally managed corporations. Such corporations will be in the league of worldwide values-driven global corporations and help the Indian economy in becoming one of the world's largest developed economies.

CHAPTER TEN

Critical Analysis of Performance and Sustainability of the Companies Studied

'Research means that you don't know, but are willing to find out'

CHARLES F. KETTERING

IN THE PREVIOUS CHAPTERS we presented a qualitative analysis of various factors which seem to impart sustainability in growth to organizations. We now attempt a comparative analysis of the performance of the companies studied by us in such detail with those on whom we obtained information through secondary sources such as write-ups in business magazines, newspapers and our own desk research including the works of others, such as Sumantra Ghoshal. We may mention here that Ghoshal and others have studied some of these organizations in detail in their book Managing Radical Change[1]. But it will be clear to a careful reader that there are significant differences in the approach used by Ghoshal and others and the approach of the present study. In this study we use four basic parameters to assess the sustainability of organizations. These are fairly simple and include:

1. A change in the sales turnover (compound rate of growth)
2. A change in the profits (profit before depreciation interest and taxation[2])
3. A change in the reserves and surplus and
4. A change in the market capitalization.

While the first three are predominantly intrinsic to the organization and, therefore, the organization has significant control over these, the fourth, the change in market capitalization, is based on the perception of the market regarding the value of the organization. It would be difficult to say as to what extent the change in market value of shares is influenced by long-term sustainability. But, it has been noticed that the day the news of some drug applied for licensing by a pharmaceutical firm is approved, its share price records an increase. At the same time, it is also true that the share price of an organization may register a fall consequent upon its inability to register profits equal to or more than the targeted profits for the quarter. Similar divergence in expectations regarding sales registered could once again influence the price of the shares of the company. Finally, external factors such as the outbreak of war or some political event could exert a downward trend in the prices of shares of all companies including the ones, under review. Notwithstanding these divergent influences of market valuation, external factors are important enough to be included in assessing the probability of long-term sustainability of an organization.

Literature in economics states that the long-term sustainability of a firm depends upon the rate of investment and proportion of resources reinvested in enhancing capacity. In the context of a micro level study, such as the one attempted in this exercise, undistributed profits and reserves could measure such survivability. This, however, is just one of the factors, recognizing that there are other important factors, which lead to the improved probability of sustainability. These include, among others, the allocation of resources between meeting immediate requirements and those of the long-term. This, therefore, is the standard dilemma faced by any decision-maker regarding allocation of resources to improve the short-term profitability and long-term sustainability. In this context, the work of Mariss (Optimal Rate of Growth of Firm)[3] offers a number of valuable suggestions for business practitioners. Equally important is the observation of Peter Drucker that the top management needs to have a bifocal vision: one for the short-term interests of the firm and the other for the long-term.

It is true that resources retained and invested in the firm improve its sustainability capacity. However, organizations have to be equally careful about their liquidity position. Organizations such as Arvind Mills, United Breweries and Essar Group, invested large resources in creating capacity ignoring their liquidity position and faced difficulty in paying interest and repaying installments of loans. Therefore, besides investment in the long run in capacity creation and research and development, firms need to ensure that investment in the long run does not result in excessive interest obligation leading to financial difficulty. Keeping these concerns in mind, in the paragraphs below, we review the performance of companies that have been short-listed by us in six important sectors. In each sector we have results of companies studied by us in detail. These results are compared with the performance of other companies on whom information was obtained using secondary sources.

INFORMATION TECHNOLOGY SECTOR

In this sector, we have considered the performance of five companies out of which three have been studied by us in detail. Amongst these organizations, Satyam Computer Services Ltd. emerges as the one with highest probability of sustainability. It registered 85% rate of growth (compound rate) in sales turnover; 72% rate of growth in profits and 197% rate of growth in market capitalization. These figures are way above the selective industry average of 41% for sales and 43% for profits (see table 10.1 for details). The next one, in order of prospects of sustainability, is the admired company of Infosys Technologies Ltd. It has a compound rate of growth of 71% in sales, 73% in profits and 114% in market capitalization. Wipro has registered a relatively low performance on these parameters as it has presence in sectors other than information technology also. The sectors such as edible oils and medical equipments have not registered such a high rate of growth as has been registered by the IT sector. Yet this performance is a bit disconcerting in as much as Wipro Ltd gets about 82% of its revenue from the information technology sector.

The other companies included are Digital and Polaris. Digital, of course, has only 32% rate of growth in sales and 34% in profits, which is lower than the three companies included in the study for detailed analysis. In contrast, Polaris has registered the highest rate of growth 101% in sales and 79% in profits. But the data for this company relates to a limited time period only.

When we consider the index of sustainability, as recommended in the literature in economics (rate of growth of reserves and surpluses reinvested), Wipro Ltd and Infosys Technologies registered a rate of growth of 48% and 85% respectively but Satyam, once again, registered the highest rate of growth of 95%. This, of course, excludes the information relating to Polaris for which we had data for the limited time period of 1995-2003. Polaris registered the highest rate of growth of 116%. From these rates of growths, once again, it is clear that Satyam has been investing in long-term prospects to a fairly considerable extent.

Table 10.1

Company Name	DS	DP	DRS	DMC***
Infosys Technologies Ltd.	71*	73*	85*	114#
Satyam Computer Services Ltd.	85#	72#	95#	197[1]
Wipro Ltd.	27	39	48	88
Digital	32	34&	67**	
Polaris	101+	79+	116+	
Selective Industry Average**	41	43	82	

All Figures given above are in percentages.

All Figures given have 1990 as the base year and 2003 as the terminal year.

DS - Sales Turnover DP - Profits DMC - Market Capitalisation DRS - Reserves & Surplus

* Base Year 1992 # Base Year 1994 + Base Year 1995 & Base Year 1991 ** Base Year 1993

[1]Base Year 1996 *** Base Year 1990 and Terminal Year 2001

**Selective industry average was calculated on the basis of figures for upto the twenty top companies in the industry, other than the companies included in the study.

To our mind the superior performance of Satyam is due to its entrepreneurial thrust as against the more structured approach of Infosys Technologies Ltd and Wipro Ltd. The focus of the latter companies has been to move in a planned manner to reach a predetermined destination. In the case of Infosys Technologies Ltd. this destination was to create 100 millionaires through developing world level IT solutions. In Wipro's case it is to be amongst the top most admired companies at the global level through ethical practices. But the thrust in the case of Satyam Computers is on innovativeness. This emphasis on innovativeness, by implication, means less of a structured approach including training etc. This, therefore, is a model that is close to people, processes and purpose as against the structured approach of strategy, structure and systems. We reiterate that the three-S approach does not undermine the importance of innovation in human beings and their skill upgradation but the emphasis in the case of innovativeness is more on freedom, creativity. This can be evidenced from the write-up given in the chapter on strategy, processes etc.

PHARMACEUTICAL SECTOR

In this sector, we considered two companies for in-depth analysis: Ranbaxy Laboratories Ltd and Dr. Reddy's Labs Ltd and two others from secondary sources i.e. Cipla and Nicholas Piramal. Dr. Reddy's registered a rate of growth of 38% in sales turnover, 45% in profits and 56% in market capitalization. These figures are decidedly higher than Ranbaxy Laboratories. The corresponding figures for Ranbaxy are 22% in sales turnover, 30% in profits and 53% in market capitalization. We are highlighting these two companies because both the companies have focussed on basic research. At the same time there is some difference in the two. At Dr. Reddy's, they have believed in following the inorganic route to growth (i.e. growth of business through acquisition's, mergers, etc.) whereas Ranbaxy has preferred more of organic growth (i.e. internal growth of business through expansion). Of course Ranbaxy has also acquired some companies but the level of acquisitions in the case of Dr. Reddy's Lab is of a higher order. This is particularly so when it comes to the strength of the companies acquired. In general, in Dr. Reddy's case, these acquired companies are in the areas of research whereas Ranbaxy Laboratories has acquired companies in other areas as well. The other two companies, not included for in-depth study, Cipla & Nicholas-Piramal, have a lower degree of strength for sustainability relative to Dr. Reddy's but demonstrate a higher registered rate of growth as regards sales turnover and profits. These results, of course, are influenced by the fact that these companies do not depend so critically upon basic research. As is well understood, investment in basic research is a time consuming process and gives results after a time lag. Therefore, strictly speaking, these companies should not be compared with Ranbaxy. Again, Nicholas Piramal has chosen the inorganic route to growth through acquisitions which is not so pronounced in the case of Ranbaxy Laboratories (for details see table 10.2).

Table 10.2

Company Name	ΔS	ΔP	ΔRS	ΔMC*
Ranbaxy	22	30	36	53
Dr. Reddy's Labs	38	45	67	56
Cipla	24	29	31	51
Nicholas Piramal	33	33	33	44
Selective Industry Average	**26**	**27**	**42**	

All Figures given above are in percentages.

All Figures given have 1990 as the base year and 2003 as the terminal year.

* Base Year 1990 and Terminal Year 2001

The prospects of long-term sustainability, as given by the rate of growth of reserves and surplus is again the highest for Dr. Reddy's. The rate of growth registered by Dr. Reddy's Labs is 67% as against 36% for Ranbaxy and 31% for Cipla.

AUTOMOBILE–TWO-WHEELERS SECTOR

In this sector we have included five companies for empirical assessment of their long-term sustainability one of which has been studied in detail (Hero Honda Motors Ltd.) while the remaining four have been studied based on secondary sources. These are Bajaj Auto, LML, TVS, Kinetic. A study of table 10.3 would show that Hero Honda definitely strikes as superior performer as judged by the three parameters mentioned above i.e. rate of growth of sales, profits and market capitalization. It registered a rate of growth of sales of 31% as against the selective industry average of 13%. Its rate of growth of profits was 2½ times the selective industry average, while in market capitalization it registered a rate of growth of 40% which is almost double the rate of growth of market capitalization of the nearest rival, TVS. One may recall that its unique ability to maintain relations both with vendors of input and distributors have been largely responsible for such a performance. Besides, it has been very customer friendly (would entertain the complaint even when it is known to be incorrect) and has a very good feel of the market.

The next in ability for sustainability is TVS, which has a rate of growth in sales of 25%, rate of growth of 30% in profits and rate of growth in market capitalization of 27%. There are no contradictions in the 3 parameters on which these 2 companies have been scrutinized. The other company, Bajaj Automobiles, has not come out as strong on this yardstick This company was a cash rich company but did not see the change in demand from scooters to motorcycles. It is our conjecture that partly this switch from scooters to motorcycles could be due to higher fuel efficiency of motorcycles, 80 kilometres per litre, as against the norms of about of 40 kilometres per litre in scooters. This difference in mileage can be attributed to the difference in two-stroke and four-stroke engines. Nonetheless, a motorcycle is any day a more reliable means of transportation in rural areas and even in suburban areas where roads are in an awful condition and are ill-maintained. Over and above all these factors, Hero Honda has been particularly emphatic in promoting its product through world cup series in cricket and other tournaments. Thus, it would be extremely difficult to say which factor could have been responsible for indicating a higher degree of sustainability as in the case of Hero Honda.

Hero Honda has done remarkably well as given by the prospects of long-term sustainability in the form of rate of growth of reserves and surplus. It registered a rate of growth of 42% as against 21% for Bajaj Auto and 23% for LML and 41% for Kinetic Motors. The rate of growth, as given by reserves and surplus, is the highest for TVS motors, though the data on this are for a limited period 1994-2003.

Table 10.3

Company Name	ΔS	ΔP	ΔRS	ΔMC***
Bajaj	14	14	21	10
Hero Honda	31	40	42+	40
LML	8#	-3#	23#	-15
TVS	25	30	64**	27
Kinetic	8+	2+	41*	
Selective Industry Average	**13**	**15**	**11**	

All Figures given above are in percentages.

All Figures given have 1990 as the base year and 2003 as the terminal year.

+ Base Year 1991 # Terminal Year 2002 * Base Year 1992 ** Base Year 1994

*** Base Year 1990 and Terminal Year 2001

AUTOMOBILE–FOUR-WHEELERS SECTOR

In this sector, we studied Eicher Motors in detail and three others through secondary sources. These are Telco, Swaraj Mazda and Maruti Udyog. Strictly speaking, Swaraj Mazda may be the only company which is comparable to Eicher Motors as producers of light commercial vehicles and other commercial vehicles. Telco and Maruti Udyog are in the passenger cars business too. This is particularly true of Maruti Udyog which hardly has any presence in commercial vehicle-except that it's Omni, and to a lesser extent Gypsy, could be considered falling in the category of commercial vehicle.

Eicher Motors registered a rate of growth in sales of 15% as against the selective industry average of 10%; 19% in profits (as against the selective industry average of 9%) and 7% in market capitalization as against 4% in case of Telco. (For details refer to Table 10.4). Probably the figures of Telco have been significantly influenced by its recent investment in the passenger car business which has just started yielding some profits. Nevertheless it registered 14% rate of growth in sales turnover but only 12% rate of growth in profits. It is clear that recent years have been witness to a very significant increase in intensity of competition and this has resulted in a squeeze in its profit. Swaraj Mazda is a fairly close contender to Eicher Motors but it registered a 12% rate of growth in sales and only 13% rate of growth in profits.

The results relating to the prospects of long-term sustainability are the highest for Eicher Motors as represented by rate of growth of reserves and surplus. Eicher motors registered a rate of growth of 41% as against 15% for Telco and 31% for Maruti Udyog. From this, it is clear that inclusion of Eicher Motors is again confirmed by this parameter of long-term sustainability.

Table 10.4

Company Name	ΔS	ΔP	ΔRS	ΔMC*
Telco	14	12	15	4
Swaraj Mazda	12	13		
Eicher Motors	15	19	41#	7
Maruti Udyog	18+	14+	31+	
Selective Industry Average	**10**	**9**	**12**	

All Figures given above are in percentages.

All Figures given have 1990 as the base year and 2003 as the terminal year.

* Base Year 1990 and Terminal Year 2001 # Base Year 1991 + Terminal Year 2002

FMCG SECTOR

In the FMCG sector, we considered HLL and Glaxo-SmithKline for an in-depth analysis whereas, on other firms included in the study, we obtained information from secondary sources. These are Britannia, Nestle, Colgate-Palmolive, Dabur, Godrej and Nirma. HLL registered 19% rate of growth in sales turnover, 26% rate of growth on profits (for details see table 10.5). We may mention that it registered a 40% rate of growth in market capitalization which is the highest if we exclude rate of growth of market capitalization of Dabur where the information available is only from 1995-2001. Surprisingly, Dabur comes fairly close to HLL, excluding of course Godrej & Nirma and has recorded 18% rate of growth of sales and 19% rate of growth in profits. One may recall that the selective industry average for these two are 16% and 17% respectively. It was very difficult to find firms which are strictly comparable. For instance, Britannia is in the snacks business but is not present in detergents. Glaxo-SmithKline is primarily in nutrient enhancing business but is absent in other sectors. Nestle's is in foods and beverages but is totally absent in detergents. Colgate-Palmolive is present only in personal grooming and hair care but is not present in other sectors. Dabur has been doing businesses predominantly in the Indian system of medicine besides the nutrient-enhancing sector. Godrej, till recently, was in the detergents business and many other fields and finally Nirma has been mostly dabbling in soaps and detergents. Nevertheless, the figures (see table 10.5) indicate that HLL has a very high probability of sustainability. This has been more than amply demonstrated by its recent moves of adopting a more flexible approach-people centric-and resorting to inorganic route to growth through acquisitions and mergers. This is all the more significant because HLL has been in existence for very long in India and, therefore, has acquired some inflexibility, which is normally associated with large organizations. In the chapter on Strategy and Implementation, it has been highlighted that the company has adopted a more adaptive model to growth and has been making an attempt to be as close to the customer as possible. It has been known for speed in implementation of strategy. Nirma definitely gave a very tough fight to HLL in the detergents business through its cost competitiveness and agility, which is normally associated with a young organization. It also resorted to a non-conventional approach to competing with HLL. Unlike recommendations in the literature on strategy, which suggest that small companies should avoid direct confrontations with large organizations, Nirma decided to take on HLL and yet proved successful.

Table 10.5

Company Name	ΔS	ΔP	ΔRS	ΔMC*
Britannia	12	19	22	19
Glaxo	16	15	24	14
Nestle's	18	20	13	21
Colgate	12	10	14	9
HLL	19	26	28	40
Dabur	18	19	22	52[1]
Godrej	2	24+	-17	-12
Nirma**	21	26	46	
Selective Industry Average	**16**	**17**	**24**	

All Figures given above are in percentages.

All Figures given have 1990 as the base year and 2003 as the terminal year.

* Base year 1990 and Terminal year 2001 [1] Base year 1995 + Terminal year 2000

** Base year 1991

Britannia Industries has been doing very well through their business in snack items and, particularly, through their superior promotion policies and product positioning. In the last year and a half, there has been some degree of disagreement between the promoters of the company and the CEO because of which has the company lost some grip on the market. Notwithstanding this, the company registered 12% rate of growth in sales turnover, 19% rate of growth in profits and 19% rate of growth in market capitalization. Nestle's comes fairly close to HLL on all parameters except market capitalization where it has just about 21% rate of growth as against 40% of HLL. Like HLL, Nestle's also felt the impact of recession and, to some degree, its pricing policy was out of tune with what is acceptable to the market.

Godrej has been one company which lost its preeminence but, nonetheless, has shown good performance on the parameter of rate of growth of sales and profits, because it has strong brands such as Cinthol and others, and these take time to be forgotten. However its brand equity suffered a set back resulting in a fall in market capitalization.

HLL has done better than other firms as regards long-term prospects of sustainability as measured by rate of growth of reserves and surplus except Nirma Ltd., which registered a higher rate of growth. The rate of growth for Nirma is 46% while HLL has a rate of growth of 28%. The rates of growth in reserves and surplus of other companies are 22%, 24%, 13%, 14% and 22% for Britannia Industries, GSK, Nestle's, Colgate-Palmolive, Dabur India respectively.

WHITE GOODS SECTOR

In this sector, we have reviewed the performance of 4 companies: BPL Ltd, Videocon, Philips India, Onida. On BPL Home Appliances, we obtained the information through in-depth study while for the remaining three companies through secondary sources. A scrutiny of table 10.6 would show that BPL is not as good a performer as measured by the rate of growth of sales as Videocon. But on the parameter of rate of growth of profits, it is fairly close to Videocon. Also, BPL has been unique on many accounts such as internationalization route to growth, large-scale production of components as against their import and, of late, entry into other businesses. The company's indiscriminate diversification into the cell phone business and energy sector and over-extending its debt, may have been responsible for unsatisfactory performance in market capitalization. Nevertheless, the company has a very strong base and all manufacturers of white goods use components produced by BPL. Its presence in Europe is providing it with some degree of buffer when Indian companies are experiencing sluggish demand and excess capacity. The performance of BPL is all the more encouraging if we compare these figures with selective industry averages. BPL registered 14% rate of growth in sales turnover which is 5 times the rate of growth of industry of 3%. Similarly it registered 22% rate of growth in profits, which is more than 3 times the selective industry average of 8%. Also the company possesses the necessary elements for sustainability in the long-term.

The results relating to prospects of long-term sustainability once again re-confirm the inclusion of BPL for an in-depth analysis. It registered a rate of growth of 33% in reserves and surplus, as against 43% for Videocon and 16% for Philips India.

Table 10.6

Company Name	ΔS	ΔP	ΔRS	ΔMC*
BPL Ltd	14**	22**	33**	7***
Videocon	30	28	43	
Philips	11	13	16	11
Onida	0++	-6++	-1+++	
Selective Industry Average	**3**	**8**	**6**	

All Figures given above are in percentages.

All Figures given have 1990 as the base year and 2003 as the terminal year.

* Base year 1990 and Terminal year 2001

** Terminal year 2002 *** Base year 1995 ++ Figures available from 1993-2002

+++ Base year 1997 and Terminal year 2002

WATCH SECTOR

In this sector, we considered 3 organizations – Titan Industries Ltd., HMT Ltd., and Timex Watches. HMT, as is known, is present in other sectors as well and to that extent the figures studied are strictly not comparable. On Titan Industries, we obtained information through in-depth interviews which have been quoted in various chapters. It would be recalled that, like BPL, it shows internationalization as its route to growth. It has a unique distribution network besides having a good product and very good relationship management. It registered a rate of growth of 20% in sales turnover as against the selective industry average of 0% and 14% rate of growth in profits as against a negative rate of growth of 2% for the industry. The other company, Timex, is strictly not comparable because the data for this company are available only from 1993 to 2003. Nevertheless, Timex registered 17% rate of growth in sales as against the 20% of Titan (see table 10.7 for details) whereas it registered a negative rate of growth of 15% as against the 14% of Titan. The results need to be interpreted with some degree of caution because the data relate to 1993-2003.

Table 10.7

Company Name	ΔS	ΔP	ΔMC*
HMT Ltd.	-6**	4**	76***
Titan Industries Ltd.	20	14	5
Timex	17##	-15 ##	
Selective Industry Average	**0**	**-2**	-

All Figures given above are in percentages.

All Figures given have 1990 as the base year and 2003 as the terminal year.

* Base year 1990 and Terminal year 2001 ** Terminal year 2002

*** Base year 1991 and Terminal year 1997 ## Base year 1993

From the account given above, the choice of companies included in the study for in-depth analysis is more than supported by the financial parameters. In Appendix 1, we have given information on these companies based on the trend (linear). We must mention that, in all probability, the linear trend is not a very good description of reality. On the basis of linear trend analysis, we noted that all the companies, particularly in the IT and Pharmaceuticals sector, show a negative rate of growth.

The analysis of performance of various companies in this chapter has raised some important questions about measuring relative and longitudinal performance of companies to ascertain their competitiveness and sustainability. However, on the basis of the results of this analysis, we can state that the companies included in the sample have demonstrated high levels of sustainability and competitiveness in their respective industries. The quantitative analysis has supported the choice of companies for inclusion in the sample for this research study.

REFERENCES

1. Sumantra Ghoshal, et.al., *Managing Radical Change*, (New Delhi: Viking, 2000).

2. This comes close to 'operating margin', that was emphasized by some of the respondents as a better measure of profitability relative to other measures.

3. R.L. Mariss, A Model of the Managerial Enterprise, *Quarterly Journal of Economics*, Vol. 77, 1963, 185-203.

CHAPTER ELEVEN

Learnings and Action Implications

Lessons For the Business Leaders, Entrepreneurs and Managers

'Problems cannot be solved at the same level of awareness that created them'

ALBERT EINSTEIN

'Companies die because their managers focus on the economic activity of producing goods and services, and they forget that their organization's true nature is that of a community of humans'

ARIE DE GEUS (THE LIVING COMPANY)

WE STARTED WITH THE quest to find answers to the question: What makes outstanding organizations develop and sustain their competitive edge over long spans of time in the dynamic, changing and turbulent business environment? Now that we are at the stage of completing this particular research in our journey for the eternal quest to find answers to this enigmatic question, let us pause to take a look at the learnings and action implications of this work for the practitioners.

A business leader, entrepreneur or professional manager can legitimately ask us: Tell me in simple words what are your main findings from this research and how can I apply them to my organization? How can I make my organization outstanding and sustain its competitiveness over long spans of time?

In this chapter we will attempt to answer such questions. We will present here the main findings of this work in as simple terms as possible. We will try to indicate how the practicing business leaders and managers can apply the insights and framework, based on this study in their thinking, decision-making and actions to raise their organizations to the highest possible levels of excellence, and sustain their competitiveness, over time.

Let us take a look at the main learnings from this study, highlighting the factors, characteristics and practices that distinguish the outstanding organizations and enable them to sustain their competitiveness in the long run. We shall simultaneously discuss the action implications of these learnings, i.e., how can these be utilized and applied by the practitioners.

Our findings can be classified and described at three levels: Operational, Theoretical and Paradigmatic (i.e., relating to the underlying business philosophy). We shall focus first on the operational level findings, because these are of direct and immediate interest to the practitioners.

We found that outstanding organizations sustained their competitiveness by following certain practices and ensuring distinct characteristics in five different interdependent and overlapping clusters. These clusters were like links in a chain, in which each link is important and weakness in any link can weaken the whole organization. Following are the five clusters, which are the key elements that characterize an outstanding organization:

- ***Inspiring Leadership***
- ***Innovative Strategy***
- ***Implementation Skills and Process-Driven Execution***
- ***Internal and External 'Win-Win' Relationship with all Stakeholders***
- ***Identity - Purpose, Values and Culture***

The Figure 11.1 represents these clusters and their interrelationship:

This framework can be utilized as a template to analyze an organization and diagnose its strengths and weaknesses in each of the key clusters. The findings and insights in each cluster, which are based on the experience of highly successful business leaders and professional managers of some of the most outstanding organizations, can be used as benchmark for comparison and improvement. However, it will be important to use your judgement to determine how and which of the findings and insights to apply to your organization and its unique situation.

Let us now examine the specific characteristics and practices relating to each of these key elements that were observed and inferred from the various kinds of

Figure 11.1: The Five Distinguishing Elements of Purposeful Values-driven Organizations

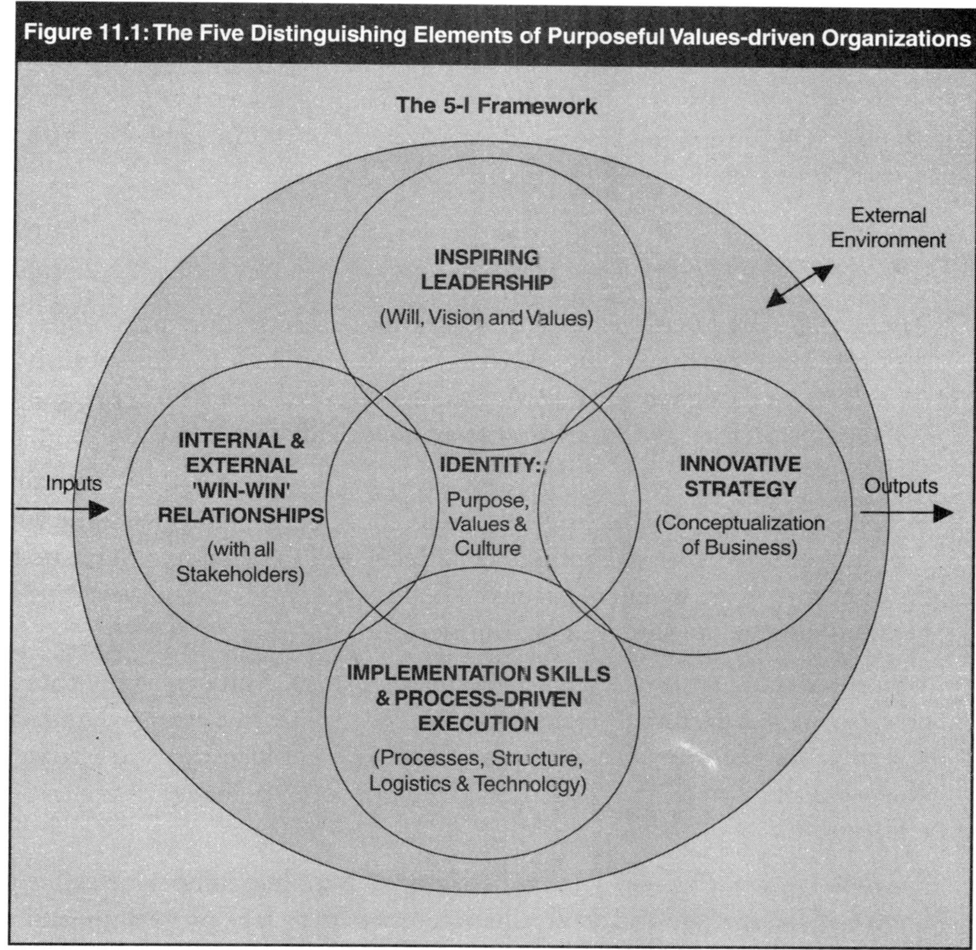

data analyzed in this study and their action implications. Following are the specific characteristics and practices in each of the five clusters that distinguished the outstanding organizations and enabled them to sustain their competitiveness. It may be pointed out here that some points may appear to be repeated in different clusters, that is because of the overlap in these clusters:

INSPIRING LEADERSHIP

Leadership is the inspiring, direction providing, influencing, energizing and driving force provided by the people in key positions at various levels in the organization.

The leadership in these organizations was not confined to only one person at the top. It consisted of a team and a network of leadership across the organization. There was high emphasis on identifying and developing leadership across the organization. **Will, Vision and Values** characterized the inspiring leadership. The main attributes of such leadership were:

Will

- ***Passion and commitment for ambitious goals*** and urge for supremacy across the organization as the driving and energizing force. The leadership of such organizations thought big. They had daring vision and dream for the future of their organization; and the tenacity, confidence and competence to convert such dreams into reality.
- ***Pro-active and positive mindset.*** Positive and developmental orientation in thinking; constructive and optimistic outlook; will to convert threats into opportunities; overcoming constraints by finding creative solutions; converting latent needs of people into business opportunities.
- ***Willingness and ability of the top leadership to change.*** Ability to anticipate change and will to initiate change innovatively even when change did not appear to be necessary. Three types of change were identified: Reactive, Adaptive and Pro-active. The proactive approach to change was most effective.
- ***Competency Building and Winning Paradigm.*** Building competencies for competitiveness. Will and determination to win in tough competition and succeed against all odds. Seeking and choosing to operate in challenging business environment (overseas in most cases), rather than protected environment that would breed mediocrity.

Vision

- ***Clear vision and mission,*** stated in most simple and understandable form, known and shared by people across the organization.
- ***Institution building, sustained leadership, nurturance of leadership and talent*** across the organization. The top management saw their role as building the organization that would last much longer beyond them. They saw their

term like one part of the relay race, in which they were keen about the success of the company and their successor to win the race. The successors built further on the past achievements and did not try to undo or undermine the good work done by predecessors.

- ***Thorough knowledge of business, attention to details and holistic view.*** The leadership acquired thorough and first-hand knowledge and understanding of the business, markets and technology. They ensured attention to details and had a holistic - not functionally myopic -- view of business problems (i.e., treating a problem narrowly as financial, marketing or operations problem). Guided by vision of raising the standards in quality, service, innovative and superior products and cost efficiencies to higher and higher levels in each area of operation.

Values

- ***Openness in communication and willingness to learn (Knowledge development).*** Encouraging openness in communication inside the organization. Fierce openness to new ideas in some organizations. Seeking relevant knowledge, information and feedback from all sources, especially from customers, consumers and employees. Investing in training and development of all levels. Exposing employees, dealers and other key stakeholders to best practices and know-how. High importance to mastering technology, Research and Development.
- ***People-Centric, generally 'egalitarian' or 'extended family-like' management style*** (in contrast to the feudal style in other organizations), treating employees with respect and dignity. Giving flexibility and empowering people down the line. Emphasis on team-based working across functions and levels, creating conditions to obtain highest possible level of involvement, commitment and sense of belonging among the employees, enabling them to contribute the best of their creative talent, abilities and energy.
- ***Simplicity, values and character; modesty and personal touch in top management leadership.*** The top leadership set personal example of values they prescribed for the organization. They demonstrated integrity and character in taking tough decisions. They were easily accessible to employees at all levels. Most of them followed simplicity and almost austerity in their personal life and work situations (as in Infosys, Wipro and Hero Honda).

Implications for Action

- Need to realize that barriers to growth and success are mainly within oneself and not so much in the external environment.
- Passion and tenacity to achieve ambitious organizational goals and supremacy in competition is the most important driving force for success.
- Positive and optimistic outlook, constructive and developmental orientation (as contrasted with negative outlook and excessive control orientation). Identifying strengths of people and organization and building on them. Converting threats, constraints and latent needs of people and client organizations into imaginative business opportunities. These are some of the important keys to success and growth in business.
- The most important factor for sustaining competitiveness is willingness and ability of the top leadership and management to change, especially to pro-actively anticipate and initiate change ahead of competition. The best time to change is when the company is doing well and has strength and resources to change.
- The most important keys for enhancing and sustaining competitiveness are to develop competencies and resourcefulness. One way to develop competencies is to operate in competitive international markets and acquire world-class technical and managerial expertise.
- Developing a shared vision and mission for the organization and stating them in the most simple and understandable form. Aligning policies, strategies and structure with them and obtaining involvement and commitment of all members of the organization through various means of communication. These factors and practices act as powerful means of inspiring people to achieve challenging goals.
- Sustaining competitiveness and growth require great attention to identifying and nurturing leadership across the organization, ensuring continuity of outstanding leadership at the top through careful succession planning and building a culture of meritocracy and professionalism.
- Building a great organization is more important than short-term gains. The main task of leadership is to build the organization as an outstanding institution that will last far beyond their life and will ensure continued business success in the dynamic and changing business environment.

- The challenge for top leadership is to have a holistic view and thorough understanding of their business, its markets and technology, ensure full attention to details and yet delegate and empower people unto the lowest possible levels for operations.
- Vision and imagination of developing innovative and superior products, raising the standards in quality, service and cost efficiencies to higher and higher levels in each area of operation is equally important along with the strategic vision.
- Openness and two-way communication within the organization is a cardinal value for organizational effectiveness, adaptability, change and competitiveness. Leaders and management must keep ear to the ground, solicit information from all sources and feedback from all stakeholders, especially from customers, consumers and employees. Closing channels of communication and blocking feedback from customers and employees is a sure way for organizations to decline and fall.
- Most of the work in organizations now is knowledge-based. Constant updating of knowledge, skills and attitudes through training and development, exposure to best practices, knowledge management, R & D, mastering and developing technology and managerial know-how has become essential for survival and growth in the highly competitive business environment. The top management leadership has to give special attention to these aspects, for upgrading and changing the knowledge and expertise profile of the company as well as to searching and inducting the best-suited talent in the organization. Some companies that have been able to change their employees' knowledge profile, have been able to improve their productivity and competitiveness phenomenally and compete globally.
- With the changing times and changing profile of employees who are mostly knowledge workers now, the style of leadership has to change. Most of the outstanding organizations now have an egalitarian and informal work environment. Employees give their best when they are treated with respect and dignity, develop feelings of involvement and commitment (as contrasted with alienation and frustration). They contribute their creative talent and energies when they develop a sense of belonging and pride in being members of the organization. The fine art of leadership is to combine high and demanding standards of performance with high care, flexibility, empowerment and development of teamwork in the organization culture. Business leaders

of successful Indian organizations have found that they get best results when they treat the employees and other key stakeholders as members of an extended family, which is more consistent with the cultural ethos of India.

- Inspiring leadership requires setting personal example. The character, integrity and values of leaders matter more than their words. People respond more to behaviour, conduct and values of the leaders than to their words. Great organizations are built by the character, values and vision of their leaders, who keep the institution-building goal of the organization above their personal needs and ego.

INNOVATIVE STRATEGY

Strategy is the process of conceptualizing value-creating propositions (consisting of better products, services and promotion) to meet the needs of customers and developing business models that will create and deliver value to the customers in the most efficient, effective and satisfying manner, leading to customer goodwill, revenue generation and profitability. Successful business strategies are imaginative and innovative strategies, based on thorough understanding and analysis of customer needs, nature of market, nature of industry, nature of competition and also insightful intuition. The following characteristics and practices were found in the strategic thinking of outstanding companies:

- ***Sensing and creating business opportunities; process-driven planning and review.*** Seeing beyond the constraints and barriers and imaginatively creating new business opportunities. They keep 'ear to the ground' to sense changes, challenges and opportunities, obtaining, processing and absorbing enormous information. They evolve flexible and streamlined systems and processes, like strategic business review meetings, technology initiative task forces, etc., to continually plan and review strategic changes.
- ***Customer-centric value-creating propositions; building brands and innovative business models.*** 'Value to the customer' was like the magic mantra to the most successful organizations. They tried hard to understand the needs of the customer/consumer and demonstrated deep concern to provide genuine value to the customer. They constantly explored and experimented with superior value propositions (in the form of better and differentiated products, quality, service, price, economy in operations, convenience, comfort, delivery

and satisfying other expressed or latent needs of the customers) and new business models that would create value for the customer. Building, sustaining, leveraging and re-positioning brands helped in sustaining value creation and competitiveness.

- ***Internationalization for competitiveness, talent and technology.*** Internationalization of all operations or benchmarking them with international standards in productivity quality and scale, as the key strategy for developing competencies and ensuring competitiveness in the global and domestic markets. A growing trend among most of the outstanding Indian organizations is to become Indian multinationals and in some cases even to become an international benchmark for others.
- ***Sustained dynamic focus.*** Highly focused strategy, maintaining a dynamic focus on selected products, services, market segments, regions, etc., responding to or initiating change in markets and technology. A multi-focused approach in diversified companies. The companies moved up the value curve as the products or services got 'commodotized'.
- ***Innovation, change and rapid response.*** Quick response and speed in initiating changes, innovation in products, service, processes of operations for higher productivity and quality and other initiatives, to meet the challenges of the changing business environment for maintaining strategic superiority.
- ***Building, sustaining and leveraging Brand Equity,*** through considerable investment and maintaining consistency with the projected image. Leveraging brand equity for new products and services.
- ***Acquiring best technology,*** mastering and developing technology through their own efforts and investment in appropriate Research and Development to stay ahead of the competition.
- ***Growth and development*** through organic (Internal Growth) and inorganic (Acquisitions and Mergers) approaches to expand operations and market coverage, specially through acquisition of related units overseas for access to international expertise, technology, management practices and international markets. Some companies are setting up multi-country bases for supply to international markets.
- ***Prudential and innovative financial policies,*** pursuing financial prudence, internal resource generation for growth and development and low debt-equity ratio.

Implications for Action

- The key to developing effective business strategy is to keep in close touch with the changing business environment, changes in markets and technology, changes in the needs of the customers/consumers and moves of the competitors. Identifying business opportunities, many of which are latent in the emerging needs of existing and potential customers, can provide immense business possibilities. Superior strategies create new value propositions to meet needs of the customers in a manner that is better than the competitors and are based on workable business models that enhance profitability. Superior strategies often lead to re-writing the rules of the game in the market.
- Development of strategy is a dynamic, iterative process. It requires constant review, experimentation, modifications and changes keeping in view the changes in the business situation, business environment and needs of customers. For this purpose suitable processes and systems need to be developed within the organization.
- Internationalization of operations as a means of developing technical, managerial and marketing competencies is one of the most effective strategies being adopted by several outstanding Indian organizations. It enables Indian companies to become competitive both in the international and domestic markets with high quality of products, access to world-class technology and international markets, while leveraging cost advantage of operations in India.
- Focus is a critical element in effective strategy. However, the focus has to be dynamic keeping in view the changes in the market, changes in tastes and preferences of customers in various market segments, competitors' moves and new technologies. A multi-focus strategy may be needed within the same product line to compete in the various segments in the market, as well as for the companies having diversified businesses.
- Innovations in strategy and rapid response to take lead in competitive situations or to cope with the challenges of change are essential elements for survival in competitive markets. Imagination and timing are, therefore, very important for success of business strategy.
- Developing, nurturing, sustaining, leveraging and re-positioning the brand enables the organizations to sustain their competitiveness. Therefore, building brands needs as much attention as building better products and services.

- Mastering and developing the best possible technology give enormous competitive advantage to companies. It is important to master and develop technology internally to reduce dependence on external sources who may not like to part with the latest technology. Companies that have been able to develop technology on their own have developed better sustainability in the long run and are not as vulnerable as those depending on external collaborators (especially those with equity partnership) for technology upgradation.
- Whereas internally driven organic growth has many benefits, in-organic growth through acquisitions and mergers can also be very advantageous. Especially when it is utilized to enhance technical capabilities, market access and synergetic combination, ensuring skilful cultural integration and 'win-win' approach. Some outstanding Indian companies have successfully utilized this approach to have access to the international markets and technology.
- Financial prudence and imaginative methods of raising and leveraging financial resources with least cost and risk are the keystones of successful business strategies. The secret of most successful and enduring business enterprises is financial prudence and probity.

IMPLEMENTATION SKILLS AND PROCESS-DRIVEN EXECUTION

The central key to success of organizations lies in effective implementation and execution. The best philosophies of business, most well conceived strategies and plans, availability of technology and resources and all other aspects of business can go haywire if the organization does not have implementation skills and ability to execute the plans most efficiently and effectively within the required time-frames. Therefore, a great deal of emphasis was laid by experienced business leaders and professional managers on the importance of implementation, execution, efficiency in logistics and suitable structures, systems and processes for them. The following main points were noted in this cluster:

- ***Centrality of outstanding implementation and execution skills and superior logistics across the value chain and supply chain as a competitive advantage.***
- ***Attention to details.***

- ***Search for talent through social networking.*** Enormous emphasis on developing and maintaining high level of competence through search for talent, training and development across the organization.
- ***Operational efficiency***
- ***Benchmarking with the best***
- ***Development of superior, streamlined processes, systems and structure*** that were reviewed from time to time to remain relevant and nimble for strategic and operational planning and performance management and alignment of activities and goals across different functions and regions.
- ***Conspicuous institutional practices in key areas like HRD, quality and productivity enhancement, cost reduction, encouraging innovation and operations improvement.***
- ***Mastery, ownership and development of technology.***
- ***Less hierarchical, adaptive, flexible and evolving structure.***
- ***Coordination mechanisms.***
- ***High level of communication and feedback across the organization*** through various platforms to ensure two-way communication and involvement of employees at different levels. Special concern and attention to employee and customers' feedback.

Implications for Action

- Need to evolve detailed processes because these obviate the need to ponder over as to what is to be done and remove ad hocism. The best manifestation of this has been found in the case of Ranbaxy, Infosys Technologies and Satyam Computers.
- Need for flexibility to cope with highly dynamic environment including the need to review organization structure, from time to time.
- Emphasis on details and the ability to understand finer nuances of technology and HR practices.
- Importance of social networking in attracting talented peoples, thereby, suggesting the importance of informal channels in execution of strategy.

- Operational efficiency highlighting the need to cut costs to their bare minimum and increase productivity to the highest levels possible.
- Benchmarking with the best companies at the global level.
- Significance of quantification in identifying responsibility and corrective measures. The best example of which is the use of six-sigma by some leading companies in their various operations.
- The urgency of timely availability of data regarding resource availability and its utilization.

INTERNAL AND EXTERNAL 'WIN-WIN' RELATIONSHIP WITH STAKEHOLDERS

The management of any business organization works in a network of relationships with its various internal and external stakeholders. The nature and quality of these relationships determine the success, profitability and survival of the organization in the long run. These relationships can be characterized by 'win-win' paradigm, or 'win-lose' paradigm. The outstanding organizations base their relationship with all its stakeholders on win-win paradigm. The nature of relationships of highly successful and enduring organizations indicated the following characteristics:

- ***A 'Win-Win' paradigm in relationship*** with the employees, suppliers, distributors and other value contributors.
- ***'Extended family-like' relationship with the key stakeholders,*** especially in Indian organizations, consistent with the Indian ethos.
- ***Concern for balancing and safeguarding the interests of all stakeholders.*** Attempt to equitably share the gains with the key stakeholders.
- ***Functional relationship with relevant business and social entities,*** such as chambers of commerce, professional bodies, regulatory and government authorities, community forums, educational and research institutions, etc.

Implications for Action

- The business leaders need to seriously examine the nature of relationships that they have with their key internal and external stakeholders, especially the employees, distributors, suppliers, customers and shareholders. These relationships can be tacitly 'win-lose', i.e., they are not treated as partners but as parties with whom there is only a contractual relationship in which the organization wants to give out minimum and extract maximum value from them. Such relationship will lead to an adversarial position, in which both parties will try to exploit each other and none is likely to gain in the long run. On the contrary, if the relationship is based on 'win-win' paradigm, i.e., both parties see each other as partners in a common enterprise, the success of which would benefit both, then the parties would extend maximum possible support to each other, create value jointly and benefit by sharing the value equitably. Organizations like Hero Honda that have developed such relationship with the employees, dealers, suppliers and other stakeholders, have demonstrated enormous gains to the organization and to the stakeholders.

- Every country has a unique cultural ethos and management practices in the country work better if they are consistent with the positive aspects of such ethos. Collective group-centered ethos of Japanese organizations and individualistic achievement oriented American style of management are effective in their organizations. Successful and outstanding Indian organizations follow management style and practices that are based on the extended family paradigm, which is a central characteristic of the Indian culture. They have also effectively incorporated Japanese practices for productivity, quality, cost reduction and constant improvement and various western techniques, best practices and concepts in their strategic and operational aspects of management. Therefore, Indian organizations can be very successful if they combine the extended family paradigm with their key stakeholders and also utilize the best management practices and concepts developed in other countries.
- Balancing the interests of all stakeholders means fair dealings with all stakeholders and not seeking the benefit of only the promoters or controlling shareholders. Stakeholders' support is essential for the survival, growth and sustainability of the enterprise. Therefore, it is important to share wealth equitably with them, while protecting the long-term interest and sustainability of the enterprise.
- Networking of the organization with other organizations having similar interests and with other important social and regulatory institutions is

important for survival and viability of the enterprise. Organizations need goodwill of the community in their enlightened self-interest.

IDENTITY: PURPOSE, VALUES AND CULTURE

The central and enduring core of an organization that provides it continuity and sustainability consists of its distinct identity, purpose, values and culture. It is like the soul of the organization. It gives a unique character to an organization and builds its brand equity. It indicates what the organization stands for and why it exists. Following are the specific elements of this cluster and their main characteristics found in the outstanding organizations:

- ***Principle-centered paradigm,*** reflected in strongly held, rigorously practiced and in some cases explicitly articulated, values and business philosophy for doing business in ethical way was stated, emphasized and practiced in almost all outstanding organizations. Some of the cornerstones of stated business ethics were: Integrity, honouring commitments, meeting delivery schedules to internal and external customers, maintaining specifications and quality standards and giving full value for money to the customer.
- ***Distinct institutional identity, framework of values and purpose,*** that uphold the cherished core organizational values, enabling the organization to pursue high levels of excellence and performance in achieving its clearly articulated purpose.
- ***High performance culture and a global mindset.*** A culture of high performance, high standards of excellence in all operations, combined with high care for employees across the entire organization.
- ***Openness, transparency, meritocracy and professionalism in management and governance.***
- ***Concern and initiative for broader socio-economic and environmental issues, as a part of Corporate Social Responsibility.***

Implications for Action

- Explicitly articulated business philosophy for doing business in a professional and ethical manner, reflected in strongly held and practiced values and a well-defined purpose, inspires all members of the organization, creates a sense of belonging and pride among them and confidence among stakeholders and customers. These factors immensely benefit the organization. Ethical business is, therefore, profitable business.

- The clarity and articulation of core values and core purpose bestow a sense of commitment, pride and alignment with the goals of the organization among its members, as they see themselves working for some higher goals. These are the hallmarks of outstanding organizations.
- Clarity of purpose, vision, mission and values and a strongly held culture and identity endow the organization with a distinct brand equity, cohesiveness, character and framework to ensure continuity and longevity of organization as a distinctive institution. The top management must, therefore, invest time in clarifying and developing shared understanding of these elements in the organization.
- The outstanding organizations compare and benchmark themselves with international organizations and seek to operate not only in the domestic markets, but also increasingly in the global markets. They demonstrate a global mindset.
- Openness, transparency, meritocracy and professionalism in management and governance attract best talent and resources. They inspire credibility, confidence and goodwill of stakeholders and customers. These characteristics and practices of organization and its management ensure its long-term survival, growth and competitiveness.
- Initiatives for environmental protection, addressing some important socio-economic issues in which organization can contribute meaningfully, transparent and responsible corporate governance are parts of Corporate Social Responsibility. Such concerns and initiatives are becoming increasingly important for societal goodwill and sustainability of business organizations.

CONCEPTUAL AND THEORETICAL FINDINGS

We have defined sustainable competitive edge as 'the distinctive intrinsic ability, resilience and endurance of an organization to maintain relative superiority in performance and growth, in a competitive and changing business environment over a reasonably long span of time (10 to 12 years for this study). It is the ability of a company to transcend trade cycles and other factors that lead to corporate demise and bounce back when everything seems to have been lost'.

We would like to highlight the main *differentiating theoretical findings* of this research study with the earlier studies on this subject as given below:

- Most of the earlier researches have identified a few key factors and sought to explain competitiveness as a function of such variables generally in **linear models.** We have noted and identified a **configuration** of interrelated factors, characteristics and practices that function as **mutually interacting variables in a dynamic system** as the keys for developing and maintaining a sustainable competitive advantage
- On the basis of five clusters of factors, characteristics and practices that distinguished the outstanding organizations and enabled them to develop and sustain competitive edge, we have developed the **'5-I framework'**. The five clusters of key elements were found to be like overlapping circles as shown in the figure above in this chapter.
- We have conceptualized our understanding of the organization as a **Socio-economic-technical Open Organic System** (Figure 9.2 in Chapter 9) that maintains continuity and change by adapting, influencing and co-evolving with the changing business environment. We have also developed a model of the **Strategic Thought Process,** based on our observations and analysis of such processes noted during our research study (Figure 5.2 in Chapter 5).

PARADIGMATIC FINDINGS

- Based on our research, findings and concepts developed by thinkers and writers earlier, we have conceptualized the organizations that demonstrate resilience, competitiveness and sustainability over long spans of time as **'Purposeful Values-driven Enterprises' (PVEs).** They have some unique identifiable factors, characteristics and practices. *They create economic value through a 'values-driven paradigm'.* These are different from the primarily **'Money-making Commercial Outfits' (MCOs).**
- The Purposeful Values-driven Enterprises (PVEs) are created and developed by entrepreneurial leaders who have a deeply felt passion to win, a clearly

articulated purpose, a long-term ambitious vision for the future and supremacy of the enterprise. They have a strong will and confidence, willingness to take risks and learn from failures. They engage in quick and intensive learning to understand the nature of business.

They develop effective management practices, acquire and master the technology and nurture mutually supportive 'edge' in partnership with their key stakeholders by innovative business propositions. They offer better and higher quality products and services at lower cost and competitive prices. They inspire trust and respect of customers and 'win-win' relationships with their stakeholders.

They maintain their competitive edge through successive chain of outstanding leadership. They sustain competitive edge by constantly creating genuine value and wealth and sharing it equitably with their stakeholders. They painstakingly build and nurture their brand equity and core competence and leverage them to compete and grow.

They are principle-centered organizations that manage their business with some strongly held values and business ethics and their governance is highly professional, based on transparency and meritocracry, keeping in view the long-term interest of the enterprise. They have demonstrated that, in the long run, ethical business is good business, because it sustains the trust, confidence and respect of stakeholders and customers.

- Organizations that deviate from the principles, values, characteristics and practices that inspire the trust, confidence and respect of the customers and stakeholders may achieve short-term gains and superior financial performance but may not be able to sustain their competitive edge in competitive situations in the long run.

RELEVANCE OF THE RESEARCH FOR INDIAN ORGANIZATIONS

The findings of this research study are **context-based** and help in understanding the various factors, characteristics and practices that seem to have specially worked in India and some of these are unique to the Indian context. We have identified and conceptualized the unique characteristics of the **'Emerging Modern Indian Corporation (EMIC)'**, that we found as an interesting combination of the Indian

'Extended family-like' Culture, Western style and techniques of management and Japanese practices for productivity and quality. The Emerging Modern Indian Corporations are aspiring to become Indian multinationals. They are changing the image of business in India, where business was usually perceived, negatively. Companies like, Infosys and Ranbaxy, are building the brand equity of India in the international markets, like Sony and Toyota did for Japan. The EMICs are playing an important role in transforming the Indian industry and economy.

Some Messages for the Indian Firms

1. A good balance sheet, sales performance and profitability of most companies operating in non-competitive markets is illusory. The heat of competition is going to be far more intense in the coming days, as the imperatives of WTO and competition from overseas as well as domestic firms increase. Such changes in the business environment may lead to disappearance of good performance and endanger the company. The time to change and develop competitiveness is when the company is doing well and has resources and capability of introducing change for improvements.
2. The barriers to growth and success are mostly within our mindset. The best in us comes out in situations that are challenging and demanding. The will and determination to set ambitious goals for the organization and the passion to excel and achieve such goals against all odds differentiate the leaders who build outstanding organizations from the mediocre performers. Indian business leaders and professional managers have demonstrated that they can build world-class organizations and succeed in the toughest competitive markets.
3. A pro-active mindset and a positive attitude, notwithstanding the forces working against such approach and behaviour, lead to success in the long run. Setbacks and failures can be put in proper perspective and help in learning to deal with such situations better. For examples, a sudden change in the government policy having a negative influence on the organization could be seen as an opportunity to impress upon the managers to realize the importance of always providing for uncertainties and emphasizing the need for contingency planning.
4. Clear purpose, vision and mission, stated in simplest possible terms, evolved through participatory processes and widely shared across the organization with high level of open communication and information sharing, develop a

sense of involvement, commitment and ownership among members of the organization for goals and targets to be achieved. This process is to be followed by setting milestones and reviewing performance with all organization members. Such approach has enabled organizations like Sundram Fasteners, Infosys, Wipro, Ranbaxy, Satyam and several other companies to achieve outstanding performance and competitive ability. For this purpose, benchmarking with the best in quality and productivity, performance management systems for monitoring and review, reward and recognition systems for excellent performance and developing a culture of openness, learning, leadership and talent development and high performance are necessary.

5. The Indian firms should seriously consider internationalization route as strategy for developing competitiveness and tapping larger markets. Besides cushioning against downturn and uncertainties in the domestic market, it would enable the Indian firms to develop world-class competencies, best practices, superior technology and management knowhow, leading to high level of competitiveness. Several outstanding Indian organizations are already following this route successfully and aiming at becoming Indian multinationals.

6. The management has to be extremely meticulous in translating any strategy into action-oriented plan and implement the same with high speed and efficiency. It requires the development of a high performance culture, and streamlined, institutionalized processes. It is specially a challenge for the large organizations, which tend to develop inflexible, cumbersome and time-consuming systems and processes. The speed in implementation of strategy and flawless and effective execution for meeting commitments and customer requirements are critical for survival and competitiveness.

7. The most effective way of getting full cooperation and support of the key stakeholders in the Indian context is to treat them as a part of an extended family with a personal touch - to the extent possible. The company must ensure profitability and gains to their key external and internal stakeholders like distributors and vendors/suppliers, employees and shareholders. The mutual gains are enormous if they are treated as partners and relationships with them are based on a 'win-win' paradigm.

8. Managing the family business requires good family management. Learning to harness the competitive spirit of family members and dealing with their aspirations through imaginative structural arrangements is necessary. Some

business houses have managed it by creating autonomous divisions or separate units. The divisions and units could then compete with each other for superior performance. Such arrangements can be a protection against complacency creeping into family organizations.

9. Transparency, meritocracy and professionalism in management and governance are important, if we want our organizations to be world-class, sustainable and internationally competitive. Companies like Infosys developed credibility and confidence of stakeholders by listing in US stock markets, which require high level of transparency in accounting and financial reporting practices.

10. Humility, modesty, access and informality in dealing with people, combined with no compromise in values and firmness in creating a high performance culture are prerequisites for success, particularly in the changing Indian business environment. Arrogance has serious disadvantages and has to be guarded against.

We would like to conclude by reminding the reader the statement, quoted earlier in this book, that *nothing great was ever achieved without passion.* If as a business leader, entrepreneur or manager, you want to build a sustainable and competitive great organization, begin and pursue your endeavour with a *passion to win.*

RESEARCH APPENDIX I

Analysis of the Linear Trend of Selected Financial Parameters in the Sample Companies

IN THIS SECTION, WE review the relative performance and probability of maintaining competitiveness of firms based on linear trend of two financial parameters.

These are:

1. Return on investment
2. Market capitalization

Before giving a descriptive account of companies belonging to different sectors, we may mention that for some companies we could not identify competitors. This was especially true for Larsen and Toubro, Bharat Electronics Limited and Reliance Industries Limited. Though it is possible to get a group of companies which would be fairly representative of the type of businesses in which these companies operate, there is an element of approximation involved. For example, L&T could be compared with companies which are in the business of manufacturing cement, engineering products, to name a few. Similarly, BEL could be evaluated with other firms in the electronics business. Finally, RIL could find its competitors in firms that are in the oil sector or in petrochemicals and in the textile sector. In this exercise we did not attempt such comparative analysis because of lack of break-up of data on the performance of the companies in different sectors from which they derived revenue.

We move over to a possible critique of picking up various parameters on which the performance of the companies has been measured. For instance, there could possibly be a very high degree of divergence between return on investment and market capitalization. Return on investment would be governed by the overall performance of the organization whereas market capitalization is governed by the perception of potential investors about the well-being of the company. Market capitalization, which is based on price of shares, could vary based on the actual performance of the firm against the globally competitive firms. Thus, it is possible to visualize lower return on investment co-existing with a rise in market capitalization. This observation is more emphatic because any deviation from expected performance is met by the usual response of shareholders. From time to time, various regulatory bodies have mentioned the futility of market capitalization. We feel that it is necessary to consider the perception of potential investors and so we included this as one factor influencing the capacity for sustainability of an organization.

The criterion suggested by Prof. Ghoshal and others that a firm is likely to survive over long period if its productivity increases at a rate faster than its weighted cost of capital is a truism. It does not prove or disprove anything. On the other hand, what results in improved productivity or reduced weighted average of cost of capital are questions of significant concern to the practitioners. In the chapter on Implementation of Strategy, it was highlighted that Reliance Industries Limited has been extremely successful in keeping its cost of capital low by coming out with innovative schemes. The innovative effort could come in other areas such as a new style of producing goods, improved marketing skills or introduction of inexpensive substitute. These have been highlighted at their appropriate places.

INFORMATION TECHNOLOGY

ROI

In this section, we present the results of the information technology sector which has shown remarkable performance both in the domestic and foreign market. On the criterion of Return on Investment, Digital Globalsoft Ltd. emerges as No. 1 with a value of trend equal to 3.07 followed by Wipro Ltd. at 2.13; Infosys Technologies Ltd. at 0.65; Satyam Computer Services Ltd. at 0.31 and Polaris Software Lab Ltd. with a negative value of 9.09. (See chart 1 for details). How does one explain this pattern of trend values? It is true that these well known companies have been investing in recruiting people in anticipation of their future demand. It is also true that it is not possible to obtain skilled people as and when desired. Hence most companies have not slowed down on their recruitment effort. The last three years have witnessed a slow down in this sector and yet these companies did not believe in retrenching people. However, in the year 2001, one company deferred the joining by new trainees, picked up from campus, due to a slowdown in demand.

It is also clear that Wipro's superior performance is due to the diversified portfolio of its businesses including vegetable oil. It is fairly well known that consumer goods do not feel the effect of a fall in the working of the economy. In fact, this sector registers the effect after all other sectors have felt the impact.

Chart 1: Information Technology Sector (Return Capital Employed)

Company Name/Year(March)	1991	1992	1993	1994	1995	1996	1997	1998	1999	2000	2001	2002	2003	LINEST*
Infosys Technologies Ltd.			60.61	50.43	31.45	36.06	41.86	46.29	43.66	46.33	64.19	54.42	47.65	0.65
Satyam Computer Services Ltd.					38.37	33.25	28.97	25.10	34.06	38.95	49.80	36.78	26.50	0.31
Wipro Ltd.	28.66	21.82	20.86	21.88	36.99	33.61	34.05	36.93	40.62	58.62	57.48	43.03	31.09	2.13
Polaris Software Lab Ltd.						104.90	66.86	35.87	50.47	47.93	36.77	29.20	22.75	-9.09
Digital Globalsoft Ltd.	5.95	21.61	29.40	6.33	18.09	31.02	42.41	49.21	36.91	21.33	46.48	56.17	42.13	3.07
Selective Industry Average#	67.33	47.21	65.41	51.42	49.56	44.42	52.05	51.19	51.23	34.02	32.45	21.16	18.36	

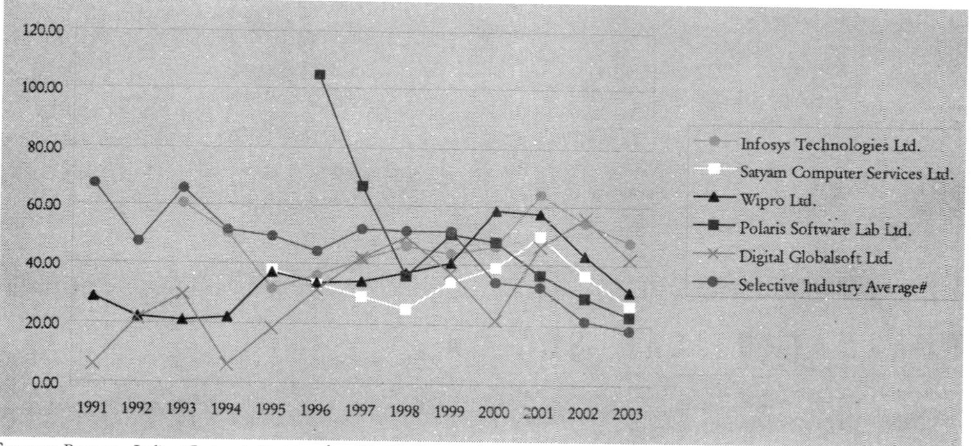

Source: *Prowess - Indian Corporate Database* by CMIE Pvt. Ltd.
Selective Industry Average# - Based on data of 14-companies in IT sector excluding those mentioned above
LINEST* - Linear Trend

Index of Market Capitalization*

The second factor considered by us is based on the evaluation of the companies by capital market. We have taken the average of the share price registered as the lowest during the year and the highest and taken the average of the two as representative for the entire year. Market capitalization is equal to average price times the number of shares issued. The index of market capitalization is given by ratio of market capitalization in the terminal year (2002) to its value in the initial period (1992). The value of the index is the highest for Wipro at 269.79 followed by Infosys Technologies at 192.78 and of Satyam at 67.56. (See chart 2).

Chart 2: Information Technology Sector Market (Capitalization Index)											
	1991	1992	1993	1994	1995	1996	1997	1998	1999	2001	2002
Infosys Index					1.157	1.507	4.268	11.974	100.727	228.619	192.780
Satyam Index							2.856	37.016	37.016	229.390	67.560
Wipro Index	1.087	1.748	1.942	4.971	4.369	7.040	15.129	59.876	190.974	1119.036	269.790
Average					**2.763**	**4.274**	**7.417**	**36.289**	**109.572**	**525.682**	**195.118**

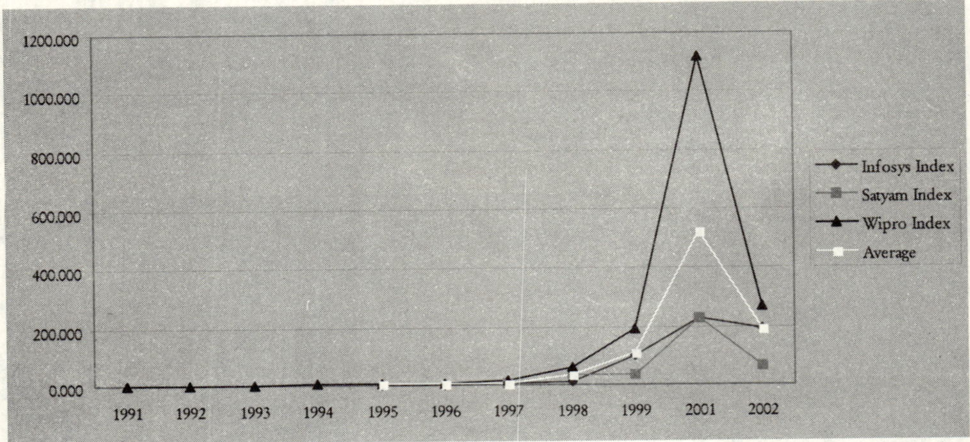

Source: Bombay Stock Exchange Directory

PHARMACEUTICAL SECTOR

ROI

The ranking of companies based on return on investment as measured by the trend over a period of last fourteen years indicates that Nicholas Piramal ranks first followed by Ranbaxy Laboratories, followed by Cipla and Dr. Reddy's Lab (mentioned as DRL for short). All companies included in the study registered a negative trend except Nicholas Piramal (+0.28) during the last fourteen years. The value of the negative trend varies from -0.43 to -2.45. This indicates that with each passing year there is a decline in return on investment in the case of Ranbaxy equal to 0.43 whereas decline in the case of Dr. Reddy's Labs is 2.45. (See chart 3). It is possible to understand a decline in return on investment in the case of Ranbaxy Laboratory and Dr. Reddy's Laboratories because they have been investing in basic drugs. It is recognized that research is a time consuming process involving time in the discovery of drug and finally getting it registered in the name of the company. It is an expensive proposition too because it takes about two years to get the drug registered in the name of the company and a considerable amount of money has to be deposited with the Federal Drug Administration's Office (USA). We were told that in the case of Ranbaxy Laboratories about 20 million dollars are deposited with the authorities for registration of the patent at any point in time.

Chart 3: Drugs & Pharmaceutical Sector (Return on Capital Employed)

Company Name/Year(March)	1990	1991	1992	1993	1994	1995	1996	1997	1998	1999	2000	2001	2002	2003	LINEST*
Ranbaxy Laboratories . Ltd	21.77	28.05	27.71	33.74	34.92	24.93	20.27	21.59	21.29	12.87	19.04	17.65	16.94	40.07	-0.43
Dr. Reddy's Laboratories Ltd.	27.99	50.07	94.51	88.42	69.76	28.60	22.30	17.45	24.53	20.74	20.80	43.81	58.48	26.90	-2.45
Cipla Ltd.	37.14	38.96	41.35	44.33	41.51	43.94	32.49	46.14	43.29	38.34	33.74	36.33	38.08	31.43	-0.46
Nicholas Piramal India Ltd.	41.01	34.58	23.73	22.15	18.17	15.95	16.00	27.05	17.73	17.65	20.82	20.97	39.42	48.15	0.28
Selective Industry Average#	27.86	26.87	28.12	29.59	33.48	30.98	28.41	30.39	25.66	23.96	25.41	25.52	28.30	29.66	

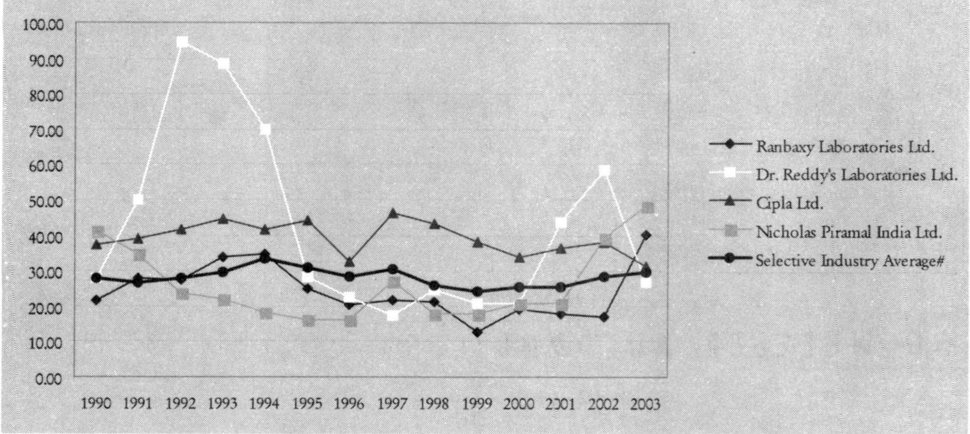

Source: *Prowess - Indian Corporate Database* by CMIE Pvt. Ltd.
Selective Industry Average# - Based on data of 17 companies in pharmaceutical sector excluding those mentioned above
LINEST* - Linear Trend

Index of Market Capitalization

On the parameter of index of market capitalization, Dr. Reddy's Labs comes no. 1 with a value of index equal to 385.82 followed by Ranbaxy at 112.27 and Cipla equal to 110.96. These results are in contrast to the trend in the first factor on return on investment where DRL emerged as the last in ranking. (See chart 4)

Chart 4: Drugs and Pharmaceutical Sector (Market Capitalization Index)

	1991	1992	1993	1994	1995	1996	1997	1998	1999	2000	2001
Ranbaxy index	4.503	13.111	18.292	53.841	65.063	62.957	79.246	65.692	210.973	116.681	112.274
DRL Index	2.160	13.589	19.547	37.213	50.162	39.392	43.487	75.659	176.229	141.183	385.828
Cipla Index	1.308	1.478	3.198	9.734	15.092	14.253	22.113	25.494		101.013	110.964
Piramal Index	2.816	8.885	7.494	27.779	26.106	14.258	17.063	38.760		58.099	86.799
Average	**2.697**	**9.266**	**12.133**	**32.141**	**39.106**	**32.715**	**40.477**	**51.401**	**193.601**	**104.244**	**173.966**

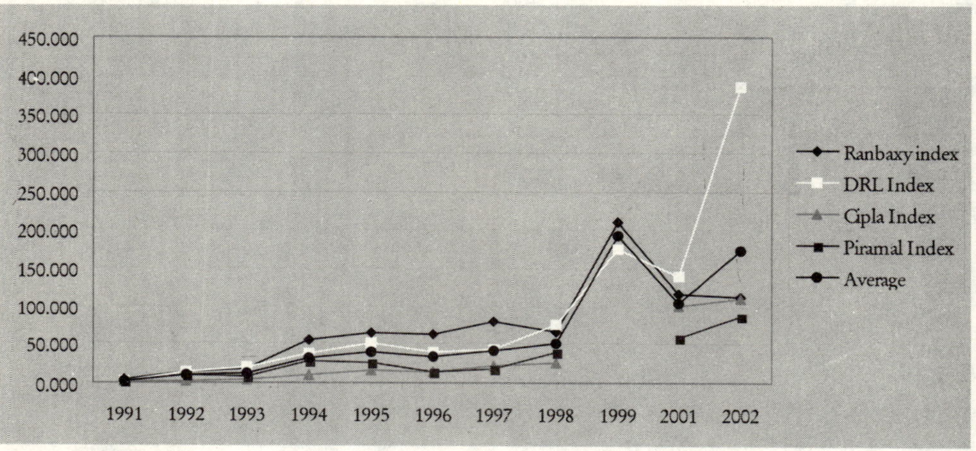

Source: *Bombay Stock Exchange Directory*

TWO WHEELER AUTOMOBILES

ROI

In this sector, Hero Honda emerges on top on the parameter of return on investment with a positive value of 5.89 followed by Kinetic at -0.14, TVS at -0.30, LML at -1.03 and Bajaj at -1.28. (For LML Ltd we have information only upto Mar-2002, see Chart 5 for details). This appears to be rather unusual because, of late, TVS has been doing exceptionally well. It is mentioned that after Suzuki left TVS, the performance of TVS has registered an increase. Nevertheless, only one company, Hero Honda, shows a positive value of the trend while the remaining have shown a negative trend.

Chart 5: Two-Wheeler Sector (Return on Capital Employed)

Company Name/Year	Mar-90	Mar-91	Mar-92	Mar-93	Mar-94	Mar-95	Mar-96	Mar-97	Mar-98	Mar-99	Mar-00	Mar-01	Mar-02	Mar-03	LINEST*
Bajaj Auto Ltd.	33.71	27.59	25.13	21.65	47.91	47.04	41.60	37.[illegible]1	29.21	26.21	20.42	9.98	17.30	21.47	-1.28
Hero Honda Motors Ltd.	13.13	35.55	28.04	26.37	24.58	35.63	45.91	50.74	53.99	61.70	71.98	70.98	96.27	94.64	5.89
Kinetic Motor Co. Ltd.		40.69	28.81	19.72	9.95	18.42	21.25	15.81	15.84	16.17	38.83	38.46	33.50	7.29	-0.14
T V S Motor Co. Ltd.	13.42	26.64	43.10	39.73	61.77	70.56	76.13	67.35	51.06	36.27	32.33	20.74	20.86	42.1	-0.30
L M L Ltd.	20.19	5.44		-19.68	29.38	70.95	53.55	32.25	36.30	36.50	9.50	-2.09	-10.86		-1.03
Selective Industry Average#	18.74	14.66	21.15	23.74	25.53	31.88	18.97	13.37	35.82	12.30	12.06	4.85	2.70	-4.65	

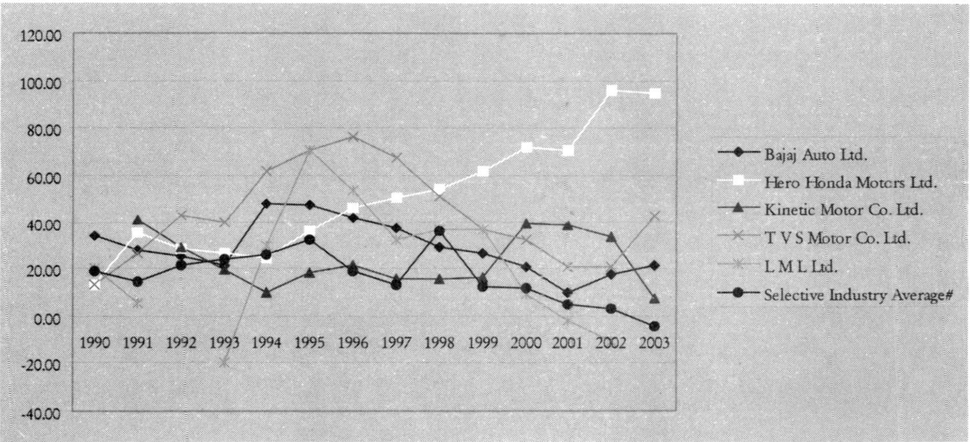

Source: *Prowess - Indian Corporate Database* by CMIE Pvt. Ltd.
Selective Industry Average# - Based on data of 7 companies in two-wheeler sector excluding those mentioned above.
LINEST* - Linear Trend

Index of Market Capitalization

On the criterion of index of market capitalization, Hero Honda emerges on top with a value equal to 60.37 followed by TVS at 11.81, Bajaj at 3.33 and finally LML with a value of 0.11. We did not have information on Kinetic. (See chart 6).

Chart 6: Two Wheeler Sector (Market Capitalization Index)

	1990	1991	1992	1993	1994	1995	1996	1997	1998	1999	2001	2002
Bajaj Index		0.942	1.684	1.733	3.671	5.611	6.341	6.145	6.583	5.502	2.969	3.332
Hero Honda Index		1.981	3.497	3.590	7.903	5.824	6.655	14.517	20.767	48.721	42.799	60.376
TVS Index		1.289	2.181	3.228	10.000	12.174	16.034	22.201	27.611		14.015	11.812
LML Index		0.124	0.179	0.164	0.392	0.450	0.276	0.287	0.468	0.276	0.165	0.115
Average		1.084	1.885	2.179	5.491	6.015	7.326	10.788	13.857	18.166	14.987	18.909

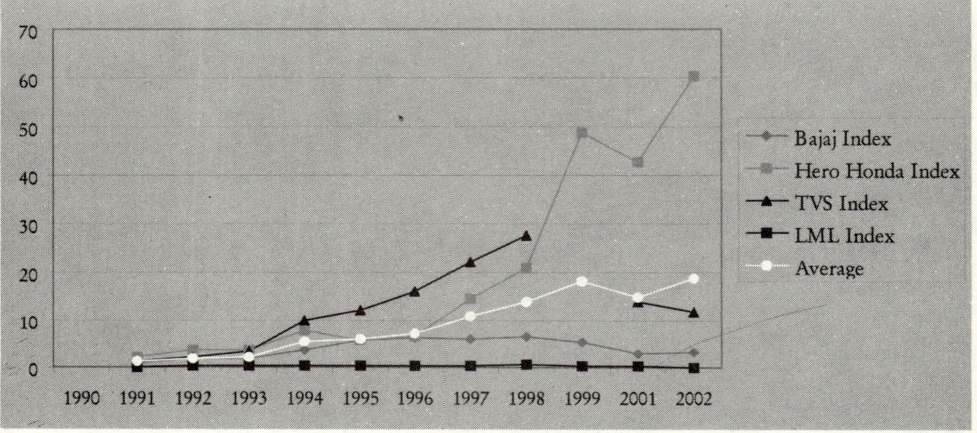

Source: *Bombay Stock Exchange Directory*

FAST MOVING CONSUMER GOODS SECTOR

ROI

On the parameter of ROI, only Nestle India and HLL have a positive value. Nestle India has a value of 5.79 while HLL has a value equal to 2.81. Other companies, in descending, order, are Dabur India, Britannia Industries, GSK Consumer Healthcare, Nirma Ltd., Godrej Foods and Colgate-Palmolive with a negative trend value of 0.64, 0.84, 2.21, 2.54, 2.96 and 5.24 respectively. (See chart 7) From the description given in the previous paragraphs, it may have been noticed that the value of trend on ROI in the case of the knowledge intense sector has been negative. We rationalized such a phenomenon on the grounds that the recession experienced during the last 2-3 years has squeezed the profits and volume as the firms have not resorted to retrenchment. It is surprising to note that even in case of FMCGs, there is a negative return on investment which suggests that the recession must have been extremely acute to lead to a fall in profits in the case of FMCG companies also. It is very well recognized in economic literature that recession invariably affects the consumer goods sector the last. In fact, when sales in supermarkets register a fall, it is taken as a matter of great concern.

Chart 7: Fast Moving Consumer Goods Sector (Return on Capital Employed)

Company Name/Year	Mar-90	Mar-91	Mar-92	Mar-93	Mar-94	Mar-95	Mar-96	Mar-97	Mar-98	Mar-99	Mar-00	Mar-01	Mar-02	Mar-03	LINEST*
Colgate-Palmolive (India) Ltd.	98.27	108.4	84.4	91.33	74.16	60.97	67.76	61.39	47.6	24.68	30.45	36.71	44.89	56.86	-5.24
Nestle India Ltd.	21.8	23.69	35.81	27.62	24.55	24.38	32.46	28.11	30.45	37.22	48.57	70.61	92.03	125.13	5.79
Hindustan Lever Ltd.	31.66	34.69	42.1	49.48	52.49	56.78	54.39	68.63	67.29	67.81	70.02	70.81	66.09	63.26	2.8[illegible]
Godrej Foods Ltd.	14.07	18.55	-16.15	-2.31	6.17	4.76	8.59	-2.16	-13.87	11.49	3.48		-79.4	-6.34	-2.95
Nirma Ltd.			42.04	36.07	47.5	42.73	27.83	37.26	29.28	24.65	21.08	17.93	19.38	19.96	-2.54
Britannia Industries Ltd.	31.75	42.44	49.18	47.75	34.58	32.34	27.71	25.39	33.25	33.89	36.22	37.22	29.33	28.23	-0.84
GSK Cons. Healthcare Ltd.	73.06	67.56	66.81	51.02	51.97	67.65	71.31	73.29	63.24	58.92	53.11	43.58	44.34	28.65	-2.21
Dabur India Ltd.	19.51	25.19	34.87	33.75	31.03	25.7	34.02	27.37	21.06	18.74	19.83	24.97	19.37	22.54	-0.64
Selective Industry Average#	38.46	41.46	53.54	45.76	40.51	33.24	31.52	27.02	29.54	23.17	12.01	-111.47	31.46	10.80	

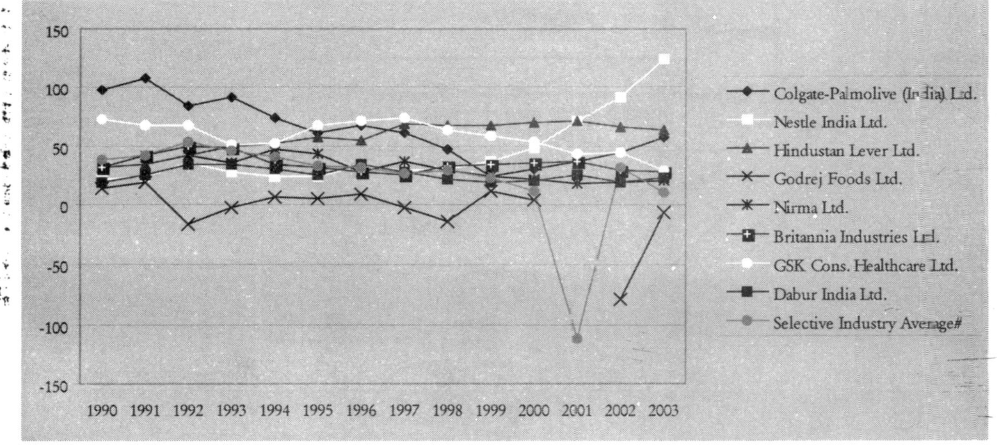

Source: *Prowess - Indian Corporate Database* by CMIE Pvt. Ltd.
Selective Industry Average# - Based on data of 12 companies in FMCG sector excluding those mentioned above.
LINEST* - Linear Trend

Index of Market Capitalization

As mentioned earlier, this index tries to express the perception of the market regarding the value of the organization and has been taken as the ratio of market capitalization at the terminal point (2002) to market capitalization in the initial period (1992 or near by year). Once again, HLL emerges on top with a value of 38.20 We did not have information on Nirma for the initial year and therefore have not indicated the value of this index for Nirma. It is interesting to know that the value of the index is about 4 times of the next company in order of the index of market capitalization. (See chart 8). It would be recalled that on the basis of ROI as well as the trend representing management of working capital, HLL was on top.

Chart 8: FMCG Sector (Market Capitalization Index)

	1990	1991	1992	1993	1994	1995	1996	1997	1998	1999	2001	2002
Colgate Index		1.329	2.650	3.626	8.125	5.170	4.257	4.976	3.785	3.740	2.717	2.656
Nestle Index		1.289	3.099	4.010	5.089	4.380	5.909	5.237	7.348	10.533	8.448	10.235
HLL Index		1.789	3.627	4.977	7.885	6.719	8.872	18.649	23.832	38.324	40.565	38.205
Godrej Foods Index		1.250	4.405	2.566	3.972	3.453	2.330	2.789	2.064	2.986	0.231	
Britannia Index		1.346	2.748	2.159	2.897	1.781	1.487	2.520	4.299	9.344	7.220	6.625
GSKB Index		1.209	1.806	1.496	2.512	3.039	1.740	3.334	4.443	6.491	4.145	3.917
Dabur Index							0.677	3.589	3.602	4.655	11.909	9.943
Average		**1.369**	**3.056**	**3.139**	**5.080**	**4.091**	**3.610**	**5.871**	**7.053**	**10.868**	**10.748**	**11.930**

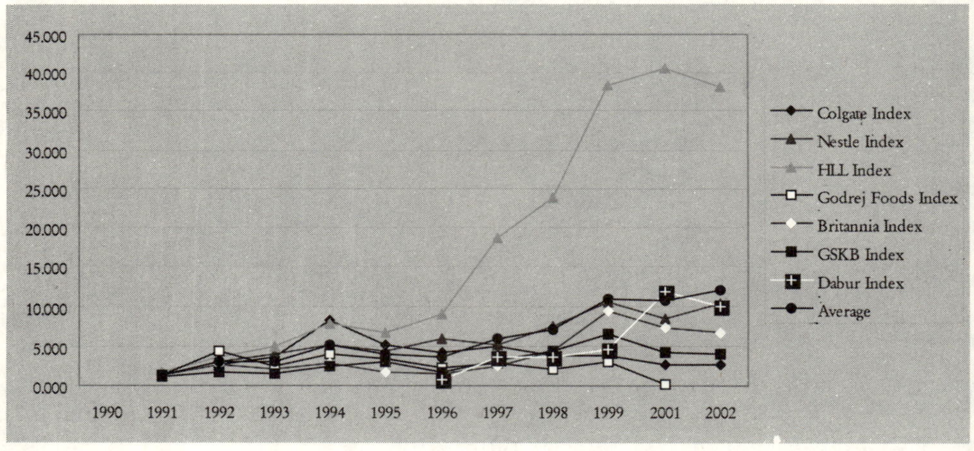

Source: *Bombay Stock Exchange Directory*

WHITE GOODS SECTOR

ROI

In this section, we analyze the results relating to companies which are in the white goods sector such as televisions, refrigerators, dish washers and music systems etc. It is true that even this sector has been very severely affected by the recent recession experienced by the economy. Consequently, on the parameter of trend of ROI, all companies, except Philips India, show a negative value. The companies (in descending order) are Philips India, Videocon Appliances Ltd., Onida Saka, BPL Ltd. The value of trend for these companies is 0.07, -0.31, -1.14 and -2.78 respectively. (See chart 9)

Chart 9: White Goods Sector (Return on Capital Employed)

Company Name/Year	Mar-90	Mar-91	Mar-92	Mar-93	Mar-94	Mar-95	Mar-96	Mar-97	Mar-98	Mar-99	Mar-00	Mar-01	Mar-02	Mar-03	LINEST*
Videocon Appliances Ltd		40.36	21.3	14.84	19.75	13.38	9.65	3.11	15.43	17.42	19.29	20.58		30.05	-0.31
B P L Ltd.	41.92	44.55	34.30	41.79	62.73	45.93	31.30	23.59	25.86	24.62	23.91	16.49	12.43		-2.78
Onida Saka Ltd.					28.62	39.12	36.62	-75.19	-34.96	22.39	25.70	14.08	11.42		-1.34
Philips India Ltd.	8.59	28.34	46.53	33.16	21.95	49.77	30.12	24.81	30.34	30.46	26.40	7.53	27.36	44.04	0.07
Selective Industry Average#	40.01	34.65	31.84	22.66	11.26	1.92	14.32	4.50	-119.89	12.92	-7.00	28.85	14.87	16.35	

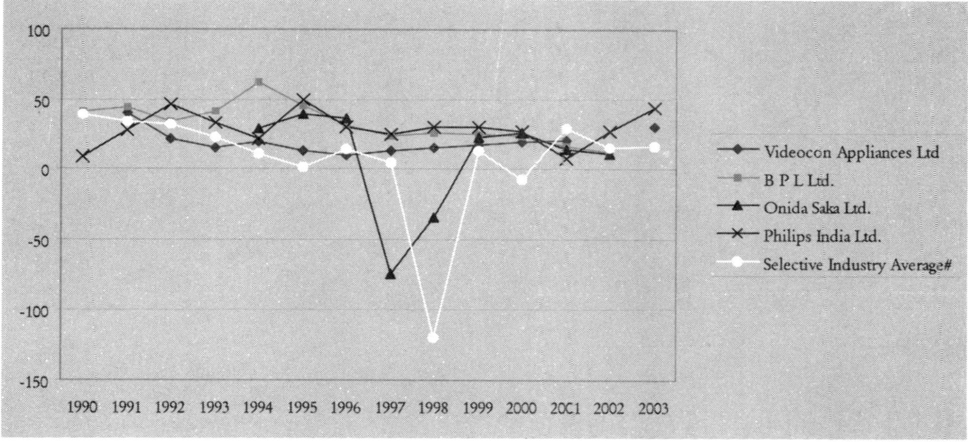

Source: *Prowess - Indian Corporate Database* by CMIE Pvt. Ltd.
Selective Industry Average# - Based on data of 17 companies in white goods sector excluding those mentioned above.
LINEST* - Linear Trend

Index of Market Capitalization

Once again, Philips India emerges on top with the value of index of 2.09 followed by BPL Home Appliances with a value of 0.59 (See chart 10). We did not have information on market capitalization for Onida in the initial period.

Chart 10: While Goods Sector (Market Capitalization Index)												
	1990	1991	1992	1993	1994	1995	1996	1997	1998	1999	2001	2002
BPL Index							0.362	0.465	1.811	2.726	1.523	0.591
Philips Index		2.119	4.723	4.112	9.063	6.779	3.284	2.402	3.066	3.802	3.181	2.099
Average							1.823	1.433	2.438	3.264	2.352	1.345

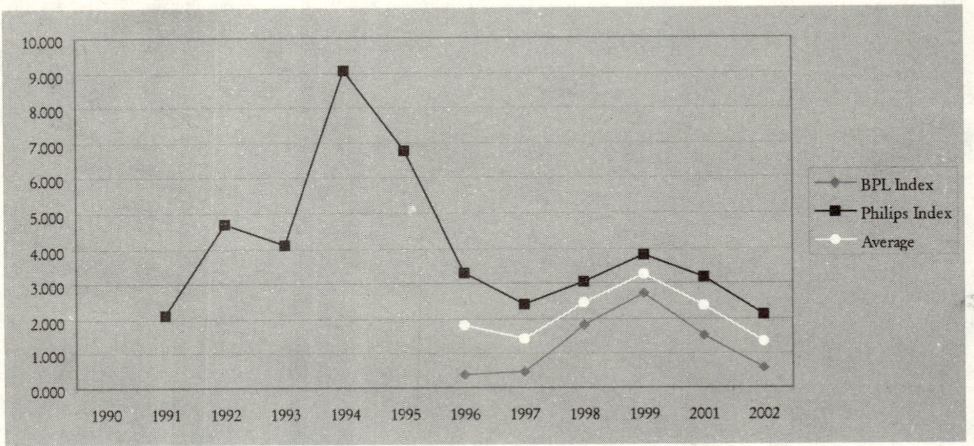

Source: *Bombay Stock Exchange Directory*

AUTOMOBILE SECTOR (FOUR-WHEELERS)

ROI

Based on this parameter, Swaraj Mazda ranks first with a value of trend of 2.09, followed by Eicher Motors at 0.88, Maruti Udyog at -0.49 and Telco at -2.17. (See chart 11). Last two years have been particularly bad for automobiles with the competition increasing manifold. In the case of Telco, the introduction of the passenger car has resulted in a huge investment, the benefit of which will accrue after some years. Notwithstanding the competition, Eicher Motors and Swaraj Mazda have done very well in the last two years. It is true that competition is not so fierce in the commercial vehicles segment. Also, Eicher Motors has been able to internalize technology unlike Maruti Udyog and some other organizations.

Chart 11: Automobile Sector (Return on Capital Employed)

Company Name/Year	Mar-90	Mar-91	Mar-92	Mar-93	Mar-94	Mar-95	Mar-96	Mar-97	Mar-98	Mar-99	Mar-00	Mar-01	Mar-02	Mar-03	LINEST*
Maruti Udyog Ltd.*	19.57	17.37	21.17	16.49	27.75	44.09	65.4[illegible]	59.79	64.8	32.75	16.51	-8.41	6.19		-0.49
Telco Ltd.	32.23	39.76	32.86	16.40	16.50	32.70	38.08	33.55	15.10	6.88	6.12	-0.05	5.89	21.32	-2.17
Eicher Motors Ltd.	36.30	40.59	19.94	-0.71	11.64	35.01	33.50	27.35	14.51	17.64	24.82	27.57	31.74	58.40	0.88
Swaraj Mazda Ltd.	36.61	31.23	-17.20	-21.90	1.28	66.21	54.10	33.76	29.93	19.34	17.76	28.86	32.62	58.33	2.09
Selective Industry Average#	**23.93**	**24.25**	**23.65**	**15.14**	**20.70**	**19.66**	**29.64**	**18.02**	**10.46**	**0.96**	**7.67**	**7.86**	**11.67**	**21.21**	

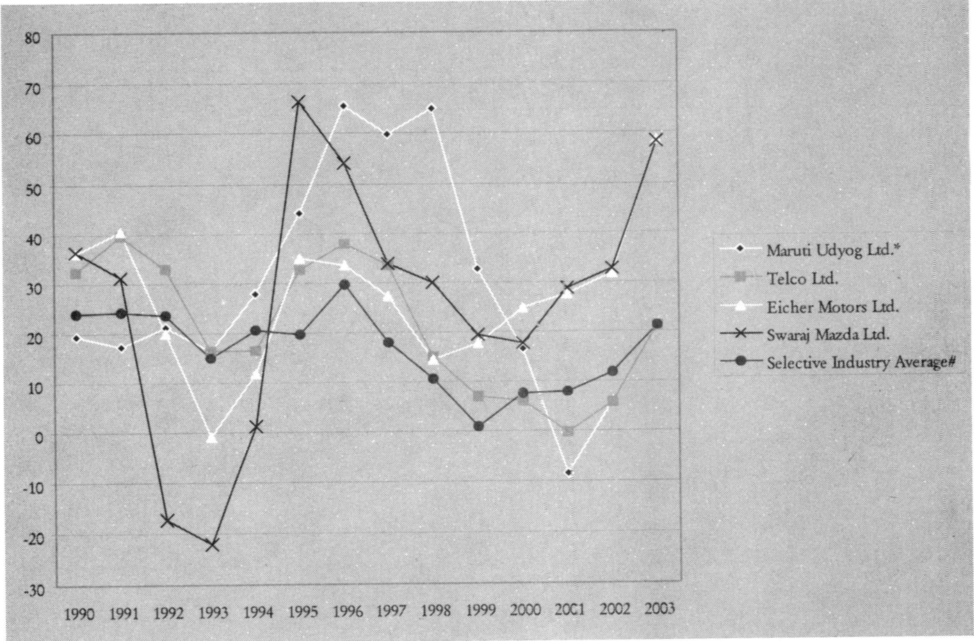

Source: *Prowess - Indian Corporate Database* by CMIE Pvt. Ltd.
Selective Industry Average# - Based on data of 2 companies in automobile sector excluding those mentioned above
Maruti Udyog Ltd* - Maruti Udyog Ltd. comes under the passenger car and multi-utility vehicle sector but we have taken it for comparison while the rest of the companies come under commercial vehicle sector.
LINEST* - Linear Trend

Index of Market Capitalization

We had information on market capitalization for only two companies, Telco and Eicher, with the value of trend of 1.69 and 2.19 respectively. (See chart 12). We may mention that the heavy investment made in the passenger car by Telco has just started yielding results. Very recently, Tata's are entering into an agreement with Rovers of England to produce cars to be sold in England. As BBC put it (18th September 2002), 'now India would be producing automobiles to be sold in England'. The unwritten message was that India has moved 'from being a bullock cart economy to an automobile economy'. Though we did not have data on Maruti for earlier years, as it has been privatized only recently, its share price is doing well. In times to come the index of its market capitalization would show an upward trend.

Chart 12: Automobile Sector (Market Capitalization Index)

	1990	1991	1992	1993	1994	1995	1996	1997	1998	1999	2001	2002
Telco Index		1.281	2.625	1.730	3.184	3.519	5.180	4.677	2.704	2.917	1.516	1.690
Eicher Index		1.279	2.347	0.805	5.374	3.046	2.647	1.311	0.820	2.205	2.056	2.198
Average		**1.280**	**2.486**	**1.268**	**4.279**	**3.282**	**3.914**	**2.994**	**1.762**	**2.561**	**1.786**	**1.944**

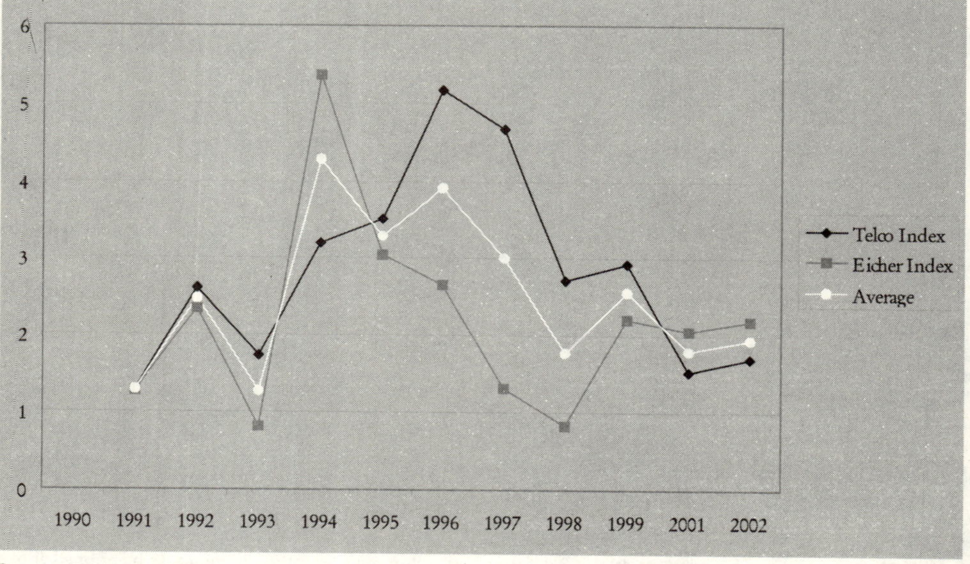

Source: *Bombay Stock Exchange Directory*

CLOCK AND WATCH SECTOR

ROI

On the parameter of trend of ROI, all companies show a negative value. Of all the companies, Titan emerges on top with a negative value of -0.28 followed by HMT and Timex with negative values of -4.22 and -21.71 respectively. (See chart 13).

Chart 13: Clocks and Watch Sector (Return on Capital Employed)

Company Name/Year	Mar-90	Mar-91	Mar-92	Mar-93	Mar-94	Mar-95	Mar-96	Mar-97	Mar-98	Mar-99	Mar-00	Mar-01	Mar-02	LINEST*
Titan Industries Ltd	13.94	19.61	22.11	15.96	14.89	17.12	17.51	16.72	14.74	15.66	14.00	14.58	15.31	-0.28
HMT Ltd	10.9	12.95	17.94	8.9	-10.78	-1.93	-0.05	11.14	8.18	11.89	-193.06	13.73	13.03	-4.22
Timex Watches Ltd					12.41	10.40	7.86	10.40	7.37	-5.56	-1.64	-102.08	-215.16	-21.71
Selective Industry Average#	**4.36**	**-0.53**	**11.15**	**9.97**	**25.55**	**33.14**	**23.14**	**2.74**	**-19.47**	**-26.40**	**14.20**	**10.93**	**-42.88**	

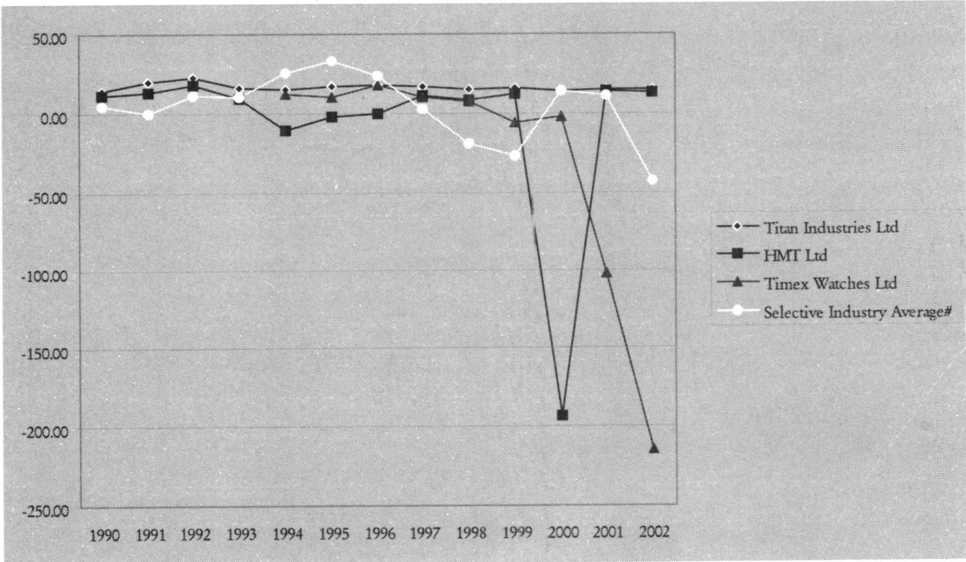

Source: *Prowess - Indian Corporate Database* by CMIE Pvt. Ltd.
Selective Industry Average# - Based on data of 8 companies in clocks and watch sector excluding those mentioned above.

Index of Market Capitalization

We do not propose to give any narration of capitalization as we have information over years for just one organization, Titan Industries. For HMT, information upto 1997 is available but that was the boom time. Independent of that, Titan Industries was in the process of establishing itself and hence its market capitalization was not of the same or similar order as given by the index of market capitalization (See chart 14).

From the details given above, it is clear that results of this section contradict the ranking of the section given in the main text. This is explicable as the compound rate of growth in the value of different parameters forms the basis of section one. The results are based on the intial year and the terminal year and do not capture what has been happening to the organization from year to year. At the same time, we do not have data for a fairly long period of time to get really reliable estimates in trends. Also, it appears that a quadratic trend, as against the linear trend, may be more representative of the actual state of things. This justifies our discussing the empirical results based on linear trend in the appendix to the chapter. A vigilant reader may find the year to year variations quite useful and the same have been presented.

Chart 14: Clocks and Watch Sector (Market Capitalization Index)

	1990	1991	1992	1993	1994	1995	1996	1997	1998	1999	2001	2002
Titan Index		1.346	1.836	2.037	3.813	2.940	2.541	1.655	1.511	2.606	1.633	1.039
HMT Index			0.677	113.767	62.572	35.290	52.203	27.581				
Average			1.257	57.902	33.193	19.115	27.372	14.618				

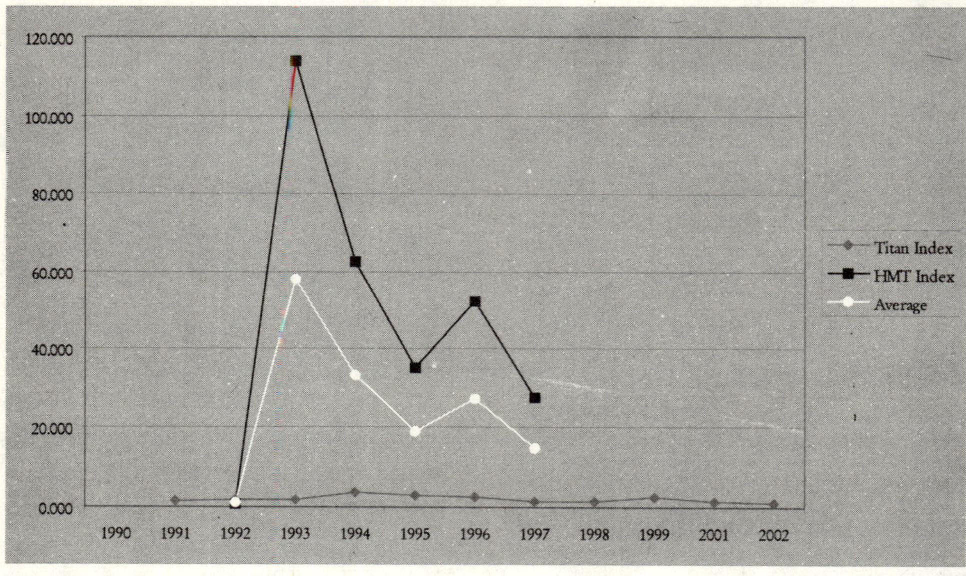

Source: *Bombay Stock Exchange Directory*

RESEARCH APPENDIX II

Rankings of the Top 100 Companies in the Year 1991 and 2002 Based on Market Capitalization

Table A-1

Company Name#	Rank* - 1991	Company Name##	Rank** - 2002
Tata Steel	1	Hindustan Lever	1
ITC	2	Wipro	2
Telco	3	Reliance Industries	3
Century Textiles	4	Infosys technologies	4
Hindustan Lever	5	ITC	5
Reliance Industries	6	Ranbaxy Laboratories	6
Grasim Industries	7	HDFC	7
GSFC	8	Satyam Computer Services	8
ACC	9	Dr. Reddy's Laboratories	9
Colgate	10	ICICI Bank	10
Hindalco	11	HCL Technologies	11
Bajaj Auto	12	Hero Honda Motors	12
Bombay Dyeing	13	Bharti Tele-ventures	13
Larsen & Toubro	14	HDFC Bank	14
Brooke Bond	15	Cipla	15
Great Eastern Shipping	16	Zee Telefilms	16
Nestle India	17	Nestle India	17
Madura Coats	18	Hindalco Industries	18
Essar Gujarat	19	Baja Auto	19
Motor Industries	20	Tata Iron & Steel Co.	20
Birla Jute	21	Tata Motors	21
Indo Gulf Fertilizers	22	Videsh Sanchar Nigam Ltd	22
Tata Tea	23	Larsen & Toubro	23
Century Enka	24	Indian Petrochemical Corpn.	24
Tata Chemicals	25	BSES	25

Table A-1 (Continued)

Company Name#	Rank* - 1991	Company Name##	Rank** - 2002
Smith Kline	26	Gujarat Ambuja Cements	26
Raymond Woolens	27	Grasim Industries	27
SKF Bearings	28	Glaxo-SmithKline Pharmaceuticals	28
Hindustan CIBA-GEIGY	29	Sun Pharmaceutical Inds	29
Ballarpur Industries	30	Associated Cement Co.	30
Castrol India	31	Castrol India	31
Indian Rayon	32	Tata Power Co.	32
Indian Aluminium	33	Asian Paints (India)	33
Ingersoll-Rand	34	Digital Globalsoft	34
Jindal Strips	35	Nirma	35
GNFC	36	I-Flex Solutions	36
Siemens	37	Colgate-Palmolive (India)	37
Kirloskar Cummins	38	Wockhardt	38
Hoechst	39	GSK Cons. Health Care	39
Gujarat Ambuja Cement	40	Dabur India	40
National Organic	41	Britannia Industries	41
Peico	42	Hindustan Zinc	42
Reliance Petrochemicals	43	Moser-Baer India	43
Glaxo	44	Ashok Leyland	44
Apollo Tyres	45	Mahindra & Mahindra	45
Britannia Industries	46	Polaris Software Lab	46
Tata Power	47	ABB	47
Escorts	48	Gillette India	48
CESC	49	East India Hotels	49
Oswal Agro	50	Pfizer	50
JaiPrakash Industries	51	TVS Motor Co.	51
ITC Bhadrachalam	52	Gillette India	52
Shaw Wallace	53	Jindal Vijayanagar Steel	53
Asian Paints	54	Tata tea	54
Godfrey Philips	55	Tata Teleservices (Maharashtra)	55
Goodricke Group	56	Siemens	56
Ashok Leyland	57	Lupin	57
Sesa Goa	58	GSK Cons. Healthcare	58
India cements	59	Nicholas Piramal India	59
Gujarat Alkalies	60	Cadia healthcare	60
Ponds India	61	Mphasis BFL	61
Nagarjuna Fertilizers	62	Sterlite Industries (India)	62
Bharat Forge	63	Kotak Mahindra Bank	63

Table A-1 (Continued)

Company Name#	Rank* - 1991	Company Name##	Rank** - 2002
Hind. Development corp.	64	Great Eastern Shipping Co.	64
Ranbaxy Laboratories	65	Indian Hotels Co.	65
Saw pipes	66	Procter & Gamble	66
VST Industries	67	East India Hotels	67
ICI India	68	Indian Aluminium Co.	68
Lipton	69	Punjab Tractors	69
Titan watches	70	Pfizer	70
JCT	71	Hughes Software Systems	71
Polyolefins Industries	72	Jaiprakash Industries	72
Mukand	73	Aurobindo Pharma	73
Spic	74	Reliance Capital	74
Excel Industries	75	Hinduja TMT	75
Tamilnadu Petro Prod.	76	Aventis Pharma	76
ABB	77	Radaan Mediaworks India	77
India Glycols	78	Jindal Steel & Power	78
Bayer India	79	Novartis India	79
Geroge Williamson	80	Ingersoll-Rand India	80
Essar Shipping	81	ING Vysya bank	81
Tea Estates	82	Century Textiles & Inds.	82
Tribeni Issues	83	Raymond	83
Usha Rectifier	84	Arvind Mills	84
Voltas	85	CMC	85
Maharashtra Seamless	86	E-Serve International	86
Eicher Tractors	87	Godrej Consumer Products	87
Lakshmi Machinery	88	Alstom Projects India	88
Crompton Greaves	89	DSP Merrill Lynch	89
Deepak Fertilizers	90	Pidilite Industries	90
Coromandel Fertilizers	91	Chambal Fertilizers & Chemicals	91
MRF	92	Indian Rayon & Inds.	92
Straw Products	93	ISPAT Industries	93
Mahavir Spinning	94	Ballarpur Industries	94
Sunflag Iron	95	DIVI's Industries	95
Chloride Industries	96	Matrix Laboratories	96
Mysore Cement	97	Wyeth	97
Alfa-Laval	98	Polaris Software Lab	98
Reckitt & Colman	99	Himachal Futuristic Communications	99
Dalmia Cement (Bharat)	100	United Phosphorus	100

Six Companies Included in the study
Eleven Companies Included in the Study

* Source: Business Today March 7-21 1992
** Source: Business Today November 9, 2003

Index

Accessibility 88, 91, 229
Accountability 31, 148, 158, 192
Adaptive 18, 147, 148, 149, 158, 172, 186, 280, 288
Adaptive style 147, 148
Ambitious goals 17, 42, 44, 46, 280, 295
Autocratic 84

Brand building strategy 111
Brand equity 21, 58, 110, 111, 117, 226, 228, 262, 272, 285, 291, 292, 294, 295
Brand leadership 57
Business ethics 13, 21
Business leadership 51, 57, 167
Business models 16, 18, 98, 106, 107, 109, 110, 112, 132, 148, 149, 159

Challenging goals 12, 38, 40, 44, 46, 49, 81, 225, 257, 282
Closed system 16, 218
Co-evolving continuity 15
Commitment 34, 35, 37, 38, 40, 44, 46, 47, 49, 51, 55, 56, 61, 68, 76, 79, 83, 87, 95, 145, 147, 280, 281, 282, 283, 291, 292, 296
Competency trap 66, 218
Continued outstanding leadership 40, 57, 58, 60, 62
Corporate governance 205, 207, 218, 221, 227, 229, 246, 252, 292
Cost reduction 20, 288, 290
Culture trap 218

Customer friendly 268
Customer leadership 57

Decentralized 30, 74
Delphi-type 5
Developing skills 20
Dharma 69, 74, 75, 237
Different paradigm 15, 26, 152, 256
Distinct identity 21, 22, 214, 215, 219, 220, 221, 234, 238, 291
Distinctive ability 25, 34
Dynamic configuration 16

Emotional bonding 85, 175
Emphasis on details 176, 288
Empowerment 28, 40, 53, 57, 64, 76, 79, 83, 87, 247, 283
Endanger sustainability 13
Entrepreneurship 11, 18, 44, 46, 79, 84, 85, 86, 87, 133, 134, 179, 197, 199, 234, 238, 240, 241, 242, 243, 245, 261
Equanimity 88, 92
Execution 12, 16, 20, 23, 29, 30, 35, 141, 168, 169, 170, 171, 177, 187, 188, 214, 215, 217, 255, 256, 278, 279, 287, 288, 296
Extended family 18, 85, 208, 245, 284, 290, 296

Field observations 5, 23
Financial security 175
Finite 27

Genetic code 215
Global mindset 220, 238, 239, 242, 245, 291, 292
Globally competitive 11, 34, 299
Good execution 30
Governance 21, 22, 28, 34, 111, 192, 200, 205, 207, 216, 218, 220, 221, 227, 229, 241, 246, 247, 252, 261, 291, 292, 294, 297

Holistic understanding 10

Indian costing 113
Indian multinational companies 20
Information technology sector 175, 300, 301, 302
Initiatives 16, 20, 30, 35, 51, 65, 88, 94, 97, 129, 133, 149, 153, 155, 167, 231, 240, 245, 285, 292
Innovation 11, 12, 13, 18, 22, 30, 33, 44, 50, 55, 65, 70, 83, 84, 99, 112, 113, 121, 132, 133, 134, 135, 136, 138, 139, 140, 141, 142, 143, 144, 145, 146, 154, 159, 168, 226, 234, 238, 239, 241, 242, 243, 244, 245, 261, 285, 286, 288
Innovation process 141, 144, 145
Innovative 16, 18, 19, 22, 53, 57, 66, 79, 80, 81, 87, 98, 100, 106, 107, 108, 112, 113, 132, 134, 136, 141, 142, 149, 153, 156, 158, 195, 197, 199, 200, 214, 215, 214, 215, 218, 231, 239, 241, 245, 246
Innovative solutions 57, 80, 81, 231
Innovative strategy 12, 16, 17, 18, 94, 97, 99, 214, 217, 255, 278, 279, 284
Inspiring leadership 16, 17, 37, 38, 40, 278, 279, 280, 284
Institution building 40, 57, 58, 59, 62, 280
Institutional characteristics 26
Integrity 222, 224, 225, 227, 229, 231, 232, 245, 281, 284, 291
Internal competence 17, 135
International markets 42, 50, 55, 58, 113, 115, 117, 118, 163, 165, 282, 285, 286, 287, 295
Intrinsic ability 25, 292

Joint family ethos 210
Joint venture partner 122, 160, 161, 162

Large sample 4
Latent needs 19, 100, 149, 280, 282, 285
Learning culture 12
Learning opportunity 85
Long tenure 27, 119

Managerial processes 4, 114, 116
Market capitalization 247, 263, 265, 267, 268, 269, 270, 272
Marketing 18, 26, 27, 32, 53, 61, 65, 75, 94, 102, 142, 143, 149, 160, 162, 173, 201, 205, 206, 209, 241, 256, 257, 281, 286
Mechanistic 26, 253, 258
Meritocracy 241, 245, 247, 248, 260, 261
Milestone-setting 69
Mission 40, 45, 51, 52, 54, 56, 57, 86, 98, 109, 123, 155, 168, 280, 282, 292, 295
Money-making commercial outfits 12, 15, 22, 255, 293
Monitoring and review 167, 244, 296
Moral development 89, 210
Motivation 12, 13, 28, 40, 61, 80, 82, 116, 198, 200, 207, 217, 235, 246, 256, 257

Need for learning 174

Open system 16, 253, 255
Openness 21, 22, 40, 63, 64, 65, 66, 73, 77, 86, 88, 91, 136, 159, 168, 199, 224, 231, 238, 239, 241, 244, 247, 281, 283, 291, 292, 296

Operating plan 105
Operational efficiency 150, 171, 173, 178, 288, 289
Organic growth 287
Organic system 293
Organizational culture 53, 226, 239, 240, 241, 260
Organizational environment 18
Outstanding organizations 38, 42, 44, 51, 62, 76, 83, 87, 93, 94, 97, 98, 99, 112, 148, 277, 278, 279, 283, 289, 291, 292, 293, 295
Outstanding performance 1, 4, 15, 17, 25, 228, 296
Ownership 12, 28, 33, 76, 79, 83, 86, 87, 120, 121, 167, 172, 184, 198, 200, 207, 212, 213, 226, 233, 246, 249, 255, 288, 296

Passion and ambition 40, 43, 44
People-centric 40, 76, 83, 84, 85, 87, 88, 281
People leadership 57
Pro-active approach 149
Proactive style 147, 148, 152
Process management 29, 74, 194, 227
Procuring technology 162, 163, 185
Productivity 13, 19, 20, 174, 178, 179, 185, 256, 257, 259, 260, 261, 283, 285, 288, 289, 290, 295, 296, 300
Productivity measures 26
Professional approach 245
Professionalism 21, 22, 91, 92, 221, 241, 245, 248, 249, 260, 261, 282, 291, 292, 297
Profitability 26, 27, 31, 54, 60, 90, 107, 108, 128, 144, 160, 168, 223, 227, 241, 247, 255, 256, 264, 275
Purposeful values-driven enterprises 10, 12, 15, 22, 187, 188, 250, 255, 259, 293

Rapid response 99, 132, 133, 153, 155, 285, 286
Reactive style 147, 148
Reliability 27, 111, 127, 207, 226, 231
Resilience 25, 26, 204, 292, 293

Six sigma 31, 35, 57, 143, 149, 231, 260
Social networking 171, 288
Speed 22, 30, 102, 133, 136, 137, 153, 154, 155, 231, 233, 285, 296
Stakeholders 12, 13, 14, 15, 17, 18, 21, 22, 28, 31, 32, 35, 97, 113
Statistical analysis 4
Stock offer plan 85, 174
Strategic fit 26
Strategic intent 35, 53, 95, 131, 168
Strategic orientations 4
Strategic plan 45, 105
Strategic planning 29, 87, 100, 105, 227
Structure 16, 17, 20, 21, 195, 199, 217, 219, 220, 249, 256, 258, 261, 266, 279, 282, 287, 288
Style of leadership 18, 65, 76, 79, 80, 82, 84, 85, 283
Superior execution 12
Supply chain 28, 116, 140, 171, 184, 192
Survive 1, 2, 15, 22, 26, 34, 43, 61, 73, 137, 142, 146, 147, 168, 192, 204, 258, 300
Sustain 1, 15, 22, 25, 29, 31, 40, 43, 68, 97, 106, 110, 111, 121, 128, 208, 219, 236, 246, 255, 261, 277, 278, 279, 286, 293, 294
Sustainable competitive edge 4, 16, 20, 40, 60, 63, 75, 292
Sustained dynamic focus 98, 122, 124, 285
Swift communication 187
Synergetic growth models 99, 158, 167
System-based models 29

Tacit knowledge 10
Timing 27, 143, 286
Transformation 26, 37, 38, 55, 58, 117

Transformational leadership 12
Transparency 64, 65, 192, 195, 221, 232, 246, 247, 249, 291, 292, 294, 297

Unique purpose 21, 215

Values framework 226, 227, 230, 249

Vision 32, 35, 39, 40, 44, 45, 46, 51, 52, 53, 54, 55, 56, 57, 64, 68, 69, 72, 82, 97, 98, 120, 122, 123, 126, 137, 143, 150, 161, 166
Vision statement 51, 53, 54, 56, 57, 123

'Win-Win' relationship 12, 16, 17, 21, 22, 191, 194, 214, 250, 259, 278, 279, 289, 294